Cisco Wireless LAN Security

Krishna Sankar
Sri Sundaralingam
Andrew Balinsky
Darrin Miller

Cisco Press

800 East 96th Street
Indianapolis, IN 46290 USA

Cisco Wireless LAN Security

Krishna Sankar, Sri Sundaralingam, Andrew Balinsky, Darrin Miller

Copyright© 2005 Cisco Systems, Inc.

Cisco Press logo is a trademark of Cisco Systems, Inc.

Published by:
Cisco Press
800 East 96th Street
Indianapolis, IN 46240 USA

All rights reserved. No part of this book may be reproduced or transmitted in any form or by any means, electronic or mechanical, including photocopying, recording, or by any information storage and retrieval system, without written permission from the publisher, except for the inclusion of brief quotations in a review.

Printed in the United States of America   5 6 7 8 9 0

Fifth Printing August 2007

Library of Congress Cataloging-in-Publication Number: 2003100133

ISBN: 1-58705-154-0

Trademark Acknowledgments

All terms mentioned in this book that are known to be trademarks or service marks have been appropriately capitalized. Cisco Press or Cisco Systems, Inc. cannot attest to the accuracy of this information. Airopeek is a trademark of WildPackets, Inc. Sniffer is a trademark of Network Associates Technology, Inc. Use of a term in this book should not be regarded as affecting the validity of any trademark or service mark.

Warning and Disclaimer

This book is designed to provide information about wireless LANs. Every effort has been made to make this book as complete and as accurate as possible, but no warranty or fitness is implied.

The information is provided on an "as is" basis. The authors, Cisco Press, and Cisco Systems, Inc. shall have neither liability nor responsibility to any person or entity with respect to any loss or damages arising from the information contained in this book or from the use of the discs or programs that may accompany it.

The opinions expressed in this book belong to the authors and are not necessarily those of Cisco Systems, Inc.

Corporate and Government Sales

Cisco Press offers excellent discounts on this book when ordered in quantity for bulk purchases or special sales.

For more information, please contact: U.S. Corporate and Government Sales 1-800-382-3419
corpsales@pearsontechgroup.com

For sales outside the U.S., please contact: International Sales international@pearsoned.com

Feedback Information

At Cisco Press, our goal is to create in-depth technical books of the highest quality and value. Each book is crafted with care and precision, undergoing rigorous development that involves the unique expertise of members from the professional technical community.

Readers' feedback is a natural continuation of this process. If you have any comments regarding how we could improve the quality of this book or otherwise alter it to better suit your needs, you can contact us through e-mail at feedback@ciscopress.com. Please make sure to include the book title and ISBN in your message.

We greatly appreciate your assistance.

Publisher	John Wait
Editor-in-Chief	John Kane
Executive Editor	Brett Bartow
Acquisition Editor	Michelle Grandin
Cisco Representative	Anthony Wolfenden
Cisco Press Program Manager	Nannette M. Noble
Production Manager	Patrick Kanouse
Development Editor	Ginny Bess Munroe
Senior Copy Editor	Amy Lepore
Technical Editors	Brian Cox, David Pollino, Dr. Peter Welcher, and Nancy Cam-Winget
Editorial Assistant	Tammi Barnett
Cover Designer	Louisa Adair
Project Management	Argosy Publishing
Composition	Prospect Hill Publishing Services
Indexer	Eric T. Schroeder
Proofreader	Karen A. Gill

CISCO SYSTEMS

Corporate Headquarters
Cisco Systems, Inc.
170 West Tasman Drive
San Jose, CA 95134-1706
USA
www.cisco.com
Tel: 408 526-4000
        800 553-NETS (6387)
Fax: 408 526-4100

European Headquarters
Cisco Systems International BV
Haarlerbergpark
Haarlerbergweg 13-19
1101 CH Amsterdam
The Netherlands
www-europe.cisco.com
Tel: 31 0 20 357 1000
Fax: 31 0 20 357 1100

Americas Headquarters
Cisco Systems, Inc.
170 West Tasman Drive
San Jose, CA 95134-1706
USA
www.cisco.com
Tel: 408 526-7660
Fax: 408 527-0883

Asia Pacific Headquarters
Cisco Systems, Inc.
Capital Tower
168 Robinson Road
#22-01 to #29-01
Singapore 068912
www.cisco.com
Tel: +65 6317 7777
Fax: +65 6317 7799

Cisco Systems has more than 200 offices in the following countries and regions. Addresses, phone numbers, and fax numbers are listed on the
Cisco.com Web site at www.cisco.com/go/offices.

Argentina • Australia • Austria • Belgium • Brazil • Bulgaria • Canada • Chile • China PRC • Colombia • Costa Rica • Croatia • Czech Republic
Denmark • Dubai, UAE • Finland • France • Germany • Greece • Hong Kong SAR • Hungary • India • Indonesia • Ireland • Israel • Italy
Japan • Korea • Luxembourg • Malaysia • Mexico • The Netherlands • New Zealand • Norway • Peru • Philippines • Poland • Portugal
Puerto Rico • Romania • Russia • Saudi Arabia • Scotland • Singapore • Slovakia • Slovenia • South Africa • Spain • Sweden
Switzerland • Taiwan • Thailand • Turkey • Ukraine • United Kingdom • United States • Venezuela • Vietnam • Zimbabwe

Copyright © 2003 Cisco Systems, Inc. All rights reserved. CCIP, CCSP, the Cisco Arrow logo, the Cisco *Powered* Network mark, the Cisco Systems Verified logo, Cisco Unity, Follow Me Browsing, FormShare, iQ Net Readiness Scorecard, Networking Academy, and ScriptShare are trademarks of Cisco Systems, Inc.; Changing the Way We Work, Live, Play, and Learn, The Fastest Way to Increase Your Internet Quotient, and iQuick Study are service marks of Cisco Systems, Inc.; and Aironet, ASIST, BPX, Catalyst, CCDA, CCDP, CCIE, CCNA, CCNP, Cisco, the Cisco Certified Internetwork Expert logo, Cisco IOS, the Cisco IOS logo, Cisco Press, Cisco Systems, Cisco Systems Capital, the Cisco Systems logo, Empowering the Internet Generation, Enterprise/Solver, EtherChannel, EtherSwitch, Fast Step, GigaStack, Internet Quotient, IOS, IP/TV, iQ Expertise, the iQ logo, LightStream, MGX, MICA, the Networkers logo, Network Registrar, *Packet*, PIX, Post-Routing, Pre-Routing, RateMUX, Registrar, SlideCast, SMARTnet, StrataView Plus, Stratm, SwitchProbe, TeleRouter, TransPath, and VCO are registered trademarks of Cisco Systems, Inc. and/or its affiliates in the U.S. and certain other countries.

All other trademarks mentioned in this document or Web site are the property of their respective owners. The use of the word partner does not imply a partnership relationship between Cisco and any other company. (0303R)

Printed in the USA

About the Authors

Krishna Sankar is currently with Cisco Systems as a distinguished engineer in the Global Government Solutions Group. He has about 20 years of experience ranging from software architecture and development to industrial engineering to author, speaker, teacher, entrepreneur, and technology evangelist. He has worked with many organizations including the U.S. Air Force, the U.S. Navy, Hewlett-Packard, Qantas Airlines, Air Canada, and Ford.

He is part of (either by observing or as a member) many web services, security, and networking standards bodies. He also has worked with security bodies in the European Union: Electronic Signature Infrastructure and Comité Européen de Normalisation (CEN).

His technology interests include network-centric operations and transformation; dynamic self-configuring and adaptive networks; multihop, sensor, and identity networks; peer-to-peer and grid networks; distributed security; and Linux kernel security. Krishna lives in Silicon Valley with his wife, Usha, and son, Kaushik.

Sri Sundaralingam is currently a technical marketing manager in the Wireless Networking Business Unit at Cisco Systems, Inc. Sri has extensive customer contact and is responsible for developing and marketing enterprise and carrier networking solutions using the Cisco Aironet series of wireless LAN products. Sri has focused in the areas of wireless LAN security and wireless/wired LAN integration in the past three years at Cisco. Prior to joining the Wireless Networking Business Unit, Sri was a network consulting engineer in the Cisco Customer Advocacy organization. In this role, he worked with service providers and Fortune 500 companies to design and deploy IP-, DSL-, and ATM-based networks. Sri has been in the data communications and networking industry for the past 10 years. Before joining Cisco, Sri was a consulting engineer at Newbridge Networks and focused on designing and deploying Core Carrier networks. Sri attended University of Waterloo in Ontario, Canada where he majored in computer engineering.

Andrew Balinsky is a birdwatcher who supports his habit with professional computer security work. His love of computers dates back to a Commodore PET and has continued through a bachelor's degree in computer science at Harvard and master's degree in computer science at the University of Maryland at College Park. His introduction to computer security was through the Air Force Information Warfare Center, where he did everything from tracking hackers to developing security software. He continued this work at WheelGroup and at Cisco. His work at Cisco includes testing for security vulnerabilities and educating others how to do so.

Darrin Miller has been in the networking industry for more than 15 years. He has been an IT security manager, a security consultant, and a consulting systems engineer. Darrin currently works as a security researcher at Cisco Systems, Inc. and has authored several whitepapers on the subject of network security. Darrin holds a bachelor's degree in computer science from the University of Cincinnati. When not working in the area of network security, he enjoys spending time with his wife and three daughters.

About the Technical Reviewers

Nancy Cam-Winget has more than 20 years of experience in architecture and systems design. She is currently a security architect for the Wireless Networking Business Unit at Cisco Systems. She is an active participant in both the IEEE 802.11 security standards and Wi-Fi security task groups. Prior to joining Cisco, Nancy was lead engineer in wireless security at Atheros. She has also designed and developed 3D graphics and image-processing systems at Intrinsic and Silicon Graphics.

Brian Cox is a network consulting engineer with Cisco Advanced Services—Wireless at Cisco Systems. He holds his CCIE in routing and switching and received his master's degree in engineering at RMIT. Brian has 25 years of industry experience.

David Pollino has a strong background in security and networking and leads research focusing on wireless and security technologies. During his career, he has worked for an industry-leading security consulting company, a large financial services company, and a tier 1 Internet service provider. David often speaks at security events and has been frequently quoted in the press on security issues in online and printed journals. During his career as a consultant and network engineer, David has worked for clients across multiple industries, including financial services, service providers, high technology, manufacturing, and government. David has authored such books as RSA Press's *Wireless Security* and Osbourne's *The Hacker's Challenge* Books 1 and 2.

Dr. Peter J. Welcher, CCIE No. 1773, has a Ph.D. in math from MIT. He started out teaching math at the U.S. Naval Academy while simultaneously buying and maintaining UNIX systems, writing a book, and writing a major computer program in C. He saw the light in 1993 and then taught a wide variety of the Cisco courses for Mentor Technologies, formerly Chesapeake Computer Consultants, while also doing network consulting whenever possible. Pete is now doing high-level network consulting with Chesapeake Netcraftsmen, with tasks including network design, security, QoS, and IP telephony for several major enterprise customers. He has reviewed a large number of books for Cisco Press and other publishers and has authored or managed development of several courses for Cisco and others. Pete writes articles for *Enterprise Networking* magazine. He can also sometimes be found presenting his own seminars at East Coast Cisco offices, on topics ranging from campus design to WLAN security. The articles and seminars can be found at http://www.netcraftsmen.net/welcher. Pete also holds the CCIP certification and is a certified Cisco Systems instructor.

Dedications

Krishna Sankar—To my mother and Usha's mom and dad

Sri Sundaralingam—For Amma and Appa

Andrew Balinsky—For Julia and Rufus

Darrin Miller—For Jill, Megan, Beth, and Katie

Acknowledgments

Krishna Sankar—Of course, this book would not be in your hands without perseverance and hard work from a lot of folks. In particular, the coauthors Sri, Darrin, and Andy, from whom I learned a lot and it has been a pleasure to work with. We owe thanks to Michelle, who has been our mentor; she really kept the chapters from mushrooming (by promising us another book with infinite time and resources). The direction and gentle guidance from the reviewers, Nancy Cam-Winget, Brian Cox, David Pollino, and Peter Welcher, made this work complete and correct; the hard work by editors Ginny Bess Munroe and San Dee Phillips has made this book readable and cohesive. Tammi Barnett has been the glue that holds this well-oiled team together. I want to thank Merike Kaeo for materials in Chapter 2.

On a personal note, I am standing on the shoulders of giants. I want to thank Sue Stemel and Greg Akers for their guidance and encouragement. They have tremendous positive influence, and I hope all of you get to know, watch, learn from, and be led by gurus like Greg and Sue. In the same vein, Lt. Col. Terry Morgan USMC (Ret.), Col. Pat Ryan USAF (Ret.), Cdr. Charlie Booth USN (Ret.), Paige Atkins, Jim Massa, Rick Sanford, Brett Biddington, Bob Maskell, and Tom Frommack have been my support system. I could bounce my crazy ideas off them and always receive well-thought-out, rational encouragement and gentle prodding toward various forms of appropriateness. Finally—the best for last—I thank my family, who give me pride and joy (and grief occasionally, when I start veering from track): Usha (my North Star, friend, philosopher, and guide), little Kaushik, and our extended family—Usha's and my parents and our respective siblings.

Sri Sundaralingam—I want to thank my family, including Amma, Appa, my sisters Nalayini and Pathanchali and their families, my friends, and my coworkers who have inspired me to achieve above and beyond. This book is a result of hard work by many, including my coauthors Krishna, Andy, and Darrin. I would like to thank Krishna for inspiring us to author this book. I also want to thank Michelle Grandin at Cisco Press for her patience and dedication for making this happen. Last but not least, I want to thank our editors, Brian, Dave, Nancy, and Peter, who gave us timely and detailed feedback on our chapters.

Andrew Balinsky—First and foremost, I give thanks to my wife, Julia, and our canine companion, Rufus, who spent many evenings urging me to finish. Thanks also to Mum, who encouraged me to accept the challenge, and Dad, who would have been proud to see another generation of Balinskys in print. I'm grateful to my coworkers on the STAT team at Cisco who endured far-too-detailed descriptions of some of these protocols. Thanks go to Krishna for asking me to participate and my fellow authors for their feedback. At Cisco Press, I thank Michelle Grandin for keeping us on task and reminding us of the realities of authorship. I thank the trees that gave their lives for this book to be printed. Finally, I'm indebted to the nesting screech owls in our back yard that kept a watchful eye on the writing process from their perches. Their dedication to their family and their work kept me on track.

Darrin Miller—I want to thank my wife, Jill, and our daughters, Megan, Beth, and Katie, for their love, patience, and support. They remind me that there are more interesting things in life than network security. Thanks also to Mom, Dad, and my brothers for their support and the important life lessons that they teach me. I'm grateful to all of my coworkers at Cisco who challenged me with new and exciting problems to solve on a daily basis. Thanks go to my coauthors for asking me to participate. Finally, I would like to thank Michelle Grandin at Cisco Press for keeping us focused on the end goal.

Contents at a Glance

Introduction   xxi

Chapter 1   Securing WLANs Overview   3

Chapter 2   Basic Security Mechanics and Mechanisms   13

Chapter 3   WLAN Standards   59

Chapter 4   WLAN Fundamentals   81

Chapter 5   WLAN Basic Authentication and Privacy Methods   111

Chapter 6   Wireless Vulnerabilities   125

Chapter 7   EAP Authentication Protocols for WLANs   157

Chapter 8   WLAN Encryption and Data Integrity Protocols   195

Chapter 9   SWAN: End-to-End Security Deployment   233

Chapter 10   Design Guidelines for Secure WLAN   255

Chapter 11   Operational and Design Considerations for Secure WLANs   287

Chapter 12   WLAN Security Configuration Guidelines and Examples   307

Chapter 13   WLAN Deployment Examples   355

Appendix A   Resources and References   399

Index   405

Table of Contents

Introduction   xxi

Chapter 1   Securing WLANs Overview   3

WLAN: A Perspective   3

Wireless LAN Components and Terminology   5

WLAN Standards   7

WLAN Security   8

WLAN Security Domain Conceptual Model   8

Navigating This Book and Chapter Contexts   10

Summary   11

Chapter 2   Basic Security Mechanics and Mechanisms   13

Security Mechanics   13
Confidentiality Mechanisms   15
Symmetric Key Encryption   15
Asymmetric Encryption   19
Encryption Algorithm Strengths and Weaknesses   23
Integrity Mechanisms   24
Hash Functions   24
Digital Signatures   26
Key Management   29

Authentication and Identity Protocols   34
PPP Authentication Protocols   34
PPP Password Authentication Protocol   35
PPP Challenge Handshake Authentication Protocol   37
PPP Extensible Authentication Protocol   40
The TACACS+ Protocol   42
TACACS+ Authentication   43
TACACS+ Authorization   43
TACACS+ Accounting   44
TACACS+ Transactions   44
The RADIUS Protocol   45
RADIUS Authentication   46
RADIUS Authorization   46
RADIUS Accounting   47
RADIUS Transactions   47

The Kerberos Protocol   48
    Kerberos Authentication Request and Reply   49
    Kerberos Application Request and Response   51
IPv6   52
    IPv6 Address Structure and Representation   53
    IPv6 Header   53
    Scalability   54
    Adoption   54
IPSec   54
    Authentication Header   55
    Encapsulating Security Payload   55
    Security Associations   55
    Key Management   56

Summary   56

Chapter 3   WLAN Standards   59

Standards Organizations, Position, Context, and Influence   59
    IEEE   60
        IEEE 802 Standards   60
    Wi-Fi Alliance   65
        WPA Overview   65
    Wireless LAN Association   67

Hardware/Radio/Waves and Modulation   67

FCC Regulations   67
    Radio Technologies in 802.11   68

Brief Discussion on Relevant Standards   69
    IEEE 802.11   69
    IEEE 802.11b   70
    Channel Allocation   70
    IEEE 802.11a   70
    IEEE 802.11g   72
    IEEE 802.11f   73
    IEEE 802.11e   73
        QoS Capabilities   74
        QoS Mechanisms   74
        QoS-Related Entities   75
        Association Based on QoS Capabilities   75
    IEEE 802.11k   75

IEEE 802.11h   76
European Standard Organizations and Regulations: ERO   76
European Standard Organizations and Regulations: ETSI   77
802.11h Details   78
Light Weight Access Point Protocol   79

Summary   79

Chapter 4   WLAN Fundamentals   81

WLAN: Elements and Characteristics   81

WLAN Basic Topology   84

WLAN Building Blocks   86
Services   87
Frames   89

WLAN State Diagram   91

Basic Choreography   93
Beacon   94
Probe   95
Authentication   96
Deauthentication   99
Association   100
Reassociation   101
Disassociation   102
Data   103
Reason and Status Codes   104
WEP   108

Summary   109

Chapter 5   WLAN Basic Authentication and Privacy Methods   111

Authentication Mechanics   111

Open Authentication   113
Trust Model and Assumptions   114
Supporting AAA Infrastructure   114
Applications, Vulnerabilities, and Countermeasures   114
Auditing and Accounting   114

MAC-Based Authentication   115
Trust Model and Assumptions   115
Supporting AAA Infrastructure   116
Auditing and Accounting   116
Applications, Vulnerabilities, and Countermeasures   116

Shared-Key Authentication   116
    Protocol Choreography   117
    Trust Model and Assumptions   118
    Supporting AAA Infrastructure   118
    Auditing and Accounting   118
    Applications, Vulnerabilities, and Countermeasures   118

WEP Privacy Mechanics   119
    WEP Processing Model   120
        RC4 Algorithm   121
        Data and Integrity   121
        Seed and Keylength   121
        IV Generation   122
        Key Generation and Selection   122
        Packaging   123
        Decryption   123
    Vulnerabilities   123

Summary   123

Chapter 6   Wireless Vulnerabilities   125

Attacker Objectives   126
    Attack Trees   126
        Reconnaissance   127
        DoS   127
        Network Access   128

Reconnaissance Attacks   130
    Sniffing and SSIDs   130
    Sniffing Tools   131
        Prismdump   132
        Ethereal and Tcpdump   132
        Commercial Sniffers   132
    Wardriving and Its Tools   133
        Network Stumbler and Mini Stumbler   134
        Macintosh Tools   135
        Kismet   135
        Wellenreiter   135
        bsd-airtools   136

DoS Attacks   138
    Disassociation and Deauthentication Attacks   139
    Transmit Duration Attack   140

Authentication Attacks   140
    Shared-Key Authentication Attacks   140
    MAC Address Spoofing   141

WEP Keystream and Plaintext Recovery   141
    Keystream Dictionaries   141
    Methods for Recovering RC4 Keystreams   142
        Known Plaintext Attack   142
        IV Collisions and the Birthday Paradox   143
        Reaction Attack   143
        Inductive Attack   144
    Uses for Recovered Keystreams   145
        Traffic Injection: Choosing Your Own IVs   145
        Message Modification and Replay   145
        Decryption   146
        A Brief Note on Solutions   146

WEP Key Recovery Attacks   146
    Dictionary-Based Key Attacks   146
    The Fluhrer-Mantin-Shamir Attack   147
        FMS Tools   149

Attacks on EAP Protocols   150
    Summary of 802.1x and EAP   150
    Dictionary Attack on LEAP   151
    PEAP Man-in-the-Middle Attack   153

Rogue APs   154

Ad-Hoc Mode Security   155

Summary   155

Chapter 7   EAP Authentication Protocols for WLANs   157

Access Control and Authentication Mechanisms   157
    The Three-Party Model   158
    Layered Framework for Authentication   159

EAP   163
    EAP Frames, Messages, and Choreography   163
    EAP Authentication Mechanisms   170
        EAP-MD5   170
        EAP-OTP   171
        EAP-GTC   171
        EAP-TLS   171
        EAP-TTLS   176

PEAP   176
    PEAP Frame Format   177
        PEAP Arbitrary Parameter Exchange   178
    PEAP Choreography   180

802.1x: Introduction and General Principles   183
    EAPOL   184

Cisco LEAP (EAP-Cisco Wireless)   185

EAP-FAST   187
    EAP-FAST Frame Format   189
    EAP-FAST Choreography   189

Summary   192

Chapter 8   WLAN Encryption and Data Integrity Protocols   195

IEEE 802.11i   195

Encryption Protocols   197
    WEP   197
        RC4   198
        WEP Encapsulation   200
        WEP Decapsulation   202
    TKIP (802.11i/WPA)   203
        Michael MIC (802.11i/WPA)   204
        Preventing Replay Attacks   206
        Key Mixing Algorithm   207
        TKIP Packet Construction   208
        TKIP Encapsulation   209
        TKIP Decapsulation   210
    CCMP   211
        CCMP Encapsulation   212
        CCMP Decapsulation   214
        CCM Algorithm   215

Key Management   217
    Master Key Establishment   218
    Key Hierarchy   218
        Pairwise Key Hierarchy   220
        Group Key Hierarchy   221
    Key Exchange   222
        The 4-Way Handshake   222
        The Group Key Handshake   223

Security Associations   224
PMKSA   225
PTKSA   225
GTKSA   225
Security Association Destruction   225

WPA and Cisco Protocols   225
Cisco Protocols   226
WPA   226

Security Problems Addressed   227
Reconnaissance   227
DoS Attacks   227
Shared-Key Authentication Attacks   227
MAC Address Spoofing   227
Message Modification and Replay   228
Dictionary-Based WEP Key Recovery   228
WEP Keystream Recovery   228
Fluhrer-Mantin-Shamir Weak Key Attack   228
Rogue APs   229
Security Considerations of EAP   229

Summary   229

Chapter 9   SWAN: End-to-End Security Deployment   233

Overview of SWAN Security Features   233

WLAN Deployment Modes and Security Features   235

SWAN Infrastructure Authentication   240

Radio Management and Wireless Intrusion Detection   241

SWAN Fast Secure Roaming (CCKM)   246

Local 802.1x RADIUS Authentication Service   250

Summary   252

Chapter 10   Design Guidelines for Secure WLAN   255

WLAN Design Fundamentals   255
WLAN Security Policy   256
Device Support   256
Authentication Support   257
Network Services Placement   257
Mobility   257
Application Support   258
Management of the APs   258

Radio Coverage Design   258
Multigroup Access   259

General Security Recommendations   259
AP Recommendations   259
WLAN Client Recommendations   260
Infrastructure Recommendations   260

New WLAN Deployments   261
Embedded Security Solutions   261
Threat Mitigation   263
Design Fundamentals and Embedded Security   264
VPN Overlays   265
Threat Mitigation   266
VPN Overlay Technologies   267
Design Fundamentals and VPN Overlays   270
Combined VPN and Embedded Security Design   271
Threat Mitigation   272
Design Fundamentals and the Combined VPN and Embedded Security
Design   273

Integration with Existing WLAN Deployments   275
WPA Upgradeable, WEP Only, and Pre-WEP Devices   275
Integrated Deployments   275
Threat Mitigation   278
Design Fundamentals   279

SWAN Central Switch Design Considerations   281

Admission Control Design   282

Summary   284

Chapter 11   Operational and Design Considerations for Secure WLANs   287

Rogue AP Detection and Prevention   287
SWAN Rogue AP Detection   288
Manual Rogue AP Detection   289
Network-Based Rogue AP Detection   291

WLAN Services Scaling   292
RADIUS Best Practices   292
VPN Best Practices   296
IPSec VPN Clustering   296
IPSec External Load Balancer   299
SSL External Load Balancing   299

Enterprise Guest Access   300

Enterprise Guest Access Requirements   301
    Open Authentication Guest VLAN   301
    Traffic Separation of the Guest VLAN to the Edge of the Enterprise   302
    Plug-and-Play Connectivity   302
    Cost-Effective and Secure Access Codes   302
Enterprise Guest Access Design   302

Summary   305

Chapter 12   WLAN Security Configuration Guidelines and Examples   307

Cisco Enterprise Class Wireless LAN Products   307
    Cisco Aironet AP1200 Access Point   308
    Cisco Aironet AP1100 Access Point   308
    Cisco Aironet AP350 Access Point   308
    Cisco Aironet BR350 Bridge   309
    Cisco Aironet BR1410 Bridge   309
    Cisco Aironet 802.11b/a/g and Cisco Client Extensions–Enabled Devices   309
    Cisco Secure Access Server   310
    Cisco Wireless LAN Solution Engine   310
    Catalyst 6500 Wireless LAN Services Module   310

WLAN Security Methods: Configuration Guidelines and Examples   311
    Navigating the HTML GUI Configuration Pages   311
    IOS CLI Configuration Examples and Guidelines   313
        Open/No WEP Configuration   313
        Open/with WEP and WPA-PSK Configurations   313
        MAC Address Authentication Configuration   316
        EAP with Dynamic WEP Configuration   317
        WPA-DOT1x Configuration   324
        IPSec VPN over WLAN Configuration   329
        Multiple Security Profiles (SSIDs/VLANs) Configuration   332

SWAN Nonswitching Deployment: Configuration Guidelines and Examples   336
    Basic WDS Configuration   336
    Fast Secure Roaming (CCKM) Configuration   338
    RF Aggregation Configuration and Rogue AP Detection   340
    Local Authentication Configuration (RADIUS Fall-Back Service)   343

Securing Bridge-to-Bridge Links   344

Secure WLAN Management Configuration Guidelines   346

SWAN Central Switching Deployment: Configuration Guidelines and Examples   348

Summary   353

Chapter 13 WLAN Deployment Examples 355

    Large Enterprise Deployment Examples 355
        Large Enterprise WLAN Deployment Example I 355
            WLAN Security Deployment Details 356
            Wired/Wireless LAN Integration and WLAN Infrastructure and User Management Details 357
            AAA and External User Database Infrastructure Implementation Details 358
            VoIP and Guest Services Deployment Details 360
            Summary of Large Enterprise WLAN Deployment Example I 361
        Large Enterprise WLAN Deployment Example II 362
            WLAN Security Deployment Details 363
            Wired/Wireless LAN Integration 364
            Deployment Challenges 364
            AAA Infrastructure Implementation Details 364
            Summary of Large Enterprise WLAN Deployment Example II 365

    Vertical Deployment Examples 365
        Retail WLAN Deployment Example I 366
            WLAN Security Deployment Details 367
            WDS and AAA Infrastructure Implementation Details 369
            Deployment Challenges 370
            Summary of Retail WLAN Deployment Example I 370
        Retail WLAN Deployment Example II 370
        University WLAN Deployment Example 373
        Financial WLAN Deployment Example I 376
        Financial WLAN Deployment Example II 378
        Healthcare WLAN Deployment Example I 379
        Healthcare WLAN Deployment Example II 383
        Manufacturing WLAN Deployment Example 386

    Small and Medium Businesses and SOHO WLAN Deployments 389
        Medium Enterprise WLAN Deployment Scenario Example 389
        Small Office WLAN Deployment Example 390
        SOHO WLAN Deployment Scenario Example 391

    Hotspot (Public WLAN) Deployment Examples 391
        Coffee Shop WLAN Hotspot Deployment Example 392
        Airport WLAN Deployment Example 394

    Summary 395

Appendix A Resources and References 399

Index 405

Icons Used in This Book

Throughout this book, you will see the following icons used for networking devices:

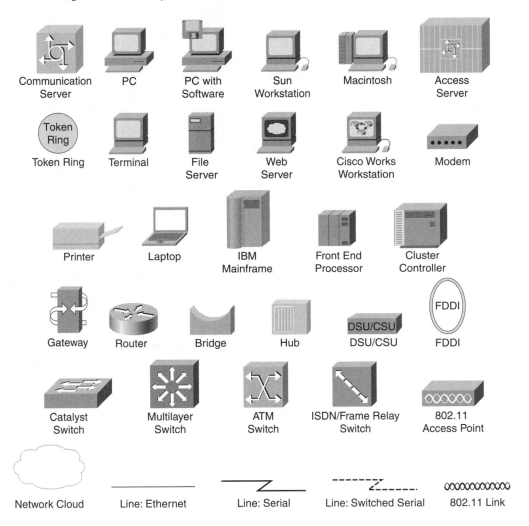

Introduction

The WLAN industry has all the thrills and chills of a well-written (and -directed) drama. WLAN is a disruptive technology that questions conventional wisdom in many ways. The domain is shaped by regulations and standards, vendors who sometimes try to compensate for inadequacies and idiosyncrasies of standards and regulations, an overheated technology adoption with an impatient user base for ever-increasing features, and most importantly, a security space that has some vulnerabilities, to say the very least.

This book covers the spectrum of WLAN security—the standards, the protocols, the specifications, and above all, deployment patterns and design guidelines. What makes this book unique is the combination of theory and practice, and we, as authors, hope we have the right balance. In the same vein, the authors (and editors) also hope that we have hit the sweet spot on breadth and depth in terms of details. In one corner, there are the 30,000-foot views, and on the other side, we have the intimate, minute details of algorithms, security considerations, and protocols. This book covers the protocols and formats—enough to satisfy inquiring minds—and includes pointers for the most detailed minds to ponder. This book also has a wealth of knowledge gleaned from the authors' experience in terms of guidelines, deployments, and configuration.

The field of WLANs is continually changing; therefore, covering all aspects, especially the emerging ones, is challenging. This book achieves the new-old balance by covering not only the older methods (such as classical WEP) but also newer concepts and architectures (such as EAP and switching).

Who Should Read This Book?

This book is planned and written for network engineers who design, configure, implement, and maintain secure WLANs. Because the topic is security, the audience also includes security practitioners in enterprise—anybody who wants to gain a good understanding on wireless LAN security. With that in mind, this book has three aims: to articulate the various aspects of wireless LAN security, to illustrate how security is implemented in Cisco products, and finally to implement in the architecture, design, and configuration of wireless networks (of different types such as campus, hotspots, office, and so on). On the way, this book also covers the big hairy topics like 802.x standards and vulnerabilities.

How This Book Is Organized

This book includes seven chapters covering all the standards and theoretical aspects of WLAN concepts and six chapters that cover the practical aspects of applying the fundamental concepts. The chapters are of varying length depending on the topic. We believe in the "brevity is the soul of wit" paradigm and have tried to be as brief as required to describe the various mechanics and mechanisms.

NOTE   For those who wonder what exactly is the difference between mechanics and mechanisms:

Mechanics is the technology, the working, the processes, and the details of how something works or the way something is done. For example, WEP is the mechanics for providing confidentiality in the WLAN world.

Mechanism is the machinery that implements the mechanics. For example, different vendors could have different mechanisms to implement WEP.

Chapter 1, "Securing WLANs Overview," is an introduction to the WLAN domain, and it covers the basic concepts and lexicon of WLAN.

Chapter 2, "Basic Security Mechanics and Mechanisms," deals with the basics of cryptography so that the uninitiated will not feel overwhelmed. This chapter covers the security concepts relevant to the WLAN domain.

Chapter 3, "WLAN Standards," describes the various standards one will encounter when dealing with the WLAN domain. This chapter covers in brief the IEEE 802 family of standards, hardware standards from ETSI, and authentication standards from IETF.

Chapter 4, "WLAN Fundamentals," gives a detailed introduction to all the aspects of WLAN security. This chapter covers the essential basics of the WLAN technology: services, messages, choreographies, and interaction primitives. It also talks a bit about the WLAN security model.

Chapter 5, "WLAN Basic Authentication and Privacy Methods," describes the various authentication methods, with the major one being the WEP. It covers open authentication, MAC-based authentication, shared-key authentication, and WEP. The methods are analyzed in terms of the AAA infrastructure requirements, auditing and accounting requirements, and the vulnerabilities and countermeasures.

Chapter 6, "Wireless Vulnerabilities," builds on the earlier chapters and describes the vulnerabilities of WLAN in detail. This chapter introduces wireless attacks via attack trees; describes reconnaissance, denial-of-service (DoS), authentication, encryption, and EAP protocol attacks; describes the tools that attackers use; discusses problems with rogue access points; and briefly discusses ad-hoc mode security.

Chapter 7, "EAP Authentication Protocols for WLANs," deals with the Extensible Authentication Protocol (EAP) methods: the various standards and specifications, how they interact with each other, and the protocols. This chapter covers the access control and authentication mechanics such as EAP, PEAP, 802.1x, LEAP, and EAP-FAST.

Chapter 8, "WLAN Encryption and Data Integrity Protocols," covers the security enhancements in the 802.11i and WPA standards; discusses wireless encryption and data integrity protocols, including WEP, TKIP, and CCMP; discusses security associations; describes key management processes; and analyzes which of the security vulnerabilities (introduced in Chapter 6) 802.11i addresses and which it does not.

Chapter 9, "SWAN: End-to-End Security Deployment," covers the Structured Wireless Aware Network solution. It details the fine points of the SWAN elements: WLSE, 802.1x authentication server, IOS-enabled access points, and wired elements such as routers and switches.

Chapters 10 through 13 aggregate the concepts from the previous chapters to depict WLAN architectures: best practices, design guidelines, configurations, and deployment examples.

Chapter 10, "Design Guidelines for Secure WLAN," provides WLAN design guidelines and fundamentals for various technologies including VPN overlay technologies, IPSec, authentication support, and threat mitigation.

Chapter 11, "Operational and Design Considerations for Secure WLANs," covers the security component best practices. This chapter addresses rogue AP detection and prevention, WLAN monitoring and intrusion detection, WLAN services scaling, and enterprise guest access.

Chapter 12, "WLAN Security Configuration Guidelines and Examples," covers the detailed configuration examples and guidelines for various security implementations such as guest access (open/no WEP), static-WEP, MAC-address authentication, EAP/802.1x with dynamic WEP, EAP/802.1x with WPA, WPA-PSK, multiple SSIDs/VLANs, and IPSec VPN. It provides secure management configuration examples to secure management traffic to the WLAN infrastructure devices and discusses secure wired policies (for example, layer-3/layer-4 ACLs) to match wireless policies.

Chapter 13, "WLAN Deployment Examples," is the deployment chapter. This chapter discusses several WLAN deployment examples across large, medium, and small enterprise networks and across vertical markets such as retail, education, healthcare, and manufacturing. It summarizes the authors' WLAN security architecture experience. We have tried to abstract and extract common patterns out of the WLAN architectures that we have encountered.

Appendix A, "Resources and References," contains the reference materials for the various chapters. This should help readers dig deeper into technologies they care about and that have relevance in their day-to-day job.

We wish you the very best on your journey through the exciting world of WLAN security . . . . If you think we have done a good job, please tell others. If you have any comments about our work, please do tell us . . . .

CHAPTER 1

Securing WLANs Overview

This chapter takes a bird's-eye view of the WLAN space in terms of entities, terminology, standards, and naturally, security. You will, of course, dig deeper into these various aspects in the rest of the book. The purpose of this chapter is to give you information in context to act as a good introduction to the WLAN world. This chapter also includes a section that acts as a forward glance to the rest of this book.

WLAN: A Perspective

A wireless LAN (WLAN) is, in some sense, nothing but radio—with different frequencies and characteristics—acting as the medium for networks. The concept of WLAN fundamentally changes the networking you are accustomed to: wired connections through some form of jacks attached to structures. The lack of hard wires in WLANs ushers in an era in which mobility, pervasive and ubiquitous connectivity, and all the associated interaction models prevail. As hyped as this technology is, there is still a belief in the industry that WLANs are not hyped enough.

It is true that, eventually, this technology will find itself in almost all the everyday things in our homes and elsewhere, from connecting the different devices in home entertainment to connecting to the Internet in public places, in addition to different ways of interacting in our workplace. In the future, mobile networks will be the norm, and wired networks will be used in special cases only, rather than the current situation in which the opposite is true.

The wireless world will move into other areas aside from just data networks, and it will open opportunity for a variety of unconventional services. There are already wireless phones (which employ voice over IP [VoIP] technologies) that operate over WLAN, devices that pipe music over WLAN, and TV recorders that have features to access the recorded shows over WLAN from other parts of the home. Ubiquitous location services over WLAN, in addition to WLANs in automobiles, are almost here. Just recently, there was news about the Federal Communications Commission's (FCC) proposal to allow the extending of the unused spectrum between the TV channels 2 and 51 for unlicensed wireless devices. The significance of this initiative is multifold: The TV signals operate at lower signals, resulting in higher range and better penetration through walls and other structures. They also offer more strength. The other dimension is the capability for the TV infrastructure to offer innovative interactive services based on WLANs operating in this spectrum.

However, the WLAN domain is also filled with various barriers—security, a limited range, nonuniform signal strength, and lack of efficient handover/roaming mechanisms between the WLAN access points (APs). WLAN also adds overhead in terms of messages for the discovery of APs and additional messages for roaming, management, and handover.

Major WLAN deployments, such an enterprise-level deployment, need to address various aspects including mobility, security, management (both network management and radio frequency [RF] management), and integration into existing infrastructure.

The key aspect of the WLAN network is secure mobility, which is the topic of this book. The challenge in the WLAN world is the security aspects, especially authentication, access control, and confidentiality. WLAN obsoletes the major assumptions in the static wired-network world and challenges the designers, architects, and administrators of networks to achieve similar or more secure LANs.

The design of WLAN is evolving—from distributed/decentralized deployment of access points and clients to centralized deployments and more integration with existing infrastructure. For example, the latest products from Cisco exemplify this trend:

- Cisco Structured Wireless Aware Network (SWAN) solution extends the "wireless awareness" into the wired infrastructure. The SWAN framework addresses WLAN deployments of different scale—from small businesses to enterprises to universities to public WLANs—and it offers the capability to integrate and extend wired and wireless networks. The wired and wireless infrastructure can be highly integrated, or the WLAN can be an overlay over the existing wired infrastructure. Chapter 9, "SWAN: End-to-End Security Deployment," covers SWAN in more detail.

- Cisco Wireless LAN Services Module (WLSM) for the Catalyst 6500 series adds fast, secure, campus-wide, wireless Layer 3 roaming and simplifies wireless deployments and ongoing network operations. The WLSM also enables you to extend the Catalyst 6500 features through the following:

  — It extends Layers 2 and 3 of the Catalyst 6500 series supervisor Nonstop Forwarding/Stateful Switchover (NSF/SSO) to wireless traffic.

  — It applies a full range of ACLs for traffic inspection, filtering, and rate limiting based on Layers 2 through 4 header information to wireless traffic.

  — Quality of service (QoS) preservation and policy enforcement of all wireless traffic on a per-mobility-group basis.

  — Hardware-based denial-of-service (DoS) protection mechanisms such as control plane rate limiters and Unicast Reverse Path Forwarding (uRPF).

  — Interoperability with intrusion detection, network analysis, IPSec VPN, and firewall services modules.

- The Cisco Compatible Extensions (CCX) for WLANs initiative provides the capability to achieve interoperability while evolving through various standards and specifications to achieve security, performance, and rich functionality. The industry should not diverge and fragment while rapid advancements occur.

In summary, the security in WLAN network deployment is of utmost importance, and the mechanics and mechanisms of the security in WLAN are the focus of this book.

Wireless LAN Components and Terminology

Components of a traditional WLAN network include APs, network interface cards (NICs) or client adapters, bridges, repeaters, and antennae. Additionally, an authentication, authorization, and accounting (AAA) server (specifically a Remote Address Dial-In User Service [RADIUS] server), network management server (NMS), and "wireless-aware" switches and routers are considered as part of an enterprise WLAN network.

Figure 1-1 illustrates WLAN components in an enterprise network architecture. Note that only components related to building a Cisco WLAN network are defined in the figure.

Figure 1-1   *Components of WLAN System*

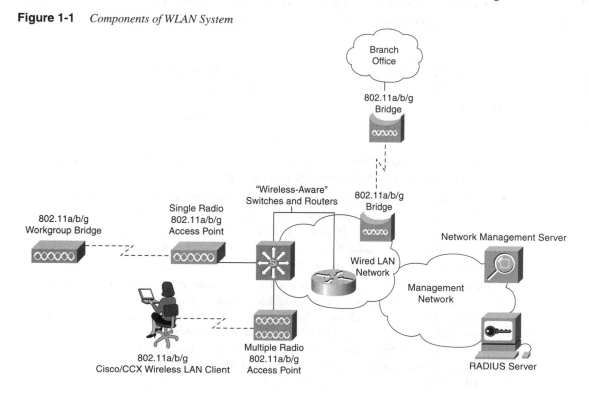

The following list describes in further detail the WLAN components depicted in Figure 1-1:

- **Access point (AP)**—An AP operates within a specific frequency spectrum and uses an 802.11 standard modulation technique. It also informs the wireless clients of its availability and authenticates and associates wireless clients to the wireless network. An AP also coordinates the wireless clients' use of wired resources. It should be noted that there are several kinds of APs, including single radio and multiple radios, based on different 802.11 technologies.

- **NIC or client adapter**—A PC or workstation uses a wireless NIC or client adapter to connect to the wireless network. The NIC scans the available frequency spectrum for connectivity and associates it to an AP or another wireless client. The NIC is coupled to the PC or workstation operating system (OS) using a software driver. Various client adapters are available from Cisco and CCX vendors.

- **Bridge**—Wireless bridges are used to connect multiple LANs (both wired and wireless) at the Media Access Control (MAC) layer level. Used in building-to-building wireless connections, wireless bridges can cover longer distances than APs. (The Institute of Electrical and Electronics Engineers [IEEE] 802.11 standard specifies one mile as the maximum coverage range for an AP.) Bridges are available for deployment using different 802.11 technologies.

NOTE   Currently, bridges are not defined in the 802.11 standards; hence, the bridges do not operate on open standards. This means the bridges must be from the same vendor as the WLAN infrastructure.

- **Workgroup bridge (WGB)**—A workgroup bridge is a smaller-scale bridge that can be used to support a limited number of wired clients.

- **Antenna**—An antenna radiates the modulated signal through the air so that wireless clients can receive it. Characteristics of an antenna are defined by propagation pattern (directional versus omnidirectional), gain, transmit power, and so on. Antennas are needed on the APs, bridges, and clients. The antennas need not be conspicuous at all; for example, many PC manufacturers build the antenna inside the LCD screen.

- **AAA server**—AAA services are needed to secure a WLAN network. The AAA server is used for both user and administrator authentication in a WLAN network. It is used for enterprise networks, not home WLANs. The AAA server can be used to pass policy such as virtual LAN (VLAN) and SSID for clients, to grant different levels of authorization rights to administrative users, and to generate dynamic encryption keys for WLAN users. Furthermore, accounting features of a AAA server can be used to track WLAN user activities.

- **Network management server (NMS)**—The NMS is needed to ease the complexity of deployment and management of large WLAN networks. The NMS should support firmware/software management, configuration management, performance trending and reporting, and client association reporting capabilities in a WLAN network. Furthermore, additional capabilities to manage the RF spectrum and detect rogue APs are needed in an enterprise WLAN network. The NMS should be supported by other normal management systems for syslogs, traps, and so on.

- **"Wireless-aware" switches and routers**—To scale and manage WLAN networks, integration between traditional WLAN elements (such as APs, bridges, WGBs, and WLAN clients) and wired network elements (such as switches, access/distribution switches, and routers) is provided by Cisco. Roaming, network management, security, and additional services can be enabled on the wired infrastructure to manage, scale, and provide end-to-end security.

Components discussed in the preceding list integrate with each other to create an end-to-end network to enable mobility in enterprise and vertical markets.

NOTE   One source of confusion in the WLAN world is that because the WLAN domain leverages many different standards, the same entity is known by many names in different standards and specifications.

The *client adapter* is also called "STA" (station) or "supplicant" or "peer" in many of the standards. The *access point* is also known as an "authenticator" or "network access server," because it acts as the point where the client interfaces with the network. The *AAA server* is also known as an "authentication server," "RADUIS server," or even "access control server (ACS)."

WLAN Standards

The various aspects of the WLAN domain are based on public standards from various bodies—the IEEE, the European Telecommunications Standards Institute (ETSI), and the Internet Engineering Task Force (IETF). The fundamental standard is the IEEE 802.11, which specifies the WLAN protocols, data frames, various layers, and frequencies. The IETF standards are in the security protocols and methods domain, whereas ETSI specifies the frequencies and other radio regulatory matters. Chapter 3, "WLAN Standards," describes the various standards in detail.

WLAN Security

The very fundamentals of WLAN that make this technology disruptive also make it a challenge in terms of security. LANs are based on the wired fundamentals, especially in terms of confidentiality and access control. In the wired world, the wires protect the communication to some extent—one needs to connect to a physical jack to communicate. In the wireless world, however, the signals are in the air, open for all to listen. Also, the wireless signals cross the physical boundaries of an organization. This same signals-in-the-air property of WLANs makes it important that there be strong confidentiality (based on encryption) and access control based on authentication mechanisms. In some sense, most of WLAN security is about achieving this balance.

WLAN Security Domain Conceptual Model

First, look at the WLAN security domain from a conceptual modeling perspective. Figure 1-2 shows the domain conceptual model and the relationship between the various components and acts as a backdrop for this book. This model defines the entities, functionalities, and relationships between them. Further, the mechanisms are the technologies and protocols through which the functionalities are implemented.

In a nutshell, the WLAN system consists of entities [1] in Figure 1-2. Entities include users, wireless cards, APs, corporate networks, and service provider network access. Each entity is identified by an identity attribute or identifier [2]. Table 1-1 shows the common identifiers for each type of entity.

Table 1-1   *Common Identifiers for Entities*

Identifier	Entity
Principals	Username, DN in a certificate
Client cards	MAC ID, IP address
Access points	SSID

You need to know how the entities are identified because, in most cases, the identities could be spoofed, so you need forms of authentication to establish the identity. Entities, of course, have credentials [3] for authentication and authorization that are exchanged using authentication protocols [7]. Entities communicate over channels that need to be secured against different types of attacks (passive and active). The final goal is to securely authenticate the entities using authentication systems [6]. The corporate AAA systems [6] hold the various required elements such as keys, usernames, password hashes, policies, and so on. Authentication protocols [7] facilitate authentication mechanisms to exchange credentials and challenge/response handshakes.

Figure 1-2   *WLAN Security Domain Conceptual Model*

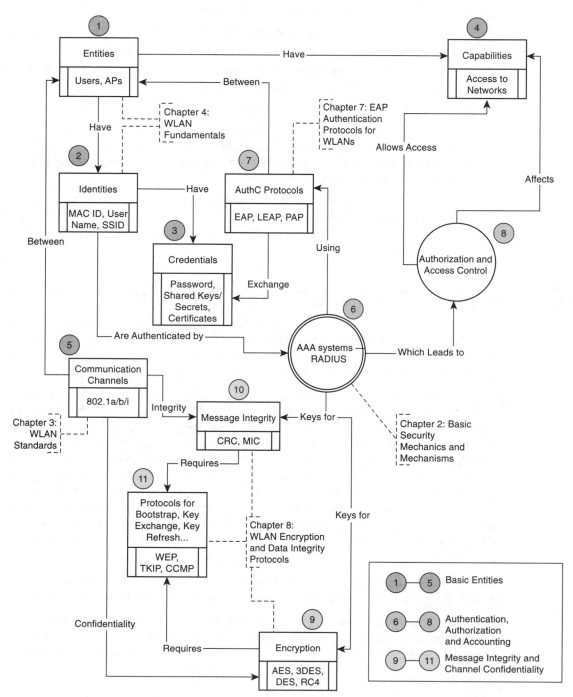

After a client is authenticated to satisfaction (based on the network policies in place), the client is authorized [8]. This authorization can take many forms:

- In the case of enterprises, the client might get full network privilege or access to restricted areas in the network (such as Internet access for guests and visitors).

- For public WLANs, this might involve payment gateways, account checks with WSP, and so on, with access provided depending on the level of service.

- Authorization would also include expiration of connections and other similar functions.

- In many cases, such as conferences, the authorization might be null in the sense that, after it is authenticated, the clients have access to the network resources. Remember in these cases that the network is just a connection to the Internet and possibly a server with conference-related materials.

The other security aspect is the integrity and confidentiality of the communication channels [5]. The confidentiality is achieved by encryption [9], and message integrity is achieved by digital signatures [10] with suitable mechanisms for bootstrapping, key exchange, and key refresh [11].

Navigating This Book and Chapter Contexts

This book focuses primarily on the security of WLANs; hence, all the chapters are directly and indirectly related to the various aspects of WLAN security. This book is virtually divided into two parts: Chapters 1 through 8 cover the underpinnings and concepts, and Chapters 9 through 13 cover the design, best practices, configuration, and deployment.

Figure 1-2 shows some of the chapters that cover the basic concepts. You might wonder about the utility of reading rigorously through the sometimes dry standards and protocol choreography materials. Some of you might be in the habit of skipping the chapters dealing with standards because they are opaque and more difficult to read. Hopefully, you are motivated to read through the standards chapters in this book. As one of the reviewers pointed out, in this case, because of rapid evolution, an understanding of the standards represents new technology that improves the operation and management of wireless networks. In many cases, such as with EAP-FAST, implementing a secure infrastructure requires the basics of authentication protocols such as EAP. Furthermore, the domain of WLAN is evolving at a fast pace—it has advanced at least two generations since we started this book! So the only defense against becoming out of date is to keep up with the fundamentals.

Chapter 2, "Basic Security Mechanics and Mechanisms," contains the concise and basic background material for cryptography and various security-related protocols and methods.

Chapter 3, "WLAN Standards," might seem dry, but it is a good introduction to various standards. When you need more information on a particular standard, you can refer to the standard directly. A basic perspective on the major IEEE and IETF standards is essential to comprehend and improve on the WLAN security space. Chapter 4, "WLAN Fundamentals," details the WLAN basics in even more depth.

A deep knowledge of the vulnerabilities of existing implementations will prevent you from repeating mistakes. In this regard, understanding the "classic" WEP implementation in Chapter 5, "WLAN Basic Authentication and Privacy Methods," is a good approach. Then dig deeper into the security aspects in Chapter 6, "Wireless Vulnerabilities." Finally, as mentioned previously, you need an understanding of protocols to implement a secure infrastructure. Chapter 7, "EAP Authentication Protocols for WLANs," and Chapter 8, "WLAN Encryption and Data Integrity Protocols," provide this requirement.

Chapters 9 through 13 address the most interesting aspects—the design, configuration, and deployment of WLAN. Chapter 9, "SWAN: End-to-End Security Deployment," covers the Cisco Structured Wireless Aware Network (SWAN), which enables scalability, manageability, reliability, and ease of deployment for small, medium, and large enterprise and vertical networks. Chapter 10, "Design Guidelines for Secure WLAN," and Chapter 11, "Operational and Design Considerations for Secure WLANs," provide an excellent opportunity to transcend the technological underpinnings to design guidelines and operational best practices. Chapter 12, "WLAN Security Configuration Guidelines and Examples," covers configuration for Cisco products, which come in handy when working with the Aironet products. Chapter 13, "WLAN Deployment Examples," is an opportunity to understand and gain a comprehensive knowledge of deployment patterns that you can extend to real-world implementations.

This book was conceived and written to be read sequentially from Chapter 1 to the end. The various concepts are introduced and discussed with minimum requirement for prior knowledge. In addition, the topics are elaborated on in a progressive manner so that you do not encounter a new concept technology without proper introduction.

Summary

This short chapter introduced the WLAN concept and the terminology you will need to understand throughout the book. It also introduced a basic security model for WLANs and described the various upcoming chapters in this book.

CHAPTER 2

Basic Security Mechanics and Mechanisms

This chapter covers the essential topics you will encounter during your journey through the wireless world, ranging from cryptography to various security protocols used in the industry. This chapter also examines some of the cryptographic primitives—the building blocks and concepts that are part of security mechanisms.

Because each topic itself requires a book, this chapter tries to capture the essence of each concept. You will also get a glimpse of the vulnerabilities that are detailed in later chapters.

This book defines *mechanics* as the general capability (for example, confidentiality) and *mechanisms* as the detailed technologies, protocols, and implementations (for example, encryption, message formats to exchange essential information, and key exchange).

Security Mechanics

The basic security mechanics are confidentiality, integrity, and availability. In the case of the wireless world (as in many other worlds), authentication, authorization, and access control are also the basic security mechanics to be achieved. Many times, availability is viewed as a quality-of-service (QoS) feature rather than a security issue. Cryptography, in some sense, is the mechanism to achieve the security goals. The topics of interest to the wireless world are digital signature, encryption, and key management.

The following list provides the formal definitions of the basic security mechanics:

- Confidentiality

  Definition: The capability to send (and receive) data without divulging any part to unauthorized entities during the transmission of data.

  Mechanisms: Encryption—symmetric and asymmetric.

- Integrity

  Definition: The capability to send (and receive) data such that unauthorized entities cannot change any part of the exchanged data without the sender/receiver detecting the change. If only integrity mechanics are in place, data can be changed, but the integrity will detect tampering.

  Mechanisms: Digital signatures using one-way hash functions.

- Availability

  Definition: Here, *availability* is defined as the capability to receive and send data. For example, if a system is under a DoS attack, it will not be able to receive or send data.

  Mechanisms: Availability mechanisms are mostly defense mechanisms that detect various forms of DoS attacks and guard against them.

- Authentication

  Definition: Authentication establishes the identity of the sender or receiver of information. Any integrity check or confidential information is often meaningless if the identity of the sending or receiving party is not properly established.

  Mechanisms: Multiple levels and protocols such as 802.1x, RADIUS, PAP/ CHAP, MS-CHAP, and so on.

- Authorization

  Definition: Authorization is tightly coupled with authentication in most network resource access requirements. Authorization establishes what you are allowed to do after you have identified yourself. (It is also called *access control*, *capabilities*, and *permissions*.) It can be argued that authorization does not always require *a priori* authentication. However, in this book, authentication and authorization are tightly coupled; authorization usually follows any authentication procedure.

  Mechanisms: Multiple levels and protocols.

- Access control

  Definition: The capability to control access of entities to resources based on various properties: attributes, authentication, policies, and so on.

  Mechanisms: At the access point (AP) based on authentication or knowledge of the WEP key.

- Encryption

  Definition: The capability to transform data (or plain text) into meaningless bytes (cipher text) based on some algorithm. Decryption is the act of turning the meaningless bytes to meaningful data again.

  Mechanisms: The main issue related to authentication and authorization in the wireless space is the robustness of the methods used in verifying an entity's identity.

The second issue is maintaining the confidentiality of the "wire" and connection and keeping it bulletproof.

In the wireless case, the wire is the air, so the problem of confidentiality becomes more difficult because anybody could potentially be a passive listener to the airwaves. The relevant point is that, in the WLAN space, encryption is needed if you are to trust the authentication. The wireless domain employs mechanisms such as WEP, CKIP, and TKIP.

- Key management

   Definition: A key is a digital code that can be used to encrypt, decrypt, and sign information. Some keys are kept private, and others are shared and must be distributed in a secure manner. *Key management* refers to the process of distributing keys for the processes previously mentioned (for example, changing keys, not signing information).

   Mechanisms: The challenge in the wireless area is the key distribution—secure and scaleable in an automated fashion.

Next, look at each of the mechanics in a little more detail.

Confidentiality Mechanisms

Confidentiality is achieved using data encryption. Encryption can be done using either the symmetric key paradigm or the asymmetric key paradigm.

Symmetric Key Encryption

Symmetric key encryption, often referred to as *secret key encryption*, uses a common key and the same cryptographic algorithm to scramble and unscramble a message.

NOTE   Symmetric key encryption and decryption are mathematically inexpensive compared to asymmetric key; therefore, they have a major performance advantage. For any bulk encryption, the preferred method is symmetric encryption.

Figure 2-1 shows two users, Alice and Bob, who want to communicate securely with each other. Both Alice and Bob have to agree on the same cryptographic algorithm to use for encrypting and decrypting data. They also have to agree on a common key—the secret key—to use with their chosen encryption/decryption algorithm. There are negotiation protocols to arrive at mutually agreeable algorithms and keys.

Figure 2-1 *Symmetric Key Encryption*

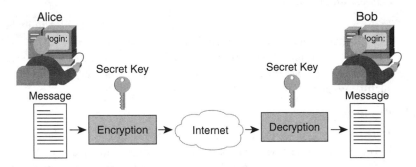

The symmetric key algorithms fall into two categories:

- **Block ciphers**—Operate on 64-bit message blocks. Even though most of the block ciphers operate on a 64-bit block, it is not an absolute requirement.

- **Stream ciphers**—Operate on a stream of data, which basically means they operate on a byte at a time.

One point to note is that you don't get to choose which method to employ for a given algorithm. The algorithms employed by the WLAN methods use the block cipher method, so let's look closely at this method and the associated challenges.

NOTE   The newer WLAN security algorithms use the Advanced Encryption Standard (AES), which uses the stream cipher method. But it is still informative to understand and learn from the vulnerabilities of the "classic" WLAN security methods.

Chaining Mechanics in Block Cipher

In the block ciphers, it is necessary to break up larger messages into 64-bit blocks and somehow chain them together. Four common chaining mechanisms called *modes* exist, and each mode defines a method of combining the plain text (the message that is not encrypted), the secret key, and the cipher text (the encrypted text) to generate the stream of cipher text that is actually transmitted to the recipient. These four modes are as follows:

- Electronic codebook (ECB)
- Cipher block chaining (CBC)
- Cipher feedback (CFB)
- Output feedback (OFB)

The ECB chaining mechanism encodes each 64-bit block independently but uses the same key. The result is that the same plain text will *always* result in the same cipher text. This weakness can be exploited in multiple ways. For example, if a snooper knows the plain text and the corresponding cipher text, that person can at least understand some parts of a message. Another vulnerability is the opportunity for an eavesdropper to analyze and perform pattern matching. A much simpler vulnerability is that an eavesdropper can recognize a change of information (when the cipher text changes) and make inferences without knowing the contents. For example, consider someone snooping a certain employee's automatic payroll transactions to a bank. Assuming that the amount is the same for each paycheck, each ECB-encoded cipher text message would appear the same. However, if the cipher text changes, the snooper could conclude that the payroll recipient received a raise and perhaps was promoted.

NOTE   Remember, in the wireless world, encryption has one and only one function: to prevent an eavesdropper from reading (or, for that matter, making any intelligent inferences of) the data passing.

Because an eavesdropper can capture the packets and analyze them later, the task of achieving confidentiality is much more difficult, so the goal is achieving confidentiality for a time limit; the strength used depends on how long the data should remain unreadable.

Another vulnerability is information leakage through pattern matching and recognizing a change in fixed data. An eavesdropper could capture the WLAN packets, look for changes, and make some inferences about the information. This makes WLAN confidentiality dynamic, so achieving confidentiality in the WLAN world becomes more difficult than in a static environment.

The remaining three algorithms—CBC, CFB, and OFB—have inherent properties that add an element of randomness to the encrypted messages. If you send the same plain text block through one of these three algorithms, you get back different cipher text blocks each time. Most secret key algorithms use one of these four modes to provide additional security for the transmitted data.

In CBC, the current block is XORed with the previous block. This still leaves the first block vunerable, and for that, the CBC uses an *initialization vector* (IV). An IV is an encrypted block of random data used as the first 64-bit block to begin the chaining process.

The CFB mode uses the cipher text of the preceding block rather than the plain text.

The OFB mode is similar to the CFB, but the XORed block is generated randomly and is therefore independent of the preceding plain text.

NOTE   The wireless world uses a stream cipher with an IV to achieve the randomness. In the case of Wired Equivalent Privacy (WEP), the IV is sent as plain text with the encrypted data. As you will see later, one of the weaknesses in wireless security deals with the implementation of the encryption algorithm and how the IV is handled.

Symmetric Key Encryption Algorithms

The following are some of the more common symmetric key algorithms used today:

- **Advanced Encryption Standard (AES)**—AES was developed as part of the U.S. Department of Commerce's effort to develop the next-generation encryption standard. You can find more information at the National Institute of Standards and Technology website: http://www.nist.gov/public_affairs/releases/g00-176.htm. Currently, among all the encryption algorithms, AES is the strongest encryption algorithm, so all new implementations are moving toward AES. For example, the IEEE specification 802.11i requires AES encryption.

- **Data Encryption Standard (DES)**—DES is the most widely used encryption scheme today. It operates on 64-bit message blocks. The algorithm uses a series of steps to transform 64 input bits into 64 output bits. In its standard form, the algorithm uses 64-bit keys, of which 56 bits are chosen randomly. The remaining 8 bits are parity bits (one for each 7-bit block of the 56-bit random value). DES is widely employed in many commercial applications today and can be used in all four modes: ECB, CBC, CFB, and OFB. Generally, however, DES operates in either CBC mode or CFB mode.

NOTE   The standard DES key length is 64 bits. Due to export regulations, you will see that 40-bit DES is also a standard. In the 40-bit DES, all but 40 bits of the key are disclosed by the implementation of the communications mechanism. For example, you can implement 40-bit DES by prefacing each message with the same 24 bits of the DES key used to encrypt the data. 40-bit DES exists solely as an artifact of U.S. government export controls; there is no technical reason that you should not use standard DES at all times.

- **3DES (read "triple DES")**—3DES is an alternative to DES that preserves the existing investment in software but makes a brute-force attack more difficult. 3DES takes a 64-bit block of data and performs the encrypt, decrypt, and encrypt operations. 3DES can use one, two, or three different keys. The advantage of using one key is that, with the exception of the additional processing time required, 3DES with one key is the same as standard DES (for backward compatibility). 3DES is defined only in ECB mode, mainly for performance reasons: it compromises speed for the sake of a more secure algorithm. Both the DES and 3DES algorithms are in the public domain and are freely available.

- **Rivest Cipher 4 (RC4)**—RC4 is a proprietary algorithm invented by Ron Rivest and marketed by RSA Data Security. It is used often with a 128-bit key, although its key size can vary. RC4 uses the block cipher mode. It is unpatented but is protected as a trade secret; however, it was leaked to the Internet in September 1994. Because the U.S. government allows it to be exported when using secret key lengths of 40 bits or less, some implementations use a very short key length. WEP uses the RC4 algorithm.

- **International Data Encryption Algorithm (IDEA)**—IDEA was developed to replace DES. It also operates on 64-bit message blocks but uses a 128-bit key. As with DES, IDEA can operate in all four modes: ECB, CBC, CFB, and OFB. IDEA was designed to be efficient in both hardware and software implementations. It is a patented algorithm and requires a license for commercial use.

Symmetric key encryption is most often used for data confidentiality because most symmetric key algorithms have been designed to be implemented in hardware and have been optimized for encrypting large amounts of data at one time. Challenges with symmetric key encryption include the following:

- Changing the secret keys frequently to avoid the risk of compromising the keys
- Securely generating the secret keys
- Securely distributing the secret keys

Asymmetric encryption is commonly used to facilitate distribution of symmetric keys. A commonly used mechanism to derive and exchange secret keys securely is the Diffie-Hellman algorithm. This algorithm is explained in the "Key Management" section later in this chapter.

Asymmetric Encryption

Asymmetric encryption is often referred to as public key encryption. It can use either the same algorithm or different but complementary algorithms to scramble and unscramble data. Two different but related key values are required: a public key and a private key. With the keys, if plain text is encrypted using the public key, it can only be decrypted using the private key (and vice versa).

Some of the more common uses of public key algorithms are listed here:

- Data integrity
- Data confidentiality
- Sender nonrepudiation
- Sender authentication

Data confidentiality and sender authentication can be achieved using the public key algorithm. Figure 2-2 shows how data integrity and confidentiality are provided using public key encryption.

Figure 2-2 *Ensuring Data Integrity and Confidentiality with Public Key Encryption*

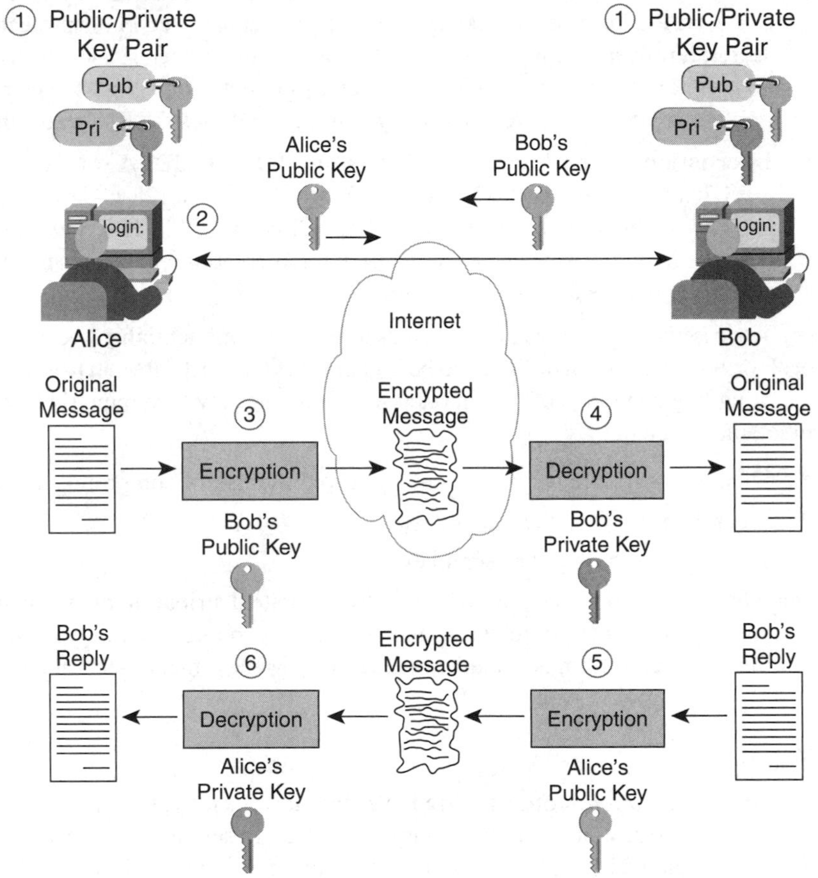

The following steps must take place if Alice and Bob are to have confidential data exchange:

Step 1 Both Alice and Bob create their individual public/private key pairs.

Step 2 Alice and Bob exchange their public keys.

Step 3 Alice writes a message to Bob and uses his public key to encrypt her message. Then she sends the encrypted data to Bob over the Internet.

Step 4 Bob uses his private key to decrypt the message.

Step 5 Bob writes a reply, encrypts the reply with Alice's public key, and sends the encrypted reply over the Internet to Alice.

Step 6 Alice uses her private key to decrypt the reply.

Data confidentiality is ensured when Alice sends the initial message because only Bob can decrypt the message with his private key. Data integrity is also preserved because, to modify the message, a malicious attacker would need Bob's private key again. Data integrity and confidentiality are also ensured for the reply because only Alice has access to her private key, and she is the only one who can modify or decrypt the reply with her private key.

However, this exchange is not very reassuring because it is easy for a third party to pretend to be Alice and send a message to Bob encrypted with Bob's public key. The public key is, after all, widely available. Verification that it was Alice who sent the initial message is important.

Figure 2-3 shows how public key cryptography resolves this problem and provides for sender authentication and nonrepudiation.

Figure 2-3   *Sender Authentication and Nonrepudiation Using Public Key Encryption*

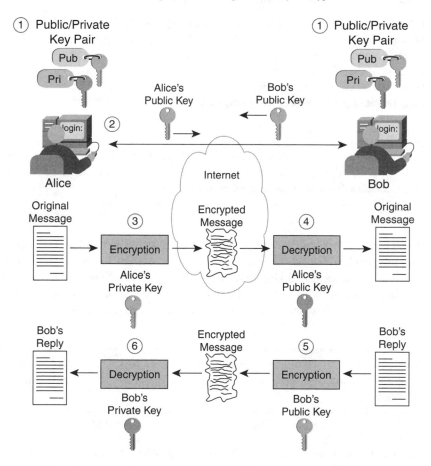

The following steps have to take place if Alice and Bob are to have an *authenticated data exchange*:

Step 1 Both Alice and Bob create their public/private key pairs.

Step 2 Alice and Bob exchange their public keys.

Step 3 Alice writes a message for Bob, uses her private key to encrypt the message, and then sends the encrypted data over the Internet to Bob.

Step 4 Bob uses Alice's public key to decrypt the message.

Step 5 Bob writes a reply, encrypts the reply with his private key, and sends the encrypted reply over the Internet to Alice.

Step 6 Alice uses Bob's public key to decrypt the reply.

Here the encryption is done using the private keys. An authenticated exchange is ensured because only Bob and Alice have access to their respective private keys. Bob and Alice should meet the requirement of nonrepudiation—that is, they cannot later deny sending the given message if their keys have not been compromised. This, of course, lends itself to a hot debate about how honest Bob and Alice are; they can deny sending messages by simply stating that their private keys have been compromised.

NOTE This scenario assumes a secure out-of-band exchange of the public keys between Alice and Bob. This would be practical for a one-time point-to-point exchange between two entities but is not scalable for a large number of entities.

If you want to use public key cryptography to perform an authenticated exchange and to ensure data integrity and confidentiality, double encryption needs to occur. Alice would first encrypt her confidential message to Bob with his public key and then encrypt again with her private key. Anyone would be able to decrypt the first message to get the embedded cipher text, but only Bob would be able to decrypt the cipher text with his private key.

NOTE A crucial aspect of asymmetric encryption is that the private key must be kept private. If the private key is compromised, an evil attacker can impersonate you and send and receive your messages.

The mechanisms used to generate these public/private key pairs are complex, but they result in the generation of two large random numbers, one of which becomes the public key and the other the private key. Because these numbers and their product must adhere to stringent mathematical criteria to preserve the uniqueness of each public/private key pair, generating these numbers is fairly processor intensive.

NOTE   Key pairs are not guaranteed to be unique by any mathematical criteria. However, the math ensures that no weak keys are generated.

Because of their performance constraints, they require much more computation and are not as amenable to hardware (chip) offload; public key encryption algorithms are rarely used for data confidentiality. Instead, public key encryption algorithms are typically used in applications involving authentication using digital signatures and key management. Public keys are also used to encrypt session keys, which are symmetric keys, so that they can be exchanged or sent across a public network without being compromised.

Some of the more common public key algorithms are the Ron Rivest, Adi Shamir, and Leonard Adleman (RSA) algorithm and the El Gamal algorithm.

Encryption Algorithm Strengths and Weaknesses

No discussion is complete without mentioning the relative strengths, weaknesses, and performance aspects of encryption algorithms.

One issue occurs when choosing between block versus stream ciphers. The general approach is that because hardware sees a bit at a time, stream ciphers are more efficient for hardware-based encryption. For software-based encryption, block cipher in CBC mode or higher is suitable.

A related issue is comparing the symmetric and asymmetric key operations. Symmetric encryption is much faster than asymmetric key encryption, and as a result, for encrypting any reasonable amount of data, symmetric key is better. So, usually, a session symmetric key is generated that is exchanged securely. Key exchange protocols use the asymmetric key for authentication and the exchange of the session symmetric keys.

The next question is the key length and the strength of the algorithms. The key strength is basically the time, effort, and resources required to "break" a key. The strength is very much related to current technologies, especially the processing power, so it is a relative term. In fact, nonrepudiation mechanisms, such as the ETSI specifications, have mechanics to "re-encrypt" data (at a later time, when the "strength" of the original encryption is diminished by technological advances) that is to be kept for long-term arbitration.

The number of bits required in a key to ensure secure encryption in a given environment can be controversial. The longer the *keyspace*—the range of possible values of the key—the more difficult it is to break the key in a brute-force attack. In a brute-force attack, you apply all combinations of a key to the algorithm until you succeed in deciphering the message. Table 2-1 shows the number of keys that must be tried to exhaust all possibilities, given a specified key length.

Table 2-1   *Brute-Force Attack Combinations*

Key Length (in Bits)	Number of Combinations
40	$2^{40}= 1,099,511,627,776$
56	$2^{56}= 7.205759403793 * 10^{16}$
64	$2^{64}= 1.844674407371 * 10^{19}$
112	$2^{112}= 5.192296858535 * 10^{33}$
128	$2^{128}= 3.402823669209 * 10^{38}$

A natural inclination is to use the longest available key, which makes the key more difficult to break. However, the longer the key, the more computationally expensive the encryption and decryption process can be. The goal is to make breaking a key "cost" more than the worth of the information that the key is protecting.

NOTE   If confidential messages are to be exchanged on an international level, you must understand the current government policies and regulations. Many countries have controversial import and export regulations for encryption products based on the length of the key. The U.S. export controls on cryptography have a lot of nuances, so beware.

Another important issue is the initialization vector. WEP uses the RC4 algorithm and a 24-bit IV, which is sent in clear text. The 24-bit IV gives around 16 million combinations, so theoretically, one has to capture millions of packets before seeing a key IV reuse. But, in fact, researchers have proven that key collision could occur at around 5000 packets or so. This aspect and other vulnerabilities are discussed in Chapter 6, "Wireless Vulnerabilities."

Integrity Mechanisms

Integrity mechanisms are aimed at detecting any changes to a set of bytes. The next two sections look at the integrity mechanisms using hash functions and digital signatures. Digital signatures use the hash function mechanism and encrypt the resultant hash.

Hash Functions

A *hash function* takes an input message of arbitrary length and outputs fixed-length code. The fixed-length output is called the *hash*, or the *message digest*, of the original input message.

If an algorithm is to be considered cryptographically suitable (that is, secure) for a hash function, it must exhibit the following properties:

- It must be consistent; that is, the same input must always create the same output.
- It must be random—or give the appearance of randomness—to prevent guessing of the original message.
- It must be unique; that is, it should be nearly impossible to find two messages that produce the same message digest.
- It must be one way; that is, if you are given the output, it must be extremely difficult, if not impossible, to ascertain the input message.

One-way hash functions typically are used to provide a fingerprint of a message or file. Much like a human fingerprint, a hash fingerprint is unique and thereby proves the integrity and authenticity of the message.

Let's take a look at how hash functions are used. Use Figure 2-4 to clarify this discussion. Alice and Bob are using a one-way hash function to verify that no one has tampered with the contents of the message during transit.

Figure 2-4   *Using a One-Way Hash Function for Data Integrity*

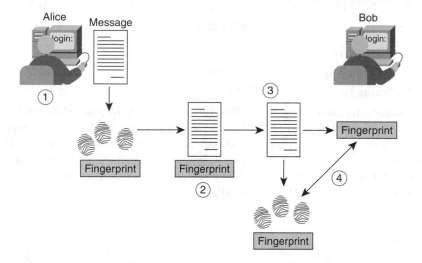

The following steps have to take place if Alice and Bob are to keep the integrity of their data:

Step 1   Alice writes a message and uses the message as input to a one-way hash function.

Step 2   The result of the hash function is appended as the fingerprint to the message that is sent to Bob.

Step 3   Bob separates the message and the appended fingerprint and uses the message as input to the same one-way hash function that Alice used.

Step 4   If the hashes match, Bob can be assured that the message was not tampered with.

The problem with this simplistic approach is that the fingerprint itself could be tampered with, and it is subject to man-in-the-middle (MitM) attacks.

NOTE   An *MitM attack* refers to an entity listening to a believed-to-be-secure communication and impersonating either the sender or receiver. This entity intercepts the message from the sender, adds its own content, and finally substitutes the correct hash for the altered message. The receiver, who is unaware of the middle entity, verifies the hash (which, of course, would be correct) and comes to the conclusion that the altered message was sent by the sender. This deception works because the hash itself is not protected.

To effectively use hash functions as fingerprints, you can combine them with public key technology to provide digital signatures, which are discussed in the next section.

Common hash functions include the following:

- Message Digest 4 (MD4) algorithm
- Message Digest 5 (MD5) algorithm
- Secure Hash Algorithm (SHA)

MD4 and MD5 were designed by Ron Rivest of MIT. SHA was developed by the National Institute of Standards and Technology (NIST). MD5 and SHA are the hash functions used most often in current security product implementations; both are based on MD4. MD5 processes its input in 512-bit blocks and produces a 128-bit message digest. SHA also processes its input in 512-bit blocks but produces a 160-bit message digest. SHA is more processor intensive and might run a little more slowly than MD5.

Digital Signatures

A *digital signature* is an encrypted message digest that is appended to a document. It can be used to confirm the identity of the sender and the integrity of the document. Digital signatures are based on a combination of public key encryption and one-way secure hash function algorithms. Figure 2-5 shows an example of how to create a digital signature.

Figure 2-5   *Creating a Digital Signature*

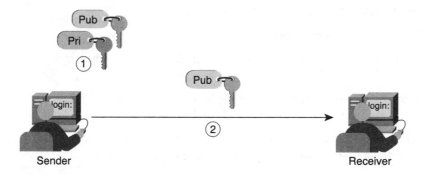

① Sender creates a public/private key pair.

② Sender sends his public key to the receiver.

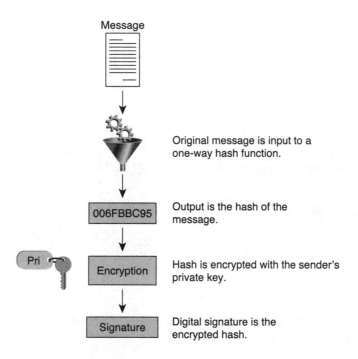

Original message is input to a
one-way hash function.

Output is the hash of the
message.

Hash is encrypted with the sender's
private key.

Digital signature is the
encrypted hash.

The following steps must be followed for Bob to create a digital signature:

Step 1 Bob creates a public/private key pair.

Step 2 Bob gives his public key to Alice.

Step 3 Bob writes a message for Alice and uses the document as input to a one-way hash function.

Step 4 Bob encrypts the output of the hash algorithm—the message digest—with his private key, resulting in the digital signature.

The combination of the document and the digital signature is the message that Bob sends to Alice. Figure 2-6 shows the verification of the digital signature.

Figure 2-6 *Verifying a Digital Signature*

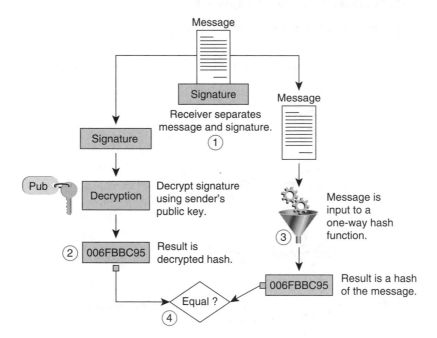

On the receiving side, these are the steps that Alice follows to verify that the message is indeed from Bob (that is, to verify the digital signature):

Step 1 Alice separates the received message into the original document and the digital signature.

Step 2 Alice uses Bob's public key to decrypt the digital signature, which results in the original message digest.

Step 3   Alice takes the original document and uses it as input to the same hash function that Bob used, which results in a message digest.

Step 4   Alice compares both of the message digests to see whether they match.

If Alice's calculation of the message digest matches Bob's decrypted message digest, the integrity of the document and the authentication of the sender are proven.

NOTE   The initial public key exchange must be performed in a trusted manner to preserve security. This is critical and is the fundamental reason for digital certificates. A digital certificate is a message that is digitally signed with the private key of a trusted third party, stating that a specific public key belongs to someone or something with a specified name and set of attributes. If the initial public key exchange wasn't performed in a trusted manner, someone could easily impersonate a given entity. As an example, if A is a spy and A knows through a wiretap that you're going to send your public key to someone via e-mail, then A could block your message and substitute A's public key instead. That would buy A the capability to forge messages. In the real world, if you send your public key to someone, what are the odds that somebody else cares? Unless secrets or money depend on this, why would anyone care? And if you're worried about that, you can always call the person and (re-)establish trust. These are some of the questions and challenges for establishing trust.

Digital signatures do not provide confidentiality of message contents. However, it is frequently more imperative to produce proof of the originator of a message than to conceal the contents of a message. It is plausible that you might want authentication and integrity of messages without confidentiality, such as when routing updates are passed in a core network. The routing contents might not be confidential, but it is important to verify that the originator of the routing update is a trusted source. An additional example of the importance of authenticating the originator of a message is in online commerce and banking transactions, for which proof of origin is imperative before acting on any transactions.

Some of the more common public key digital signature algorithms are the Ron Rivest, Adi Shamir, and Leonard Adleman (RSA) algorithm and the Digital Signature Standard (DSS) algorithm. DSS was proposed by NIST and is based on the El Gamal public key algorithm. Compared to RSA, DSS is faster for key generation and has about the same performance for generating signatures but is much slower for signature verification.

Key Management

Key management is a difficult problem in secure communications, largely due to social rather than technical factors. In the wireless world, scalability and manageability are two important factors. Current wireless technologies use symmetric key encryption. For a small number of access points (APs) and clients, it is reasonable to create a key and manually enter it. However, in most wide-scale corporations, this mechanism is awkward and outdated.

A common method used to create secret session keys in a distributed manner is the Diffie-Hellman algorithm. The Diffie-Hellman algorithm provides a way for two parties to establish a shared secret key that only those two parties know, even though they are communicating over an insecure channel. This secret key is then used to encrypt data using their favorite secret key encryption algorithm. Figure 2-7 shows how the Diffie-Hellman algorithm works.

Figure 2-7   *Establishing Secret Keys Using the Diffie-Hellman Algorithm*

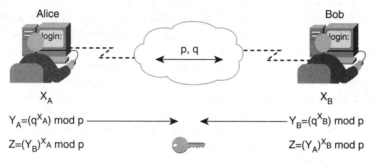

By exchanging numbers (p,q) in the clear, two entities can determine
a new unique number (z) known only to them.

The following steps are used in the Diffie-Hellman algorithm:

Step 1   Alice initiates the exchange and transmits two large numbers (p and q) to Bob.

Step 2   Alice chooses a random large integer X_A and computes the following equation:

$$Y_A = (qX_A) \bmod p$$

Step 3   Bob chooses a random large integer X_B and computes this equation:

$$Y_B = (qX_B) \bmod p$$

Step 4   Alice sends Y_A to Bob. Bob sends Y_B to Alice.

Step 5   Alice computes the following equation:

$$Z = (Y_B)X_A \bmod p$$

Step 6   Bob computes this equation:

$$Z = (Y_A)X_B \bmod p$$

The resulting shared secret key is as follows:

$$Z = Z = q(X_A X_B) \bmod p$$

The security of Diffie-Hellman relies on two difficult mathematical problems:

- Any eavesdropper has to compute a discrete logarithm to recover X_A and X_B. (That is, the eavesdropper has to figure out X_A from seeing qX_A or figure out X_B from seeing qX_B.)
- Any eavesdropper has to factor large prime numbers—numbers on the order of 100 to 200 digits can be considered large. Both p and q should be large prime numbers and (p-1)/2 should be prime.

Key management and bootstrap of trust are broad domains that are still evolving.

Creating and Distributing Public Keys

For public key algorithms, creating the public/private key pairs is complex. The pairs adhere to stringent rules as defined by varying public key algorithms to ensure the uniqueness of each public/private key pair. Uniqueness is "statistically" guaranteed; that is, the odds of two identical keys being generated independently are astronomical. The complexity associated with generating public/private key pairs is the creation of sets of parameters that meet the needs of the algorithm (for example, prime numbers for RSA and many other algorithms). Just the method for generating or finding large prime numbers is computationally hard.

NOTE   It is ideal for the end user (the person or thing being identified by the key) to generate the key pair himself. The private key should never leave the end user's possession. In corporate environments in which this might not be practical or in which key escrow is required, different rules apply. But all technical solutions should attempt self-generation as the first goal of a design architecture so that the private key is known only to the entity creating the key pair.

The problem is how you can distribute the public keys in a secure manner and how you can trust the entity that gives you the key. For a small number of wireless entities, it might be manageable to call each other or to meet face to face and give out your public key. A more scaleable approach is to use digital certificates to distribute public keys. Digital certificates require the use of a trusted third party: the certificate authority.

Digital Certificates

A digital certificate is a digitally signed message that typically is used to attest to the validity of a public key of an entity. Certificates require a common format and are largely based on the

ITU-T X.509 standard today. (ITU-T stands for International Telecommunication Union-Telecommunication Standardization Sector, the standards body that has many of the common standards like the v.32, V.42, and V.90 series for data communication over telephone networks using modems, the X series for data communications, and the H series for audio-visual multimedia systems.) The general format of an X.509 V3 certificate includes the following elements:

- Version number
- Serial number of the certificate
- Issuer algorithm information
- Issuer of certificate
- Valid to/from date
- Subject's public key
- Public key algorithm information of the subject of the certificate
- Digital signature of the issuing authority
- Optional extensions

Digital certificates are a way to prove the validity of an entity's public key and might well be the future mechanism to provide single login capabilities in today's corporate networks. However, this technology is still in its infancy as far as deployment is concerned. Much of the format of certificates has been defined, but there is still the need to ensure that certificates are valid, are manageable, and have consistent semantic interpretation. By semantic, we mean answers to questions, such as what is and what is not to be trusted and what level of trust and security the certificate implies.

NOTE   Some people disagree with the comment about digital certificates being in their infancy (among them one of the reviewers). SSL/TLS, the most widely used cryptographic standard, uses digital certificates. This is a mature technology, but enterprise deployments for system or user authentication using digital certificates are still not widely deployed.

Certificate Authorities

As noted, the certificate authority (CA) is the trusted third party that vouches for the validity of the certificate. It is up to the CA to enroll certificates, distribute certificates, and remove (revoke) certificates when the information they contain becomes invalid. Figure 2-8 shows how Bob can obtain Alice's public key in a trusted manner using a CA.

Figure 2-8   *Obtaining a Public Key in a Trusted Manner Using a CA*

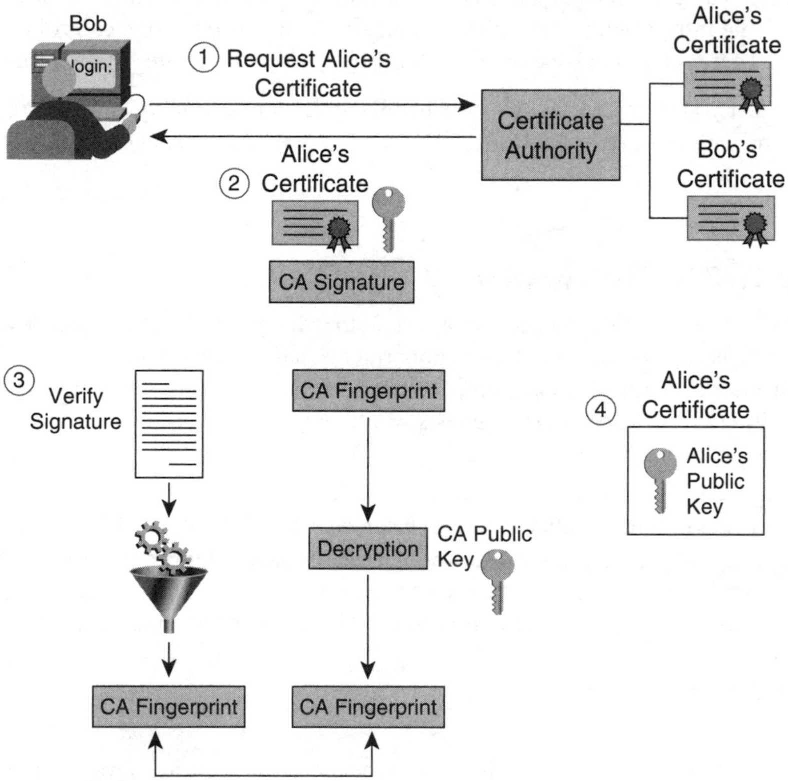

Assume that Alice has a valid certificate stored in the CA and that Bob has securely obtained the CA's public key. The steps that Bob follows to obtain Alice's public key in a reliable manner are as follows:

Step 1   Bob requests Alice's digital certificate from the CA.

Step 2   The CA sends Alice's certificate, which is signed by the CA's private key.

Step 3   Bob receives the certificate and verifies the CA's signature.

Step 4   Because Alice's certificate contains her public key, Bob now has a "notarized" version of Alice's public key.

This scheme relies on the CA's public key being distributed to users in a secure way. Most likely, this occurs using an out-of-band mechanism. There is still much debate over who should maintain CAs on the Internet. Many organizations (including financial institutions, government agencies, and application vendors) have expressed interest in offering certificate services. In all cases, it's a decision based on trust. Some corporations might want to control their own certificate infrastructure, and others might choose to outsource the control to a trusted third party. There is also the issue of cost—third-party CAs' prices are too high for many enterprises.

Now that you have looked into some details of the confidentiality and integrity mechanics and at some methods to exchange keys, let's change gears and look at the next level: authentication and identity.

Authentication and Identity Protocols

In the wireless world, you need to ascertain the identity of the users (and devices) using authentication mechanisms. This is important because access control is established depending on the user's identity. For example, users belonging to an organization would be allowed access to its internal network, whereas guests would only be allowed Internet access.

NOTE	In many environments, after you establish a peer-to-peer link-level connection, additional access control mechanisms you can sometimes deploy at higher levels of the protocol stack— for example, permitting access to hosts with certain IP addresses accessing specific applications. Also, you can assign virtual LANs and subnets to users depending on their identity.

The following sections look at, in brief, some protocols that are relevant to the wireless domain.

PPP Authentication Protocols

Passwords are incorporated into many protocols that provide authentication services. For dial-in connections, the Point-to-Point Protocol (PPP) is most often used to establish a dial-in connection over serial lines or ISDN. PPP authentication mechanisms include the Password Authentication Protocol (PAP), the Challenge Handshake Authentication Protocol (CHAP), and the Extensible Authentication Protocol (EAP). In all these cases, the user of the device is being authenticated rather than the peer device.

NOTE	PPP is relevant to the wireless domain because the evolution of PPP authentication protocols lead to EAP, which is the basis for many WLAN security protocols.

PPP is a standardized Internet encapsulation of IP over point-to-point links. PPP addresses issues such as assignment and management of IP addresses, asynchronous (start/stop) and bit-oriented synchronous encapsulation, network protocol multiplexing, link configuration, link quality testing, error detection, and option negotiation for such capabilities as network-layer address negotiation and data compression negotiation. PPP addresses these issues by providing an extensible Link Control Protocol (LCP) and a family of Network Control Protocols (NCPs) to negotiate optional configuration parameters and facilities. After the link has been established, PPP provides for an optional authentication phase before proceeding to the network-layer protocol phase.

The PPP protocol data unit (PDU) uses the high-level data link control (HDLC) frame as stipulated in ISO 3309-1979 (and amended by ISO 3309-1984/PDAD1).

PPP negotiation consists of LCP and NCP negotiation. LCP is responsible for establishing the connection with certain negotiated options, maintaining the connection, and providing procedures to terminate the connection. To perform these functions, LCP is organized into the following four phases:

1 Link establishment and configuration negotiation

2 Link quality determination

3 Network-layer protocol configuration negotiation

4 Link termination

To establish communications over a point-to-point link, each end of the PPP link must first send LCP packets to configure the data link during the link establishment phase. After the link has been established, PPP provides for an optional authentication phase before proceeding to the network-layer protocol phase. The NCP phase then establishes and configures different network layer protocols such as IP.

By default, authentication before the NCP phase is not mandatory. If authentication of the link is desired, an implementation will specify the authentication protocol configuration option during the link establishment phase. These authentication protocols are intended for use primarily by hosts and routers that connect to a PPP network server through switched circuits or dial-up lines, but they also can be applied to dedicated links. The server can use the identification of the connecting host or router in the selection of options for network layer negotiations.

PPP Password Authentication Protocol

The Password Authentication Protocol (PAP) provides a simple way for a peer to establish its identity to the authenticator using a two-way handshake. This is done only at initial link establishment. The three PAP frame types are shown in Figure 2-9.

Figure 2-9 *Three PPP PAP Frame Types*

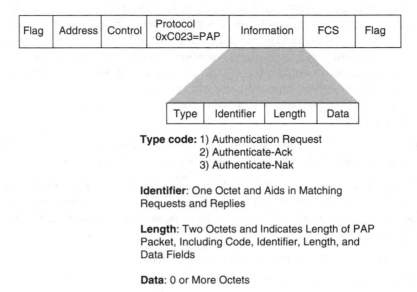

After the link establishment phase is completed, the authenticate-request packet is used to initiate the PAP authentication. This packet contains the peer name and password, as shown in Figure 2-10.

Figure 2-10 *PPP PAP Authentication Request*

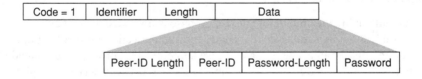

This request packet is sent repeatedly until a valid reply packet is received or an optional retry counter expires. If the authenticator receives a Peer-ID/Password pair that is both recognizable and acceptable, it should reply with an Authenticate-Ack (where Ack is short for *acknowledge*). If the Peer-ID/Password pair is not recognizable or acceptable, the authenticator should reply with an Authenticate-Nak (where Nak is short for *negative acknowledge*).

NOTE   Most implementations of PPP only allow for a single attempt at a correct Peer-ID/Password.

Figure 2-11 shows the sequence of PPP negotiations for a branch router (the peer) trying to authenticate to the network access server (NAS), which is the authenticator.

Figure 2-11   *PPP PAP Authentication*

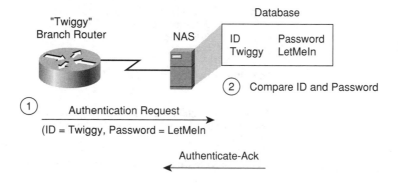

PAP is not a strong authentication method. PAP authenticates only the peer, and passwords are sent over the circuit "in the clear." There is no protection from replay attacks or repeated trial-and-error attacks. The peer is in control of the frequency and timing of the attempts. As PAP assumes, there is no chance of "wiretapping"; this renders it unfit for use in a wireless setting.

PPP Challenge Handshake Authentication Protocol

The Challenge Handshake Authentication Protocol (CHAP) is used to periodically verify the identity of a host or end user using a three-way handshake. CHAP is performed at initial link establishment and can be repeated any time after the link has been established. The four CHAP frame types are shown in Figure 2-12.

Figure 2-12   *PPP CHAP Frame Types*

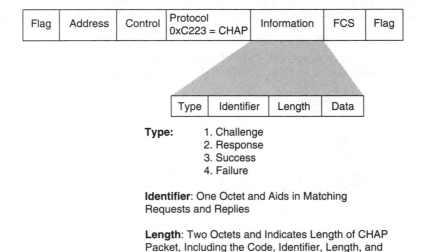

Type: 1. Challenge
           2. Response
           3. Success
           4. Failure

Identifier: One Octet and Aids in Matching
Requests and Replies

Length: Two Octets and Indicates Length of CHAP
Packet, Including the Code, Identifier, Length, and
Data Fields

Data: 0 or More Octets

Figure 2-13 shows a scenario in which a branch router (the peer) tries to authenticate to the NAS (the authenticator).

CHAP imposes network security by requiring that the peers share a plain text secret. This secret is never sent over the link. The secret is exchanged or installed out of band. (In Figure 2-13, the string "trustme" is this shared secret. The following sequence of steps is carried out:

Step 1   After the link establishment phase is complete, the authenticator sends a challenge message to the peer. The challenge consists of an identifier (ID), a random number, and either the hostname of the local device or the name of the user on the remote device.

Step 2   The receiving peer calculates a hash value of the random number using a one-way hash function; the secret (in this scenario, the string "trustme") is the input to the one-way hash function.

Figure 2-13   *PPP CHAP Authentication*

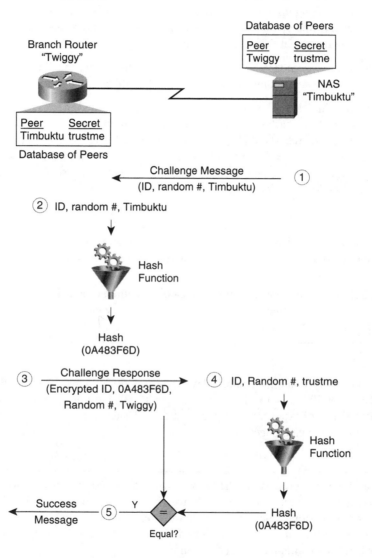

Step 3   The peer sends the challenge response, which consists of the following:

— An encrypted version of the ID

— A secret password (the calculated hash value [the string "0A483F6D" in this scenario])

— The random number

— Either the host name of the remote device or the name of the user on the remote device

Step 4 When the authenticator receives the challenge response, it verifies the secret by looking up the name given in the response and performing the same encryption operation. The authenticator checks the response against its own calculation of the expected hash value.

Step 5 If the values match, the authenticator acknowledges the authentication and sends a success message, and the LCP establishes the link.

As the figure indicates, the shared secret is never transmitted over the wire—just the response to the challenge as a hash value. The secret passwords must be identical on the remote and local devices. These secrets should be agreed on, generated, and exchanged out of band in a secure manner. Because the secret is never transmitted, other devices are prevented from stealing it and gaining illegal access to the system. Without the proper response, the remote device cannot connect to the local device.

NOTE   It is important to understand that CHAP is not compatible with some authentication implementations based on having the password in cleartext or having access to a common hash function.

Also, CHAP is vulnerable to offline brute-force/dictionary attacks. That is, the challenge and response can be captured and eventually will give away enough data to recover the secret (for example, via an offline dictionary attack).

CHAP provides protection against playback attack through the use of an incrementally changing identifier and a variable challenge value. The use of repeated challenges is intended to limit the time of exposure to any single attack. The authenticator is in control of the frequency and timing of the challenges.

NOTE   Typically, MD5 is used as the CHAP one-way hash function; it is required that the shared secrets be stored in plain-text form. Microsoft has a variation of CHAP (MS-CHAP) in which the password is stored encrypted in both the peer and the authenticator. Therefore, MS-CHAP can take advantage of irreversibly encrypted password databases that are commonly available, whereas the standards-based CHAP cannot.

PPP Extensible Authentication Protocol

The PPP Extensible Authentication Protocol (EAP) is a general protocol for PPP authentication that supports multiple authentication mechanisms. EAP does not select a specific authentication mechanism at the link control phase; rather, it postpones this until the authentication phase so that the authenticator can request more information before determining the specific authentication mechanism. This arrangement also permits the use of a "back-end" server, which actually implements the various authentication mechanisms, whereas the PPP authenticator merely passes through the authentication exchange.

Figure 2-14 shows how PPP EAP works.

Figure 2-14   *PPP EAP Authentication*

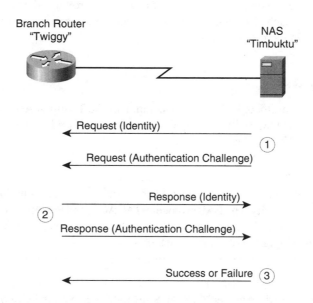

In the figure, the branch router (the peer) is trying to authenticate to the NAS (the authenticator). The sequence of steps is as follows:

Step 1   When the link establishment phase is complete, the authenticator sends one or more requests to authenticate the peer. The request has a type field to indicate what is being requested. Examples of request types include identity, MD5-challenge, S/Key, generic token card, and so on. The MD5-challenge type corresponds closely to the CHAP authentication protocol.

NOTE   Typically, the authenticator sends an initial identity request followed by one or more requests for authentication information. However, an initial identity request is not required and can be bypassed in cases in which the identity is presumed (for example, with leased lines, dedicated dial-ups, and so on).

Step 2 The peer sends a response packet in reply to each request. As with the request packet, the response packet contains a type field that corresponds to the type field of the request.

Step 3 The authenticator ends the authentication phase with a success or failure packet.

EAP adds more flexibility to PPP authentication and provides the capability to use new technologies—such as digital certificates—when they become widely available (hence, the "Extensible" in the protocol name).

The TACACS+ Protocol

The *TACACS+* protocol is the latest generation of the Terminal Access Controller Access Control System (TACACS). TACACS is a simple UDP-based access control protocol originally developed by BBN for the MILNET.

NOTE   Integration with enterprise authentication, authorization, and accounting (AAA) is an important part of WLAN security. The EAP protocols, TACACS, and RADIUS are all part of an integrated WLAN security solution, and that is why these topics are covered in this chapter. Later chapters cover the security protocols in more detail.

Cisco has enhanced (extended) TACACS several times, and the Cisco implementation, based on the original TACACS, is referred to as *XTACACS*. The fundamental differences between TACACS, XTACACS, and TACACS+ are as follows:

- **TACACS**—Combined authentication and authorization process.
- **XTACACS**—Separated AAA.
- **TACACS+**—XTACACS with extended attribute control and accounting. This is the most common implementation.

TACACS+ uses TCP for its transport. The server daemon usually listens at port 49, the login port assigned for the TACACS protocol. This port is reserved in the assigned number's RFC for both UDP and TCP. Current TACACS and extended TACACS implementations also use port 49.

TACACS+ is a client/server protocol; the TACACS+ client is typically a NAS, and the TACACS+ server is usually a daemon process running on some UNIX or NT machine. A fundamental design component of TACACS+ is the separation of AAA.

TACACS+ Authentication

TACACS+ allows for arbitrary length and content authentication exchanges, which allow any authentication mechanism to be used with TACACS+ clients (including PPP PAP, PPP CHAP, PPP EAP, token cards, and Kerberos). Authentication is not mandatory; it is a site-configured option. Some sites do not require it at all; others require it only for certain services.

TACACS+ authentication has three packet types:

- START, which is always sent by the client
- CONTINUE, which is always sent by the client
- REPLY, which is always sent by the server

Authentication begins with the client sending a START message to the server. The START message describes the type of authentication to be performed (for example, simple cleartext password, PAP, or CHAP) and might contain the username and some authentication data. The START packet is sent only as the first message in a TACACS+ authentication session or as the packet immediately following a restart. (A restart might be requested by the server in a REPLY packet.) A START packet always has a sequence number equal to 1.

In response to a START packet, the server sends a REPLY. The REPLY message indicates whether the authentication is finished or should continue. If the REPLY indicates that authentication should continue, the message also indicates what new information is requested. The client gets that information and returns it in a CONTINUE message. This process repeats until all authentication information is gathered, and then the authentication process concludes.

TACACS+ Authorization

Authorization is the action of determining what a user is allowed to do. Generally, authentication precedes authorization, but this is not required. An authorization request might indicate that the user is not authenticated (that is, it is not known who he or she is). In this case, it is up to the authorization agent to determine whether an unauthenticated user is allowed the services in question.

When authentication is completed (if authentication is used), the client can start the authorization process, if authorization is required. An *authorization session* is defined as a single pair of messages: a REQUEST followed by a RESPONSE. The authorization REQUEST message contains a fixed set of fields that describes the authenticity of the user or process, and a variable set of arguments that describes the services and options for which authorization is requested.

NOTE	In TACACS+, authorization does not merely provide yes or no answers; it might also customize the service for the particular user. Here are some examples of when authorization would be performed: when a user first logs in and wants to start a shell or when a user starts PPP and wants to use IP over PPP with a particular IP address. The TACACS+ server daemon might respond to these requests by allowing the service, by placing a time restriction on the login shell, or by requiring IP access lists on the PPP connection.

TACACS+ Accounting

Accounting is typically the third action after authentication and authorization. Accounting is the action of recording what a user is doing or has done. Accounting in TACACS+ can serve two purposes:

- It can be used to account for services used, such as in a billing environment.
- It can be used as an auditing tool for security services.

To this end, TACACS+ supports three types of accounting records:

- Start records indicate that a service is about to begin.
- Stop records indicate that a service has just terminated.
- Update records are intermediate notices that indicate that a service is still being performed.

TACACS+ accounting records contain all the information used in the authorization records and also contain accounting-specific information such as start and stop times (when appropriate) and resource usage information.

TACACS+ Transactions

Transactions between the TACACS+ client and TACACS+ server are authenticated through the use of a shared secret, which is never sent over the network. Typically, the secret is manually configured in both entities. TACACS+ encrypts all traffic between the TACACS+ client and the TACACS+ server daemon.

Figure 2-15 shows the interaction between a dial-in user and the TACACS+ client and server.

Figure 2-15   *A TACACS+ Exchange*

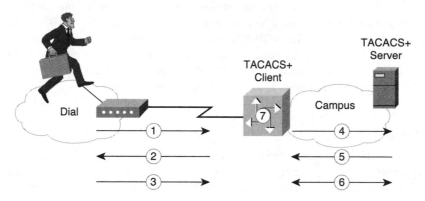

1. User initiates PPP authentication to NAS.

2. NAS prompts user for username/password (PAP) or challenge (CHAP).

3. User replies.

4. TACACS+ client sends encrypted packet to TACACS+ server.

5. TACACS+ server responds with authentication result.

6. TACACS+ client and server exchange authorization requests and replies.

7. TACACS+ client acts upon authorization exchange.

The RADIUS Protocol

The *Remote Address Dial-In User Service (RADIUS)* protocol was developed by Livingston Enterprises, Inc., as an access server authentication and accounting protocol. In June 1996, the RADIUS protocol specification was submitted to the Internet Engineering Task Force (IETF). The RADIUS specification (RFC 2058) and RADIUS accounting standard (RFC 2059) are now proposed standard protocols.

RADIUS uses UDP as its transport. Generally, the RADIUS protocol is considered to be a connectionless service. Issues related to server availability, retransmission, and timeouts are handled by the RADIUS-enabled devices rather than by the transmission protocol.

RADIUS is a client/server protocol. The RADIUS client is typically a NAS; the RADIUS server is usually a daemon process running on some UNIX or NT machine. The client is responsible for passing user information to designated RADIUS servers and then acting on the response that is returned. RADIUS servers are responsible for receiving user connection requests, authenticating the user, and then returning all configuration information necessary for the client to deliver the service to the user. A RADIUS server can act as a proxy client to other RADIUS servers or to other kinds of authentication servers.

RADIUS Authentication

The RADIUS server can support a variety of methods to authenticate a user. When the server is provided with the username and user's original password, the server can support PPP PAP or CHAP, UNIX login, and other authentication mechanisms. What is supported depends on what a vendor has implemented.

Typically, a user login consists of a query (Access-Request) from the NAS to the RADIUS server and a corresponding response (Access-Accept or Access-Reject) from the server. The Access-Request packet contains the username, password, or shared secret between the NAS and the RADIUS server, NAS IP address, and port. The format of the request also provides information about the type of session that the user wants to initiate.

When the RADIUS server receives the Access-Request packet from the NAS, it searches a database for the username listed. If the username does not exist in the database, either a default profile is loaded or the RADIUS server immediately sends an Access-Reject message. This Access-Reject message can be accompanied by an optional text message, which can indicate the reason for the refusal.

RADIUS Authorization

In RADIUS, the authentication and authorization functionalities are coupled together. If the username is found and the password is correct, the RADIUS server returns an Access-Accept response, including a list of attribute-value pairs that describe the parameters to be used for this session. Typical parameters include service type (shell or framed), protocol type, IP address to assign the user (static or dynamic), access list to apply, and a static route to install in the NAS routing table. The configuration information in the RADIUS server defines what will be installed on the NAS.

RADIUS Accounting

The accounting features of the RADIUS protocol can be used independently of RADIUS authentication or authorization. The RADIUS accounting functions allow data to be sent at the start and end of sessions, indicating the amount of resources (such as time, packets, bytes, and so on) used during the session. An Internet service provider (ISP) might use RADIUS access control and accounting software to meet special security and billing needs.

RADIUS Transactions

Transactions between the client and the RADIUS server are authenticated through the use of a shared secret, which is never sent over the network. In addition, any user passwords are sent encrypted between the client and the RADIUS server to eliminate the possibility that someone snooping on an unsecure network could determine a user's password.

Figure 2-16 shows the RADIUS login and authentication process.

Figure 2-16   *RADIUS Login and Authentication*

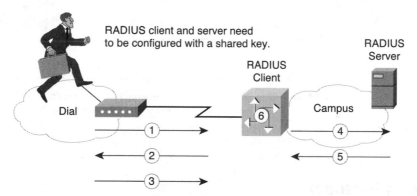

1. User initiates PPP authentication to NAS.

2. NAS prompts user for username/password (PAP) or challenge (CHAP).

3. User replies.

4. RADIUS client sends username and encrypted password to RADIUS server.

5. RADIUS server responds with Accept, Reject, or Challenge.

6. RADIUS client acts upon services and service parameters bundled with Accept or Reject.

NOTE With both TACACS+ and RADIUS, it is important to remember that encryption is performed between the TACACS+/RADIUS client and the TACACS+/RADIUS server. If the TACACS+/ RADIUS client is a NAS and not the client PC, any communication between the PC and the NAS is not encrypted (see Figure 2-17).

Also, not all information between the NAS and the RADIUS server is encrypted.

The exchange can be made more secure in CHAP and other protocols, which might use encryption or a hash between the user and the RADIUS client.

Figure 2-17   *TACACS+/RADIUS Encryption*

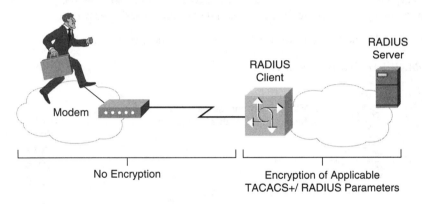

The Kerberos Protocol

Kerberos is a secret-key network authentication protocol, developed at Massachusetts Institute of Technology (MIT), that uses the data encryption standard (DES) cryptographic algorithm for encryption and authentication. The Kerberos Version 5 protocol is an Internet standard specified by RFC 1510.

Kerberos was designed to authenticate user requests for network resources. Kerberos is based on the concept of a trusted third party that performs secure verification of users and services.

In the Kerberos protocol, this trusted third party is called the *key distribution center (KDC)*, sometimes also called the *authentication server*. The primary use of Kerberos is to verify that users and the network services they use are really who and what they claim to be. To accomplish this, a trusted Kerberos server issues "tickets" to users. These tickets have a limited lifespan and are stored in the user's credential cache. They can later be used in place of the standard username-and-password authentication mechanism.

Kerberos Authentication Request and Reply

Initially, the Kerberos client has knowledge of an encryption key known only to the user and the KDC: K_{client}. Similarly, each application server shares an encryption key with the KDC, K_{server} (see Figure 2-18).

Figure 2-18   *Kerberos Keys*

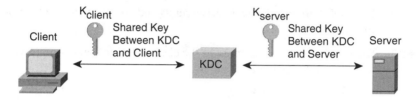

When the client wants to create an association with a particular application server, the client uses the authentication request and response to first obtain a ticket and a session key from the KDC (see Figure 2-19).

Figure 2-19   *Kerberos Authentication Request and Reply*

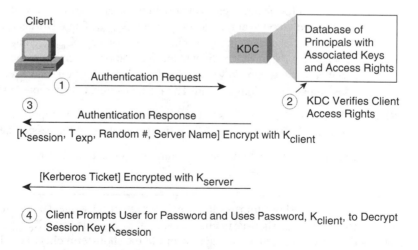

The steps are as follows:

Step 1   The client sends an authentication request to the KDC. This request contains the following information:

— Its claimed identity

— The name of the application server

— A requested expiration time for the ticket

— A random number that will be used to match the authentication response with the request

Step 2   The KDC verifies the client access rights and creates an authentication response.

Step 3   The KDC returns the response to the client. The authentication response contains the following information:

— The session key, $K_{session}$

— The assigned expiration time

— The random number from the request

— The name of the application server

— Other information from the ticket

All this information is encrypted with the user's password, which was registered with the authentication server, K_{client}. The KDC also returns a Kerberos ticket containing the random session key, $K_{session}$, that will be used for authentication of the client to the application server; the name of the client to whom the session key was issued; and an expiration time after which the session key is no longer valid. The Kerberos ticket is encrypted using K_{server}.

Step 4   When the client receives the authentication reply, it prompts the user for the password. This password, K_{client}, is used to decrypt the session key, $K_{session}$.

Now the client is ready to communicate with the application server.

NOTE K_{client} is used as the bootstrap mechanism; however, in subsequent communication between the KDC and the client, a short-term client key, $K_{client-session}$, is used. $K_{client-session}$ is created by having the KDC convert the user's password to the short-term client key. The KDC sends the short-term client key, $K_{client-session}$, encrypted with the user's password, to the client. The user decrypts the short-term client key, and the subsequent KDC-to-client communication uses $K_{client-session}$.

Kerberos Application Request and Response

The application request and response is the exchange in which a client proves to an application server that it knows the session key embedded in a Kerberos ticket. The exchange is shown in Figure 2-20.

Figure 2-20   *Kerberos Application Request and Reply*

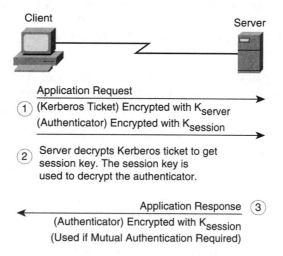

The steps in the application request and response are as follows:

Step 1   The client sends two things to the application server as part of the application request:

—   The Kerberos ticket (described in the preceding section)

—   An authenticator, which includes the following (among other fields):

•   The current time

•   A checksum

•   An optional encryption key

All these elements are encrypted with the session key, $K_{session}$, from the accompanying ticket.

Step 2   After receiving the application request, the application server decrypts the ticket with K_{server}; extracts the session key, $K_{session}$; and uses the session key to decrypt the authenticator.

If the same key was used to encrypt the authenticator as was used to decrypt it, the checksum will match, and the verifier can assume that the authenticator was generated by the client named in the ticket and to whom the session key was issued. By itself, this check is not sufficient for authentication because an attacker can intercept an authenticator and replay it later to impersonate the user. For this reason, the verifier also checks the timestamp. If the timestamp is within a specified window (typically five minutes) centered around the current time on the verifier, and if the timestamp has not been seen on other requests within that window, the verifier accepts the request as authentic.

At this point, the server has verified the identity of the client. For some applications, the client also wants to be sure of the server's identity. If such mutual authentication is required, a third step is necessary.

Step 3 The application server generates an application response by extracting the client's time from the authenticator and then returns it to the client with other information, all encrypted using the session key, $K_{session}$.

IPv6

IPv6 started out as IPng (IP: The Next Generation). Since the first RFC in early 1993, there have been about 120 or so RFCs on various aspects of this technology. Counting all versions, the list could be around 700 entries long.

Earlier proposals for IPng focused on the address space (which is constrained in IPv4) from a routing perspective and assumed a migratory universal protocol (that is, no bifurcation of "access" protocols and long-haul protocols [RFC 1454]). IPv4 thus needed to be replaced by a better scheme. The fractured network with artificial boundaries to accommodate for IPv4 gets in the way of implementing various features such as integrated security and mobility. In addition to the unambiguous address capability, IPv6 also offers the capability to develop innovative applications with end-to-end QoS, security, flow, and so on. RFC 1726 laid out the requirements as follows:

- Architectural simplicity
- Implement what is possible and don't stand in the way of other layers that will extend the functionality
- One protocol
- Provide a point of commonality between protocols
- Live long (address the longevity by thinking about a longer-term solution than a quick and dirty one)
- Build in long-term vision and migration capability

- Live long and prosper (build in extensibility and flexibility—assume that, to prosper, others will extend your artifacts)
- Provide operational benefits such as larger address space
- Cooperative anarchy
- Decentralization and loose coupling

NOTE   It is amusing to observe that many of these goals fit other current software layers such as the web services and services-oriented architecture (SOA) paradigms.

One of the major issues addressed by IPv6 is the scalability of the Internet by tackling the limited address space due to the "class" way of adding partitioning the address space in IPv4. IPv6 uses a 128-bit address as opposed to IPv4, which uses a 32-bit address (RFC 3513). This increases the number of addresses from 4×10^9 in IPv4 to 3×10^{38} in IPv6! This enables features such as wireless mobility, addressing wirelessly networked appliances and devices. In fact, in the recent RFID domain, many of the RFID tags are IPv6 addresses.

IPv6 Address Structure and Representation

The addresses in IPv6 are expressed in eight chunks of 16-bit hexadecimal numbers as x:x:x:x:x:x:x:x. One set of consecutive zeros can be collapsed by the :: notation. For example, x:x:x:0:0:0:0:x can be shortened by x:x:x::x.

The three types of IPv6 addresses are Unicast (to a single address), Anycast (to the nearest interface), and Multicast (to a set of interfaces).

The Multicast is an interesting one; the Broadcast type in IPv4 is a special case of Multicast (all-nodes Multicast). You can also construct the Manycast with this type. The scope field (4 bits wide) turns the Multicast into node interface local, link local, site/admin local, organization local, and global scope.

The requirement that each network interface have a unique IP address (in IPv4) is not carried over to IPv6; in IPv6, multiple interfaces can have the same IP address, the assumption being that there is enough intelligence inside the interfaces to differentiate.

IPv6 Header

IPv6 simplified the header (as compared to IPv4) while adding extensibility. Whereas IPv4 had one IP header (with around 12 fields and variable length), the IPv6 header has eight fields (with a fixed size of 40 bytes) and adds optional IPv6 extension headers. The two extensions relevant to security (RFC 2401) are the authentication header (AH; RFC 2402) and the encapsulating security payload (ESP) header (RFC 2406). RFC 2401 defines IPSec, the goal of which is to provide interoperable cryptographic security for IPV4 and IPV6. You will look more closely at these headers in the "IPSec" section later in this chapter.

Scalability

On the scalability side, IPv6 adds ICMPv6 (which includes neighbor discovery protocols), RIPng (RFC 2080), flow labels (for QoS), and DHCPv6 (which has a few automatic configuration and mobile IP features).

Adoption

The main barrier to adoption of IPv6 is the transition from IPv4, which still is a big hurdle. The two main mechanisms (RFC 1933) are dual IP stack architecture (where devices would have IPv4 and IPv6 stacks) and tunneling (IPv6 in IPV4).

IPSec

IP security (IPSec) adds protocols, message formats, and concepts to achieve confidential pipes across an untrusted network like the Internet. One of the most important features of IPSec is the capability to bootstrap trust anchors. The virtual private network (VPN) implementations leverage the IPSec mechanisms.

IPSec is expressed as a collection of RFCs that provide mechanisms (including cryptographic algorithms), protocols, and message formats to achieve point-to-point confidentiality and integrity for the IP. The RFCs also detail the protocols and message formats for authentication, which is a prerequisite for achieving confidentiality and integrity. Table 2-2 shows a summary view of the IPSec mechanisms.

Table 2-2   *IPSec Mechanisms: Summary View*

Mechanic	Mechanism	Format	Protocol
Confidentiality	Encryption	ESP header, ESP packet	ESP protocol and processing rules
Integrity	Origin authentication	—	—
	Antireply	Sequence number in the ESP header	—
	Data integrity	Integrity check value (ICV)	—
Authentication		Authentication header (AH)	Security association mechanics
	Key management	—	Internet Key Exchange (IKE)

The following subsections provide an introductory summary of the major IPSec formats and protocols. Refer to IPSec-specific books for more in-depth discussion.

Authentication Header

When added to an IP datagram, this header ensures the data integrity and origin authentication, including the invariant fields in the outer IP header. It does not provide confidentiality protection. Authentication header (AH) commonly uses a keyed hash function rather than digital signatures because digital signature technology is too slow and greatly reduces network throughput. AH is an appropriate protocol to employ when confidentiality is not required (or not permitted, as when government regulations restrict the use of encryption).

Encapsulating Security Payload

When added to an IP datagram, this header protects data confidentiality, integrity, and origin authentication. The scope of the authentication offered by ESP is narrower than it is for AH. (The IP header that is "outside" of the ESP header is not protected.) If only the upper-layer protocols must be authenticated, ESP authentication is an appropriate choice and is more space efficient than using AH to encapsulate ESP.

Security Associations

The concept of a security association (SA) is fundamental to IPSec. An SA is a relationship between two or more entities that describes how the entities use security services to communicate securely. The SA includes the following:

- An encryption algorithm
- An authentication algorithm
- A shared session key

Because an SA is unidirectional, two SAs (one in each direction) are required to secure typical, bidirectional communication between two entities. The security services associated with an SA can be used for AH or ESP but not both. If both AH and ESP protection is applied to a traffic stream, two (or more) SAs are created for each direction to protect the traffic stream.

The SA is uniquely identified by a randomly chosen unique number called the *security parameter index (SPI)* and the destination IP address of the destination. When a system sends a packet that requires IPSec protection, it looks up the SA in its database and applies the specified processing and security protocol (AH/ESP), inserting the SPI from the SA into the IPSec header. When the IPSec peer receives the packet, it looks up the SA in its database by destination address, protocol, and SPI and then processes the packet as required.

Key Management

IPSec uses cryptographic keys for authentication/integrity and encryption services. Both manual and automatic distribution of keys is supported.

The lowest (but least desirable) level of management is manual management, in which a person manually configures each system by keying material and SA management data relevant to secure communication with other systems. Manual techniques are practical in small, static environments, but they do not scale well. If the number of sites using IPSec security services is small, and if all the sites come under a single administrative domain, manual key management techniques might be appropriate. Manual key management might also be appropriate when only selected communications must be secured within an organization for a small number of hosts or gateways. Manual management techniques often employ statically configured, symmetric keys; however, other options also exist.

The default automated key management protocol selected for use with IPSec is the Internet Key Management Protocol (IKMP), sometimes simply referred to as the Internet Key Exchange (IKE). IKE authenticates each peer involved in IPSec, negotiates the security policy, and handles the exchange of session keys.

Summary

This chapter covered the basics of the various mechanics (Confidentiality, Integrity, Availability, Key Management, and Encryption) and how they are achieved using the basic mechanisms of cryptography, various protocols, and methods. In later chapters, you will learn about how these basic primitives are employed in the realm of wireless security, the various vulnerabilities because of the way the mechanics are combined, and the advances to mitigate the vulnerabilities. The authors would like to thank Cisco Press and Merike Kaeo for the materials from the excellent Cisco Press book, *Designing Network Security*.

CHAPTER 3

WLAN Standards

Like many other industries, the WLAN world is bound to external forces—advances in technology, regulations of various bodies including governments, and the emergence of different standards and market demands. This chapter looks at standards and regulations, and it explores how market demands create "temporary" standards to address weaknesses in the WLAN industry while waiting for standard bodies to hammer out a more detailed solution. The WLAN industry has mastered this balance while still maintaining interoperability and by doing so with little technology or market fragmentation.

Standards Organizations, Position, Context, and Influence

WLAN is mostly defined by the IEEE 802 family of standards. The good news is that adherence to these standards gives unparalleled interoperability. On the other hand, it also requires that the IEEE committees be innovative in areas such as security, which is an area where work is still being done. To bridge the gap between the leading market readiness requirement and lagging security standards, organizations like Wi-Fi Alliance and Cisco (with LEAP and Flexible Authentication via Secure Tunnel [EAP-FAST]) have implemented security mechanisms (with associated specifications). The IEEE security committees are developing standards that will eventually fill the gaps.

Why Do Standards Take More Time?

Standardization is always a deliberate effort at coordinating different insights, opinions, and ideas into a cohesive and comprehensive specification. Finalizing the precise language of a standard and reaching consensus takes time. Also, standards need to be relatively static, which means the specifications need to be mature. All this work takes time, but it is worth the effort.

IEEE

The Institute of Electrical and Electronic Engineers (IEEE) is, among other things, a standards body. IEEE publishes standards for many types of systems, ranging from power and energy systems to voting systems. The organization is well known for its standards on information exchange between computers—from best practices to IT infrastructure to LAN/MAN standards to portable applications standards. The following are some examples of systems that use IEEE standards:

- Binary floating-point arithmetic handling by computers
- IEEE-488—standard for instruments to communicate with each other
- Versa Module Eurocard (VME) bus, which is an electronic architecture specification for controllers and cards mainly used in the industrial real-time process control world
- Portable Operating System Interface (POSIX)
- Utility meter reading via telephone

The standards work is done by volunteer committees, which usually consist of experts employed in the computer industry. The committees consider a large amount of input during their standards development work, and they have formal voting procedures. After deliberation, they publish their standards, which are owned by the IEEE and are available to the public. Initially, they charge for the standards, but six months after publication, the standards are available for free download. You can access the standards by visiting http://standards.ieee.org/.

NOTE   IEEE is not the only standards organization of interest from the WLAN perspective. As you will see later in this chapter, the WLAN domain incorporates standards from the Internet Engineering Task Force (IETF), ETSI, and other standards bodies.

Of interest, of course, is the 802 family of standards that covers the local- and metropolitan-area networks. You can access the current 802 standards at the website http://standards.ieee.org/getieee802/.

IEEE 802 Standards

The IEEE 802 defines reference architecture for packet-based, shared-medium communications for the LAN/MAN. As shown in Figure 3-1, this standard defines the LAN/MAN Reference Model (RM) and a LAN/MAN Implementation Model (IM) based on the OSI seven-layer model.

Figure 3-1   *ISO and IEEE 802 Reference Model*

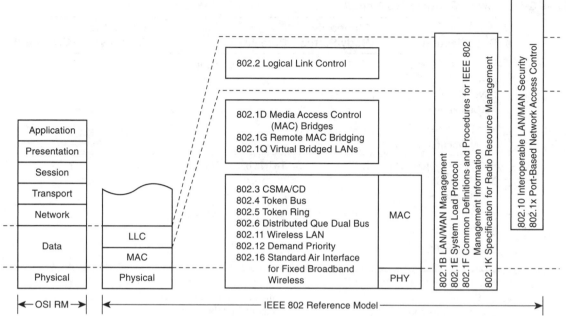

The 802 RM defines the ISO data-link layer in terms of the MAC sublayer and the Logical Link Control (LLC) sublayer, which operate over the MAC layer. The MAC handles the data transmission standards for the physical medium and bridging, and the LLC deals with the connectivity protocols. As the name implies, the LLC maintains the link independent of the physical characteristic of the link—radio, frequency, and other transmission mechanisms.

NOTE   Some interesting 802 specifications include the 802.3 Ethernet, the 802.11 wireless standards, and the 802.1x port-based network access control security standard.

Table 3-1 shows the various IEEE and related standards that are relevant to this discussion, including their domain and pertinence.

Table 3-1 *WLAN Standards in a Nutshell*

Specification	Standards Body/Status	Domain	Interest to Security	H/W	Radio
802.11: Wireless LAN MAC and Physical Layer (PHY) Specifications 802.11d-2001: Amendment 3	IEEE	Hardware, signaling	Low	Y	Y
802.11a: Wireless LAN MAC and PHY Specifications	IEEE	5-GHz band PHY layer	Low	Y	Y
802.11a: Wireless LAN MAC and PHY Specifications and Corrigendum 1	IEEE	2.4-GHz band PHY layer	Low	Y	Y
802.11g: Wireless LAN MAC and PHY Specifications and Amendment 4	IEEE	Higher data rate extension in the 2.4-GHz band (from a max of 11 Mbps to 54 Mbps)	Low	Y	Y
802.11h: Wireless LAN MAC and PHY Specifications	IEEE/Draft	Defines mechanisms for Dynamic Frequency Selection (DFS) and Transmit Power Control (TPC) that might be used to satisfy regulatory requirements for operation in the 5-GHz band in Europe	Low	Y	Y
802.15: Wireless Personal Area Networks	IEEE	802.15.1, 802.15.2, 802.15.3, and 802.15.4 specifications deal with the WPANs, which are derived from the Bluetooth specifications	Low	Y	Y
802.11i: Wireless LAN MAC and PHY Specifications: Amendment 6: MAC Security Enhancements	IEEE	Specification for enhanced security	High		

Table 3-1   *WLAN Standards in a Nutshell (Continued)*

Specification	Standards Body/Status	Domain	Interest to Security	H/W	Radio
WPA (Wi-Fi Protected Access)	Wi-Fi Alliance	Authentication, encryption Subset of 802.11i	High		
802.1x: Port-Based Network Access Control	IEEE	Authentication framework (using EAP), access control mechanisms, protocols between entities participating in authentication, basis for the WEP	High		
802.11f: IEEE Trial-Use Recommended Practice for Multi-Vendor Access Point Interoperability via an Inter-Access Point Protocol Across Distribution Systems Supporting IEEE 802.11 Operation	IEEE	Exchange information between access points, use of RADIUS protocol, and context handling for faster roaming	Medium		
802.11e: Wireless LAN MAC and PHY Specifications: Amendment 7: MAC Quality of Service (QoS) Enhancements	IEEE/In progress	MAC enhancements to support applications that require QoS, such as audio and video over 802.11 WLANs	Low		
802.11n	IEEE/High Throughput Study Group (HTSG) starting to work on the standard	Standard for high throughput 108 Mbps to 320 Mbps; plan to concentrate on throughput rather than data transfer rates. ETA: 2005 to 2006	Low		

continues

Table 3-1   *WLAN Standards in a Nutshell (Continued)*

Specification	Standards Body/Status	Domain	Interest to Security	H/W	Radio
802.11k: Wireless LAN MAC and PHY Specifications: Specification for Radio Resource Measurement	IEEE/In progress	Defines information (radio and network) for management, maintenance, and enhanced data, which could be the basis for various services	Low		
LWAPP	IETF/ Experimental	Protocol for routers and switches to manage access points	Low		
Extensible Authentication Protocol (EAP) RFC 2284	IETF	Original RFC defining an authentication method for the Point-to-Point Protocol (PPP)	High		
EAP-TLS RFC 2716	IETF	Adds Transport Level Security (TLS), which is a derivative of SSL, mechanisms to EAP	Medium		
Protected EAP (PEAP)	IETF	Addresses gaps in EAP by securing the initial exchange	High		
Cisco Wireless EAP or Lightweight EAP (LEAP)	Cisco	Based on mutual authentication between a wireless client and AP, with an access server (usually a RADIUS server) Dynamic key generation and key exchange for confidentiality/encryption	High		
EAP-FAST	IETF/ Informational	Adds a mutually authenticated tunnel to EAP and flexibility to use different security mechanisms for credential provisioning, authentication, and authorization.	High		

As you can see, IEEE and IETF play key roles in defining the security standards for WLAN. Note that the work is in progress, and many newer ways of securing WLANs are emerging.

Wi-Fi Alliance

The Wi-Fi Alliance is a nonprofit organization that specializes in the 802.11 WLAN industry. It was formed in 1999 (as WECA—Wireless Ethernet Compatibility Alliance) to address the interoperability of WLANs by certification; the devices that successfully passed the test would display the Wi-Fi CERTIFIED logo. The Wi-Fi CERTIFIED brand carries a high level of interoperability. In the security space, the Wi-Fi Alliance developed Wi-Fi Protected Access (WPA) to address the security gaps in the Wired Equivalent Privacy (WEP) offered by the 802.11 specification. You can access the various presentations and other information from the Wi-Fi Alliance website at http://www.wi-fi.org/.

WPA Overview

The WPA specification is an essential subset of the 802.11i specification. WEP provided inadequate security, so the Wi-Fi Alliance developed a pragmatic solution that preserves interoperability and compatibility with the eventual 802.11i specification while providing the necessary security. Details of the security gaps in WEP are covered later in this chapter.

The main reason for the WPA specification is that industry requirements preempt the standards work, which needs to be systematic, deliberate, and complete. So the Wi-Fi Alliance developed the WPA as a pragmatic improvement over the current implementations of WEP—pragmatic in the sense that the WPA would require only a firmware upgrade and would be interoperable by virtue of being certified by the Wi-Fi Alliance, while providing the required security features and maintaining the 802.11i compatibility. It was a tough task, indeed.

Looking at the comparison between the 802.11 specification and WPA (and the 802.11i specification), you can see that the various feature sets are evolving. Table 3-2 shows this aggregate comparison of features.

Table 3-2 *802.11 Specification Compared to WPA*

Feature	802.11/ WEP	802.1x	WPA	802.11i
Identity	Machine (the WEP key)	User	User	User
Authentication	Shared key/ EAP	UN/PW/PEAP— certificates	UN/PW (with RADIUS) or preshared key PEAP	UN/PW (with RADIUS) PEAP
Integrity	32-bit Integrity Check Value (ICV)	32-bit ICV	64-bit Message Integrity Code (MIC)	CCM
Encryption	Static keys	Session keys	Key rotation using TKIP	CCMP
Key distribution	One time, manual	Session keys automatic upon authentication	Automatic, rotation	Automatic, rotation
Initialization vector	Plain text, 24 bits	Plain text, 24 bits	Extended IV—64 bits with selection/sequencing rules	
Algorithm	RC4	RC4	RC4, AES (optional)	AES
Key strength	64-bit/128-bit	64-bit/128-bit	128-bit	128-bit
Supporting infrastructure	Static ACL	RADIUS infrastructure for user authentication	RADIUS infrastructure for user authentication	Radius infrastructure for user authentication
Evolutionary/ revolutionary			Evolutionary Adds configuration and algorithm information in beacon for cipher suite and authentication modes' negotiation APs and clients need AES capability for stronger encryption All WPA mandatory requirements achieved by firmware update	Revolutionary APs and clients need AES capability for stronger encryption

For the next few years, the 802.11i specification will be the standard to implement WLAN. While the standard is being developed, however, as an interim solution, WPA is the required security implementation in a WLAN infrastructure.

NOTE   The most important WLAN security specification is the 802.11i specification, approved June 24, 2004. The Wi-Fi Alliance is releasing Wireless Protected Access 2 (WPA2) testing and certification to reflect the 802.11i and incorporates the full implementation of 802.11i. The major advancements in WPA2 (from WPA) are the key management/encryption and optional preauthentication mechanisms. Similar to WPA, WPA2 offers two classes of certification: WPA2-Enterprise and WPA2-Personal. Whereas the WPAs-Enterprise requires support for Radius/802.1X-based authentication and Pre-Shared Key, the WPA2-Personal requires only the Pre-Shared Key.

Wireless LAN Association

The Wireless LAN Association (WLANA) is a nonprofit association that concentrates on the educational aspects of WLAN. You can achieve various levels of certification, including Certified Wireless Network Administrator (CWNA), Certified Wireless Security Professional (CWSP), Certified Wireless Network Integration (CWNI), and Certified Wireless Network Expert (CWNE). You can find more information at http://www.wlana.org/.

Hardware/Radio/Waves and Modulation

WLAN hardware is influenced and shaped by the standards and regulations. The following sections examine the relevant principles quickly without delving into too much detail.

FCC Regulations

The Federal Communications Commission (FCC) regulates the devices operating in all frequency bands and provides unlicensed spectrums. The FCC is specific to the United States; other countries have different guidelines and regulatory organizations.

For devices that fall in the licensed spectrum, the consumer must register the devices, perform tests, and so on. The industrial, scientific, and medical band (ISM band), which includes 2.4 GHz (802.11b and 802.11g) and 5 GHz (802.11a), falls in the unlicensed spectrum category. In most countries, the ISM band is in the range of 902 MHz to 5.850 GHz. Cordless phones (900 MHz, 2.4 GHz, and 5 GHz), microwave ovens (2.4 GHz), garage door openers, and so on fall into this unlicensed spectrum category; this is why you do not have to register your cordless phones and ovens with the FCC and get a license to operate them. The disadvantage of using the unlicensed spectrum is the interference—many devices (in homes, for example) use the same frequency and cause interference. The 902-MHz and 2.4-GHz ranges are used by most of the devices, and the 5-GHz range is relatively sparse in terms of usage by appliances and devices.

NOTE	The FCC rules are under title 47 of the Code of Federal Regulations, and Part 15 (47CFR15) covers the unlicensed ISM band employing the spread spectrum modulation. Quoting the CFR 15.47, it "sets out the regulations under which an intentional, unintentional, or incidental radiator may be operated without an individual license."
	The FCC website is http://www.fcc.gov/, and you can find Part 15 at http://www.fcc.gov/oet/info/rules/PART15_8-26-03.pdf.

NOTE	Since its initial publishing in 1985, the 47CFR15 has changed with the times; the August 2003 version describes such twentieth century necessities as digital TV, picture-in-picture (PIP), and more.

Radio Technologies in 802.11

It is interesting to follow the radio technologies and trace the capabilities as the 802.11 standard evolved from 1997 to present day. The capabilities are as follows:

- The original 802.11 PHY standard supported 1 and 2 Mbps using the 2.4-GHz spectrum. The original specification included Direct Sequence Spread Spectrum (DSSS), infrared, and Frequency Hopping Spread Spectrum (FHSS).

- The 802.11b specification added the 5- and 11-Mbps speeds to the 2.4-GHz spectrum. It was considered high speed at the time of its introduction. The 802.11b specification includes only DSSS.

- The 802.11g specification is attempting to add 22 and 54 Mbps to the 2.4-GHz spectrum.

- The 802.11b and 802.11g specifications use the DSSS modulation.

- The preceding PHY specifications used the 2.4-GHz spectrum, but the 802.11a PHY specification introduced the 54-Mbps speed in the 5-GHz spectrum using Orthogonal Frequency Division Multiplexing (OFDM). (Technically speaking, the 802.11a specification operates in the UNII-1 and UNII-2 bands—Unlicensed National Information Infrastructure bands were set aside by the FCC in 1997 in the unlicensed spectrum in the 5.15-GHz to 5.825-GHz band.)

- As throughput increases, range decreases. (Moreover, higher frequencies are more susceptible to degradation and thus possibly result in reduced range.) Hence, the 802.11a has less range than the 802.11b specification.

- Range and other characteristics can be improved by methods such as increasing power, but the manufacturers are limited by the FCC rules. For example, the CFR15.47 limits the power to 1 watt for the 802.11, 802.11b, and 802.11g specifications. The UNII-1 and UNII-2 bands limit the power at 40 to 800mW. As a result, the manufacturers resort to optimizing the range based on the allowed power characteristics.
- IEEE standards are worldwide and might conflict with the FCC rules.

Brief Discussion on Relevant Standards

The following sections cover the relevant standards and basic concepts discussed throughout the rest of this book. The IEEE standards are long, detailed, and thorough; for example, the 802.11 document is 528 pages. This chapter highlights the discussions that focus on what you need to know to implement security without bogging you down with details. Of course, these discussions are not a substitute for the actual standard. Also, note that later chapters will cover all the security standards in detail.

IEEE 802.11

This standard, titled "Part 11: Wireless LAN Media Access Control (MAC) and Physical Layer (PHY) Specifications," is the fundamental standard for the WLAN; hence, the WLAN is called the 802.11 WLAN. The standard is extensive and defines the mechanics and mechanisms in detail. It is the authoritative source for the definitions, topologies, and ontology covered in Chapter 1, "Securing WLANs Overview." The messages, choreographies, and other WLAN characteristics are covered in Chapter 4, "WLAN Fundamentals," and beyond, and they are also derived from this specification.

In essence, the 802.11 specification defines the following:

- WLAN architecture
- Various services such as association, reassociation, authentication, and privacy
- Frame formats, including the MAC and PHY sublayer functionalities
- FHSS and DSSS functions, including the frames
- WEP algorithm and process for confidentiality

The next few chapters in this book cover these concepts in detail.

IEEE 802.11b

This specification, titled "Higher-Speed Physical Layer Extension in the 2.4-GHz Band," details the famous WLAN in the 2.4-GHz band, 5 and 11 Mbps using the Complementary Code Keying (CCK) modulation scheme for the DSSS scheme. The original 802.11 specification supported 1-Mbps and 2-Mbps data rates.

In addition to the HR/DSSS feature, this specification adds some technologies to the WLAN domain. The new features include the following:

- Short preamble option (72 bits) in Layer 2 for faster synchronization; the 802.11 specification has the long preamble (144 bits). Of course, the 802.11b specification works with the long preamble, and the short preamble is optional. The preamble is the Physical Layer Convergence Protocol (PLCP) Preamble in the PLCP Protocol Data Unit (PPDU).

- Channel agility feature, which counteracts the limitation of the static channel allocation in the 802.11 specification.

The specification, which is approximately 100 pages, covers the PHY and MAC aspects of the high-rate extension, including the message formats, different codes, values, state machines, service primitives' semantics, and choreographies.

Channel Allocation

It is interesting to see the channel allocation across different countries. In addition to the original 802.11 and 802.11b specifications, 802.11b Corrigendum 1 adds more frequencies as per the Ministry of Public Management, Home Affairs, Post, and Telecommunication (MPHPT) Ordinance for Regulating Radio Equipment, Article 49-20 in Japan. Figure 3-2 shows the combined channel layout in the 2.4-GHz spectrum for different countries.

IEEE 802.11a

The IEEE 802.11a specification, titled "Higher-Speed Physical Layer Extension in the 5-GHz Band," defines the artifacts required to support the 5.15-GHz to 5.25-GHz, 5.25-GHz to 5.35-GHz (actual 5.18-GHz to 5.32-GHz), and 5.725-GHz to 5.825-GHz (actual 5.745-GHz to 5.825-GHz) unlicensed National Information Infrastructure (U-NII) spectrum using OFDM modulation scheme and supports the 6-, 9-, 12-, 18-, 24-, 36-, 48-, and 54-Mbps speeds. Figure 3-3 shows the channel plan.

Figure 3-2 *802.11b Channel Plan*

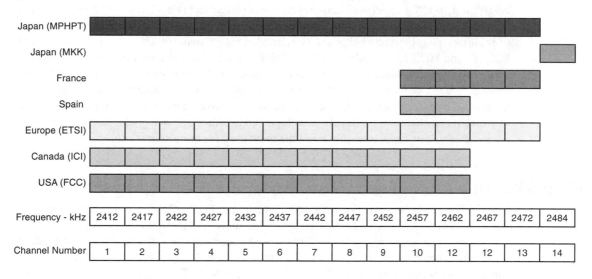

Figure 3-3 *802.11a Channel Plan*

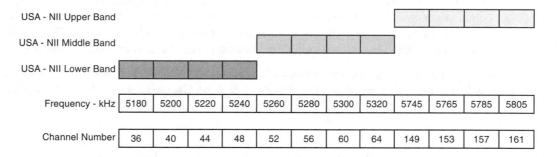

The specification, which is approximately 91 pages, describes in detail the various codes, equations, wave forms, and Layer 2 and Layer 1 implementations for achieving the radio LAN. The 802.11a was named as "Wi-Fi5" to differentiate it from the 802.11b, but the name didn't stick, and as a result, the term "Wi-Fi" includes the .b, .a, and .g.

Although it offers higher bandwidths, the 802.11a technology also results in shorter range. This makes it ideal for places where there is a concentration of many users or many high-bandwidth applications. Another advantage is that the 5-GHz spectrum is a relatively free spectrum in terms of interference from appliances and devices. But the 5-GHz electronic components are costly, and an 802.11a network requires new equipment and is not backward compatible with the more popular 802.11b devices. As a result, even though the 802.11a specification had a lot of promise, it has currently become an intermediate-stage mainstream technology, between the 802.11b and 802.11g technologies. Some think that 802.11a has a future in home networks, especially in audio-video equipment, which requires a high-fidelity bandwidth in a relatively short distance. Others think it is a waste to relegate 802.11a to the home when the extra channels are needed by enterprises, and hence 802.11a will also have long-term application in enterprises in which more channels, small cells, and high bandwidth are design goals. Dual-mode devices are inexpensive and will probably continue to be used for quite some time.

IEEE 802.11g

The IEEE 802.11g specification, titled "Amendment 4: Further Higher Data Rate Extension in the 2.4-GHz Band," adds the frame formats, fields, and codes to add the higher rates to the basic 802.11 specification using the DSSS-OFDM modulation scheme in the 2.4-GHz ISM band. The new higher data rates added by this specification are 6, 9, 12, 18, 22, 24, 33, 36, 48, and 54 Mbps. This specification, like its siblings 802.11a and 802.11b, is unassuming and functional, yet it is influential and will be discussed for a long time.

There are discussions about whether 802.11g will be the ultimate specification or a temporary compromise that will give way to a more firm specification. One reason is that the 802.11g is a combination of different technologies and has four modes to satisfy all constituents. It has higher speed, using the OFDM technologies (similar to the 802.11a), in the 2.4-GHz range (similar to the 802.11b) and has only three channels. (The channels are nonoverlapping).

One advantage of 802.11g over the 802.11a specification is that it has backward compatibility (and co-existence); you can still use the older 802.11b CCK modulation scheme, throughputs, and channels—but at the 802.11b speeds, of course.

NOTE   A recent article pointed out that the throughput of 802.11g implementations goes down if they are supporting mixed 802.11g and 802.11b cards, and the degradation of speed persists even when the 802.11b cards are inactive. This failure happens when the 802.11b cards become inactive after having been active.

Another advantage of the 802.11g specification is the use of the 2.4-GHz spectrum with its less costly electronic components and higher range and penetrability. Of course, it is susceptible to interference from microwaves, cordless phones, and other devices in the 2.4-GHz spectrum.

IEEE 802.11f

Titled "IEEE Trial-Use Recommended for Multi-Vendor Access Point Interoperability via an Inter-Access Point Protocol Across Distribution Systems Supporting IEEE 802.11 Operation," the IEEE 802.11f specification defines service primitives and protocols for access points (APs) to exchange information.

This standard is relatively unknown and less complex (as compared to other IEEE 802.11 standards); approximately 78 pages, it details the mechanisms at the higher layers. The Inter-Access Point Protocol (IAPP) can be used not only among the APs but also among switches and bridges that require the exchange of WLAN information. The IAPP uses a distribution service network using TCP and UDP and is, therefore, independent of the WLAN traffic and security mechanisms.

Because the various detailed mechanisms are beyond the scope of this book, this subsection examines the abbreviated features.

The 802.11f specification introduces a higher-layer entity called the *Access Point Management Entity (APME)*, which interacts with the IAPP using a Service Access Point (SAP) layer. The SAP layer has four primitives: requests, confirms (that the request has been completed), responses (to requests), and indications (of events/triggers).

The Remote Authentication Dial-In User Service (RADIUS) protocol provides the security and authentication services. The RADIUS protocol provides the BSSID to IP address resolution of the APs, in addition to key distribution for encrypting the AP-to-AP traffic. Some RADIUS interactions require changes in the RADIUS RFC and are being addressed by an appropriate IETF document (http://www.ietf.org/internet-drafts/draft-moskowitz-radius-client-kickstart-01.txt).

The specification adds capability for faster roaming by proactive caching of STA (STAtion or client) context between neighboring APs. This capability is enhanced by adding the dynamic learning of neighboring AP graphs and caching the graphs. There is a station move process to "move" an STA to a different AP without the STA doing the association process all over again.

IEEE 802.11e

The IEEE 802.11e specification, titled "Media Access Control (MAC) Quality of Service (QoS) Enhancements," adds the QoS capability and essential features for multimedia support to WLANs. The QoS functionality is required for audio, voice, and video applications that are highly sensitive to delay and require guaranteed throughput and tight limits on jitter. The specification, affectionately called the *Wireless Multimedia Enhancements (WME)*, is approximately 165 pages. Because of the underlying protocols and transmission medium, the specification does not guarantee deterministic levels of throughput, jitter, delay, or any such properties—the final result is still best effort. Therefore, QoS addressed by the 802.11e provides better effort but is not guaranteed.

The following sections look at some of the most important WME features that are addressed in this specification.

QoS Capabilities

The WME defines QoS in terms of mechanisms and the ability to recognize, classify, and prioritize four access categories and eight traffic streams. The access categories are Voice, Video, Best Effort, and Background. The 802.11e specification adds frame formats, elements, messages, and other artifacts to specify, classify, and distinguish between the various traffic streams.

QoS Mechanisms

The WME features are basically implemented at Layer 2 with the ability to set policies at the higher layers. As you have seen, the upper layers set the priorities or traffic categories, and the Layer 2 mechanisms are adjusted appropriately.

The specification provides two mechanisms: EDCA and HCCA. The following is a general description of these two mechanisms:

- The Enhanced Distributed Channel Access (EDCA) provides a method to poll a channel more frequently based on user priorities (UP) set by the application layer; higher-priority traffic will have a shorter waiting period. The eight priorities 7 to 0 are as identified in the 802.1D priority tags. Table 3-3 shows the mapping between access categories and the priority designators.

Table 3-3 *User Priorities (UP) Mapping to an Access Category*

UP	Category	Priority
1	Background	Lowest
2	Background	
0	Best Effort	
3	Best Effort	
4	Video	
5	Video	
6	Voice	
7	Voice	Highest

- The HCF (Hybrid Coordination Function) Controlled Channel Access (HCCA) is a reservation-based mechanism that is initiated by the voice/video application through management primitives.

NOTE   Recent research (http://mosquitonet.stanford.edu/software/802.11e/ipc84.pdf) on the characteristics of these mechanisms observed that EDCF provides significant improvements for higher-priority traffic but causes worse performance for lower priorities; the HCCA provides efficient use of the medium when the load is high. Of course, you can expect that when some traffic gets better performance, the rest gets worse because of the limited resource being allocated differently. The point is that these mechanisms are not absolute and would require tuning for different performance characteristics and load conditions.

The QoS traffic-scheduling service and the higher-layer timer-synchronization service are added to implement the QoS functionalities.

QoS-Related Entities

The WME specification adds QSTA, QAP, QoS enhanced basic service set (QBSS), and QoS independent basic service set (QIBSS).

QSTA (QoS STAtion) and QAP (QoS Access Point) denote the STA and AP that are capable of performing the QoS facility—message exchange, the ability to handle frame formats, and the ability to selectively handle streams. The basic service set (BSS) and independent basic service set (IBSS) that are capable of QoS are called *QIBSS* and *QBSS*, respectively.

Association Based on QoS Capabilities

The final basic feature is the ability to distinguish and differentiate APs and STAs based on the QoS capabilities during the association process.

IEEE 802.11k

The IEEE 802.11k specification, titled "Specification for Radio Resource Measurement," adds the measurement and reporting functionality from an STA. The factors measured include the load, noise, beacons, hidden nodes, medium sensing events, a site report that shows the list of APs that the STA recognizes, and data (voice- and video-related features such as delay, jitter, device processor, and encryption information). This enables the measurement of environment and performance data on the radio substrate. The 802.11k specification not only specifies the information but also the MIB.

As you can see, the rich information that an STA can provide helps a management station make intelligent inferences; an AP with the management function; or a WLAN switch and router with regard to load, QoS, security, and topology. In essence, the radio information (in Layers 1 and 2) is not available at higher layers, so they make decisions based on local (and most probably device-level) optimization. The 802.11k Radio Resource Measurement (RRM) specification makes the lower-level radio data available at higher layers.

Remember that the 802.11k RRM standard provides the means to request and receive the information but does not make specific recommendations about interpreting the data.

The potential impacts of the 802.11k standard include better diagnostics, new services based on the data (such as location-based services), and reconfiguration based on operating context.

IEEE 802.11h

Titled "Spectrum and Transmit Power Management Extensions in the 5-GHz Band in Europe," the IEEE 802.11h specification adds the spectrum services to the 802.11 specification. The two spectrum services—Dynamic Frequency Selection (DFS) and Transmit Power Control (TPC)—are required to comply with the ERC/DEC/(99)23 and the EN 301 893.

NOTE   Even though the 802.11h specification is not of much interest from a security point of view, this brief discussion illustrates how government regulations and international forces influence and affect the WLAN domain. For example, this standard focuses on defining the services requirements for the 5-GHz, OFDM band for the 19- to 20-MHz channels based on European regulations.

National and international standards and opinions do matter; while we were writing this book, a new controversy erupted with respect to WLAN security in China. The country developed a new WLAN security standard and issued a decree to make all products (sold in China) comply with its standard. At least for now, this directive has been relaxed; however, a competing WLAN security standard now exists in China.

The reason for the European standards to incorporate the DFS is twofold: to adjust dynamically to different frequencies to avoid interference (for example, radar systems) and to distribute the load (that is, to "provide aggregate uniform loading of spectrum across all devices").

European Standard Organizations and Regulations: ERO

The European Radiocommunications Office (ERO) is based in Denmark (http://www.ero.dk). In its "ERC Decision of 29 November 1999 on the harmonized frequency bands to be designated for the introduction of High-Performance Radio Local Area Networks (HIPERLANs)

(ERC/DEC/(99)23)" (available at http://www.ero.dk/documentation/docs/doc98/official/pdf/ DEC9923E.PDF), the ERO mandated that the radio LAN (RLAN) devices should have two features: transmitter power control and a dynamic frequency channel-selection mechanism to spread the load uniformly (and for channel avoidance) in the 5250-MHz to 5350-MHz and 5470-MHz to 5725-MHz spectrum. Figure 3-4 shows the channel plan.

Figure 3-4   *802.11h Channel Plan*

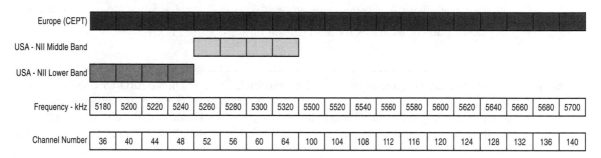

The decision also limits the power of the 5150-MHz to 5350-MHz spectrum to a maximum of 200 mW and restricts this spectrum to indoor. The 5470-Mhz to 5725-MHz spectrum can be used indoors or outdoors, with a maximum power restriction of 1000 mW (1 watt). The directive is 7 pages.

NOTE   It is interesting to note that the ERC/DEC/(99)23 uses different terminology. Rather than WLANs, it uses the term "HIPERLANs" (High-Performance Radio LANs), which are "intended for connectivity between traditional business products such as PCs, laptops, workstations, servers, printers, and other networking equipment, as well as digital consumer electronic equipment in the wireless home network environment." WLANs are called "cordless LANs" in some recommendations.

European Standard Organizations and Regulations: ETSI

The European Telecommunications Standards Institute (ETSI), which develops telecommunication standards for Europe, is based in the hills of Sophia Antipolis, South France. The standards are also referred to and used outside Europe.

The relevant document for this discussion is the ETSI EN 301 893, "Broadband Radio Access Networks (BRAN); 5-GHz high performance RLAN; Harmonized EN covering essential requirements of article 3.2 of the R&TTE (Radio and Telecommunications Terminal Equipment) Directive," which is available at http://webapp.etsi.org/exchangefolder/ en_301893v010203p.pdf.

The EN 301 893 is approximately 43 pages. The current version 1.2.3, dated August 2003, includes the following:

- Stipulation of the mechanisms and mechanics to perform dynamic frequency selection such as Interference Detection Threshold, Channel Availability Check time, and Uniform Spreading
- Definition of the frequencies and channels
- Description of the test sites and methods for testing compliance with the requirements
- Description of the limits for the Transmit Power Control (TPC)

NOTE   In 1996, the ERO originally designated the HIPERLAN bands in the ERO/DEC/(96)03. In 1998, the ERO (with ETSI) realized that more spectrum was necessary for multimedia applications. By the decision ERO/DEC/(99)24, the ERO withdrew the ERO/DEC/(96)03 and the EN 301 893, and the ERO became the authoritative standard for the spectrum and the DFS and TPC.

802.11h Details

The 802.11h standard defines the choreographies, message formats, and other required elements to implement the European standards in an interoperable way. To achieve this, you must add corresponding services to the WLAN specification. As you might expect, the two spectrum management services—Dynamic Frequency Selection and the Transmit Power Control—have been added to the architecture and the station services clauses.

The Transmit Power Control service adds functionality to associate STAs with APs based on power capability. It also covers methods to specify, select, and manage power of channels based on the respective regulations.

The Dynamic Frequency Selection (DFS) services add functionality to associate STAs with APs based on channels supported, quieting, testing, detecting radar channels, and discontinuing channels based on radar interference.

As a result, the various artifacts added to the 802.11 specification include the following:

- Fields such as country code, power constraint, channel selection, quiet, and power are added to the beacon and probe response.
- Power capability and supported channels fields are added to the association and reassociation request.
- The reason and status codes reflect the state of power and channel attributes.
- Elements that reflect the power and channels supported are added.
- Messages to start power measurement and report the results are added.

- Channel switch announcement is added.

- Quiet element to silence a channel to aid interference measurement is added.

- The specification also describes the TPC and DFS procedures based on the preceding message types and elements, including selection and announcement of new channels, requesting and getting reports on measurements, quieting channels for testing radar interference, procedures for detecting radars, and discontinuing operations on a channel.

Light Weight Access Point Protocol

This IETF draft, titled "draft-calhoun-seamoby-lwapp-03.txt," defines the Light Weight Access Point Protocol (LWAPP) to enable routers and switches to manage WLAN access points. This proposal is a little different from other specifications because it treats the AP as a thin device that acts primarily as a collector of 802.11 frames. The frames are transmitted to an access router (AR) in a point-to-point topology, which then manages the frames.

The APs go through a discovery, configuration exchange, and update phase with the AR before starting to work. After the AP-AR pair is enabled, the LWPP encapsulates the 802.11 data and management frames and transports them between the AP and AR. There are also message choreographies and formats for encryption session key update. The keys, of course, are managed by the AR and are updated to the AP as required. The transport layer between the AP and AR can be Layer 2 802.3 frames or Layer 3 UDP.

Summary

This chapter covered some of the more interesting and relevant standards in the WLAN space. It also gave a perspective of the forces acting in the standards space—customer requirements, government regulations, and the time it takes to mature a standard. As discussed previously in this book, the WLAN space is a young domain, which means there will be many more new standards and regulations in the next few years as the domain matures.

CHAPTER 4

WLAN Fundamentals

This chapter discusses the essential basics of the WLAN technology: the services, the messages, the choreographies, and the interaction primitives. Chapter 3, "WLAN Standards," touched on the standards and discussed them at a high level. This chapter gets into the relevant details of the 802.11 standard, the 802.11a, 802.11b, and 802.11g. The rest of this book dives into the various security aspects—standards, design, best practices, configuration, and deployment examples.

NOTE   As one of the reviewers pointed out, you might be wondering when this wireless security book is going to start talking about wireless security. WLAN security is a complex subject and has a lot of context. So an understanding of these fundamentals is required to fully comprehend and analyze wireless security.

WLAN: Elements and Characteristics

The basic elements in a WLAN domain are as follows:

- The wireless client, also known as the *STA (station)* or *supplicant*, is usually a card or embedded chip in a device. These devices include PCs, PDAs, tablets, or smart phones. They communicate over a radio link.

- The access point (AP) is the receiving (or sending, depending on the context) end of the radio link, and it has the capability to reach back to the LAN. The AP, obviously, has a range called the *coverage area* (actually, it is three-dimensional and should be called coverage volume). The coverage area could overlap or be disjointed between the APs. The AP's signal strength and antenna characteristics usually determine the coverage area. The antenna determines the shape and volume of the coverage area, and the power of the AP determines the signal strength. Factors like interference (from other devices) and objects (like walls) affect the overall coverage area.

- The coverage area is also essentially a Basic Service Set (BSS), the lowest membership, group, or organizational granularity in a WLAN.

NOTE   Unless there are mechanisms to coordinate between the APs, a mobile device jumping from one coverage area/BSS to another loses the connectivity. That is, the BSSs are independent; one device can be associated with only one BSS, and the STA-BSS association is dynamic. Later you will learn how the Extended Service Set (ESS) solves this problem of disjointed BSS and provides continuity for a client to move from one AP to another seamlessly.

- The distribution service (DS) is the wired network that provides connectivity from the WLAN to the rest of the world. This could be a corporate LAN, access provider, wireless service provider (WSP), or even the Internet.

Figure 4-1 shows these elements.

Figure 4-1   *WLAN Basic Elements*

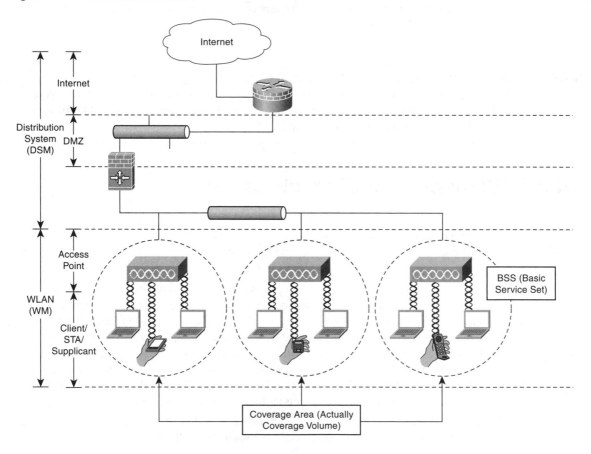

There are two modes of WLAN operation: independent BSS (IBSS) and ESS. Figure 4-2 shows the topology of the two modes.

Figure 4-2   *WLAN Operation Modes*

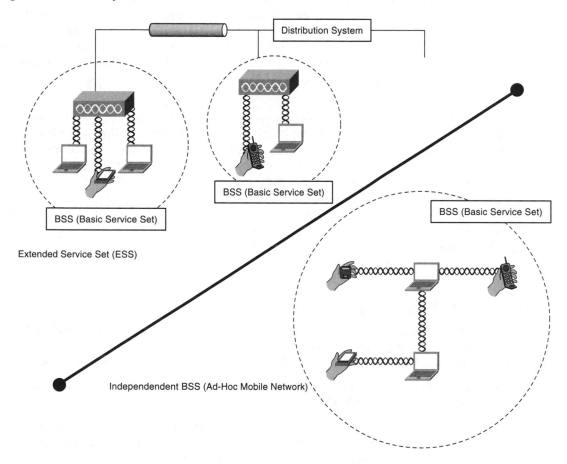

In the IBSS mode, the devices form ad-hoc connections with each other. IBSS mode is not used very often, but it has the potential to add a lot of value to the Internet—military, peer-to-peer, ad-hoc networks, sensor networks, mesh networks, and other applications are emerging in this space. The Mobile Ad-Hoc Network (MANet) protocols such as Ad-Hoc On-Demand Distance Vector (AODDV) and Adaptive Demand Driven Multicast Routing (ADMR) are being worked on at the standards level (IETF) and at research labs.

The ESS consists of STAs connected to APs that, in turn, are connected to the DS. The APs and the DS enable the STAs to reach back and connect to a network infrastructure with more "permanency." ESS mode is the most common WLAN mode, at least for now. ESS provides the capability for sustained mobility—that is, a client/STA can move from AP to AP or from BSS to BSS connected to the same ESS and will not lose the connectivity context. However, the connectivity context is lost when an STA moves between ESSs. In plain words, the concept of an ESS is to give mobility across APs in an organization, but moving across organizations is not supported. Also remember that the applications might not be able to tolerate the connection transition time from one BSS to another in the same ESS.

NOTE   IEEE 802.11 distinguishes between the distribution system medium (DSM), which is usually the wired environment, and the wireless medium (WM), which is usually radio signals over the air. But the specification does not assume or mandate any specific DS infrastructure; rather, it specifies a set of services that the DS would provide to support a WLAN. This level of decoupling has proved to be a good architecture to evolve the 802.11 in terms of security, speed, and functionality. As you saw in Chapter 3, the various subsequent standards were able to add QoS, 802.1x security primitives, support for video, and audio to the basic 802.11 standard incrementally.

WLAN Basic Topology

As previously discussed, even though the distribution system and the wired medium could be different, usually there are only two infrastructures: a wireless environment/infrastructure consisting of STAs/clients that is connected to a wired environment/infrastructure through APs.

Figure 4-3 shows one possible simplified topology as a perspective to compare and contrast functionalities of DS and WLAN.

The authentication, authorization, and accounting (AAA) infrastructure is part of the distribution system. Usually the RADIUS server is specific to the WLAN environment, and once authenticated, the WLAN users are authorized by the corporate AAA system. As you will see in the "Enterprise Guest Access" section of Chapter 11, "Operational and Design Considerations for Secure WLANs," this topology could allow guest users access to the Internet but not to any corporate network resources. This topology works well not only for big corporate organizations but also for universities and small businesses.

Figure 4-3   *Simplified WLAN Topology—Corporate*

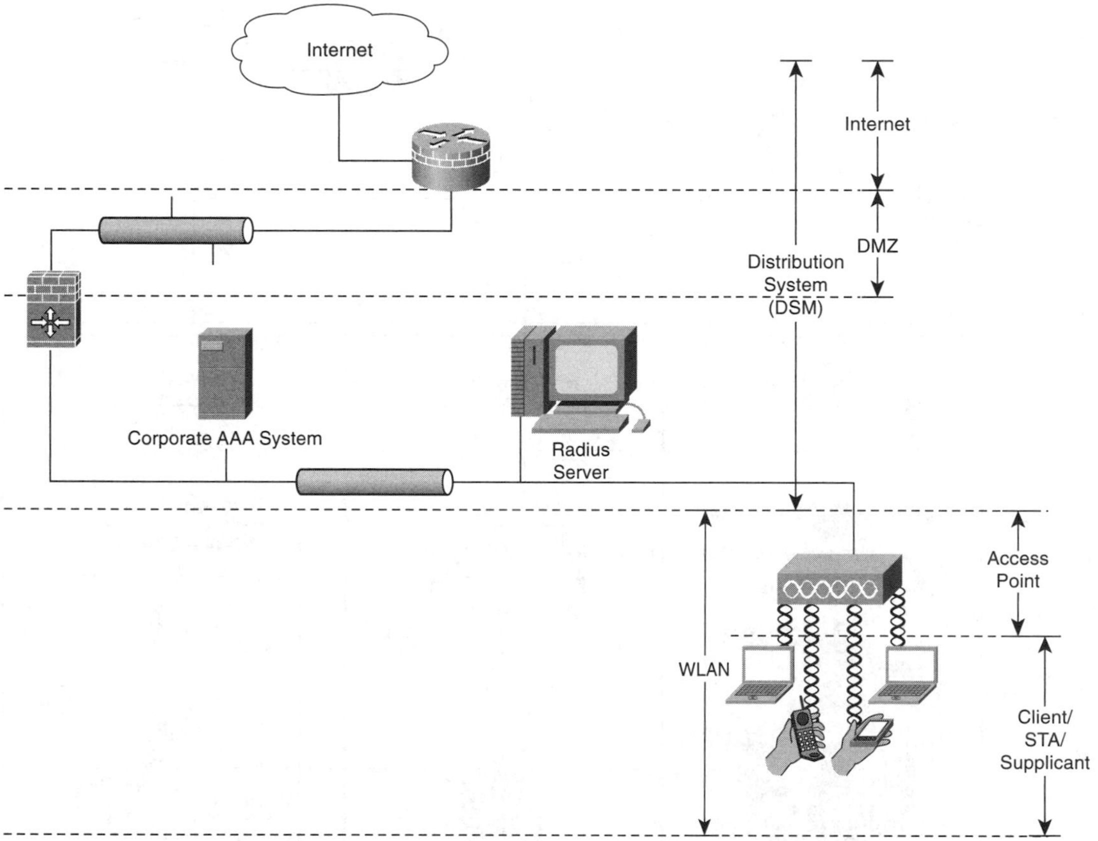

Figure 4-4 shows another possible scenario: an aggregator or wireless service provider (WSP).

In this scenario, there is a WSP cloud and an access provider layer. This scenario is usually employed in what is called *public WLAN (PWLAN)*. The WSP provides multiple establishments, such as conferences, hotels, or airports, with Internet access. The establishments provide the WLAN infrastructure and an access layer to the WSP. The WSP usually handles the AAA functions in addition to billing and related services.

Recently, all the carriers and a few service providers have emerged in the WSP layer, whereas the airports, coffee houses, and burger joints have started providing the WLAN access. The attractive feature (at least to the SPs) is that if a user has an account or service with the service provider, the user can ubiquitously access the Internet anywhere he or she travels.

Figure 4-4 *Simplified WLAN Topology—WSP/PWLAN*

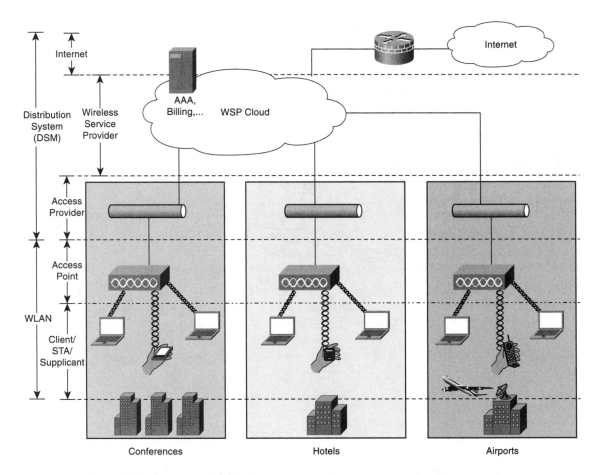

Please bear in mind that Figures 4-3 and 4-4 are provided simply to gain a perspective. Chapter 11 and Chapter 13, "WLAN Deployment Examples," cover more detailed designs.

WLAN Building Blocks

Let's examine the building blocks of an 802 WLAN. The 802.11 WLAN consists of a set of services that are defined as architectural artifacts, independent of implementations and layers. The services are achieved by messages between the entities, mainly the STA/client, the APs, and the distribution system. In turn, messages are composed of frames.

Services

As discussed previously, the 802.11 architecture consists of essential services implemented by the STAs, APs, and the distribution system. Table 4-1 shows the essential services, the specification that defined the services, and the entity that implements the services. The services implemented by the APs and STAs are collectively known as *station services (SS)*, and the services implemented by the backend DS are called the *distribution system services (DSS)*. The type of service represents the flexibility that an entity has; a "request" type can be denied, but a "notification" type is final, should be honored, and cannot be refused by either party.

Table 4-1   *802.11 Services*

Service	Description	Specification	Group	Type
Authentication	This service establishes the identity of a client entity to the satisfaction of the server.	802.11	SS	Request
	The preauthentication of an already authenticated STA is also part of this service.			
	An STA can be authenticated with many APs.			
Deauthentication	This service terminates an existing authentication.	802.11	SS	Notification
Association	This service establishes the STA-AP relationship. An STA would be associated with at most one AP.	802.11	Straddles the line between SS and DSS	Request
	With specifications like the 802.11e, association can be conditional based on capabilities; for example, with 802.11e, the required qualtiy of service (QoS) functionality would determine whether an association would be entertained.			

continues

Table 4-1 *802.11 Services (Continued)*

Service	Description	Specification	Group	Type
Disassociation	This service terminates an existing STA-AP association.	802.11	Straddles the line between SS and DSS	Notification
Reassociation	This service "moves" an STA from one AP to another (or, effectively, one BSS to another), obviously within an ESS. This service is also used to change the attributes of an STA-AP association (kind of a virtual reassociation).	802.11	DSS	Request
Privacy (802.11i renames this service as confidentiality.)	The confidentiality of messages to achieve the equivalent of wires. The privacy service is invoked only for the data frames.	802.11	SS (DSS contributes to key material.)	Request
Distribution	The delivery of messages between the various entities. The 802.11 describes the message formats and the "what" part. It leaves the "how" to the implementers.	802.11	DSS	Request
Integration	This service is invoked after the distribution and is responsible for the connectivity between the WLAN and the back-end LAN.	802.11	DSS	Request
MSDU delivery	Delivery of data between MAC service access points; consists of functionalities such as asynchronous data service to transfer data and data units reordering.	802.11	SS	Request

Table 4-1 *802.11 Services (Continued)*

Service	Description	Specification	Group	Type
Higher-layer timer synchronization	For QoS.	802.11e	SS and DSS	Request
QoS traffic scheduling	For QoS.	802.11e	SS and DSS	Request

Frames

The 802.11 devices communicate with each other by exchanging frames at the MAC layer. Figure 4-5 shows the frame format.

Figure 4-5 *MAC Frames*

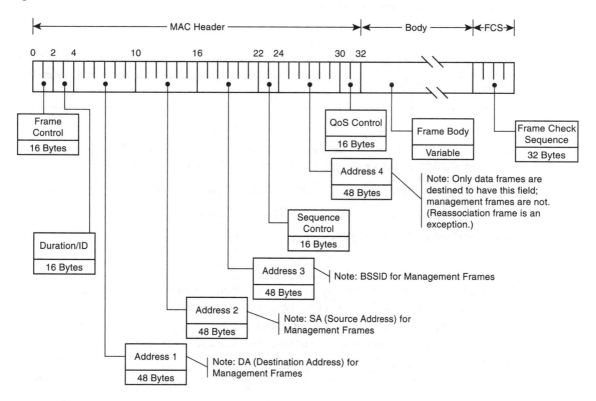

The basic 802.11 MAC frame consists of a header that is 32 octets long, a variable length body, and a 4-octet CRC.

The MAC frame itself consists of seven fields:

- Frame Control.
- Duration/ID.
- Three Address Fields (Source, Destination, and BSSID).
- Sequence Control.
- QoS Control. (This field is being added by the 802.11E WG.)

Not all fields are present at all times; the presence and convention (convention as to which field is used for which information) of the fields depends on the type of messages. For example, there is space for four address fields corresponding to the BSSID, destination address (DA), source address (SA), and the receiver address (RA).

NOTE   The addresses are 48 bytes long and are organized according to clause 5.2 of IEEE 802-1990. Individual addresses are MAC addresses; if the address represents a multicast or broadcast address, it is as defined by the domain convention.

The frame control is of interest because it contains fields that are required for the security mechanisms; therefore, let's examine the frame control in a bit more detail.

Figure 4-6 shows the contents of the frame control field at a bit level.

The protocol version is 0. It changes only if there is an incompatibility.

The type bits (bits 2 and 3) signify management, control, and data frames.

NOTE   The management frames include the request and response frames from the association/ reassociation service, the authentication, beacon, and probe request/probe response.

The control frames include Clear to Send (CTS), acknowledgement (ACK), and Request to Send (RTS) frames for controlling the transmission at the medium layer.

The data frames include the actual data bits.

Figure 4-6   *Frame Control Field Bits*

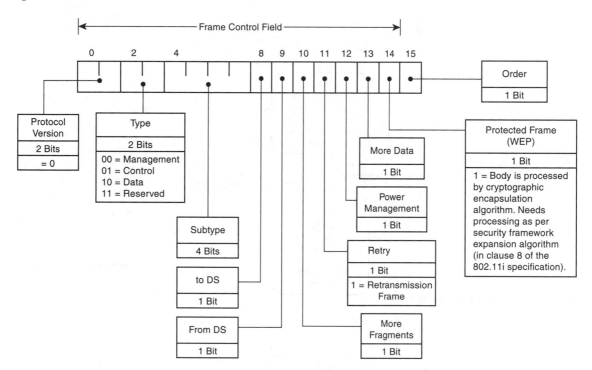

The subtype bits signify a more granular description of the type. Some examples include association request (00-0000), association response (00-0001), and data (10-0000).

The WEP bit signifies that the WEP has processed the frame body, so the receiver would apply the WEP unpacking algorithms. The 802.11i standard renames this field to Protected Frame.

WLAN State Diagram

Now look at the state diagram of an STA. The state diagram in Figure 4-7 defines the states of STA with respect to a wireless medium in an ESS.

Figure 4-7 *STA State Diagram*

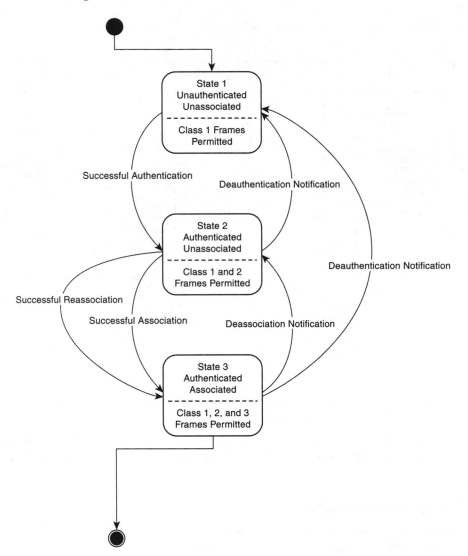

The state transitions occur based on the outcome of the WLAN services. The STA/client starts out in an unauthenticated, unassociated state. The first step is to authenticate utilizing the authentication service; the authentication steps needed depend on the authentication requirements of the APs and DS. Perhaps open authentication is sufficient, or perhaps 802.11i authentication is required. A successful authentication transitions the STA to state 2. The next step is to associate, and a successful association transitions the STA to fully functional. The state transitions also happen through the deauthentication, disassociation, and reassociation services.

Note that the deauthentication and disassociation services are notifications; as discussed previously, a notification cannot be denied. Therefore, after an STA sends or receives these messages, the state transition is automatic.

The authentication process, of course, is based on the type of authentication, the policies in place for the APs, and the back-end network (for example, DS). Similarly, the association process can be based on capabilities including QoS, throughput, and load. The authentication, association, and disassociation requests can be denied; hence, the messages that are associated with these processes require the successful result from these services to transition the state.

Another important point to note is about the frames permitted at each state. Each state has associated frames that can be exchanged. The class 1 frames include essential communication frames, probe, beacon, authentication, and deauthentication. Class 2 frames include association, disassociation, and reassociation frames. Class 3 includes all data frames. Figure 4-7 shows which frames are allowed at each state.

NOTE   Note the following points:

- The importance of the "authentication" frames pertains only to 802.11, and the frames are pre-802.1x authentication.

- You should note the lack of state or acknowledgement of these frames. This information might be relevant to protocol-based security discussions.

- The frames that aren't allowed are blocked.

- Because authentication takes a relatively long time, optimizations are sought out in which either authentication information is cached in such a way that different APs can access it, or one-time authentication is done with multiple APs. This way, a client can roam between APs by changing the association and without requiring authentication.

Basic Choreography

Let's look at some of the relevant message exchanges to understand how the frames fit together to form cohesive and meaningful interactions.

Beacon

An AP sends the beacon message on a periodic basis. Figure 4-8 shows the beacon frame.

Figure 4-8   *Beacon Frame*

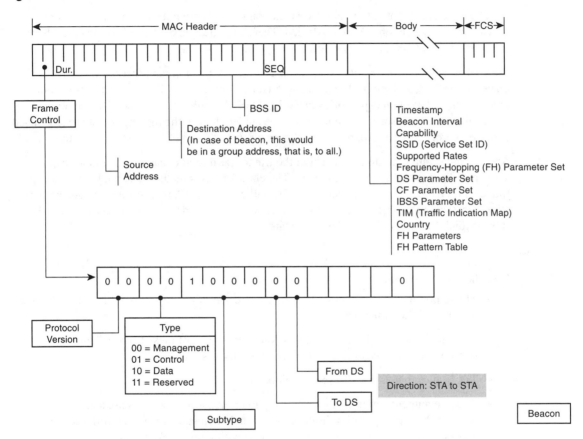

The beacon was designed as the primary discovery mechanism for the STAs to get a list of all APs in a BSS. However, this is terrible in terms of security because any wanderer can get the list of all APs, SSID, and capabilities. Therefore, inside enterprises, the periodic broadcasting of beacons is usually turned off. But for public WLANs and ad-hoc networks, this is turned on.

Probe

The probe exchange typically occurs between an STA and an AP. Figures 4-9 and 4-10 show the probe request and response frames.

Figure 4-9   *Probe Request Frame*

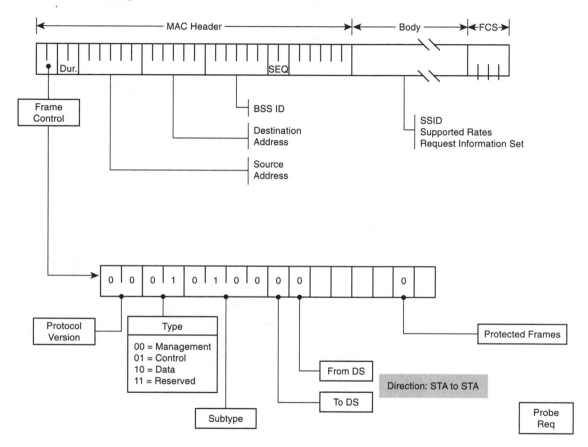

The request information set field in the probe request frame is interesting; it is a list of element IDs for which the initiator wants details. The probe response would include the IDs and the appropriate information.

The probe response contains almost all the information in the beacon.

Figure 4-10   *Probe Response Frame*

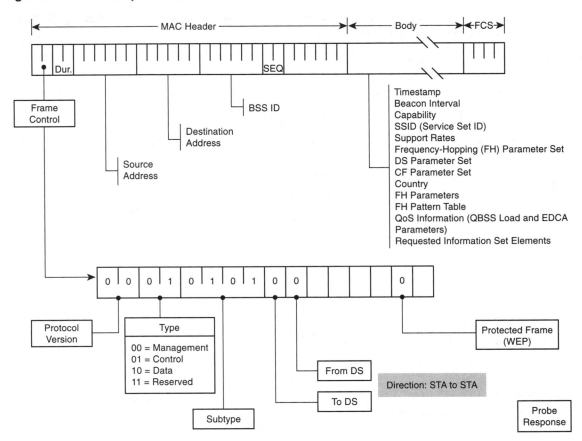

Authentication

Authentication involves a set of exchanges; Figures 4-11 and 4-12 show the pattern and the framework. The specific exchanges depend on the algorithm and the protocols. You will see them in detail in Chapter 5, "WLAN Basic Authentication and Privacy Methods," and Chapter 7, "EAP Authentication Protocols for WLANs."

Figure 4-11   *Authentication Request Frame*

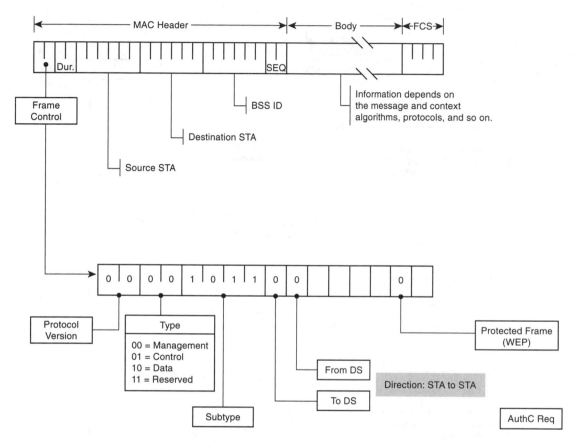

Figure 4-11 shows how the authentication request frame would look with the relevant fields. The type is management (00), and the subtype is authentication (1011). The data field would depend on the actual algorithms and protocols.

The 802.11 specification defines the open and shared-key authentication. This is for device authentication only and uses MAC addresses as authentication criteria. The reason for this authentication is to achieve confidentiality of data transmission. Chapter 5 covers this in more detail.

For user authentication, the mechanics are based on EAP, which is covered in detail in Chapter 7.

Figure 4-12 shows a general, conceptual choreography framework and pattern that covers both device and user authentication.

Figure 4-12 *Authentication Framework Pattern Choreography*

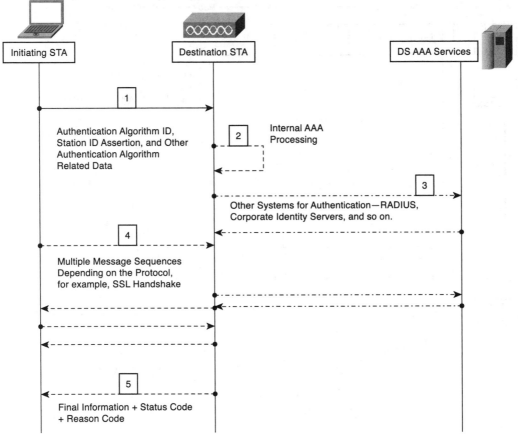

In Step 1, the initiating STA (usually a laptop or a PDA) sends the authentication request frame with various pieces of information. The target STA (usually an AP) performs internal processing (2) or communicates with AAA systems such as RADIUS server (3).

NOTE   For device authentication, Step 2 is usually sufficient, whereas for user authentication, corporate AAA systems would also be used.

Many exchanges are possible and will happen between the initiating STA and the AP (4). Finally, the AP sends the result frame (5) with information and reason or status code.

Deauthentication

This is a one-way notification message with the frame format shown in Figure 4-13.

Figure 4-13   *Deauthentication Frame*

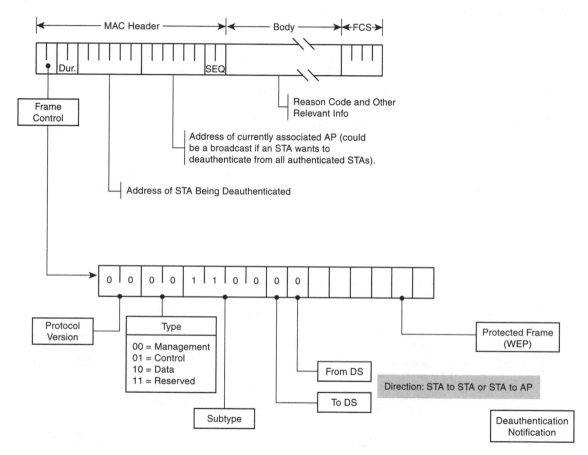

If an STA/client wants to deauthenticate from all APs, it inserts a broadcast address to the destination address field. The frame type is management (00) and subtype deauthentication (1100). The frame also contains a reason code.

Association

As shown in Figures 4-14 and 4-15, the association frames (request and response) are simpler frames than the authentication frames.

Figure 4-14 *Association Request Frame*

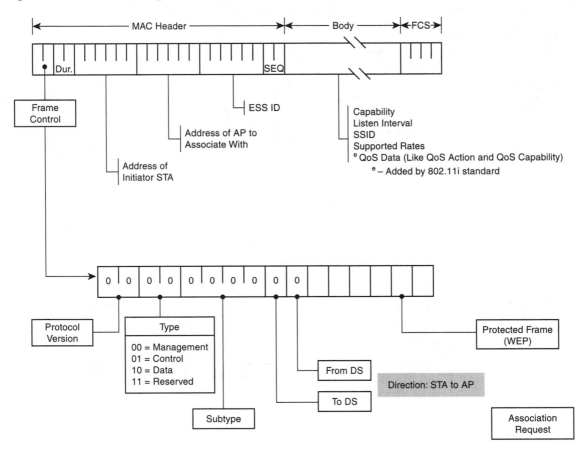

The data might include capability information, supported data rates, QoS features, and so on for the AP to decide whether an association would result in required performance characteristics. The response frame would include a status code and (optionally) a reason code.

Figure 4-15   *Association Response Frame*

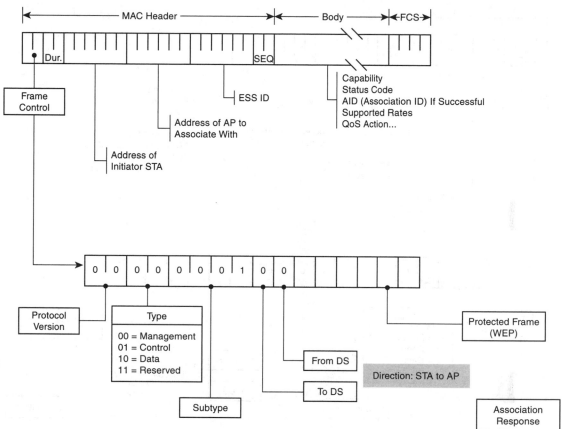

Reassociation

The reassociation frames are similar to the association frames, as shown in Figure 4-16.

This frame has four addresses: the STA, the AP to be associated with, the AP it is currently associated with, and the BSS ID.

Figure 4-16 *Reassociation Frame*

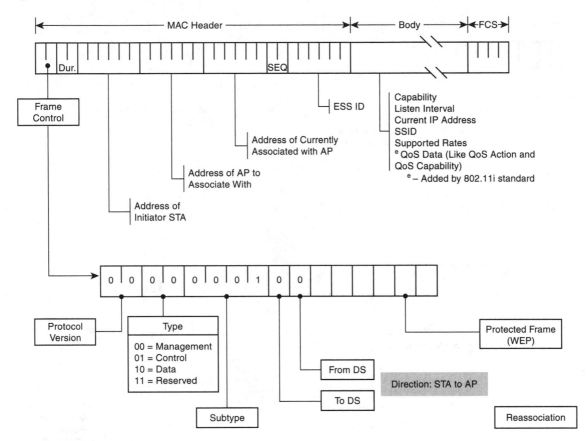

Disassociation

Like the deauthentication message, this message is a one-way notification, as shown in Figure 4-17.

The destination address could be a broadcast address if an AP wants to disassociate with all associated STAs—for example, if it is shutting down or reorganizing for better performance.

Figure 4-17   *Disassociation Frame*

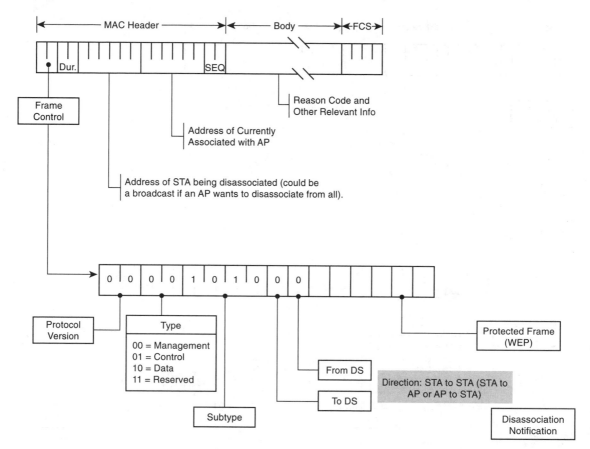

Data

The generic data frame is shown in Figure 4-18.

The following are a couple of points to note:

- The type is data (10), as is the subtype (0000).
- The source, destination, and BSS ID would be embedded in the control frame.

Figure 4-18   *Generic Data Frame*

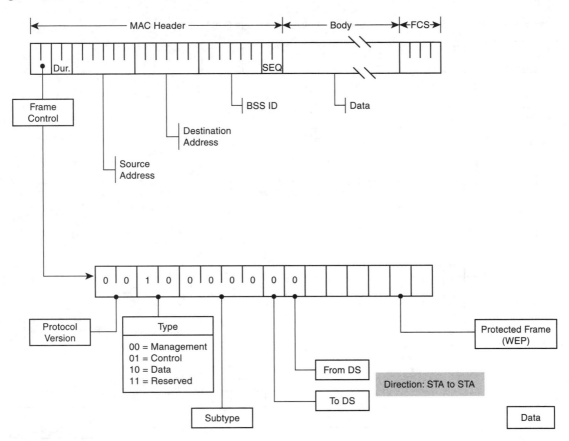

Reason and Status Codes

Many of the responses and notifications incorporate information and context in the form of reason and status codes. Both the reason code and the status code are 2 bytes long and thus can carry 65,536 values. When 802.11 was first introduced, there were fewer than 15 reason codes and status codes. As more and more specifications are being developed, the reason and code tables are also getting bigger. In fact, while writing this book, an overlap was found for status codes 40 to 43 between the 802.11e and 802.11i working specifications; both had defined those four status codes. But after 802.11i was published, the 802.11e revised the codes to 47 through 50. Table 4-2 lists the reason and status codes.

Table 4-2   *Reason Code Table*

Reason Code	Description
0	Reserved.
1	Unspecified reason.
2	Previous authentications no longer valid.
3	Deauthenticated because sending station is leaving (or has left) IBSS or ESS.
4	Disassociated due to inactivity.
5	Disassociated because AP is unable to handle all currently associated stations.
6	Class 2 frame received from nonauthenticated station.
7	Class 3 frame received from nonassociated station.
8	Disassociated because sending station is leaving (or has left) BSS.
9	Station requesting (re)association is not authenticated with responding station.
10–12	Reserved.
13	Invalid information element.
14[i]	MIC failure.
15[i]	4-Way Handshake timeout.
16[i]	Group key update timeout.
17[i]	Information element in 4-Way Handshake different from (Re)Associate Request/Probe Response/Beacon.
18[i]	Multicast cipher is not valid.
19[i]	Invalid pairwise cipher.
20[i]	Invalid AKMP.
21[i]	Unsupported RSN IE version.
22[i]	Invalid RSN IE capabilities.
23[i]	IEEE 802.1X authentication failed.
24[i]	Cipher suite is rejected per security policy.
25–31	Reserved.

continues

Table 4-2 *Reason Code Table (Continued)*

Reason Code	Description
32^i	Disassociated for unspecified, QoS-related reason.
33^i	Disassociated because QAP lacks sufficient bandwidth for this QSTA.
34^e	Disassociated because of excessive number of frames that need to be acknowledged but are not acknowledged for AP transmissions or poor channel conditions.
35^e	Disassociated because QSTA is transmitting outside the limits of its TXOPs.
36–65,535	Reserved.
36^e	Requested from peer QSTA because the QSTA is leaving the QBSS (or resetting).
37^e	Requested from peer QSTA because it does not want to use the mechanism.
38^e	Requested from peer QSTA because the QSTA received frames using the mechanism for which a setup is required.
39^e	Requested from peer QSTA due to time out.
40–655,535	Reserved.

Legend:

^{i}Added by 802.11i standard

^{e}Added by 802.11e standard

Table 4-3 *Status Code Table*

Status Code	Description
0	Successful.
1	Unspecified failure.
2–9	Reserved.
10	Cannot support all requested capabilities in the capability information field.
11	Reassociation denied due to inability to confirm that association exists.
12	Association denied due to reason outside the scope of this standard.
13	Responding station does not support the specified authentication algorithm.
14	Received an authentication frame with an authentication transaction sequence number out of the expected sequence.
15	Authentication rejected because of challenge failure.
16	Authentication rejected due to timeout waiting for next frame in sequence.
17	Association denied because AP is unable to handle additional associated stations.

Table 4-3   *Status Code Table (Continued)*

Status Code	Description
18	Association denied due to requesting station not supporting all of the data rates in the BSSBasicRateSet parameter.
19[b]	Association denied due to requesting station not supporting the Short Preamble option.
20[b]	Association denied due to requesting station not supporting the PBCC Modulation option.
21[b]	Association denied due to requesting station not supporting the Channel Agility option.
22[g]–24[g]	Reserved.
25[g]	Association denied due to requesting station not supporting the Short Slot Time option.
26[g]	Association denied due to requesting station not supporting the DSSS-OFDM option.
27–31	Reserved.
32[e]	Unspecified, QoS-related failure.
33[e]	Association denied due to QAP having insufficient bandwidth to handle another QSTA.
34[e]	Association denied due to excessive frame loss rates or poor conditions on current operating channel.
35[e]	Association (with QBSS) denied due to requesting station not supporting the QoS facility.
36[e]	Association denied due to requesting station not supporting Block Ack.
37[e]	The request has been declined.
38[e]	The request has not been successful because one or more parameters have invalid values.
39[e]	The TS has not been created because the request cannot be honored. However, a suggested TSPEC is provided so that the initiating QSTA can attempt to set another TS with the suggested changes to the TSPEC.
47[e]	The TS has not been created. However, the HC might be capable of creating a TS in response to a request after the time indicated in the TS Delay element.
48[e]	Direct Link is not allowed in the BSS by policy.
49[e]	Destination STA is not present within this QBSS.
50[e]	Destination STA is not a QSTA.
40[i]	Invalid information element.
41[i]	Invalid group cipher.
42[i]	Invalid pairwise cipher.
43[i]	Invalid AKMP.

continues

Table 4-3 *Status Code Table (Continued)*

Status Code	Description
44[i]	Unsupported RSN IE version.
45[i]	Invalid RSN IE capabilities.
46[i]	Cipher suite is rejected per security policy.
51–65,535	Reserved.

Legend:

[b]Added by 802.11b standard   [e]Added by 802.11e standard

[g]Added by 802.11g standard   [i]Added by 802.11i standard

WEP

Now that we have dealt with the basic mechanisms, the natural progression is to discuss the main feature of this book: security. The wireless nature of the medium adds two difficulties with respect to the wired medium:

- The packets can be captured by anybody in the coverage area (as compared to the wired medium, where a person needs to connect to a jack using cables).

  Moreover, the coverage area does not conform to the physical organizational boundaries; the area often spans to outside the buildings, which enables the war-driving phenomenon. An attacker could be miles away. It is rumored that a person could drive down busy office streets of major cities and become connected to the LANs of Fortune 500 companies that have offices there.

- Because anyone in the coverage volume can be connected to the wireless medium, we also need authentication mechanisms to interact with the medium.

The challenge is "securing the medium," so to speak, which is taken for granted in a wired environment. The 802.11 specification defines two authentication mechanisms and one confidentiality mechanism to balance the aforementioned difficulties.

NOTE   Remember, the pervasiveness and ubiquity of the wireless medium makes it attractive in many places and domains. For example, one would find it useful to have wireless connecting all home entertainment pieces; the same goes for guest access in enterprises, attendee access in conference centers, or access in airports, coffee houses, and other public places. So the key word is balance—achieving symmetry between the security mechanisms and the domain requirements.

The authentication methods defined in the 802.11 standard are open authentication and shared-key authentication, which are mainly aimed at device authentication. Chapter 5 covers the authentication methods and WEP in detail.

To achieve a robust wireless LAN, the specification defines WEP mechanisms, which aim to achieve the confidentiality equivalence of wires. Needless to say, the WEP proved to be less secure than intended and was deemed unsuitable for a secure wireless LAN. Chapter 6, "Wireless Vulnerabilities," delves into the common vulnerabilities of WLAN.

Summary

In this chapter, you saw a bird's-eye view of the WLAN security domain. This chapter covered not only the basic elements and characteristics but also the services, messages, and frames. Now you are ready to dive into the various WLAN security mechanisms, scrutinize the vulnerabilities, and explore how they are remediated.

WLAN Basic Authentication and Privacy Methods

This chapter is the first of a trilogy of chapters that looks at the authentication aspects of WLAN security—the bootstrap, the initialization, the security measures they support, the trust models, and the processes.

Although the WLAN domain is young, its security has gone through three generations. This chapter looks at the basic authentication services—the open authentication and shared-key authentication methods—of the 802.11 specification. This chapter also dives into Wired Equivalent Privacy (WEP) mechanisms. Although these mechanisms are quickly becoming legacy, a thorough knowledge of them enables you to have a good understanding of and proper perspective on current and future WLAN security mechanics.

NOTE   Currently, only point-to-point authentication is supported; no multicast authentication is allowed. Multicast authentication can be useful for mobility in which a client can authenticate to multiple access points (APs)—it is one way of enabling seamless mobility, quality of service (QoS), or even channel aggregation.

Also, the authentication is session, user, or device authentication; it is not message authentication.

Authentication Mechanics

The IEEE 802.11 standard defines the authentication service, frames, and associated semantics for achieving this function. Chapter 4, "WLAN Fundamentals," discussed the general frame elements and the top-level choreography of authentication. This chapter concentrates on the payload and the next-level details of the authentication process.

Figure 5-1 shows the elements in the authentication frame body.

Figure 5-1   *Authentication Frame Body*

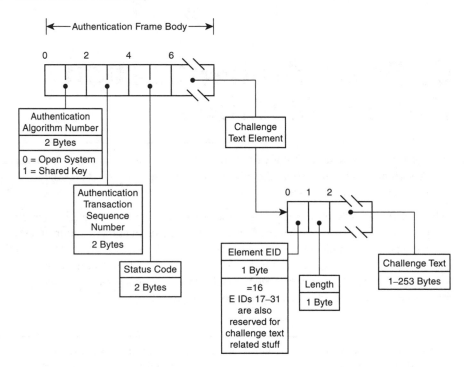

The authentication frame body consists of the algorithm number, transaction sequence number, status code, and challenge text. Two algorithms are supported now (as of this point in the evolution of the standards): open (number=0) and shared key (number=1). The challenge text element has the ID 16.

NOTE   Authentication can be between a client's station (STA) and an AP or between two clients' STAs in the case of ad-hoc networks.

Open Authentication

Open authentication is a simple exchange of messages. The choreography is shown in Figure 5-2.

Figure 5-2   *Open System Authentication*

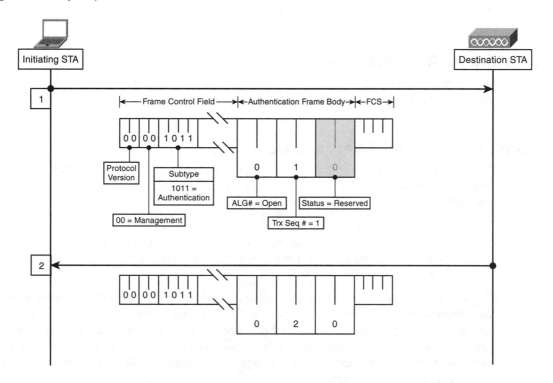

The initiating STA (usually a WLAN client, a laptop, or a PDA) sends message 1 out to an AP. The AP goes through its internal processing and sends a reply, which is either a success or a failure with a reason code. The status code is relevant only for the reply from the AP.

NOTE   Open system authentication, in general, is a null authentication that can typically enable any client to authenticate to an AP. However, it is possible for the AP to impose policy decisions (for example, load constraint) to turn down particular clients from using open authentication.

Trust Model and Assumptions

Open authentication provides no security because of the "open" nature of this protocol. The default is to trust all STAs that ask to be connected. The only security aspect is that the STAs should know the Service Set Identifier (SSID) of the AP. The AP's policy could base its access on the client's MAC address, too (not that this is secure either), so open authentication equates to no secure authentication or null authentication.

Supporting AAA Infrastructure

The open authentication method does not rely on, require, or use any AAA mechanisms; therefore, no AAA infrastructure is required.

Applications, Vulnerabilities, and Countermeasures

The open authentication method has no security whatsoever. If an STA can find and communicate with an AP, it will be allowed access. The advantage is the simplicity and ease, precisely because no setup is required.

Open authentication is suitable for public WLANs, including the ones available in hotels, coffee shops, airport lounges, and conference halls. Usually, the users use IPSec/VPN solutions to connect to their corporate network; hence, the open authentication to an AP is perfectly appropriate as a connectivity mechanism.

If you use open authentication to connect to the Internet directly, you should also use a hardware or software firewall. In many installations, the APs that employ open authentication are located in the demilitarized zone (DMZ), so your computer is not fully secure against threats from the Internet. When you use a VPN solution, the VPNs usually filter out and disable local connections. So with a VPN connection, because all traffic is through the VPN, your computer is safe from the DMZ vulnerabilities.

NOTE   With a VPN, the traffic is protected, but the accessing PC is not. If the hacker compromises the PC, he can then do as he will via the IPSec VPN.

Auditing and Accounting

Special auditing and accounting capabilities are not required or provided by the open authentication method.

As previously discussed, there would be a billing, accounting, and auditing infrastructure beyond the WLAN infrastructure for public WLANs. Often, a wireless service provider (WSP) offers this service. Usually after the association with an AP, there are accounting servers to gather user credentials such as username and password, e-commerce servers to provide billing and payment services (usually by credit card), and proxies to audit the time. (The billing is usually based on expired time, say $10 for 24 hours.) The interface for these services usually is a Web-based interface.

NOTE   It is important to make the distinction between auditing and accounting requirements and motivations at the different protocol stacks.

In the case of hotspots, the accounting/billing is achieved through higher layers (because mobility might come into play and the accounting is to remain whole as the session is transferred from one access point to another).

However, at Layer 2, there may be required auditing and other accounting to improve network management.

MAC-Based Authentication

The MAC-based authentication is actually an internal policy processing by the AP. The AP has an internal table of MAC addresses from which it allows access to the network. The MAC address authentication configuration is described in Chapter 12, "WLAN Security Configuration Guidelines and Examples."

NOTE   Because MAC-based authentication is not part of the 802.11 standard, different implementations can vary. For example, some block association, whereas others simply block the traffic.

In many APs, MAC-based authentication can be achieved when using either open authentication or shared-key authentication, with the enhancement that the AP enforces the policy of matching the authenticating MAC address to the AP's table of valid MAC addresses.

Trust Model and Assumptions

The MAC-based authentication method trusts the registered MAC addresses and assumes their integrity—that is, it assumes that the MAC addresses belong to the devices. The method also presumes that the receiver trusts the message because the message is not integrity protected.

Supporting AAA Infrastructure

Although no AAA mechanisms are used, there is a need for out-of-band registration of client MAC addresses. The APs require the STAs' MAC addresses, which must be manually entered into the APs. That is, registration can be done centrally but must be configured/provisioned on every AP. Although configuration tools can enable propagation of registration tables to many APs, population of the registration table (with MAC addresses) has no means for automation.

NOTE   The manual population of the registration table does a fair amount of work for little security. If only a couple of MAC addresses are registered, this might be worth the effort. For more than a few, it is unlikely to be worth the bother.

Auditing and Accounting

There are no special auditing and accounting capabilities. The auditing and accounting of the open authentication method apply here, too.

Applications, Vulnerabilities, and Countermeasures

The MAC-based authentication method is suitable for home LANs and for small offices where the number of computers (and hence the registration table) is small. This method can be used as the first layer of defense to deny access to any arbitrary STA. This is not a convenient mechanism for public WLANs because it adds the burden of configuring the MAC addresses without additional security benefits.

MAC addresses are visible and prone to theft. For example, a hacker can hide the device's built-in MAC address and spoof other MAC addresses using a firmware overlay. In fact, the MAC address can be spoofed by many other mechanisms, such as driver support. There is no means to prevent an adversary from impersonating a valid client by simply using that device's identity (for example, its MAC address).

All the countermeasures of the open authentication method also apply to this method. Use VPN for a secure connection and, if someone is surfing the Internet, use a firewall (hardware or software).

Shared-Key Authentication

In the realm of WLANs, the shared key is one of the more secure methods of authentication; it is based on a challenge-response protocol. The shared-key authentication requires WEP mechanisms and thus depends on a WEP infrastructure.

NOTE   Shared-key authentication is not a true authentication mechanism per se. Looking at the messages, it is a protocol that merely establishes proof that both parties share the same secret, but it does not prove or authenticate each party's identity.

Protocol Choreography

Shared-key authentication requires a six-step process with four messages, as detailed in Figure 5-3.

Figure 5-3   *Shared-Key Authentication*

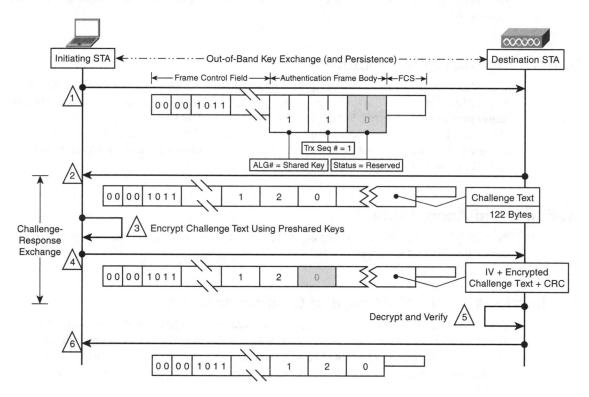

Step 1 is the authentication request to an AP, followed by Step 2, which is the challenge from the AP. In Step 3, the requester encrypts the challenge text as per the WEP algorithm and then responds to the AP in Step 4. If the AP can successfully decrypt the challenge text (Step 5) and all other conditions are satisfied, the authentication will be successful (Step 6).

NOTE	Generally speaking, the authentication happens between a requester or initiator and a responder. In the case of infrastructure mode, the requestor is normally a laptop or a PDA, and the responder is an AP.

Trust Model and Assumptions

There is an explicit trust model in the shared-key authentication that is based on WEP primitives. The trust model hinges on the key distribution (such as the ability to distribute to and keep the keys in only the intended devices) and the strength of WEP algorithms. Both of these have been under attack (this is discussed in Chapter 6, "Wireless Vulnerabilities") and are now considered fairly vulnerable.

Supporting AAA Infrastructure

Shared key-authentication requires a WEP infrastructure. No other special infrastructure is required except the out-of-band entry of the encryption keys. The APs and the STAs require the keys (such as shared secret) in their configuration tables. The keys need to be entered into the APs and STAs manually. There are no standard, automated ways to enter the keys. However, some wireless network configuration tools (provided by companies such as Wavelink) enable the distribution of configuration profiles, including keys.

Auditing and Accounting

No special auditing and accounting capabilities exist. The auditing and accounting of the open authentication method apply.

Applications, Vulnerabilities, and Countermeasures

The main difficulty is the out-of-band, manual authentication key distribution to all STAs. Because WEP uses symmetric key cryptography, establishing the key-mapping relationships between entities (either you should have a key mapping of an AP to a client for every client-AP combination, or you should have an arbitrarily grouped key mapping between entities) is not scalable.

In fact, the use of multiple keys is painful; therefore, keys tend to be common across multiple APs and clients. Thus, paired sharing of keys becomes a communal sharing of keys. This situation has two weaknesses:

- When an employee leaves or a laptop is compromised, reissuance of keys to the group and to the APs can be painful. Thus, this only scales to small numbers.

- This mechanism also makes itself vulnerable to implementation or deployment constraints. The configuration of the same key on all the APs (because of the configuration demands) results in the compromise of not just a target AP but of the whole edge infrastructure.

WEP, as detailed in 802.11 (R2003) and if practiced rigorously, has limited usages in small, bounded WLANs in small organizations and home networks where the number of APs and clients is deterministic and small.

NOTE   There is a well-documented vulnerability with shared-key authentication. The authentication process leaks information about the key stream and is generally regarded as insecure. Many configuration screens on Cisco APs have discouraged the use of shared key.

WEP Privacy Mechanics

Let's look at WEP mechanics in more detail. This section looks at the various aspects of WEP, including the encryption exchanges and mechanics, RC4, how an initialization vector (IV) is generated and handled, and finally, how keys are generated and distributed.

WEP mechanisms (the encapsulation of data frames to attempt to provide message confidentiality and message integrity) are aimed at achieving wired characteristics on the wireless connection.

NOTE   The main difference between the wired world and the wireless world—besides the lack of wires—is the signals being transmitted in the air. All the assumptions made in the wired world (resilience against casual eavesdropping, the signals being confined to a wire, and the ability to curtail LAN connections to a physical jack in the wall) are invalid. In the wired world, a connection can be detected, but in the wireless world, anyone can listen and capture packets (actually not anybody, but clients in the coverage area) without a trace—in other words, undetectable passive sniffing.

In WEP, the packets are encrypted so that listeners cannot make sense of the garbled bits; this achieves the confidentiality equivalent of the wired environment. Moreover, entities are authenticated before they are allowed to join the network and get the keys to decrypt the information. In a way, this gives the equivalency of a "wall jack."

NOTE   The first version of WEP is the mobility-as-an-exception-to-static-networks view. Actually, as you will see in Chapter 7, "EAP Authentication Protocols for WLANs," and Chapter 8, "WLAN Encryption and Data Integrity Protocols," by applying 802.11i and 802.1x paradigms, the standards consider the mobility natively by treating wireless in its own right and enhance the security, management, and control. Also note that the standardization work is still in progress and has a long way to go before becoming truly mobile.

WEP Processing Model

The 802.11 specification details the WEP processing model, as shown in Figure 5-4. The following sections look at each part of the diagram.

Figure 5-4   *WEP Processing Model*

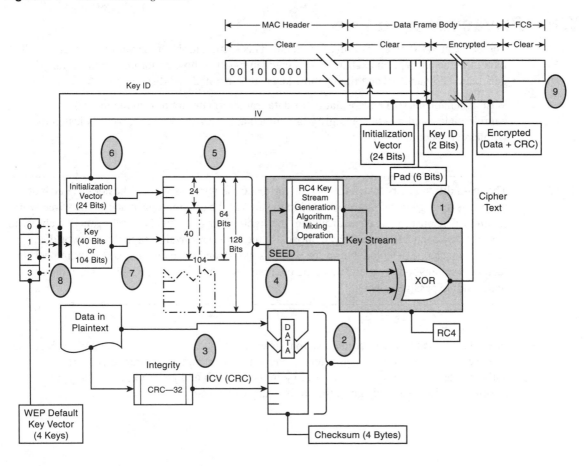

RC4 Algorithm

The encryption algorithm used by WEP is the RC4. RC4 is a symmetric algorithm (it uses the same key for encryption and decryption) and is a stream cipher. (The key is a stream that is operated against the plaintext to produce the cipher text.)

NOTE   A stream cipher can encipher various sizes of data, as opposed to a block cipher, which is constrained to a fixed block size.

RC4 has two phases: key stream generation and encryption. Key stream generation is a set of state machine and mixing operations that result in a pseudorandom stream of bits. The key setup takes a seed, which is the key as referred to outside the RC4 machine. After the state table is initialized, the values are used to generate a key stream. The fundamental encryption operation really is an XOR of the plaintext with the generated key stream.

NOTE   RC4 has an interesting history. It was invented in 1987 by Ron Rivest of RSA Security Inc. and was never published. It was a trade secret until 1994, when a program to encrypt and decrypt using RC4 was anonymously published in the cyberpunks mailer—the only public documentation. RSA still holds the trademark on the name RC4 (not on the algorithm), so one needs to license it to use the name RC4 in products. Some people call it ARCFOUR and try to circumvent this, but the legality is questionable.

RC4 is used in many products, including Lotus Notes, and is indicated in many specifications, including the cellular digital packet data (CDPD) specification for wireless packet data access over cellular networks.

Data and Integrity

WEP includes the data and the integrity as plaintext to the RC4 engine #3 in Figure 5-4. The CRC-32 algorithm is employed to generate an integrity check value (ICV) 4 bytes long, and the ICV is concatenated to the data. The CRC-32 algorithm is specified in RFC 3309.

Seed and Keylength

The RC4 engine takes the data (#2 in Figure 5-4, the plaintext + ICV) and the seed (#4 in Figure 5-4, essentially the "key"). The seed is generated using a 24-bit initialization vector (IV) and a 40-bit key, which essentially gives the 64-bit key length. Implementations improved on this and have added a 104-bit key, thus achieving a 128-bit key length.

NOTE	RC4 can use key lengths of 1 to 256 bytes (for example, 1 to 2048 bits). Initially, 802.11 chose the 40-bit key because of export restrictions.

IV Generation

The IV is usually generated starting at 0 and incrementing by one. Some implementations might start at a random number and count forward. In any case, because the IV is only 24 bits, it has a finite value and needs to be reset. The IV is sent, in clear, as a part of the data frame.

NOTE	You might ask the significance of an IV. An IV adds the randomness to the encryption. Without the IV, the same plaintext and key would result in the same cipher text, which can result in some interesting forms of data leakage (called the residual effect). The IV essentially alters the key stream even when used with the same key.
	The importance of the IV in this instance is to prevent collisions; therefore, the randomness of the IVs themselves is not a requirement. The IV can indeed be a counter. One of the problems with WEP is that the industry failed to define this requirement; therefore, implementations exist that enable the IV to wrap or remain static. This has been fixed, but there are still a few legacy systems that do not adhere to IV generation to avoid collisions.

Key Generation and Selection

WEP uses static preshared keys. There are many mechanisms to share keys. WEP defines a key vector that can hold four keys, distributed out of band. The key ID used in each communication is sent as part of the data frame. As previously discussed, it also has facilities to have a key mapped to arbitrary pairs of communicating entities. The key can be 40 bits or 104 bits in length and can be generated by a paraphrase in some installations. In most installations, the key is entered as a set of hexadecimal digits.

NOTE	The use of the four keys is independent of WEP. 802.11i and WPA make use of these four key IDs for temporal key integrity protocol (TKIP) and cyberblock-chaining message-authentication-code (CCMP).
	It is important to note that WEP lacks key management mechanisms. Thus, these static keys are used to perpetually improve the adversary's chance of discovering the keys over a period of time.

Packaging

The data frame consists of the IV, the key ID, and the encrypted data resulting from the RC4 engine. The header and FCS are always there as part of the standard frame. From #9 in Figure 5-4, you can see that the frame, IV, and FCS are all clear, whereas the data and ICV (CRC-32) are encrypted as a result of a cryptographic operation.

Decryption

The decryption process is almost the reverse of the encryption process. The receiver is able to resolve the key (either by the key number or, if it is null, the first key, key0) and the IV. Using those two inputs, the RC4 engine can decrypt the data stream. The receiver then extracts the last 4 bytes, calculates the ICV of the remaining stream using the CRC-32 algorithm, and verifies the integrity.

NOTE   The advantage of the stream cipher is implementation optimization. That is, only the encipher logic (such as the keystream generation) is required because the XOR is a symmetric operation.

Vulnerabilities

WEP, as defined in the 802.11 specification, was deemed unsecure by the community for a variety of reasons (which Chapter 6 describes in detail). The choice of IV, the transmission of the IV, the ICV mechanisms, weak IVs and RC4 weak keys, and the nonscalability of key distribution all came under close scrutiny and were found to be less secure. (The IV can be predicted, and IVs can be reused, leading to cryptographic insecurities because the strength of the key is diminished, the IV is transmitted in cleartext, and moreover, 802.11 does not specify how IVs are selected.) There are well-documented vulnerabilities with WEP that could allow a passive attacker to actually devise the key. WEP also does not provide suitable message integrity, because CRC32 is a checksum mechanism and not a message integrity mechanism. Above all, WEP lacks strong mutual authentication, which is a requirement for establishing a secure channel. To provide a secure WLAN, various mechanisms are being developed by extending and augmenting the WEP security to true mobility (including guest access), still maintaining the administrative control in the wired world. The following chapters exhibit many aspects of this.

Summary

This chapter looked at authentication mechanisms and the WEP method. Chapter 6 looks into the vulnerabilities of wireless networks.

CHAPTER 6

Wireless Vulnerabilities

Wireless networks are particularly vulnerable to attacks because it is difficult to prevent physical access to them. The only advantage they have in this respect is that an attacker must be in physical proximity to the network, which can limit the pool of potential attackers. However, with cheap antennae, such as those at http://www.cantenna.com, an attacker can pick up or send signals from up to a few miles away. To secure a wireless network, an administrator should know what types of vulnerabilities exist and what types of attacks can exploit them.

Wireless networks are subject to both passive and active attacks. A passive attack is one in which an attacker just captures signals, whereas an active attack is one in which an attacker sends signals, too. Passive attacks are exceedingly easy to carry out with wireless antennae and are undetectable. Any good security mechanism must start with the assumption that an attacker can see everything.

This chapter presents a methodology for understanding how the various wireless networking vulnerabilities relate to each other. It also describes each type of vulnerability and provides examples, both real and theoretical. Although this chapter focuses primarily on basic 802.11, it also delves into EAP-based protocols, ad-hoc mode security, and rogue access points (APs).

Note that the purpose of mentioning attack tools in this chapter is not to teach people how to attack networks. That is already better documented on many websites. The purpose is to give network administrators an introduction to what they will be facing. A demonstration of attacks can be a useful tactic for an administrator who is facing the task of justifying a security budget request to a skeptical superior. The attackers already understand the attacks and the tools. Many administrators need to catch up quickly, and this chapter aims to help them. By knowing the threat, they can better plan and deploy their defenses.

Attacker Objectives

Attackers have many reasons for targeting wireless networks. They might want to access resources on a network, such as confidential files. Many organizations focus on perimeter defenses and are rather open after an attacker gets through them. A wireless network might represent the easiest attack avenue to the inside if adequate defenses are not in place. Other attackers might simply want to use a wireless site's network. This could be as simple as a traveler not wanting to pay for network access while on the road, or it could be as nefarious as a spammer wanting to send millions of objectionable e-mails that won't be traced back to him, or a virus writer wanting a good anonymous location from which to launch the latest worm. Finally, it could be an attacker wanting to disrupt a wireless network, whether for simple vandalistic glee, for revenge, or to harm a competitor in some way. Sometimes these attacks can be combined. For example, an attacker could execute a denial-of-service (DoS) attack against the legitimate wireless infrastructure to redirect clients to a rogue AP that the attacker controls. Attack trees illustrate these goals and some of the methods that an attacker uses to achieve them.

Attack Trees

Attackers follow a process when they attack networks. Usually there is an initial reconnaissance phase, followed by the actual attack. In the reconnaissance phase, an attacker discovers the presence of the network and then explores potential targets within it. This chapter considers three main goals that attackers have when attacking wireless networks: denying service, gaining read access, and gaining write access. It also considers the fourth goal of reconnaissance, which is a necessary subgoal of the main three goals. The attack trees illustrate each of these goals.

NOTE   Introduced by Bruce Schneier, attack trees are a means of describing vulnerabilities in a system. They can also be used as analysis tools to assist in planning defenses against those vulnerabilities. Each tree starts with a goal, which is broken into subgoals. Subgoals can be broken down further. At each node, the attack tree creator denotes whether all the steps must be taken ("AND") or whether any one of them will do ("OR"). The best way to illustrate this is with a simplified example:

```
GOAL: Rob bank.
    OR
    Bribe guard for entry during off hours.
    Become trusted employee of the bank and embezzle.
        AND
        Get hired by bank.
        Work long enough to learn system and gain trust.
    Conduct an armed robbery.
        AND
        Obtain weapons.
        Plan carefully.
```

This tree shows that the bank robber has three OR subgoals, any one of which will get him the money. He can choose the easiest one. The embezzlement subgoal has two AND subgoals. If he chooses embezzlement, he must perform both of these to be successful. From a defensive perspective, a bank must prevent all branches of the tree from succeeding. The defender must prevent all OR branches, which in this example means preventing all three avenues of attack. Where there are AND branches, the defender only has to prevent one from succeeding. Thus, in this example, the bank can either improve its interview screening or institute an oversight system for its trusted employees to prevent the embezzlement option from succeeding.

Reconnaissance

An attacker must discover a target network before attacking it. This can be a targeted attack in which an attacker goes after a particular organization or user, or it could be an attack of convenience in which an attacker just looks for the first network that meets his criteria. Such criteria include proximity, fast bandwidth, and of course, the presence of vulnerabilities.

In the wired networking world, intrusion-detection systems or firewalls can often detect this reconnaissance activity. In the wireless world, portions of the discovery can be completely passive and undetectable. There could, however, be active components to a wireless attack reconnaissance, such as network scans, which would be detectable. Attack Tree 1 outlines reconnaissance attacks:

```
Attack Tree 1
GOAL: Discover target network.
    AND
    Discover presence of a network.
        OR
        Conduct wardriving.
        Passive sniffing of specific targets ("parking lot sniffing").
    Discover more information about the network.
        OR
        Conduct active host and port scanning.
        Conduct passive sniffing.
```

DoS

DoS is an attack on network availability that can serve several purposes for an attacker. These purposes range from disruption to assisting man-in-the-middle attacks (MitM) and are explored later in this chapter. An attacker might want to set up wireless equipment to take over the communications path for legitimate clients. By disrupting particular parts of the network, an attacker can remove interference from the legitimate equipment and have the rogue path be the only one available. Attack Tree 2 describes these goals:

```
Attack Tree 2
GOAL: Deny wireless service.
    AND
    Discover target network (using Attack Tree 1).
    Deny service.
        OR
        Deny service to an entire network.
            OR
            Use radio jamming equipment.
            Continually broadcast frames to fill up network bandwidth.
            Disassociation/deauthentication attack against all users.
            Conduct transmit duration attack.
            Flood associations to fill up access point tables.
            Set up a rogue access point and associate users to a bogus network.
        Deny service to a particular user.
            Conduct disassociation/deauthentication attack against
            a user.
```

Network Access

The most frequent goal of a network attacker is to gain either read access or write access to a network. Read access includes the capability to intercept and read traffic from the network and includes attacks on encryption, authentication, and other protection methods. Write access includes the capability to send traffic to a network entity and usually implies read access because the attacker often needs to read response packets to communicate over some network protocols. However, in some cases, an attacker can place packets on a network without being able to decode any of the return traffic.

Attack Tree 3 describes read-access goals:

```
Attack Tree 3
GOAL: Gain read access.
    AND
    Discover target network (using Attack Tree 1).
    Read traffic.
        OR
        Read unencrypted traffic.
            Capture traffic using sniffer.
        Read encrypted traffic.
            AND
            Capture encrypted traffic using sniffer.
            Gain key material.
                OR
                Recover keys.
                Recover keystream.
        Set up rogue access point and control network parameters, such as
        encryption keys (most feasible as a man-in-the-middle).
```

```
    AND
    Compromise client.
    Penetrate client via ad-hoc network via misconfiguration or unpatched
    operating system vulnerability.
    Install spying software on client.
    Spying software forwards data to attacker by some means
```

Attack Tree 4 describes write-access goals:

```
Attack Tree 4
GOAL: Gain write access.
    AND
    Discover target network (using Attack Tree 1).
    Bypass authentication schemes to gain network access privileges.
        OR
        Network has no authentication. No bypass needed.
        Use MAC address spoofing to evade MAC-based filtering.
        Use shared-key authentication bypass attack.
            If network is using 802.1x for authentication, use LEAP dictionary
            attack or PEAP man-in-the-middle attack documented later in this
            attack tree.
    Inject data packets.
        OR
        Network is not using encryption. Inject the data.
        Write encrypted data by replaying captured keystream.
            Recover keystream.
        Encrypt data with key and write it to network.
            Recover key.
        Penetrate client via ad-hoc network. Install malicious code on client,
 which writes your traffic using the client's credentials.
        Perform LEAP dictionary attack.
            AND
            Capture a LEAP session.
            Run an offline dictionary attack to recover the password.
            Authenticate using the captured credentials.
            Once authenticated, write your data.
        Perform PEAP man-in-the-middle attack.
            AND
            Set up rogue AP to which the client can connect.
            Establish session to real AP.
            Capture client credentials and use them to authenticate to the back-
 end server.
            Take over the connection in place of the client.
            Write the data.
```

The rest of this chapter expands on the attacks described in the attack trees.

Reconnaissance Attacks

The most obvious security problem with wireless LANs is also their chief virtue: Data can be received by anyone who is anywhere in range of the signal. The signal passes through walls, outside buildings, and off property boundaries. Attackers can both capture and transmit wireless signals provided they are within range. Powerful antennae allow attackers to receive and transmit 802.11 packets from up to several miles away.

NOTE	An attacker uses reconnaissance to discover and analyze the targets of his attack. During this analysis, he tries to determine what protocols and security mechanisms are being used so that he can choose which tools to use to attack them. Although sniffing and wardriving are not attacks and have legitimate purposes for system administrators, they can serve as the reconnaissance stage of an attack.

Sniffing and SSIDs

Sniffing is a general networking term that refers to eavesdropping packets on any medium, but it is especially easy over the airwaves. In the wireless medium, sniffing is undetectable. Several groups have written free drivers to perform sniffing on most of the major vendors' client adapters. There are also commercial sniffing tools. The chipsets most commonly used for sniffing are Prism2 (used by Linksys, D-Link, SMC, and others), Orinoco (used by Lucent), and Aironet (used by Cisco). Many of the free drivers allow the sending of any packets the attacker wants.

Service Set Identifiers (SSIDs) are sometimes touted as a security mechanism to keep outsiders off your network. However, they were not designed as security mechanisms. SSIDs should be thought of as a method of separating wireless networks for convenience only. SSIDs are broadcast in beacons from APs and in probes from stations. Tools such as Network Stumbler, Kismet, and Wellenreiter sniff and record SSIDs that they hear. Most vendors allow SSID broadcasts to be turned off. This can lower your profile for random drive-by attacks, but several tools sniff SSIDs from association packets, which must still include the SSID in the clear. At least one vendor has a security solution that treats SSIDs as an access control mechanism. Such "closed" networks are secure only in name.

In Figure 6-1, a packet capture shows the SSID 5ECUR3w3p5TOR3 in a probe packet.

Figure 6-1   *Packet Dump Showing a Cleartext SSID*

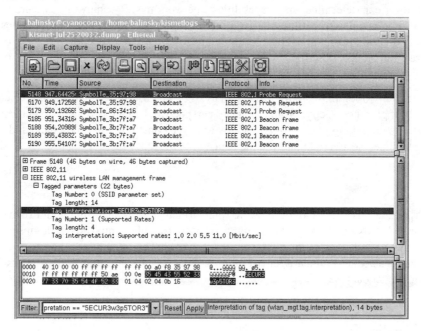

This odd SSID is hard to type, so it appears that it is being used for access control. Hopefully, the site using this SSID does not use the obscure string for security, because anybody can sniff it.

Sniffing Tools

One of the best ways to figure out what is happening on a network is sniffing. Sniffing is useful for both attackers and defenders of a network, and as a result, there are a wide variety of tools to do this. Some of these tools are commercial, and some are available free of charge, usually with open-source code.

Sniffing tools must perform two key functions: packet capture and useful packet analysis and display. Some of the open-source tools only capture packets, but most of the tools perform some level of display.

Packet analysis is a key reconnaissance tool for an attacker. By analyzing probe packets, an attacker can determine what capabilities a network has. By analyzing captured packets, an attacker can also sometimes discover interesting information such as usernames or other confidential information. Packet capture is also important, especially for some of the WEP key-cracking attacks described later. An attacker can capture traffic and analyze it or run cracking tools on it later.

For a network administrator, packet analysis can be useful for determining whether a network is configured correctly. From a security perspective, he can also use it to determine whether attacks are taking place. This is usually too time consuming to do by hand and relies on specialized software to analyze the data.

Prismdump

Prismdump is a text-based, freeware Linux tool that allows sniffing with Prism2 chipset-based cards. It only performs packet capture and is not capable of analysis. It dumps packets in a pcap format, which each of the next two tools can read. The open-source software community uses pcap as a de facto standard format for files of packets. Prismdump's reliability makes it valuable for packet capture.

Ethereal and Tcpdump

Ethereal (http://ethereal.com) and tcpdump (http://tcpdump.org) are network sniffers based on the libpcap (http://tcpdump.org) packet capture library. Both are open-source tools that are available free of charge. Tcpdump is text based, whereas Ethereal can be used in text or GUI mode. Tcpdump is primarily useful for packet capture because it does not allow for graphical analysis of packets. It has some powerful filtering capabilities that can permit selective packet capture. Ethereal's graphical user interface makes it a great tool for viewing captured packets and becoming familiar with the structure of wireless protocols. Figure 6-1 shows Ethereal's interface.

Commercial Sniffers

Several commercial tools can capture and display wireless packets. The two most widely used are AiroPeek from WildPackets and Sniffer Wireless from Network Associates.

Wardriving and Its Tools

Wardriving is a term that refers to surveying wireless networks, typically from a car. The term goes back to wardialing, which is an old technique for finding computer modems by automatically dialing thousands of numbers. Wardriving has been made easy by programs such as Network Stumbler and Wellenreiter, which use consumer WiFi cards to automatically scan the airwaves for networks. Sites such as http://netstumbler.com have online databases of unprotected wireless networks. These wardriving programs and databases are often correlated with global positioning system (GPS) data so that physical maps of these networks can be made. Websites sell cheap antennae and describe how to make your own. Therefore, all it takes for your network to become a potential target is for *someone* to wardrive by it and post it on a website.

NOTE   *Warchalking* is the practice of signposting open access points, often with chalk or spray paint on a sidewalk or wall. Most often, the owners of these devices do not intend for the public to access them and are simply ignorant of their insecure configuration. If you find one of the warchalk symbols in Figure 6-2 on your sidewalk, you might want to check that your wireless configuration is secure. Some public wireless access hotspots have even started incorporating the warchalking symbols in their signage. Warchalking is documented at http://www.warchalking.org.

Warstrolling is simply walking around with wireless equipment looking for networks. Some have even done warflying by mounting antennas on a plane and flying around a city.

Figure 6-2   *Standard Set of Basic Warchalking Symbols*

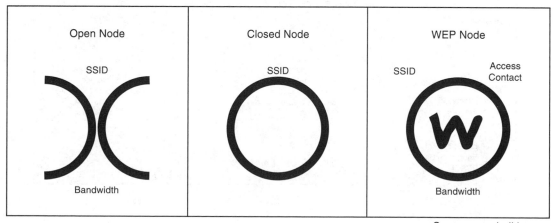

Source: warchalking.org

A number of tools can assist in mapping networks. They are available under nearly every major operating system (Linux, Windows, Macintosh, FreeBSD) and for many types of devices, including laptops and handhelds. Some of these tools are free of charge and use open-source software, whereas others are commercial tools marketed to security personnel. The commercial tools often have additional features that are useful for doing site surveys and troubleshooting of wireless networks.

Network Stumbler and Mini Stumbler

Network Stumbler (http://netstumbler.com) is a popular tool. It is Windows-based and is easy to use. It records SSIDs in beacons it sniffs and can interface with various GPS systems to make a spatial database. This data can be used to create maps of networks. Mini Stumbler is a version that runs on PDAs running PocketPC. PDAs are easy to conceal, and an attacker can use them for surreptitious warstrolling in an environment where having a laptop might look suspicious. Figure 6-3 shows Network Stumbler in action.

Figure 6-3 *Network Stumbler Displays the Networks It Has Discovered*

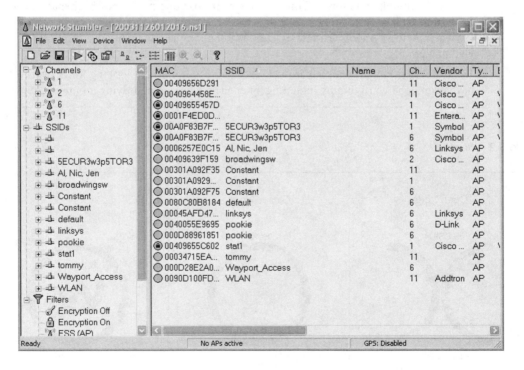

Macintosh Tools

MacStumbler (http://www.macstumbler.com) is unrelated to Network Stumbler and brings wardriving capability to the Macintosh. It works by sending out probe requests and listening for responses. It cannot discover "closed" networks, which don't respond to probes.

KisMAC (http://www.binaervarianz.de/projekte/programmieren/kismac) is another Macintosh wardriving application. It has good mapping capabilities and a good user interface. KisMAC is not related to the next tool, despite the similar name.

Kismet

Kismet (http://kismetwireless.net) is a powerful Linux-based wardriving tool. It sniffs and displays networks and clients and can use most client cards, including cards based on the Aironet, Orinoco, and Prism2 chipsets.

The software records ESSIDs, BSSIDs, channels, signal levels, and any IP addresses seen in the traffic. Like Network Stumbler, it can integrate with GPS devices and add location data to its records. It has a fun feature that uses a voice generator to read out names of networks as they are discovered. This is an "eyes-free" feature for drivers.

Kismet can dump printable strings (which might include passwords). For an attacker, this is a key advantage over Network Stumbler. Kismet saves several files for each session, including a list of networks in both CSV and XML format, a listing of Cisco CDP packets, a dump of all packets sniffed during the session, and a dump of weak initialization vectors. These packets with weak IVs (called *interesting packets*) can be used for the Fluhrer-Mantin-Shamir attack on the key (described later in this chapter). Although Kismet doesn't crack the keys, it can save the interesting packets to a pcap file to feed to other programs. All in all, Kismet is the most complete free wardriving tool around. Figure 6-4 shows its main interface.

Wellenreiter

Wellenreiter (available from http://www.wellenreiter.net) is a Perl-based wardriving tool for Linux or BSD. It integrates GPS data and has sound output. Wellenreiter is more graphically oriented than Kismet. It has the ability to save its status to a file, but it does not save packet dumps. Wellenreiter is primarily a tool for discovering networks. It does not save data for use in breaking WEP keys offline.

Figure 6-5 shows Wellenreiter's interface.

Figure 6-4   *Kismet Displays Networks It Finds (The Networks with N in the W (WEP) Column Have No Encryption Configured)*

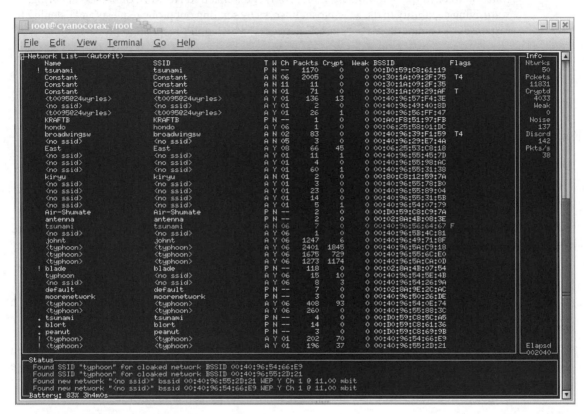

bsd-airtools

bsd-airtools is a set of utility tools for the FreeBSD operating system. It includes the following tools:

- *dstumbler* is the wardriving component of bsd-airtools. It is modeled after Network Stumbler and has GPS capabilities.

- *prism2dump* is a sniffing program for putting Prism2-based cards into promiscuous mode and displaying the packets.

Figure 6-5   *Wellenreiter Displays Networks, Channels, and APs*

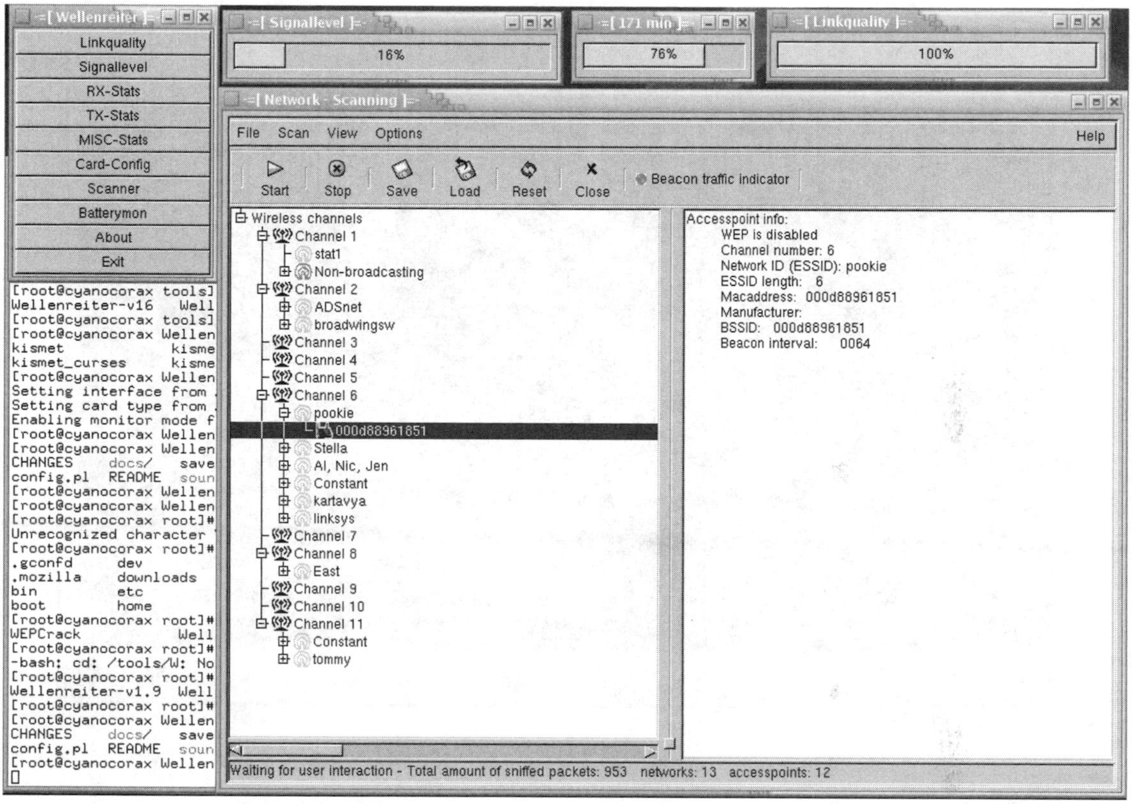

bsd-airtools also has some tools for cracking and creating WEP keys. (They are described in the "WEP Key Recovery Attacks" section later in this chapter.) bsd-airtools is available from http://www.dachb0den.com/projects/bsd-airtools.html. It is also available on a bootable CD-ROM called WarBSD (http://www.warbsd.com), which eliminates the need for installation and configuration.

NOTE   Several distributions of Linux and the BSD UNIX variants are trimmed down to fit on a bootable CD-ROM. These distributions (known as live CDs) are valuable for security testing because they allow you to run a preinstalled operating system that is completely independent of what is on the hard drive. They run in memory and do not touch the hard drive. Live CDs also allow for rapid testing of tools without having to install an operating system or compile tools. Many of the tools in this chapter are available on bootable CD-ROM distributions such as *WarBSD* (http://www.warbsd.com) or *WarLinux* (http://sourceforge.net/projects/warlinux). Network administrators should be aware of how easy it is for their adversaries to run various wireless attack tools. Figure 6-6 shows what a user sees after booting with the WarBSD CD.

Figure 6-6 *Bootable WarBSD CD Makes It Easy for an Attacker to Use Wireless Attack Tools*

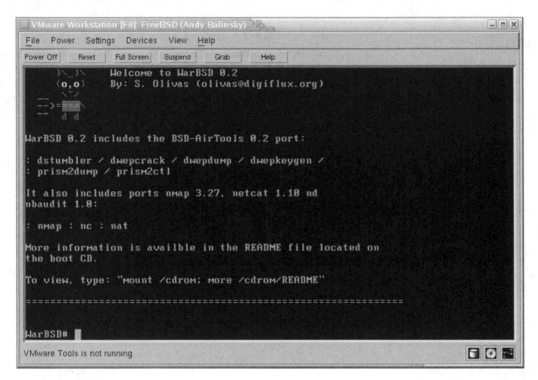

DoS Attacks

DoS is a common network security problem, and it refers to an attempt to disrupt the function of a service. The disruption can range from physical destruction of network equipment to attacks that are designed to use all of a network's bandwidth. It could even be an attempt to deny a particular person from using the service. DoS is particularly problematic in the wireless realm because of the ease of network access. An attacker can do a simple DoS attack with radio-jamming equipment, but such equipment is more difficult to find than 802.11 cards, and it has no means of being selective. Attacks that use the consumer-grade 802.11 cards are much easier to carry out and can be just as effective. Several DoS attacks can target particular stations or networks.

Disassociation and Deauthentication Attacks

Disassociation and deauthentication attacks exploit the unauthenticated nature of 802.11 management frames. Chapter 3, "WLAN Standards," showed that when a station wants to connect to an AP, it first exchanges authentication frames and then association frames. It can participate in the network after it is authenticated and associated. However, any station can spoof a disassociate or deauthenticate message, pretending to be another station. The AP disassociates the targeted station, which cannot send traffic until it is associated again. By repeatedly sending these frames, an attacker can keep one or more stations off a network indefinitely. This attack is documented in a paper by John Bellardo and Stephan Savage. The following are several implementations of this attack.

Mike Schiffman released one such implementation in a tool called *Omerta* (named after the Sicilian code of silence). This tool listens for packets and simply sends a disassociate message for every data packet it sees. To his credit, Schiffman delayed releasing Omerta until other tools just like it were already public. Omerta is written using Schiffman's libradiate package, which allows creation of custom 802.11 packets. Omerta is available in a posting to the bugtraq mailing list (http://www.securityfocus.com/archive/89/326248).

The *AirJack* package (http://802.11ninja.net) comes with a tool called *essid_jack*, which implements a deauthentication attack to discover "hidden" networks. These are networks in which the AP does not send beacon packets advertising the SSID. However, by disassociating a user, the attacker forces that user to send probe packets with the SSID in them. This tool demonstrates why SSIDs are not, and should never be considered, a security mechanism. AirJack also includes *wlan_jack*, which is a simple disassociation attack. A variation on this theme is *fata_jack*. It sends invalid authentication requests spoofing legitimate clients, causing the AP to disassociate the real client.

A more nefarious use of this attack would be to knock somebody off a network with the goal of posing as a server. This technique is useful in the MitM attack on PEAP. Monkey_jack is a proof-of-concept attack that deauthenticates a victim and then poses as the AP when the victim comes back up. If the victim does not have a method of verifying the AP's identity, he could be fooled into giving up useful information.

Reyk Floeter wrote void11 (http://www.wlsec.net/void11), which includes two attacks based on this principle. One is the deauthentication attack described earlier. The other attack floods authenticate requests to an AP, with the goal of crashing the AP or denying service by filling up tables of associated stations.

Given all of the preceding attacks, you can see that the lack of strong authentication for management frames in 802.11 leads to some critical vulnerabilities.

Transmit Duration Attack

Bellardo and Savage describe another denial-of-service attack based on the Transmit Duration field of the 802.11 frame. Transmit Duration is the collision avoidance mechanism for 802.11 that announces to other nodes how long a frame transmission will last. All stations on the network are then supposed to stay quiet for that amount of time to avoid colliding with that transmission. An attacker can send a stream of packets with the maximum Transmit Duration (1/30th of a second) set, which prevents other nodes from sending for that amount of time. Thus, a relatively slow 30-packets-per-second rate keeps the network occupied. Currently, many cards ignore the Transmit Duration field, so the attack is not effective now. However, they will have to respect it to support QoS in the future, and this attack could become practical.

Authentication Attacks

DoS attacks are simple, but they can achieve only limited goals. Network access can provide an attacker with much greater benefits. Because gaining physical access to a wireless network is trivial, various schemes have been developed to provide access control. The original 802.11 specification defines a rather broken authentication mechanism to limit which stations can connect to the network. The IEEE has introduced new authentication mechanisms based on 802.1x and EAP. These authentication mechanisms are covered in Chapter 7, "EAP Authentication Protocols for WLANs," and Chapter 8, "WLAN Encryption and Data Integrity Protocols." In addition, some vendors have implemented other schemes for access control, such as MAC address filters. This section describes attacks on the shared-key and MAC address filtering schemes. Attacks on the 802.1x protocols are also authentication attacks and are covered in their own section later in this chapter.

Shared-Key Authentication Attacks

The 802.11 designers created an authentication mechanism, but unfortunately, what they came up with was badly flawed. The mechanism, called shared-key authentication, is easy to forge and leaks keystream information. Fortunately, it is optional. The default authentication mechanism is open authentication, which basically doesn't do authentication, and is preferable to shared-key authentication. Even better than both of these is EAP-based authentication; this comes in various forms and is discussed in Chapter 7.

Shared-key authentication is a mutual authentication mechanism in which each side sends a random challenge. Each side proves its knowledge of the WEP key by encrypting the challenge sent by the other party. The mechanism is inherently broken because an attacker can gain enough information by observing a single successful authentication to generate his own successful authentication responses in the future.

By simply XORing together the challenge and the response, an attacker can figure out a chunk of keystream corresponding to that *IV*. Now the attacker has enough information to authenticate because he can reuse the IV he has sniffed and the keystream he has calculated. He simply encrypts whatever challenge is thrown at him with this keystream, and he is authenticated.

A much worse result of this flaw is that the attacker can use this mechanism to build up a dictionary of per-IV keystreams. He can do this by passive observation or successful authentication. These dictionaries are useful for decrypting messages that the attacker observes. Thus, shared-key authentication has the curious property of being more dangerous than using no authentication at all. It is quite rightly considered obsolete.

MAC Address Spoofing

Several vendors' APs have the ability to limit which stations can connect based on the MAC address. This approach has two key flaws. The first, nonsecurity flaw is that it is time-consuming to configure and is thus unlikely to be used other than by small sites. More seriously, however, is the ease with which attackers can spoof their MAC addresses. Several 802.11 card drivers allow users to specify whatever MAC address they want. An attacker can easily glean valid MAC addresses from an active network by sniffing.

WEP Keystream and Plaintext Recovery

There are two means of breaking WEP-encrypted data. The most obvious is to discover the key itself. The other is to discover all possible keystreams that a key can generate. This section deals with recovering and using keystreams. The section titled "WEP Key Recovery Attacks" deals with how to crack the keys. Attack Trees 3 and 4 (from earlier in this chapter) show that recovering the key or the keystream enables reading and writing of encrypted data.

RC4 encryption involves XORing the keystream (K) with the plaintext (P) data to produce the ciphertext (C). If an attacker knows any two of these three elements, he can calculate the third. An attacker can always know C because it is broadcast. Thus, if an attacker knows P, he can get K. After he has K, he can recover P in future jackets.

Keystream Dictionaries

The security of RC4, which is the underlying encryption method in WEP, depends in part on not repeating the same keystream. WEP does this by using the initialization vector (IV) to permit 2^{24} (about 16 million) possible keystreams for each key. As previously mentioned, an alternative to breaking the key is to break each of the keystreams. One method is to wait for repeated keystreams, known as a *collision*, which reveals information about the data and the keystream. Another method is to know some or all of the data that was encrypted, called a *known plaintext attack.* After an attacker has built up a dictionary of all 16 million keystreams, he can then decrypt anything that is sent using that WEP key. A dictionary of all keystreams that are 1500 bytes long only takes about 24 GB to store, which easily fits on a laptop hard drive. No tools, as of yet, can implement this attack. Fortunately, as the per-packet key algorithms in WPA and 802.11i become more widely implemented, the usefulness of this attack might disappear before a tool is written.

Methods for Recovering RC4 Keystreams

There are several techniques for recovering keystreams and building keystream dictionaries. The attacks that this section describes have fortunately only been practiced in the academic world. No real-world tool has yet implemented them. The likely reason is that tools that attack and recover the key itself have been more practical and perhaps easier to implement.

Known Plaintext Attack

The simplest method of recovering keystreams is the known plaintext attack. The attacker sends data over a wired network to a machine on the wireless network. The AP encrypts it and sends it to the client. The attacker captures the encrypted wireless traffic. Finally, the attacker can apply the XOR operation to the plaintext and the captured traffic and recover the keystream. There are many ways to get known plaintext sent to a wireless user, from sending ping packets to sending e-mails to getting a user to visit a known website. Because the attacker knows the content of each message, he can match it with the encrypted traffic and recover the keystreams used to encrypt it. An attacker can send data rapidly to build up his keystream dictionary. Figure 6-7 illustrates the known plaintext attack.

Figure 6-7 *Attacker Sends Known Plaintext to Client, Sniffs the Resulting Ciphertext, and XORs the Two to Recover the Keystream*

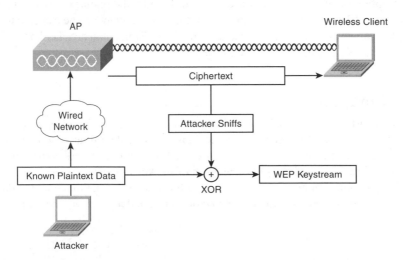

IV Collisions and the Birthday Paradox

The *birthday paradox* refers to the seemingly counterintuitive idea that if you have a room of 23 people, chances are greater than 50 percent that two of them have the same birthday (month and day). By the time you get to 50 people, the chances rise to 97 percent. This result arises from the difficulty of adding random birth dates to a list without "colliding with" one of the birth dates already on the list.

A similar concept applies to the avoidance of repeating an IV. After a small fraction of the possible IVs have already been broadcast, it becomes difficult for a random algorithm not to rebroadcast one. When you do have an IV collision, it is relatively easy to compromise the data in those two packets. It takes some cryptographic techniques, but it is considered an easy problem for a computer. If the data is compromised, the keystream corresponding to that IV can also be compromised. This can help an attacker build up a dictionary of keystreams.

The cards of several manufacturers use IVs that start at 0 and increase by 1 with each packet. These cards reset to 0 each time they lose power, which can be quite frequent on a laptop. Thus, it is virtually guaranteed that the first few thousand IVs will be reused at least once per day. It is not difficult for an attacker to build up a dictionary of these IVs.

A partial solution that avoids both the birthday paradox and the reset problem is to start at a random number on power-up and then count sequentially up. 802.11i solves these problems by replacing the IV with a longer sequence number, counting sequentially, and forbidding repeated sequence numbers.

NOTE WEP has an insecure checksum called the *Integrity Check Vector (ICV)*. It is a linear sum, which means that the sum depends in a predictable and reversible way on the message data. Changing one bit in the message changes a predictable bit in the ICV. An attacker can therefore change a bit in an encrypted message and know which bit of the encrypted ICV will change as a result. Repetition of this process allows an attacker to change any arbitrary parts of the encrypted message and fix the ICV so that is still valid. To perform this bit-flipping attack, the attacker is not required to know the contents of the message. Bit flipping is used in the reaction and inductive attacks described in this section.

Reaction Attack

Nikita Borisov and his colleagues at Berkeley discovered an interesting flaw in WEP based on the insecure checksum that 802.11 uses. This attack assumes that an attacker can guess some of the bits in a message, and it allows him to determine the value of the bits he does not know. Given the highly predictable nature of certain fields of TCP/IP packets, an attacker usually know some bits in the message. The attacker then flips certain bits in the message, rebroadcasts it, and views whether the packet had a valid TCP checksum by looking for a recognizably short, encrypted TCP acknowledgement (ACK) packet. Although encrypted, an ACK packet can be recognized by its length. By flipping selected bits, the attacker can deduce whether other bits were 0 or 1 by the absence or presence of an ACK response. By repeating this procedure, some or all of the keystream for a particular IV can be recovered. This is known as a *reaction attack*.

Inductive Attack

One of the more ingenious methods of recovering keystreams relies on methodical trial and error. Bill Arbaugh's inductive attack relies on WEP to serve as an oracle to tell the attacker when she correctly guesses parts of the keystream. The attack is a method for extending a chunk of known keystream for a given IV.

Assume that an attacker starts with a given amount, *n*, of keystream (K) for a given IV and a given WEP key. She can obtain this initial K by watching for an easily guessed packet, such as a DHCP request, or by conducting a known plaintext attack. Now the attacker begins the inductive attack. She creates a packet such as an ICMP ping packet or ARP request that demands a reply. She chooses the length of her packet, including the 802.11 checksum, to be *n*+1. But the attacker only has *n* bytes of keystream, so she must guess the *n*+1st byte. She does this by sending 256 versions of the packet with all possibilities for that last byte. The AP silently discards the incorrect ones. But the correct one has the proper encrypted checksum, and the AP accepts it and responds. The attacker now knows which was correct and knows *n*+1 bytes of keystream. She can repeat this process until she knows a full-length (1500-byte) keystream for that IV. Figure 6-8 illustrates one round of this process.

As you can see, the insecure ICV enables bit-flipping attacks. These enable the reaction and inductive attacks. Plaintext attacks and reuse of keystreams from IV collisions allow an attacker to recover keystream fragments and build up keystream dictionaries.

Figure 6-8 *In the Arbaugh Inductive Attack, the Attacker Repeatedly Guesses One Byte of the Keystream and Encodes a Packet to the AP—A Response from the AP Indicates a Successful Guess*

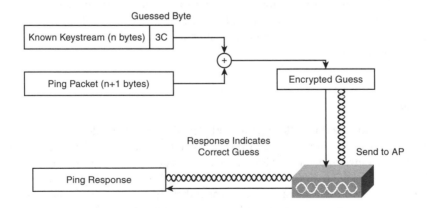

Uses for Recovered Keystreams

Now that an attacker has recovered the keystreams relating to one or more IVs, how can he use them?

Traffic Injection: Choosing Your Own IVs

In legacy systems not using WPA or 802.11i, an attacker only needs one keystream to inject packets. This is because the original 802.11 specification unfortunately allows a sender to choose his own IV and does not prohibit reuse of IVs. So an attacker can just repeatedly reuse the same IV for which he has the keystream and inject an unlimited number of packets into a network. Fortunately, some vendors, including Cisco, have implemented mechanisms that reject repeated IVs. Message integrity check algorithms, described in Chapter 8, also solve this problem.

Message Modification and Replay

A slightly weaker form of injection attack is possible if an attacker cannot get an entire keystream. This attack is called *message modification*, also known as a *bit-flipping attack*. Because the ICV can be recalculated even in its encrypted form, an attacker can take a message that he can only partially understand, flip arbitrary bits, and recalculate a proper ICV. He can then rebroadcast the message, and it is valid. An application of this attack might be for an attacker to try to change the destination IP address of a message so that it goes to his own machine instead of its intended recipient. He will then receive the entire packet, unencrypted, via a wired interface!

Another application might be to capture a single TCP SYN packet and rebroadcast it many times as a SYN flood, changing a few parameters for each packet. He could not just rebroadcast the packets unmodified because they would be dropped as duplicates. Because TCP has a fixed header, the attacker knows where in the packet the appropriate fields are and can randomly flip bits in those fields to create different legitimate packets.

An attacker who has no information about the keystream can still do a packet replay attack. He does this by simply capturing and rebroadcasting one or more packets. This attack is unlikely to do much, especially in protocols such as TCP that are designed to prevent repeated packets. However, in some protocols such as UDP, sending the same packet multiple times can have a meaning and can tie up resources on the destination machine. An attacker might be able to use this attack to affect machines on wired networks that communicate with the wireless network.

Decryption

To decrypt packets from keystreams, an attacker needs a dictionary of most or all keystreams. His ability to decrypt the packets is proportional to the completeness of his keystream dictionary for that WEP key. Aftcr the attacker has a complete dictionary, he can decrypt every packet sent with that WEP key. This is equivalent to having the WEP key itself. A sophisticated attacker could capture packets, hoping to compromise the keystream in the future. If he does compromise it, he can then go back and decrypt packets from his historical cache.

A Brief Note on Solutions

Fortunately, many of these attacks are becoming obsolete with mechanisms that Cisco and other vendors have implemented. A keyed message integrity check (MIC) eliminates traffic injection and the inductive and reaction attacks. Mechanisms that avoid IV reuse prevent collisions and thus make keystream dictionaries useless. The disadvantage is that after the maximum of 2^{24} packets has been sent, the WEP key must be changed because the IVs are all used up. WPA and 802.11i include a MIC and a longer IV. These solutions are described in Chapter 8.

WEP Key Recovery Attacks

One of the juiciest targets for an attacker targeting a WEP-protected WLAN is recovering the WEP key. Because of vulnerabilities in the WEP protocol and some implementation mistakes, several attacks have been developed that compromise WEP keys. The most serious of these is the Fluhrer-Mantin-Shamir (FMS) attack, which allows a passive sniffer to recover WEP keys with as little as nine minutes of sniffing.

Dictionary-Based Key Attacks

So-called *strong* WEP keys are 104 bits, or 26 hexadecimal digits, which is a chore to type. Dynamic key distribution methods, such as those included in the Lightweight Extensible Authentication Protocol (LEAP) or the Protected Extensible Authentication Protocol (PEAP), overcome this chore. However, in small installations, manual WEP keys are the usual choice. Because of the difficulty of typing in such a long key, manufacturers have developed an alternative method based on a passphrase for configuring 40- or 104-bit WEP keys. To ensure interoperability, there is an unpublished standard for this "key-generation" algorithm. Unfortunately, this algorithm reduces the possible WEP keys that can be chosen and opens them up to a dictionary-based attack.

Tim Newsham introduced wep_crack, a tool that can crack these passphrase-based passwords. One technique it uses is to run all the words in a dictionary through the WEP key-generation algorithm. It operates on a file of captured packets. First the tool finds a WEP-encrypted packet. Then it tries to decrypt the packet using WEP keys based on all the dictionary words it has. If the integrity check vector of the packet is correct, the tool knows it has decrypted the packet correctly and has found the right WEP key. If the passphrase occurs in a dictionary, it will be cracked.

Newsham also noticed that the algorithm for 40-bit key generation allows only 2^{21} possible WEP keys, no matter how long or complex the passphrase is. This limits you to only 2 million keys, which an attacker can search exhaustively (called a *brute force attack*) in a matter of minutes on modern hardware. Newsham also wrote a simple tool called *wep_decrypt*, which decrypts a file of packets after you have the WEP key. The tool works independent of the manner in which you obtained the WEP key.

Figure 6-9 shows three runs of wep_crack. In the first run, it cracks a 40-bit WEP key by brute force. That passphrase was not based on a dictionary word. This attack took about 60 seconds. In the second run, it cracks a 40-bit key based on the word "test." In the third run, it cracks a 104-bit WEP key based on the word "yeomanry." The latter two attacks only took approximately 1 second.

The Fluhrer-Mantin-Shamir Attack

The most damaging attack on WEP was discovered by three cryptographers: Scott Fluhrer, Itsik Mantin, and Adi Shamir. In cryptographic literature, the attack often bears their initials, FMS. This attack is rooted in a flaw in the key scheduling algorithm (KSA) of the RC4 encryption protocol, on which WEP is based. The KSA is the first step of RC4, and it transforms the key into a matrix from which RC4 generates its cryptographic keystream. The flaw is a slight statistical anomaly in which, given certain keys structured in certain ways, a small portion of the key is slightly more likely to end up in the keystream than other values. This sounds like a tiny flaw that would be of interest only to mathematicians, but to cryptographers, nonrandom anomalies like this are potentially fatal to cryptographic algorithms.

Figure 6-9 *The wep_crack Tool Rapidly Cracks Passphrase-Based WEP Keys*

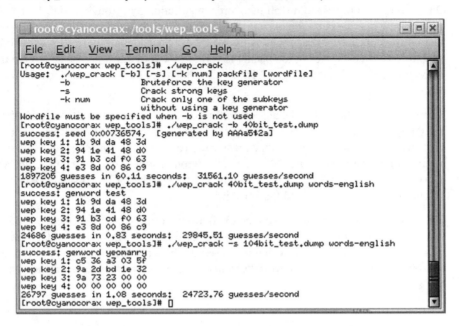

The attack relies on gathering large amounts of encrypted data and looking for the packets in which the key has the weak structure. These are so-called "interesting packets." In these interesting packets, there is only about a 5-percent chance that one byte of the key will be leaked. Therefore, the attacker gathers hundreds of interesting packets and keeps statistics. Over time, the leaked byte value shows up more than the other possible values and clearly shows up as the most frequent value. Figure 6-10 is a graph of the values for one of the key bytes from a sample packet dump. It clearly illustrates how obvious the bias is.

Figure 6-10 *After the Attacker Gathers Enough Packets, the Flaw in WEP Reveals the Bytes of the Key, One by One*

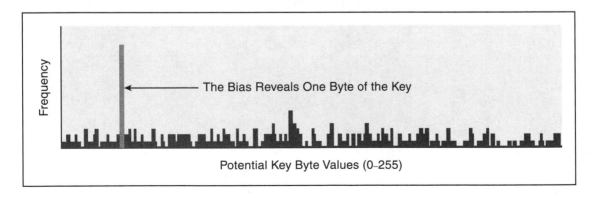

The attacker simply keeps counters for each of the 5 or 13 bytes of the keystream. After gathering enough packets, he has a reasonable assurance that the byte values with the highest totals are indeed the actual bytes of the key. The more packets he gathers, the higher the assurance that he has in fact cracked the key. Estimates are that in the worst case, an attacker can gather enough packets to crack the key with as few as 1 million packets. These can be gathered in as few as 9 minutes on a saturated network. Although the attack would likely take longer, it points to the need to have a dynamic WEP key-management scheme. With protocols such as LEAP and PEAP, WEP keys can be assigned per user and configured to be changed based on time or packet limits.

FMS Tools

Several tools implement the FMS attack:

- *WEPCrack* (http://wepcrack.sourceforge.net) was the first publicly released tool. It requires a Prism2-based card (Linksys, SMC, and others) for sniffing. WEPCrack is actually a collection of tools that requires some attacker sophistication because the attacker must figure out how to use the prismdump tool on his own. WEPCrack then analyzes the output and tries to crack the keys.

- *AirSnort* (http://airsnort.shmoo.com) is much better known, mainly because it is easier to use. It is a complete tool that has the ability to put the card in sniffing mode and has a front-end GUI. Airsnort implements an attack based on a subset of the FMS weak packets. Figure 6-11 shows a sample run of AirSnort.

Figure 6-11   *AirSnort Recovers the 104-Bit WEP Key 12:12:12:12:12:12:12:12:12:12:12:12:12 Using Only About 1.5 Million Encrypted Packets*

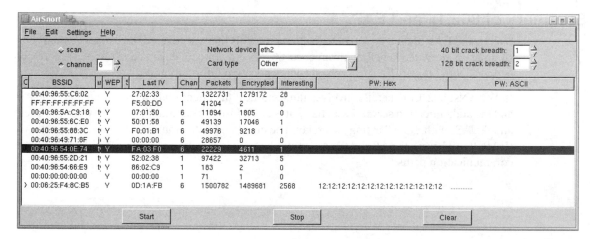

- The *bsd-airtools* package includes a pair of tools for cracking WEP keys. dwepdump captures the packets, whereas dwepcrack uses the dumps to crack WEP keys while using the FMS attack.

It should be clear at this point that WEP is seriously flawed and that many tools are readily available to exploit some of these flaws. Fortunately, the solutions in WPA and 802.11i eliminate these attacks. It should also be clear why vendors strongly recommend upgrading to these solutions.

Attacks on EAP Protocols

Cisco and others have developed several wireless protocols based on the Extensible Authentication Protocol (EAP). All these protocols involve a back-end authentication server (AS), with the AP acting mostly as a conduit for the authentication messages. An attacker can target these protocols either passively, by watching the traffic and attempting to gain useful information, or actively by becoming a participant. As a participant, the attacker can try to impersonate the client, the server, or both, as an MitM.

MitM generally refers to an active attack in which an attacker interposes between two parties for nefarious purposes. In the case of wireless networks, the physical challenge is greatly reduced, and an attacker simply needs to sniff or send the right packets to perform such attacks. Wireless protocols need protections to prevent MitM attacks. Impersonating a server usually means that the attacker must set up both an intercepting AP and a back-end AS. Several software programs exist that allow a Linux machine to act as an AP, so the AP and AS could be the same machine.

Summary of 802.1x and EAP

802.1x and EAP are network authentication protocols that are covered in Chapter 7, but a short summary is provided here for convenience. 802.1x is a protocol designed to provide security on network ports. It uses EAP to exchange authentication information.

In WLANs, 802.1x generally involves three entities: the client (called the *supplicant*), the AP, and the authentication server. Essentially, it is an end-to-end communication between the client and the AS, with the AP acting as a relay. The client and AP communicate via EAP over LAN (EAPOL), whereas the AP and the AS communicate via RADIUS. Figure 6-12 illustrates these communication paths.

Figure 6-12   *Client, Access Point, and Authentication Server Participate in 802.1x Authentication*

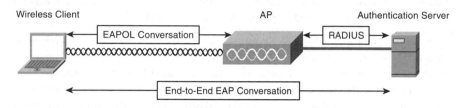

The 802.1x authentication process is generally as follows:

1 The client requests access.

2 The AS and client exchange messages so that the server can verify the client's identity. This might be mutual, with the client verifying the server, too.

3 When the AS is satisfied that the client has authenticated, it instructs the AP to let the client onto the network.

4 Optionally, the AS might pass additional information to the AP.

In LEAP, the client and AS authenticate via a modified version of Microsoft Challenge Handshake Authentication Protocol version 1 (MS-CHAPv1). The AS sends a challenge, and the client must perform a calculation based on the challenge and the password to prove that it knows the password. The challenge is there to prevent replays. In PEAP, the client and AS set up an encrypted tunnel and then do one of several possible authentication exchanges within the tunnel.

Dictionary Attack on LEAP

Lightweight Extensible Authentication Protocol (LEAP) is a Cisco-proprietary protocol described in Chapter 7. LEAP's major weakness is the use of MS-CHAPv1 in an unencrypted form for authentication. MS-CHAPv1 is vulnerable to offline dictionary attacks against dictionary-based passwords. An attacker first must sniff both the challenge and the response of a LEAP authentication. He can then run through all the words in a dictionary and attempt to obtain the response to match the challenge. When he does, he has guessed the password and can now successfully pose as the client using LEAP. The LEAP password might be identical to other network passwords, such as the active directory password. This enables an attacker to gain further access after he is on the network. There are at least two public tools that implement this attack. Figure 6-13 shows a sample run of *asleap*, written by Joshua Wright. Note the username "best" in both the challenge and response. Another implementation, much less refined, is referenced at http://www.securityfocus.com/archive/1/340184.

The main countermeasure to dictionary attacks is to enforce a strong password policy. Passwords should be changed on a regular basis. Frequency of password changes depends heavily on the security requirements of a site. A good policy should also require a password length of at least 12 characters, including numbers, mixed case, and punctuation. It should also include a requirement that passwords be based on neither words found in any dictionary nor any variant of the username. There are cracking dictionaries for hundreds of languages and commonly used words, such as names of places, people, and movies. Usually the only way to enforce strong passwords is with tools that enforce passwords at creation time. Users are good at choosing easy-to-remember passwords and tend to ignore unenforced rules. It is a good idea to run regular, automated password cracking on your organization's passwords and warn users or disable accounts with bad passwords. Your organizational environment determines what strength of password enforcement and frequency of password changes is acceptable to your user community.

Figure 6-13 *The asleap Tool Cracks the LEAP Password "test"*

PEAP Man-in-the-Middle Attack

The Protected Extensible Authentication Protocol version 1 (PEAPv1) relies on two key requirements for its security:

- The client must validate the server certificate.

- The inner, protected authentication method must not be used outside of PEAP in a form where the attacker can sniff it.

If either of these rules is violated, security can be compromised. Thus, if the client fails to validate the server's certificate, an attacker could put up a rogue AP and AS and steal the client's credentials. He could turn around and use these stolen credentials to successfully authenticate to the real server.

If the client application is poorly designed or badly configured and uses the inner PEAP authentication credentials in an unprotected wireless protocol, it violates the second requirement. An attacker can capture the password and successfully launch his own successful PEAP authentication session. Figure 6-14 illustrates the general concept of a wireless MitM attack. A rogue AP running on a laptop can act as an MitM and intercept user credentials. It can then use those credentials to authenticate to the real network. It can forward user traffic if it wants to prevent detection of the attack. The perceived connection is the connection that the wireless user thinks he has.

Figure 6-14 *Wireless MitM Attack*

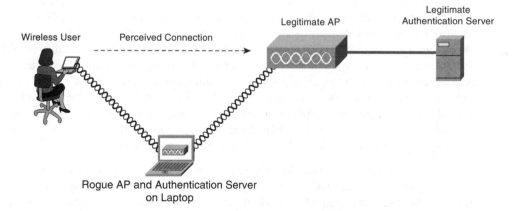

Thus, in PEAPv1, the client must properly use the protocol to be protected. In general, it is best not to allow users to override invalid server certificates. Users cannot be trusted to have the knowledge to validate a certificate and to differentiate a self-signed certificate from a real one. Any configuration that gives security-naive users the ability to weaken PEAP by merely clicking "Yes" in a dialog box is asking for trouble. EAP Tunneled Transport Layer Security (EAP-TTLS) has the same two security requirements mentioned for PEAPv1 and is similarly vulnerable to an MitM if the requirements are violated.

PEAP version 2 addresses this MitM attack by cryptographically binding the inner EAP methods to the outer tunnel. Thus, the inner authentication cannot be run outside of a protected session.

As of this writing, no publicly available tools implement these MitM attacks on PEAPv1 or EAP-TTLS.

Rogue APs

Rogue APs are unauthorized APs in a network. Network users often set them up for convenience, especially if there is no existing wireless infrastructure. APs are cheap and easy to install in a network and are frequently set up with no or minimal security. Even if rogue APs are set up with security features, such as WEP, a user is usually unable to configure more robust security mechanisms such as VPN tunnels or back-end authentication. Another potential danger is a physical intruder installing a rogue AP as a method of obtaining future access to a network.

Rogue APs do not have to be set up within a site's physical perimeter. They could be located offsite in a van or in a neighboring building. The MitM attacks discussed previously require the attacker to set up a rogue AP.

Some APs serve as public gateways, such as in airports, hotels, cafes, or other public hotspots, and many of them require a username to authenticate for wireless service. An attacker can set up a rogue AP to pose as a legitimate AP and gather user account information. One tool, Airsnarf (http://airsnarf.shmoo.com), is designed to demonstrate just that. It sets up a rogue AP and presents any web page you want to a user. You can easily mirror a hotspot's registration page and steal user credentials as the user attempts to authenticate. Unless the user has some way to authenticate the AP, such as an SSL session, he has no defense against this type of attack. Even if the service provider uses SSL, the user will probably assume that the first legitimate-looking authentication screen that pops up is genuine. The attacker has the advantage that the user has no network access, so a casual user is likely to use anything to which he can connect. Use of one-time passwords limits the scope of this attack but does not prevent it. An attacker can still steal your one-time password and use it for one session. An attacker could even set up a billing page and steal credit card numbers or other sensitive information.

An attacker can also use a rogue AP to leverage a physical compromise of a network. If an attacker is able to get physical access to a network (either directly or through an accomplice), he might be able to place an AP on a wired network. This AP can allow future access to the network without the need for further physical intrusion. An attacker can then use this "mole" on the inside to perform other attacks, such as sending confidential data to the outside.

Clearly, rogue APs can represent significant security breaches into a network. A network administrator needs a strategy for finding and eliminating any APs that are not authorized to be on his network. Best practices for dealing with rogue APs are outlined in Chapter 9, "SWAN:

End-to-End Security Deployment," and Chapter 11, "Operational and Design Considerations for Secure WLANs," but a summary of solutions is as follows:

- Provide a secure wireless alternative.
- Enforce strict policies for your users.
- Perform periodic wireless surveys to detect rogue APs.

Ad-Hoc Mode Security

In ad-hoc mode, a group of users who agree on an SSID and a channel can form a network with no AP. The security implications of this scenario are potentially serious because each user can be attacked by any of the other users in the network. At this point, each user is not protected from the other users by external firewalls. Thus, personal firewalls are essential in ad-hoc networking. Actually, they are a good idea in any networking scenario. The prevalence of network worms means that malicious code could be running on any machine, even if you trust the owner. Of course, this applies to AP-based or wired networks, too.

Many default operating system configurations allow ad-hoc networking. For example, Windows XP allows connections to both AP and ad-hoc networks by default, so a user could inadvertently join an ad-hoc network and be open to attack. Unless a user needs it, he should disable ad-hoc networking.

Summary

This chapter shows that attackers target networks for a variety of reasons and with several different attacks. Reconnaissance attacks are usually necessary precursors to any attack. They include sniffing and wardriving and are often an attacker's first step in choosing and analyzing a target. DoS attacks target network availability and can achieve some attacker goals. These attacks include dissassociation, deauthentication, and transmit-duration attacks. They can interrupt service for a particular user or for the whole network.

Access attacks aim to access network resources or to capture and, if necessary, decrypt data. Attacks on the authentication mechanisms include the shared-key authentication attack and MAC address spoofing. Attacks on 802.1x are also attacks on authentication and can give an attacker access to a network. These attacks include the LEAP dictionary attack and MitM attack on PEAPv1. WEP has many flaws that allow the recovery of data encrypted with it. There are attacks on both the keys themselves and on the keystreams generated from those keys. Rogue APs are also a significant threat that must be dealt with. Finally, the chapter shows that there are threats in ad-hoc networks, too.

You now have a good understanding of the threats you face and can plan your wireless network to avoid those threats; the remainder of this book is designed to help you accomplish this task.

CHAPTER 7

EAP Authentication Protocols for WLANs

The second in the WLAN authentication trilogy of chapters, this chapter examines the various authentication protocols such as the Extensible Authentication Protocol (EAP), Protected EAP (PEAP), the Lightweight Extensible Authentication Protocol (LEAP), and EAP- Flexible Authentication via Secure Tunneling (EAP-FAST). This chapter begins with a look at the fundamental concepts and contexts of authentication and access control; next, it discusses the various protocols such as EAP and 802.1x.

Notice the slow progression out of the basic 802.11 standards as you begin to leverage other standards: IEEE, the Internet Engineering Task Force (IETF), and sometimes even proprietary standards. You will see how the various protocols add more security features such as encrypted tunnels for exchanging various information (authentication, credentials, and other data), dynamic key distribution and rotation, authenticating the user rather than the device, and applying identity-based mechanisms and systems that are part of the administrative domain in enterprises.

Access Control and Authentication Mechanisms

Before allowing entities to access a network and its associated resources, the general mechanism is to authenticate the entity (a device and/or user) and then allow authorization based on the identity. The most common access control is binary: It either allows access or denies access based on membership in a group.

NOTE   Extending access control, especially to the wireless world, means a more finely grained authorization; for example, you can allow access to the network and its resources for internal employees and allow Internet access for guests. Employees are also working on federations, so access can be allowed based on the entity's membership in identity federations—for example, intercollege access to researchers, interorganization access based on collaboration on certain projects, and other similar groups and roles.

The different layers, standards, and conceptual entities in the EAP/802.1x world are seen in Figure 7-1.

Figure 7-1 *Layered Authentication Framework*

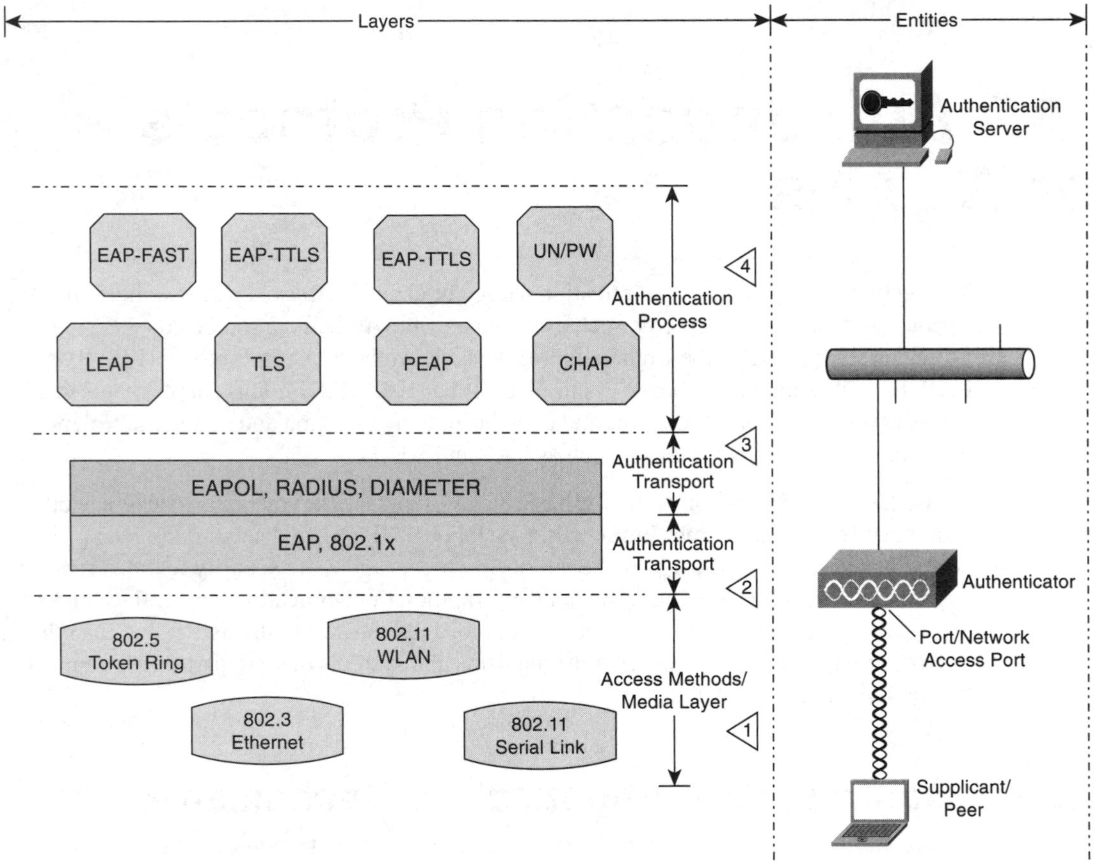

The Three-Party Model

The authentication is based on a three-party model: the supplicant, which requires access; the authenticator, which grants access; and the authentication server, which gives permission.

The supplicant has an identity and some credentials to prove that it is who it claims to be. The supplicant is connected to the network through an authenticator's port that is access controlled. The port concept is important because it acts as the choke point for the supplicant's access to the network resources. The access to the network can be controlled at a single point. The supplicant is called a *peer* in the IETF RFCs and drafts.

NOTE   In the wireless world, the most common supplicant is the STA (Station) (laptop or PDA), and the authenticator is the access point (AP). The STA to AP cardinality is 1:1. (That is, one STA can, at one time, connect to the network through only one AP.) This restriction is tailor made for the EAP/802.1x concept of an access-controlled port.

The authenticator itself does not know whether an entity can be allowed access; that is the function of the authentication server. In the IETF world, the authenticator is referred to as the *network access server (NAS)* or Remote Address Dial-In User Service (RADIUS) client.

NOTE   In many cases, the authenticator and the authentication server roles can be performed by one device, such as the 802.11 AP.

Let's look at the big picture before discussing the details. The supplicant initiates an access request, and the authenticator starts an EAP message exchange. (In the stricter sense of the standards, such as 802.1x, the supplicant does not necessarily *always* initiate the access request; the authenticator can initiate an authentication request when it senses a disabled-to-enabled state transition of a port.) At some point, the authenticator communicates with the authenticator server, which decides on an authentication protocol. A set of exchanges then occurs between the supplicant, the authenticator, and the server; at the end of this exchange, a success or failure state is reached. If the authentication succeeds, the authenticator allows network access to the supplicant through the port. The authenticator also keeps a security context with the supplicant-port pair. This context could trigger many things, including timeout if the authentication is only for a period of time (for example, the billed access in public WLAN scenario).

Layered Framework for Authentication

As shown in Figure 7-1, the authentication model is a layered one and has well-defined functionalities and protocols defining each layer and the interfaces between them. The access media (Step 1 in Figure 7-1) can be any of the 802 media: Ethernet, Token Ring, WLAN, or the original media in the serial Point-to-Point Protocol (PPP) link. The EAP specifications provide a framework for exchanging authentication information (Step 2 in Figure 7-1) after the link layer is established. The exchange does not even need IP. It is the function of the transport protocol layer (Step 3 in Figure 7-1) to specify how EAP messages can be exchanged over LAN, which is what 802.1x (and to some extent some parts of 802.11i) does. The actual authentication process (Step 4 in Figure 7-1) is the one that defines how and what credentials should be exchanged. Bear in mind that this framework still does not say how the authorization should be done, such as what decisions are made and when. This functionality is completely left to the domain.

Table 7-1 lists the major standards and efforts in the authentication framework domain. This chapter covers the different flavors of EAP. Hopefully, this table will enable you to dig deeper into the areas in which you are interested.

Table 7-1   *Specifications and Standards in the Authentication Framework Domain*

Mechanism	Specification	Description
Domain: Access Method		
PPP	RFC 1661: The Point-to-Point Protocol (PPP)	
802.3, 802.5, 802.11 and other standards	Various	IEEE access media standards
Transport Layer Security (TLS)	RFC 2246: Transport Layer Security Version 1.0	
	RFC 3268: AES Cipher Suit for TLS	
	RFC 3546: TLS extensions	
Domain: Authentication Exchange		
EAP	RFC 2284: PPP Extensible Authentication Protocol (EAP)	Original 1998 EAP standard
	RFC 3579: RADIUS Support for EAP	Was RFC 2284bis Will supersede RFC 2284
	draft-urien-eap-smartcard-03.txt	EAP-Support in SmartCard
	draft-funk-eap-md5-tunneled-00.txt	EAP MD5-tunneled authentication protocol
	draft-mancini-pppext-eap-ldap-00.txt	EAP-LDAP protocol
	draft-haverinen-pppext-eap-sim-12.txt	EAP SIM authentication
	draft-arkko-pppext-eap-aka-11.txt	EAP AKA authentication
	draft-tschofenig-eap-ikev2-02.txt	EAP IKEv2 method
	draft-salki-pppext-eap-gprs-01.txt	EAP GPRS protocol
	draft-aboba-pppext-key-problem-07.txt	EAP key management framework
	draft-jwalker-eap-archie-01.txt	EAP Archie protocol
	draft-ietf-eap-statemachine-01	State machines for EAP peer and authenticator

Table 7-1   *Specifications and Standards in the Authentication Framework Domain (Continued)*

Mechanism	Specification	Description
802.1x	IEEE Std. 802.1X-2001	Port-based network access control
	802.1aa	Revision of the 802.1x, work-in-progress
Domain: Authentication Process		
RADIUS	RFC 2865: RADIUS	Current RADIUS specification
		Supersedes RFC 2138, which in turn supersedes RFC 2058
	RFC 2866: RADIUS Accounting	Defines protocol for carrying accounting information between authenticator and authentication server
		Supersedes RFC 2139, which in turn supersedes RFC 2059
	RFC 2867: RADIUS Accounting Modifications for Tunnel Protocol Support	Updates RFC 2866
	RFC 2868: RADIUS Attributes for Tunnel Protocol Support	Updates RFC 2865
	RFC 2809: Implementation of L2TP Compulsory Tunneling via RADIUS	
	RFC 2869: RADIUS Extensions	Adds attributes for carrying AAA information between the authenticator (NAS) and authentication server (shared accounting server)
	RFC 3576: Dynamic Authorization Extensions to RADIUS	
	RFC 2548: Microsoft Vendor-Specific RADIUS Attributes	
	RFC 3575: IANA Considerations for RADIUS	Describes best practices for registering RADIUS packet types
		Updates Section 6 of RFC 2865
	RFC 3580: IEEE 802.1x Remote Authentication Dial-In User Service (RADIUS) Usage Guidelines	
	RFC 3162: RADIUS and IPV6	

continues

Table 7-1   *Specifications and Standards in the Authentication Framework Domain (Continued)*

Mechanism	Specification	Description
	RFC 2881: Network Access Server Requirements Next Generation (NASREQNG) NAS Model	Proposes a model for NAS—the authenticator
	RFC 2882: Extended RADIUS Practices	
	RFC 2618, 2619, 2620, and 2621	Various RADIUS MIBs
	RFC 2607: Proxy Chaining and Policy Implementation in Roaming	
One-Time Password (OTP)	RFC 2289: A One-Time Password System	
	RFC 2243: OTP Extended Responses	
EAP TLS (EAP Transport Layer Security)	RFC 2716: PPP EAP TLS Authentication Protocol	
EAP TTLS (EAP Tunneled TLS)	draft-ietf-pppext-eap-ttls-03.txt	EAP tunneled TLS authentication protocol
Kerberos	RFC 1510: Kerberos V5	
	RFC 2712: Addition of Kerberos Cipher Suites to Transport Layer Security (TLS)	
	RFC 3244: Microsoft Windows 2000 Kerberos Change Password and Set Password Protocols	
	RFC 3546: TLS Extensions	Updates RFC 2246
	RFC 3268: AES for TLS	
CHAP	RFC 1994: PPP Challenge Handshake Authentication Protocol (CHAP)	
	RFC 2433: Microsoft PPP CHAP Extensions	
	RFC 2759: Microsoft PPP CHAP Extensions, Version 2	
Protected EAP (PEAP)	draft-josefsson-pppext-eap-tls-eap-07.txt	PEAP V2

Table 7-1   *Specifications and Standards in the Authentication Framework Domain (Continued)*

Mechanism	Specification	Description
	draft-kamath-pppext-peapv0-00.txt	Microsoft PEAP version 0 (implementation in Windows XP SP1)
	draft-puthenkulam-eap-binding-04.txt	The compound authentication binding problem
Diameter	RFC 3588: Diameter Base Protocol	
	draft-ietf-aaa-diameter-nasreq-13.txt; Diameter Network Access Server Application	Diameter application in the AAA domain
	draft-ietf-aaa-diameter-cms-sec-04.txt	Diameter CMS security application

EAP

The EAP, a flexible protocol used to carry arbitrary authentication information, is defined in RFC 2284. (Incidentally, RFC 2284 is only 16 pages long!) A set of RFCs also defines the various authentication processes over EAP, including TLS, TTLS, SmartCard, and SIM. The IETF EAP workgroup is working on a revision of the EAP RFC and has submitted the new document as RFC 3579 (was RFC 2284bis).

EAP has two major features. First, it separates the message exchange from the process of authentication by providing an independent exchange layer. By doing so, it achieves the second characteristic: orthogonal extensibility, meaning that the authentication processes can extend the functionality by adopting a newer mechanism without necessarily effecting a corresponding change in the EAP layer.

EAP Frames, Messages, and Choreography

The basic EAP consists of a set of simple constructs: four message types, two message frames, and an extensible choreography.

The four message types are request, response, success, and failure. Figure 7-2 shows the EAP frame format.

As shown in Figure 7-3, EAP also defines a packet to negotiate the EAP protocol configuration. The EAP protocol is identified by C227 (Hex). This packet will be included in the data field of the EAP frame in Figure 7-2.

Figure 7-2 *EAP Frame Format*

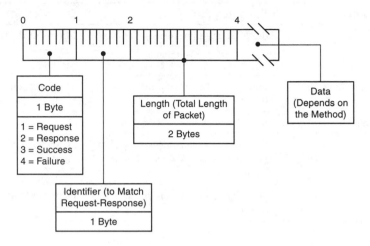

Figure 7-3 *EAP Configuration Negotiation Packet*

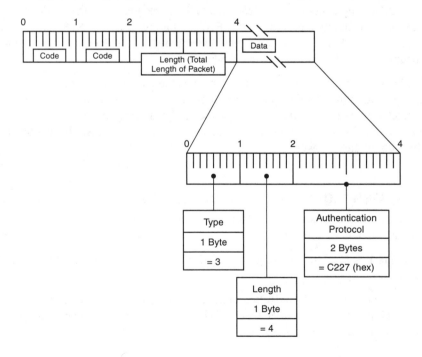

Depending on the type, the request and response packets include the type field and data, as shown in Figure 7-4.

Figure 7-4 *EAP Request/Response Frame*

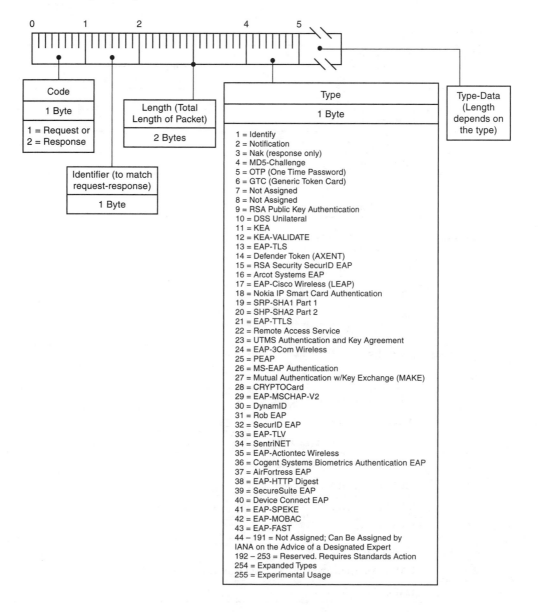

NOTE   The RFC assigns eight request/response types. The rest are assigned by the Internet Assigned Numbers Authority (IANA). The current assignments are shown in Table 7-2.

Table 7-2   *EAP Packet Types Assigned by IANA*

Type	Description
1–6	Assigned by RFC
1	Identity
2	Notification
3	Nak (response only)
4	MD5-Challenge
5	One-Time Password (OTP)
6	Generic Token Card (GTC)
7	Not assigned
8	Not assigned
9	RSA Public Key Authentication
10	DSS Unilateral
11	KEA
12	KEA-VALIDATE
13	EAP-TLS
14	Defender Token (AXENT)
15	RSA Security SecurID EAP
16	Arcot Systems EAP
17	EAP-Cisco Wireless (LEAP)
18	Nokia IP SmartCard authentication
19	SRP-SHA1 Part 1
20	SRP-SHA1 Part 2
21	EAP-TTLS
22	Remote Access Service
23	UMTS Authentication and Key Agreement
24	EAP-3Com Wireless

Table 7-2   *EAP Packet Types Assigned by IANA (Continued)*

Type	Description
25	PEAP
26	MS-EAP-Authentication
27	Mutual Authentication w/Key Exchange (MAKE)
28	CRYPTOCard
29	EAP-MSCHAP-V2
30	DynamID
31	Rob EAP
32	SecurID EAP
33	EAP-TLV
34	SentriNET
35	EAP-Actiontec Wireless
36	Cogent Systems Biometrics Authentication EAP
37	AirFortress EAP
38	EAP-HTTP Digest
39	SecureSuite EAP
40	DeviceConnect EAP
41	EAP-SPEKE
42	EAP-MOBAC
43	EAP-FAST
44–191	Not assigned; can be assigned by IANA on the advice of a designated expert
192–253	Reserved; requires standards action
254	Expanded types
255	Experimental usage

NOTE   The expanded type (254) frame includes a vendor ID; therefore, it is not deemed interoperable.

Figure 7-5 shows the success/failure frame.

Figure 7-5   *EAP Success/Failure Frame*

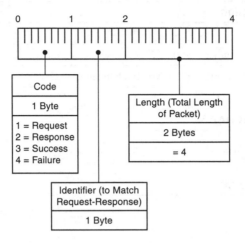

The EAP message exchange is basic, as shown in Figure 7-6. EAP starts after the supplicant has data and link layer connectivity (Step 0 in Figure 7-6). The communication between the authenticator and the supplicant is done as a request-response paradigm, meaning a message is sent and the sender waits for a response before sending another message.

NOTE   Generally, either side should be able to start EAP, not just the authenticator. But in this case, notice that the authenticator starts the EAP message, not the supplicant/client. EAP does not assume a specific protocol such as IP, so the messages are "lock-step"—an ordered exchange of messages in which a reply is sent only after receiving the earlier message. Another important observation is that EAP is a point-to-point (peer-to-peer) exchange at the transport layer, not multicast or any other many-to-many mechanism. The choreography is just a minimal framework facilitating further RFCs to define the exact processes. That is what many of the RFCs do: define EAP over various authentication processes such as EAP-SIM, EAP-over-LDAP, EAP-over-GPRS, and of course, EAP-over-802, which is the 802.1x specification.

The first exchange (Step 1 in Figure 7-6) could be an identity exchange. Even though there is an identity message type, the RFC does not guarantee identity semantics and encourages that the authentication mechanisms not depend on this exchange for identity and have their own identity-recognition mechanisms. Moreover, the initial exchange would most likely be in cleartext; therefore, it is a security vulnerability.

Figure 7-6   *EAP Message Exchange Framework*

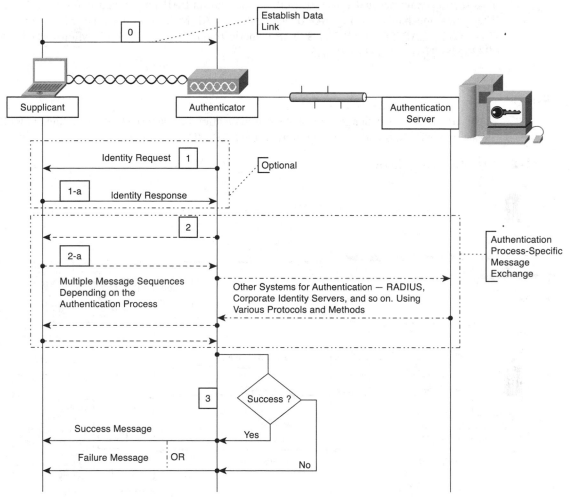

In Step 2, all the exchanges between the supplicant, authenticator, and back-end authentication systems are defined by a wide variety of specific RFCs or drafts and authentication mechanisms.

Finally, at some point, the authenticator determines whether the authentication is a success or failure and sends an appropriate message to the supplicant (Step 3 in Figure 7-6).

EAP Authentication Mechanisms

This section examines in detail some of the most relevant EAP authentication frameworks. The typical mechanisms using EAP over LANS are EAP-MD5, EAP-One-Time Password (EAP-OTP), EAP-TLS, EAP-TTLS, EAP-Generic Token Card (EAP-GTC), Microsoft CHAP (EAP-MSCHAPv2), and EAP-FAST.

EAP-MD5

The EAP-MD5 is a Challenge Handshake Authentication Protocol (CHAP), as defined in RFC 1994. Figure 7-7 shows the choreography of the EAP-MD5 mechanism.

Figure 7-7 *EAP-MD5 Choreography*

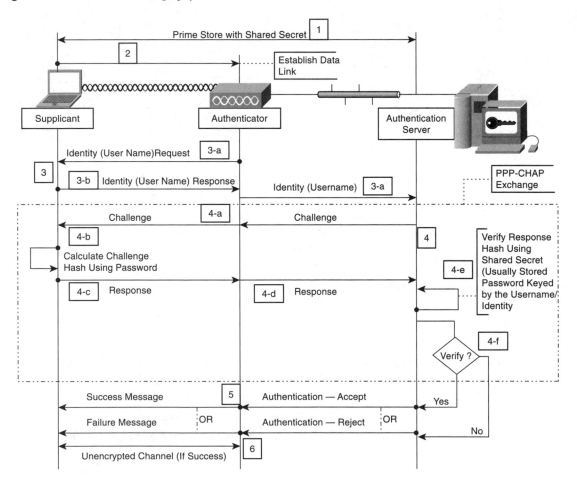

For EAP-MD5 to work, the client and the authentication server must have a shared secret, usually a password associated with an identity/username. This needs to be established out of band (Step 1 in Figure 7-7). The connectivity (Step 2 in Figure 7-7) and identity exchange (Step 3 in Figure 7-7) are required before the EAP-MD5 process. The EAP-MD5 method consists of a random challenge to the supplicant (Step 4-a in Figure 7-7) and a response from the supplicant (Step 4-c, Step 4-d in Figure 7-7), which contains the hash of the challenge created using the shared secret (Step 4-b in Figure 7-7). The authentication server verifies the hash (Step 4-e in Figure 7-7) and accepts or rejects the authentication. The authenticator allows or disallows access (Step 5 in Figure 7-7) based on this decision. If successful, the supplicant gains access (Step 6 in Figure 7-7).

EAP-MD5 is a pure authentication protocol; after the authentication, the messages are transmitted in cleartext. It is also a client authentication protocol—the server side (authenticator) is not authenticated; therefore, it cannot detect a rogue AP.

EAP-MD5 also contains a set of good features: It requires only lightweight processing (which translates to less hardware) and does not require a key/certificate infrastructure. Although pure EAP-MD5 has some value in the PPP world, it is of limited use in the wireless world. For example, Microsoft has dropped the support for EAP-MD5 for the wireless interface in Windows XP. Support was dropped because of security problems; EAP-MD5 is vulnerable to dictionary and brute-force attacks when used with Ethernet and wireless.

EAP-OTP

EAP-OTP is similar to MD5, except it uses the OTP as the response. The request contains a displayable message. The OTP method is defined in RFC 2289. The OTP mechanism is employed extensively in VPN and PPP scenarios but not in the wireless world.

EAP-GTC

The EAP-GTC (Generic Token Card) is similar to the EAP-OTP except with hardware token cards. The request contains a displayable message, and the response contains the string read from the hardware token card.

EAP-TLS

As you have seen, methods such as EAP-MD5 and EAP-GTC are specific to authentication and are confined to authenticating only the client. EAP-TLS adds more capabilities such as mutual authentication, which provides an encrypted transport layer and the capability to dynamically change the keys. On the other hand, EAP-TLS is based on digital certificates and thus requires an infrastructure to manage—issue, revoke, and verify—certificates and keys.

EAP-TLS is based on the TLS protocol that is defined in RFC 2246. The following section talks a little bit about TLS, and then you will look at which of its features carry over into EAP-TLS.

NOTE	The origin of the transport level protocol was SSLv1, proposed and implemented by Netscape for securing browser traffic. SSL 1.0 was superseded by SSL 2.0, which was the original SSL. SSL 3.0, which, of course, superseded SSL 2.0, is the most common security protocol used today. IETF chartered a working group in 1996, accepted submissions from Netscape (SSL 3.0) and Microsoft (PCT), and delivered RFC 2246—TLS 1.0.

A Brief Introduction to TLS

TLS has the concept of sessions and connection. A connection is a channel, whereas a session is governed by security context—session identifier, peer certificate, compression method, cipher spec for the session key, and MAC algorithm parameters and the shared master secret. TLS can and will securely negotiate different session parameters while maintaining the same connection—usually a TCP connection. The handshake phase establishes a session, and the session keys (symmetric) encrypt the transport during the data transfer phase. In addition to providing confidentiality, TLS provides integrity check. TLS, of course, is a point-to-point method.

TLS defines two layers: a record layer (which exchanges messages dealing with things such as fragmentation, MAC, and encryption) and a message layer (which defines different types of messages). The four message types are as follows:

- **Change cipher spec**—Used to signify change in the session context to be used by the record layer. This is an independent content type that is used to avoid getting trapped in specific protocol messages, at which point the pipe could stall.

- **Alert**—Could be warning or fatal. The alert message subtypes (approximately 26 subtypes) include close notify, decryption failed, certificate revoked, access denied, and so on.

- **Handshake protocol**—You will see these messages in Figure 7-8. The subtypes include the following:
  — Hello messages (hello_request, client_hello, and server_hello)
  — Server authentication and key exchange messages (certificate, server_key_exchange, certificate_request, and server_hello_done)
  — Client authentication and key exchange messages (certificate_verify and client_key_exchange)
  — Handshake finalization message (finished)

- **Application data**—The records themselves are transmitted over a reliable protocol such as TCP. TLS also defines a handshake protocol for authentication, exchanging cryptographic parameters and establishing session context.

Figure 7-8 shows the TLS choreography, through the lifetime of a connection, in some detail.

Figure 7-8 *TLS Choreography*

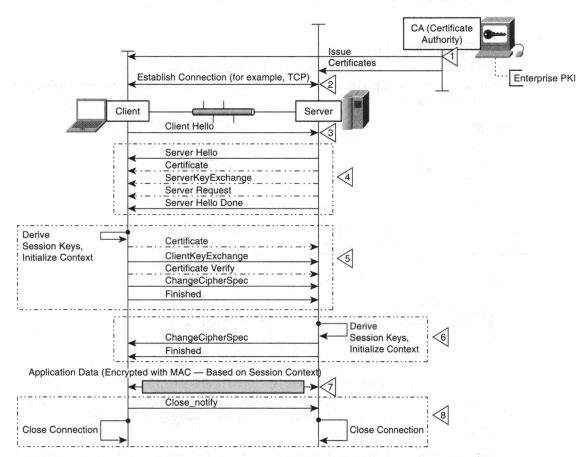

The handshake protocol (Steps 3, 4, 5, and 6 in Figure 7-8) accomplishes server authentication, algorithm negotiation, establishing session context, and (optional) client authentication. Of course, to successfully complete the handshake and arrive at the keys and secrets, the client and server should have digital certificates (Step 1 in Figure 7-8) and connectivity (Step 2 in Figure 7-8).

After the handshake is successfully completed, the client and server can exchange application data (Step 7 in Figure 7-8) using the established secure transport. Occasionally, renegotiation of session context might happen, usually for new session keys. Finally, the client or server with the close message closes the connection (Step 8 in Figure 7-8).

EAP-TLS Choreography

EAP-TLS employs selected parts of the TLS. For example, it uses the TLS handshake for mutual authentication, cipher suit negotiation, and to derive session keys; however, it does not use all parts of the TLS record protocol.

Figure 7-9 *EAP-TLS Frame Format*

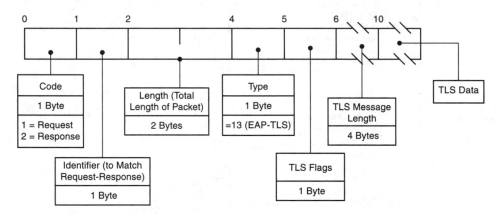

Figure 7-9 shows the frame format for EAP-TLS. The EAP type is 13 (see Table 7-2). The EAP data frame consists of TLS-specific fields. A similar approach is taken for the choreography, as shown in Figure 7-10. As expected, Figure 7-10 is a combination of Figures 7-6 and 7-8.

After the EAP identity request and response, a TLS-START request is sent (this is where Bit 2 of the TLS flag is used) to the supplicant (Step 3-a in Figure 7-10). This initiates the TLS handshake protocol (remember, TLS starts with a client-hello), which, in the end, results in authentication and establishing session keys for securing (confidentiality and integrity) the transport layer. As you saw in the TLS section, the session context contains all the relevant information. After the handshake is done, EAP-TLS does not use any of the TLS record protocols; that is, the application data is not exchanged using the TLS record protocol.

Figure 7-10   *EAP-TLS Choreography*

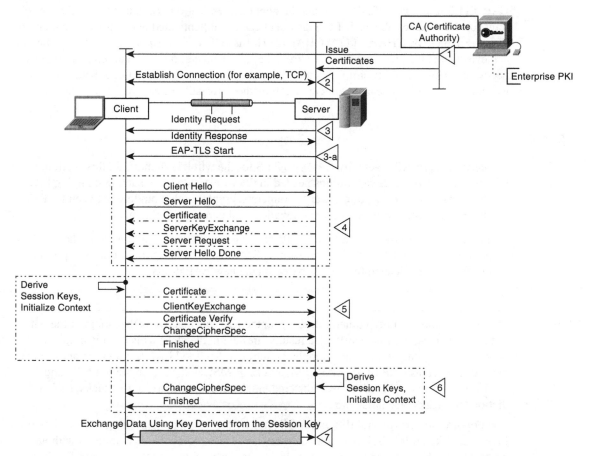

NOTE   As you can see, this still does not satisfy all the requirements of the wireless world because EAP-TLS is written for PPP, where a key and authentication are sufficient for communication and the client authenticates the server. The wireless world also has the authenticator/AP, which has to be authenticated, and the server is a RADIUS server.

In the wireless world, EAP-TLS is used as a strong and secure means for authentication and key establishment. After that, the native WEP mechanisms are used to encrypt the data. In fact, the WEP encryption key is derived from the TLS session key.

EAP-TTLS

EAP-TTLS is similar to EAP-TLS, but the client authentication is extended after the secure transport has been established. Then the client can be authenticated using any of the methods like username/PW, CHAP, and MSCHAPv2. This is called *tunneled authentication*. What this achieves is that the client does not require a digital certificate; only the authentication server needs one. This capability simplifies the client credential management. Organizations can also use currently available/legacy authentication methods (usually password-based schemes).

PEAP

In many ways, PEAP is actually EAP over TLS for the wireless domain. In this section, you will see how PEAP adds capabilities needed in the wireless domain, such as chaining EAP mechanisms and exchange of arbitrary parameters, cryptographic binding between EAP mechanism and the tunnel, session optimization, and generic reauthentication.

From a draft perspective, all the EAP drafts are generic and do not fully address the wireless domain. In addition, RFC 3579 is superseding RFC 2284. The PEAP draft aims at providing secure EAP authentication for 802.11 based on the new EAP drafts.

NOTE   One of the major security vulnerabilities from the EAP perspective is that some of the outer/initial exchanges, such as identity and results, are sent in the clear. This can result in denial-of-service (DoS) vulnerability; for example, an intruder can flood EAP failure messages. Inner exchanges such as EAP-MD5, EAP-SIM, and EAP-MSCHAPV2 also are not fully and uniformly protected. In many cases, the credential exchanges are open to attacks, such as dictionary attacks on a password.

The opportunity for vulnerability is complicated by the "compound binding problem" with PEAP and like protocols, in which two otherwise-secure protocols are combined without cryptographic handoff and might become less secure in combination than separate. On the other hand, password-based EAP protocols are simpler to manage.

PEAP aims at leveraging EAL-TLS, securing the open exchanges, and facilitating any of the EAP mechanisms over the secure channel, thus maintaining the simplicity (as far as possible) with the required level of security. For example, PEAP requires only server-side certificates, uses TLS for the secure tunnel, and extends the EAP-TLS beyond the finished message exchange to add client authentication and key exchange. The client authentication can be any of the EAP methods and thus can achieve security and the use of existing authentication paradigms. Of course, PEAP has some drawbacks. It is a little chatty (because of more message exchanges) and does require a certificate infrastructure for the servers. Also, TLS is normally implemented over a reliable transport-TCP, so implementing TLS over EAP requires small reliability and retransmit mechanisms.

The PEAP protocol has two phases. The first phase is to establish a secure tunnel using the EAP-TLS with server authentication. The second phase implements the client authentication based on EAP methods, exchange of arbitrary information, and other PEAP-specific capabilities through the secure transport established during phase 1. It will be instructive to see how PEAP manages to stay within EAP-TLS (for the most part), still adding capabilities. This is important to achieve a simpler supporting infrastructure.

PEAP Frame Format

Figure 7-11 shows the PEAP request and response format.

Figure 7-11   *PEAP Frame Format*

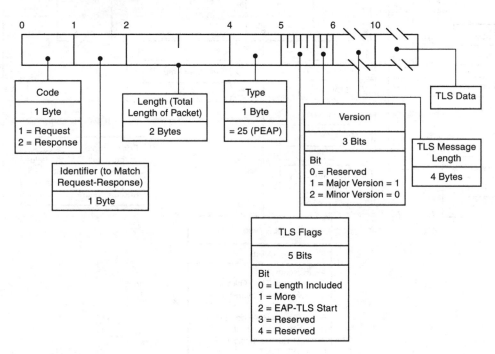

The PEAP frame format is almost the same as the EAP-TLS format, the difference being the version bits in the flags field and the type (25 for PEAP versus 13 for EAP-TLS; see Table 7-2).

PEAP Arbitrary Parameter Exchange

The type-length-value (TLV) mechanism is used to exchange arbitrary name-value pairs. Because this exchange happens in the second phase of the PEAP exchange, the frame formats are EAP formats with type 33 (see Table 7-2) but different from the TLS domain.

Figure 7-12 shows the frame format for the TLV mechanism. The RFC has defined approximately eight TLV types. Figure 7-13 shows the vendor-specific TLV. As you can see, this makes PEAP totally extensible but specific to a vendor.

Figure 7-12   *PEAP TLV Frame Format*

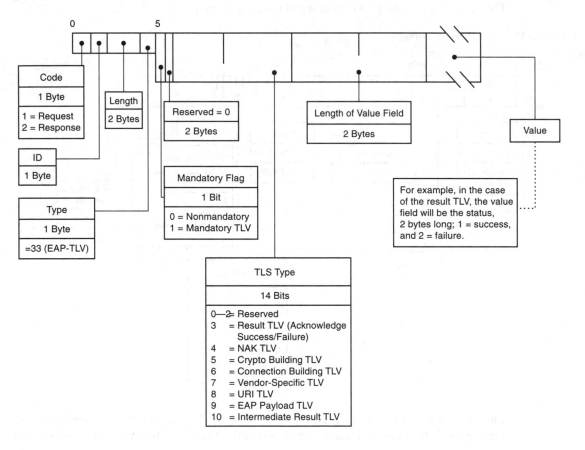

Figure 7-13 *PEAP TLV Frame Format—Vendor-Specific TLV*

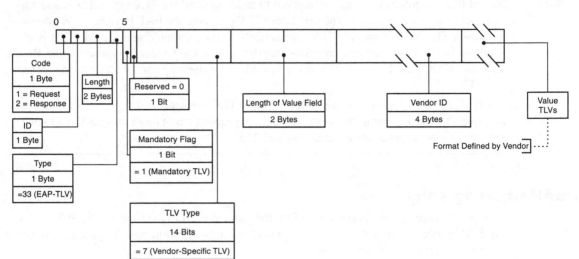

Another interesting mechanism is the EAP Payload TLV shown in Figure 7-14, which encapsulates the EAP frame in a PEAP-TLV frame. This is powerful because it can tunnel EAP methods over the secure transport. The following subsection shows how this is being used in the PEAP phase 2 choreography.

Figure 7-14 *PEAP TLV Frame Format—EAP Payload TLV*

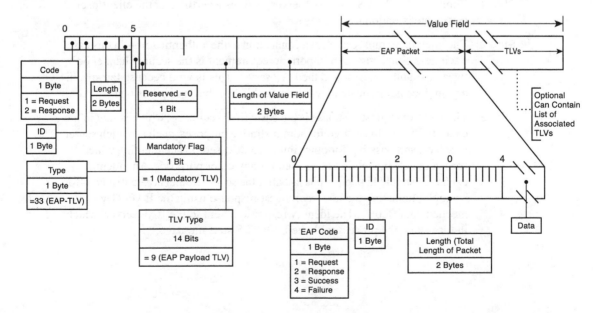

NOTE   Not all PEAP implementations are required to understand all the TLV types. The mandatory flag indicates this disposition. The mandatory TLV types are the EAP Payload TLV, Intermediate Result TLV, vendor-specific TLV (syntactical—that is, it should understand that it is a vendor-specific TLV; semantic understanding depends on the vendor implementation), Result TLV, and NAK TLV. The NAK TLV is used to indicate if an entity cannot understand the syntax of a TLV.

Another feature in the specs is the optimization of TLV message exchange; the spec allows multiple TLVs to be sent in one message—the only caveat being that multiple TLVs in one message are not allowed for the EAP Payload TLV.

PEAP Choreography

The PEAP choreography is similar (in fact, the same in most of the cases) to EAP-TLS. The main difference is that PEAP does not require client authentication, and the message exchange extends beyond where EAP-TLS stops.

Figure 7-15 shows the PEAP exchange.

As you can see, the PEAP conversation is between the EAP server and the EAP peer, and the authenticator acts as a pass-through for most of the conversation. The advantage of this scheme is that newer EAP schemes can be developed and implemented without changing the authenticator and NAS—only the peer(supplicant/client) and the EAP server need to be updated. This results in easier and simpler upgrade to the supporting infrastructure.

Step 1   Similar to EAP-TLS, the EAP server requires a certificate; the client/peer certificate is optional.

Step 2   The client/peer must establish a connection to the authenticator—in this case, a wireless connection. An important requirement is the secure channel between the authenticator and the EAP server. This is vital because the specification does not indicate how this is established, but it requires one.

Step 3   The identity request-response is the basic EAP sequence, which is sent in the clear. In PEAP, this is used for administrative purposes, such as which server to select, and possibly for other initial context setup. The identity, which is sent in the clear, should not be used for any other purposes. Any identity exchange should happen in phase 2 after the secure tunnel is established—for example, tunneling the identity request-response using the EAP-TLV mechanism (Step 7). The identity response is sent to the EAP server, which in turn starts the process with the EAP-TLS start message.

Figure 7-15   *PEAP Choreography*

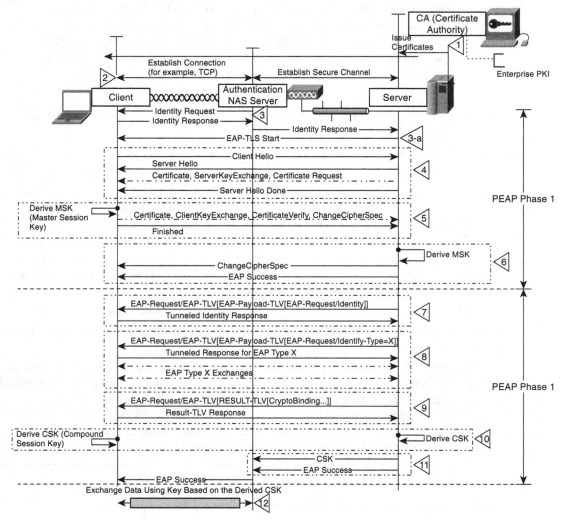

Steps 4, 5, and 6   These steps are typical EAP-TLS exchanges. Usually the client
certificate is not exchanged. The successful completion of the EAP-TLS ends
phase 1, and phase 2 leverages the secure tunnel created by phase 1.

Step 7   This is the beginning of phase 2. The EAP-TLV mechanism can be used to
tunnel the normal EAP identity exchange.

Step 8   In this step, the EAP server authenticates the client using any of the EAP mechanisms: EAP-MD5, EAP-CHAP, EAP-SIM, and so on. The exchange is fully protected by the TLS tunnel, and the EAP-TLV choreography allows a graceful mechanism to affect the EAP mechanisms. This is the heart of the PEAP method—the server with a certificate, the establishment of the tunnel by TLS, and the use of the EAP methods available in the organization's infrastructure.

Step 9   This is the final stage of crypto binding and so on between the client and the EAP server.

Step 10   In this step, the client and the server derive the required keys.

Key Derivation, Exchange, and Management

The description in this section really skipped over the more intimate details about key derivation, exchange, and management. You should read the PEAP RFC for the details; there are key derivation algorithms, key management sequences, and theory. The Compound Session Key (CSK) is actually a concatenation of the Master Session Key (MSK), which is 64 bytes, and the Extended Master Session Key (EMSK), which is 64 bytes.

The MSK and EMSK are defined in RFC 3269 (also known as RFC 2284bis) as follows:

- **Master Session Key**—Key derived between the peer and the EAP server and exported to the authenticator.

- **Extended Master Session Key**—Additional keying material derived between the peer and the EAP server and exported to the authenticator. It is reserved for future use and not defined in the current RFC. In addition, the PEAP key mechanisms are designed for future extensibility; the exchange sequences (and choreographies) and formats can be used for handling any key material; binding inner, outer, and other intermediate methods; and verifying the security between the layers that are required for future algorithms.

Step 11   This is where the authenticator receives the keys and the result of the authentication process.

Step 12   Now the client and AP can exchange information using the keys that are derived from the PEAP mechanism.

There are a lot more details and capabilities, such as reauthentication using the session resumption feature of TLS, fast roaming, fragmentation and assembly, key rotation and rekeying, and so on, in PEAP. In short, PEAP is a powerful mechanism that is in its initial stages of implementation.

802.1x: Introduction and General Principles

As you have seen, the EAP and other methods are primarily developed for dial-up connections; therefore, there are no link layer protocols for them in the 802 LAN worlds. You cannot arbitrarily open up a TCP port and start sending EAP data. That is where 802.1x comes in. It provides a set of context (such as port and supplicant), state machines between the various layers, and the EAP over LAN (EAPOL) protocol. Of course, 802.1x is not specific to WLANS; in fact, the standard is being used in wired networks successfully. 802.1x provides the access models, whereas EAP adds the authentication mechanisms.

NOTE   The 802.1x specification is clear about what 802.1x does and does not do. It provides a framework but does not specify the information (credentials and other challenge-response artifacts) or the basis of authentication (such as how to authenticate, what information is used to authenticate, how the decisions are made, and what authorizations are allowed as a result of the authentication).

The 802.1x specification starts with the concept of a port as single entry into a network for a supplicant. Hence, it covers 802.3 networks while considering a shared medium like the classical token ring out of scope. In fact, the 802.1x defines EAPOL only for 802.3 Ethernet MACs and Token Ring/FDDI MACs. As previously shown, this plays well with the 802.11 in which each client can be associated with only one AP; hence, the connection to an AP is analogous to the port in the 802.1x realm.

A controlled port is one that allows access after a successful authentication. A controlled port probably offers all the network services. The concept of an uncontrolled port also exists and is important because initial messages and authentication services would be offered through an uncontrolled port. Usually only minimal administrative services are offered by an uncontrolled port.

EAPOL

EAP encapsulation over LAN (EAPOL) is the method to transport EAP packets between a supplicant and an authenticator directly by a LAN MAC service. Figure 7-16 shows the MAC Protocol Data Unit (MPDU) for Ethernet. The header fields include Ethernet type, protocol version, packet type, and body length.

Figure 7-16   *EAPOL MPDU for 802.3/Ethernet*

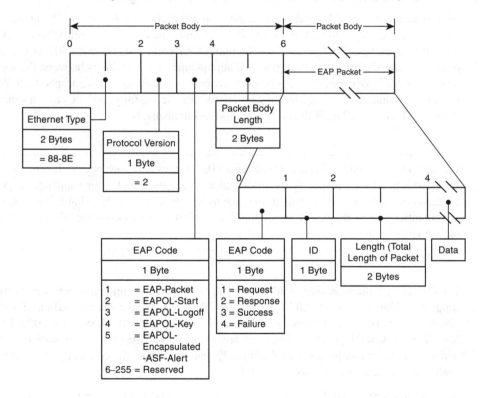

The body itself is the EAP packet you saw in earlier sections dealing with EAP.

NOTE   For the Token Ring/FDDI, the MPDU header is 12 bytes long with the first field SNAP-encoded Ethernet type.

As you might have guessed by now, a supplicant can initiate an authentication by the EAPOL-start frame. But usually a port in an authenticator becomes active (by a connection from a client), and the authenticator starts the EAP process, usually by an EAP-request-identity message encapsulated as EAP type in the EAPOL packet type field. One important packet type is the EAPOL-logoff from a supplicant to the authenticator. In the 802.11 world, this ends an association.

802.1x deals extensively with state machines, timers, handoff between the various layers, and port access control MIBs for SNMP. You can best understand these concepts by reading the standard.

Cisco LEAP (EAP-Cisco Wireless)

Cisco LEAP was developed at a time when WEP showed vulnerabilities and the full wireless security blueprint was not standardized. Moreover, instead of requiring a certificate infrastructure for clients, organizations wanted to leverage authentications that were already available within their infrastructure for secure WLAN. So Cisco developed a lightweight protocol that leveraged many of the existing features and still provided the required security features.

LEAP uses 802.1x EAPOL messages, performs server authentication, achieves username/password (over MS-CHAP) as the user authentication mechanism, uses a RADIUS server as the authentication server, and provides mechanisms for deriving and distributing encryption keys.

NOTE   The EAP type is EAP-Cisco Wireless (see Table 7-2).

Figure 7-17 details the LEAP choreography.

The entities that participate in a LEAP exchange are the RADIUS server, the AP, and the client.

In Step 1, the client and the RADIUS server should have the shared secret, usually a username-password database of all users in the RADIUS server (or access to a Microsoft Active Directory infrastructure), and each client should have its own username and password.

After a client establishes connectivity (Step 2), it initiates the authentication process by an EAPOL-start (Step 3), to which the AP responds by an EAP-request-identity message over EAPOL (Step 4).

Figure 7-17 *LEAP Choreography*

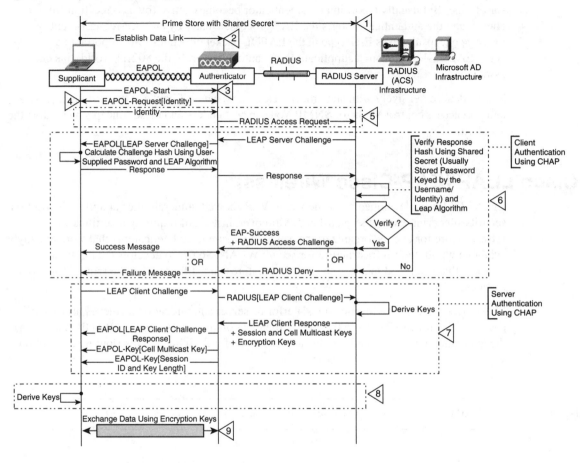

The client response with identity is sent to the RADIUS server in a RADIUS message (Step 5).

From this point on, the AP acts as a relay between the client and the RADIUS server, until after Step 7.

Step 6 is client authentication by challenge-response mechanism. The server sends a challenge, to which the client responds with a hash calculated using the password and the LEAP algorithm. The server also calculates the hash, and if they are equal, the authentication is success. As you can see, the client authentication happens based on existing infrastructure and still not transmitting the credential (here the password).

In Step 7, the server authentication happens through a similar mechanism, and at the end, the server sends the encryption keys to the AP. The AP distributes the required key material by broadcast.

The client derives the encryption key from the key materials (Step 8), and from then on, the AP and the client can use the encryption keys to have a secure conversation (Step 9).

NOTE   The LEAP key generation mechanism is proprietary and is generated every (re)authentication, thus achieving key rotation. The session timeout in RADIUS allows for periodic key rotation, thus achieving security against sniffing and hacking the keys. The RADIUS exchanges for LEAP include a couple of Cisco-specific attributes in the RADIUS messages.

EAP-FAST

Comparing the various methods, the EAP-FAST mechanism is the most comprehensive and secure WLAN scheme. LEAP was proven to be susceptible to dictionary attacks, and EAP-FAST is preferable to LEAP. In short, EAP-FAST is hardened LEAP with better crypto protecting the challenge/response mechanism.

EAP-FAST not only mitigates risks from passive dictionary attacks and man-in-the-middle (MitM) attacks, it also enables secure authentication based on currently deployed infrastructure. In addition, EAP-FAST minimizes the hardware requirement; many of the mechanisms require computational burden at the edge devices for asymmetric cryptography and certificate validation. As you have seen from your experience, secure-but-difficult-to-deploy mechanisms would not be popular; hence, EAP-FAST's features (such as flexible deployment model, support for secure provisioning, and efficiency) make it attractive for deployments.

NOTE   EAP-FAST started out as Tunneled EAP (TEAP), also known as LEAP V2. But as it evolves, it has become more than a LEAP replacement and is maturing. The final specification might be a little different from what is portrayed here, but the major concepts will not be different.

EAP-FAST is available as an informational Internet draft at http://www.ietf.org/internet-drafts/draft-cam-winget-eap-fast-00.txt.

To bootstrap the process securely, EAP-FAST establishes a shared secret (between the client and the authentication server) referred to as the *Protected Access Credential Key (PAC-Key)*. The PAC consists of the PAC-Key (32 bytes), an opaque field cached by the server, and PAC info (metadata about the PAC). The PAC is used to establish a tunnel that is then used to perform authentication. The three-phase EAP-FAST protocol is shown in Table 7-3.

Table 7-3   *EAP-FAST Phases*

Phase	Function	Description	Purpose
Phase 0	In-band provisioning— provide the peer with a shared secret to be used in secure phase 1 conversation	Uses Authenticated Diffie-Hellman Protocol (ADHP) This phase is independent of other phases; hence, any other scheme (in-band or out-of-band) can be used in the future.	Eliminate the requirement in the client to establish a master secret every time a client requires network access
Phase 1	Tunnel establishment	Authenticates using the PAC and establishes a tunnel key	Key establishment to provide confidentiality and integrity during the authentication process in phase 2
Phase 2	Authentication	Authenticates the peer	Multiple tunneled, secure authentication mechanisms

Figure 7-18 shows the functional entities involved in an EAP-FAST exchange. Of course, more than one function can be embedded in one server or software layer.

Figure 7-18   *EAP-FAST Functional Entities*

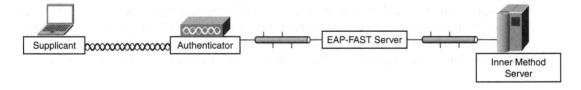

NOTE   The separation of duties between an EAP-FAST server and the inner method server adds deployment flexibility and extensibility. An organization can use the current and available authentication infrastructure and then progressively move to any other infrastructure it chooses.

EAP-FAST Frame Format

As shown in Figure 7-19, the EAP-FAST frame format is similar to the TLS format for phase 1.

Figure 7-19   *EAP-FAST Frame Format*

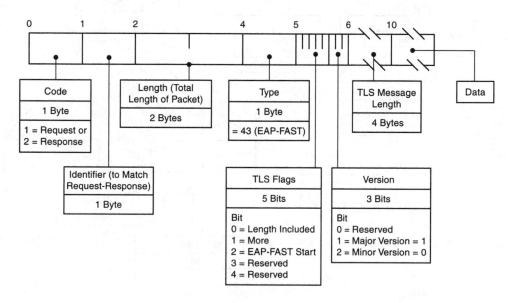

The major contribution by EAP-FAST to the frame format is the PAC fields and associated information in the phase 0 and subsequent conversations. Figure 7-20 shows the PAC-TLV.

Table 7-4 describes some of the salient fields.

EAP-FAST Choreography

The EAP-FAST choreography is a combination of multiple conversations. Figure 7-21 shows an overview of the EAP-FAST choreography.

Figure 7-20 *PAC TLV Frame Format*

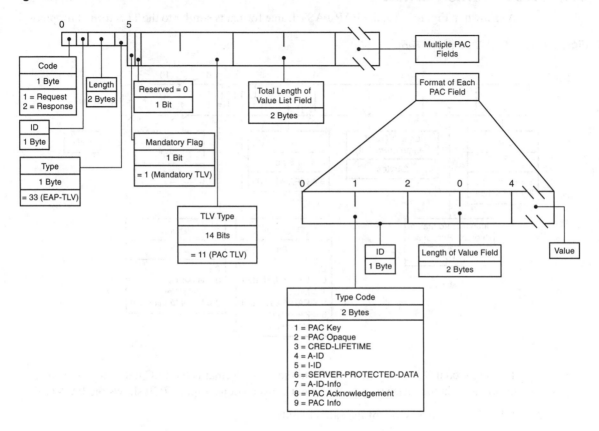

Table 7-4 *Salient Fields in EAP-FAST*

Name	Description	Relevance
A-ID	Authority identifier. This field would be in the EAP-FAST start frame.	A unique name identifying the authentication server. Will be used by the client/peer to index into the PAC and other context information.
I-ID	Initiator identifier.	A unique name identifying the peer/client.
CRED-LIFETIME	Expiration time of the credential.	This field will be in the PAC key info and used to validate a PAC key set.

Figure 7-21   *EAP-FAST Choreography Overview*

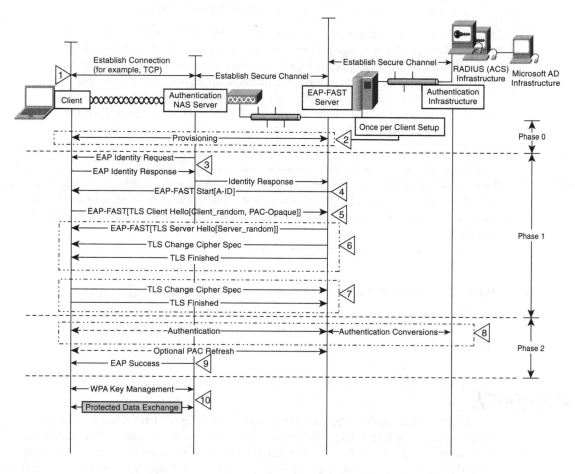

Step 1   Step 1, of course, is to have connectivity between the client/peer and AP, in addition to secure connections between the AP, EAP-FAST server, and authentication server.

Step 2   To bootstrap a secure channel, the EAP phase 0 provisioning needs to be performed. This is done once per client setup. This phase itself is an EAP-TLS exchange, with the Diffie-Hellman key exchange and fields embedded in the TLS choreography. At the end of phase 0, the PAC between the peer/client and the authentication server is established.

Step 3   This is similar to the EAP identity exchange.

Step 4   This is the EAP-FAST start message, which includes the authenticator ID.

Steps 5, 6, and 7   TLS exchanges over EAP-FAST to authenticate the peer and the server. The client sends the PAC-opaque to the server in Step 5.

Step 8   Step 8, the inner authentication method, is where the actual authentication happens. The message exchange is implemented via EAP-TLV over EAP-FAST between the peer and the EAP server and most probably RADIUS between the EAP server and the authentication server. It is also possible that the same software in one computer performs both server functions. The phase 2 inner authentication method over EAP-TLV can be EAP-SIM, EAP-OTP, EAP-GTC, or MSCHAPv2.

NOTE   One of the built-in features in EAP-FAST is the PAC refresh, which can be done after successful authentication, at the end of Step 8. This functionality adds the secure update of the PAC as part of the EAP-FAST message exchange and infrastructure, thus making maintenance easier and more secure.

Step 9   This is the mandatory EAP success message required by EAP.

Step 10 You can now use the key materials and contexts established by the three phases to use WPA methods to exchange information, thereby achieving confidentiality and integrity.

Summary

This chapter examined the authentication methods: EAP, PEAP, LEAP, and the newer, emerging paradigm EAP-FAST. The chapter also dived into basic details about port-based access control: the 802.1x. As you can see, the various solutions are at a different maturity in terms of standardization and implementation. This scheme of things will probably continue for this year, and by 2005, this area will be more stabilized. The following chapter looks at the 802.11i and the wireless security blueprint.

CHAPTER 8

WLAN Encryption and Data Integrity Protocols

Chapter 6, "Wireless Vulnerabilities," shows some serious deficiencies in the original IEEE 802.11 standard. Many of these deficiencies are in Wired Equivalent Privacy (WEP). When the Fluhrer-Mantin-Shamir attack rendered the WEP key vulnerable in 2001, it was a big blow to Wi-Fi. The members of the Wi-Fi Alliance needed a solution that could assure the general public that wireless networking was safe to use again. The IEEE 802.11i Task Group was working on enhancements, but standards bodies are slow. Cisco defined its own version of the standard to get a security solution to customers quickly. The Wi-Fi Alliance codified a well-defined subset of an early draft of 802.11i and called it Wi-Fi Protected Access (WPA). WPA, which became available in 2003, is a package of several features designed to secure 802.11 using legacy hardware. The 802.11i standard, which the IEEE Approved in June 2004, provides even more protection than WPA. It is being dubbed WPA2 by the Wi-Fi Alliance, an industry association.

802.11i adds new encryption and data integrity methods. One of these is designed to work with legacy WEP equipment, and the other is based on the Advanced Encryption Standard (AES), and will thus require a hardware upgrade in many cases.

This chapter discusses the contents of the 802.11i standard. It then describes the algorithms involved in legacy WEP and 802.11i. These include encryption algorithms to protect the data, cryptographic integrity checks to prevent message modification and replay, and dynamic key management algorithms. It describes the new security association concept associated with 802.11i. This chapter next briefly describes WPA and Cisco proprietary Cisco Key Integrity Protocol (CKIP). Finally, it ends with a review of how these solutions address the various security problems that Chapter 6 describes.

IEEE 802.11i

The IEEE and its standards are introduced in Chapter 3, "WLAN Standards." The IEEE 802.11 committee is responsible for wireless LANs and includes several subcommittees, known as Task Groups. Task Groups are charged with developing standards, which often are then rolled into the main standard, after they are adopted.

Task Group i (TGi) was formed in March 2001 as a split from the MAC Enhancements Task Group (TGe). Its charge was to "enhance the 802.11 Media Access Control (MAC) to enhance security and authentication mechanisms." TGi finished work on the 802.11i standard, and it has been approved.

The 802.11i standard enhances 802.11 with several new security mechanisms to ensure message confidentiality and integrity. Some of these mechanisms are additions, and some are complete replacements of 802.11 procedures. 802.11i also incorporates the 802.1x port authentication algorithm, another IEEE standard, to provide a framework for strong mutual authentication and key management. The additional features include the following:

- Two new network types, called *Transition Security Network (TSN)* and *Robust Security Network (RSN)*

- New data encryption and data integrity methods: Temporal Key Integrity Protocol (TKIP) and Counter mode/CBC-MAC Protocol (CCMP)

- New authentication mechanisms using the Extensible Authentication Protocol (EAP)

- Key management via security handshake protocols conducted over 802.1x

TKIP is a cipher suite and includes a key mixing algorithm and a packet counter to protect cryptographic keys. It also includes Michael, a Message Integrity Check (MIC) algorithm that, along with the packet counter, prevents packet replay and modification. TKIP and Michael are used together and are designed to work with legacy equipment, thus providing a way to secure existing networks.

CCMP is an algorithm based on AES that accomplishes encryption and data integrity. CCMP provides stronger encryption and message integrity than TKIP and is preferred, but it is not compatible with the older WEP-oriented hardware. Ultimately, vendors will be required to implement CCMP to stay in compliance with the specification.

An RSN is one that allows only machines using TKIP/Michael and CCMP. A TSN is one that supports both RSN and pre-RSN (WEP) machines to operate. TSN networks have a weakness in that broadcast packets have to be transmitted with the weakest common denominator security method. Thus, if there is a device using WEP in a network, it weakens the security of broadcast traffic for all the devices. RSN is definitely preferred, and getting all networks to use CCMP exclusively would be ideal.

802.11i specifies the use of 802.1x port management, which relies on EAP for authentication. Master keys can be established after successful EAP authentication. After master keys are established, key management is performed by one or more handshakes, which are described in the "Key Management" section later in this chapter. Chapter 3 covers 802.1x in more detail, and Chapter 7, "EAP Authentication Protocols for WLANs," covers EAP.

The next section describes WEP and the new 802.11i protocols in more detail.

Encryption Protocols

With the changes in 802.11i, the 802.11 standard has three encryption protocols: WEP, TKIP, and CCMP. These protocols serve multiple purposes. They primarily are used for confidentiality but also include message integrity. TKIP and CCMP also include replay protection. WEP does not provide robust message integrity or replay protection.

WEP

Wired Equivalent Privacy (WEP) is an algorithm that was specified in the original IEEE 802.11 specification. It had three main design goals:

- To prevent disclosure of packets in transit
- To prevent modification of packets in transit
- To provide access control for use of the network

The net effect of these mechanisms was supposed to make the wireless medium as secure as wired Ethernet, hence the term "Wired Equivalent Privacy." The designers accepted the fact that there were potential flaws, but they thought they had made attacks as difficult as physically getting onto the wired network. It turns out they were wrong, and attackers have written tools to make attacking WEP easy.

WEP Key and WEP Seed

The WEP key is the 40- or 104-bit key that is used as the base key for each packet. When combined with the 24-bit initialization vector, it is known as the WEP seed. WEP seeds are 64 or 128 bits. Many manufacturers refer to the 104-bit WEP keys as 128-bit keys for this reason. Misleading as this is, it has become part of the industry terminology.

WEP uses the RC4 algorithm from RSA Security to prevent disclosure of packets. However, RC4 is a stream cipher and is not supposed to be reused with the same key. Therefore, the designers added the initialization vector (IV), which is a value that changes for each packet. The IV is concatenated with the WEP key to form something called the *WEP seed*. The WEP seed is actually used as the RC4 key, which allows a fresh RC4 key to be used for every packet. However, the designers should have required the IV to be unique and nonrepeating for every packet. Failure to prevent repeats means that an attacker can replay packets or choose a convenient IV for an attack. Inadvertent IV collisions are possible, as are attacks on the RC4 keystream. These attacks are documented in Chapter 6. For the recipient to successfully decrypt the packet, he has to know what the IV is, so the IV is transmitted in the clear.

To prevent modification of packets in transit, the designers used the integrity check vector (ICV). The ICV is a four-octet linear checksum calculated over the packet's plaintext payload and included in the encrypted payload. It uses the 32-bit cyclic redundancy check (CRC-32) algorithm. The idea of the ICV is that if an attacker modifies a portion of the packet, the checksum will not match. The recipient can then detect the damage.

The ICV should not be confused with the frame check sequence (FCS), which is another 32-bit CRC designed to allow detection of errors in packet transmission. The FCS is attached to the end of the frame before transit. The key difference is that the ICV is encrypted to hide it from attackers. However, CRC-32 was not designed as a data integrity algorithm. Chapter 6 shows how the design choice of a linear checksum (CRC-32) combined with a stream cipher (RC4) was a poor one. Stream ciphers allow the modification of any individual bit without affecting the rest of the message. Linear checksums depend in a predictable way on the contents of the message. Changing any portion of the message results in a predictable change to the checksum. This property allows an attacker to know exactly which bits he needs to modify to keep the ICV correct. He does not have to know what the ICV is, just which bits to flip in the encrypted ICV. Thus, an attacker can modify the message and simply flip the appropriate bits in the encrypted checksum to defeat the integrity protection. Therefore, the ICV failed in its goal.

To achieve the goal of access control, the designers chose a challenge-response mechanism based on knowledge of the WEP key. This is called *shared-key authentication,* and it is documented in Chapter 5, "WLAN Basic Authentication and Privacy Methods." The idea was that a station needed to prove its knowledge of the WEP key to gain access to the network. Chapter 6 showed that this method not only is flawed, but it also compromises bits of the keystream. Thus, shared-key authentication fails in its goal, too.

RC4

RC4 is the basic encryption algorithm that WEP employs. As mentioned previously, the algorithm is a trade secret of RSA Security that has been leaked to the general public in the form of a compatible (and likely identical) algorithm called *Arcfour.* This section describes the Arcfour algorithm but refers to it as RC4 to avoid confusing the reader. RC4 is considered a secure algorithm when used according to proper guidelines, including never reusing the same key and not disclosing any portion of the key.

RC4 is a symmetric stream cipher, so it produces a keystream of the same length as the data. The symmetry refers to each party having a copy of the same key, which is used both to encrypt and decrypt the message. In WEP, this keystream is combined with the data using the exclusive OR (XOR) operation to produce the ciphertext. Chapter 5 shows how the key is formed from the 40- or 104-bit WEP key and the 24-bit initialization vector to produce a 64- or 128-bit RC4 key.

RC4 employs an S-box, which is nothing more than an array of values. These values are scrambled inside the array via a series of swapping operations; they form the basis of the pseudorandom output. The two phases in RC4 are the Key Scheduling Algorithm (KSA) and the Pseudorandom Generation Algorithm (PRGA). The purpose of the KSA is to initially scramble the S-box using the RC4 key. The PRGA then generates the bits of the keystream while continuing to scramble the S-box for each bit generated.

In the pseudocode descriptions that follow in Examples 8-1 and 8-2, all lengths are in bytes. The RC4 key is K, which has length L. The S-box is S and has 256 entries, which is the number of entries used by WEP. The generated keystream is as long as the portion of the packet that needs encryption. The swap operation refers to a simple swapping of two values within the S-box. The # symbol indicates that a comment follows.

Example 8-1 describes the RC4 Key Scheduling Algorithm.

Example 8-1 *Key Scheduling Algorithm*

```
Key Scheduling Algorithm (Key, Length)
    Key: array[Length] of int8
    Length: int8    # length of the key
    # Fill the S-box with values 0 to 255
    for i := 0 to 255
        S[i] := i
    end for
    # Scramble the S-box using the Key
    j := 0
    for i := 0 to 255
        j := ( j + S[i] + Key[i mod Length] ) mod 256
        swap (S[i], S[j])
    end for
end Key Scheduling Algorithm
```

Example 8-2 describes the RC4 Pseudorandom Generation Algorithm.

Example 8-2 *Pseudorandom Generation Algorithm*

```
Pseudorandom Generation Algorithm (Length)
    Length: integer # length of the Keystream needed
    Keystream[]: array of int8
    i := 0
    j := 0
    for k := 0 to Length - 1
        i := (i + 1) mod 256
        j := (j + S[i]) mod 256
        swap (S[i], S[j])
        # Generate one byte of the keystream
        Keystream[k] := S [ (S[i] + S[j] ) mod 256 ]
    end for
    return Keystream
end Pseudorandom Generation Algorithm
```

The resulting array returned is the keystream.

Table 8-1 defines the various symbols used in the pseudocode examples in this chapter.

Table 8-1   *Operators Used in Pseudocode*

Operator	Description
:=	Assignment
<<	Left rotate (bit shift with the leftmost bits being appended from the right)
>>	Right rotate (opposite of left rotate)
MOD	Modulo division
XOR	A bitwise XOR operator
XSWAP	Swap octets 3 and 4 with each other and octets 1 and 2 with each other
+	Simple 32-bit addition
#	Defines the beginning of a comment

WEP Encapsulation

Encapsulation is the process of transforming data from one network layer for use by a lower network layer. In the case of the algorithms in this chapter, this involves encryption, integrity check calculation, possible fragmentation, and attachment of headers. Decapsulation is the opposite. It undoes the encapsulation process so that a received packet can be passed up to a higher network layer. It involves processes such as removing headers, decryption, reassembling packets, and verifying integrity checks.

WEP encapsulation is the process of encrypting and constructing the WEP packet. Figure 8-1 illustrates the WEP packet format.

Figure 8-1   *WEP Packet Format*

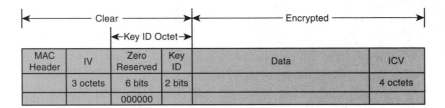

Following the MAC header are the three octets of the initialization vector. The next octet (the KeyID octet) uses 2 bits to specify which of the four stored WEP keys was used to encrypt the message. WEP allows for the storage of four different WEP keys to be used to encrypt a packet. Vendors generally implement this as a configuration option and allow the user to specify which WEP key to use at any one time.

Figure 8-2 illustrates the process of encapsulation of the WEP packet.

Figure 8-2   *WEP Encapsulation*

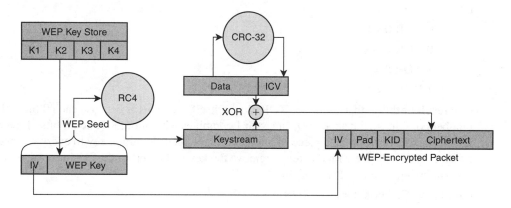

The basic WEP algorithm is as follows. (You can do some of these steps in parallel, so do not interpret the order strictly.)

First, the initialization vector is chosen. The standard does not specify how to do this. Some vendors choose the IV randomly, whereas others start at 0 and increase it by 1 with each packet transmitted. Ideally, you would want to avoid reusing IVs, which is called an *IV collision.* The easiest way to do this would be to start at 0 and count upward, with the proviso that you remember the last IV used when the card loses power. Some vendors use this model but start from 0 with each power cycle, resulting in IV reuse every time the card loses power. With card removal and reinsertion or laptop sleep modes, power loss can happen many times a day. An alternative implementation is to use random IVs, which requires a lot of memory to store all the IVs used. That is why vendors do not store them and avoid collisions. Therefore, this implementation might use a larger number space that results in fewer IV collisions, but over time collisions will still happen. (Chapter 6 discussed IV collisions in more detail.)

Next, the IV is appended to the beginning of whichever WEP key is being used to form the WEP seed. The WEP seed, in turn, is used as the key in RC4's Key Scheduling Algorithm to scramble the initial S-box. Then the RC4 Pseudorandom Generation Algorithm is run for as long as needed to produce as many bits of keystream as the data portion of the packet plus four octets.

At the same time, the CRC-32 is calculated over the data to produce a four-octet ICV. This ICV is appended to the packet. Now the data plus ICV is combined with the keystream, via the XOR operation, to produce the ciphertext. The IV and the KeyID Octet are appended to the beginning of the ciphertext. The MAC layer header is attached, and it is ready for transmission.

XOR

XOR is a bitwise logical operator that has the following properties when used to combine two bits:

$$0 \text{ XOR } 0 = 0$$
$$0 \text{ XOR } 1 = 1$$
$$1 \text{ XOR } 0 = 1$$
$$1 \text{ XOR } 1 = 0$$

One result of this is that a number XORed with itself is 0. This is because each 0 bit in the number combines with another 0, and each 1 combines with another 1. So all bits of the result are 0. Thus, in encryption, a piece of plaintext can be XORed with a key to encrypt it and XORed a second time with the key to remove the key and revert to the original plaintext data. The following algebra illustrates this:

Given that: Ciphertext = Data XOR Key

We can see that: Ciphertext XOR Key

$$= (\text{Data XOR Key}) \text{ XOR Key}$$
$$= \text{Data XOR (Key XOR Key)}$$
$$= \text{Data XOR } 0$$
$$= \text{Data}$$

WEP Decapsulation

The process of WEP decapsulation is more or less the opposite of encapsulation. It is illustrated in Figure 8-3.

Figure 8-3   *WEP Decapsulation*

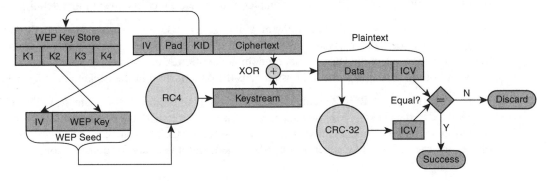

After the MAC header is stripped off, the IV and KeyID are extracted from the unencrypted header of the packet. The KeyID is used to retrieve the proper WEP key, and the IV is appended to the beginning of the WEP key to form the WEP seed. The WEP seed is used as the RC4 key for decryption. RC4 is run in the same manner as during encapsulation, which produces the identical keystream as the sender used.

When this keystream is XORed with the ciphertext, it extracts the plaintext. From this, the receiver can calculate the ICV over the data and compare it to the ICV in the received message. If they are equal, the recipient assumes the message was unmodified. Otherwise, it assumes modification has occurred and discards the message.

TKIP (802.11i/WPA)

WEP has its flaws, so the 802.11i Task Group developed TKIP and CCMP. TKIP had two main design goals. It not only had to fix the problems with WEP, but it also had to work with legacy hardware. Because many of the WEP encryption algorithms were implemented in hardware, TKIP had to stick with the basic mechanisms of WEP, including the initialization vector, RC4 encryption, and integrity check vector. Although superior encryption schemes existed, the designers had to find a method that would not obsolete the millions of legacy network interface cards (NICs) and access points (APs) already deployed.

Many of the problems in WEP stemmed from the reuse of the RC4 key and from the use of certain weak RC4 keys. The best solution for the encryption portion was to change the base WEP key with every packet.

TKIP consists of three protocols: a cryptographic message integrity algorithm, a key mixing algorithm, and an enhancement to the initialization vector. TKIP protects against capture of the WEP key by generating a different key for each packet. A cryptographic hash prevents modification of packets. TKIP also replaces the flawed IV with a longer packet counter and enforcement of replay protection. In addition, the packet counter is constructed in a manner designed to avoid known weak RC4 keys. Together, these overcome the existing attacks against WEP.

MSDU and MPDU

A MAC Service Data Unit (MSDU) is a basic packet of information that is to be transmitted to the other station. The format for transmission is called a *MAC Protocol Data Unit (MPDU)* and is what is actually transmitted via the 802.11. If an MSDU is large, it might be fragmented into more than one MPDU. At the other end, the MPDUs will be reassembled into an MSDU before being passed further up the stack. A fragmentation threshold is the maximum size that an MSDU can be before it is fragmented.

Michael MIC (802.11i/WPA)

The first of the TKIP algorithms is the Message Integrity Check (MIC), which prevents message modification. Chapter 6 shows that an attacker can easily modify messages because of the linear nature of the checksum that WEP uses in its ICV. This bit-flipping capability enables other attacks such as the reaction attack, which allows further compromise of the keystream.

The two problems with the ICV are that it depends entirely on information in the message and that it is linear, so it can be recalculated even in an encrypted stream. TKIP uses a cryptographic hash in place of a linear checksum. A hash is a mathematical calculation that uses a chunk of data with the goal of creating as unique a result as possible for each piece of data. A cryptographic hash is one that depends on something the attacker does not know: a key. It is also nonlinear in that an attacker cannot modify parts of the message and predict which parts of the hash will change as a result. Ideally, changing one bit of the message should change about half the bits of the hash.

A hashing algorithm, such as the Secure Hash Algorithm (SHA1), is usually used for cryptographic integrity checks. In the case of 802.11i, the designers felt that SHA1 was too computation-intensive to calculate on legacy hardware, so they agreed on a simpler algorithm called *Michael*. Like many hash algorithms, Michael is calculated over the length of the packet, but all of the scrambling it does is based on shift operations and XOR additions, which are quick to calculate. Michael uses a key called the *Michael key,* the derivation of which is covered in the "Pairwise Key Hierarchy" section later in this chapter. The details of Michael are covered in the "Michael Algorithm" section, also later in this chapter.

Michael Countermeasures

The output of a cryptographic hash should be long enough to make it extremely difficult to create a second piece of data that, when run through the hash algorithm, outputs the same result. Thus, without knowing the key, an attacker will have a hard time generating a packet with the correct MIC. He must take a blind guess at the correct bits of the MIC. He is unlikely to succeed.

According to the 802.11i specification, the Michael algorithm "provides only weak protection against active attack." This is a downside of making Michael easier to calculate. Thus, the specification requires additional countermeasures to safeguard against these attacks. The packet replay protections discussed in the "Preventing Replay Attacks" section are part of this defense. In addition, TKIP employs two countermeasures for the Michael algorithm:

- Logging
- Disable and deauthenticate

The first countermeasure is a suggestion that Michael failures be logged as an indication of attack. In addition, the ICV is checked before the Michael value is checked to make it harder for an attacker to create packets that will intentionally cause a Michael failure. The second countermeasure states that if two Michael failures occur within one minute, both ends should disable all packet reception and transmission. In addition, the AP should deauthenticate all stations and delete all security associations. This will result in the station having to negotiate new keys. The AP will not allow new key negotiation for 60 seconds. Key negotiation is described later in this chapter in the "Key Management" section. Stations also report MIC failures to their AP, which counts them as active attacks.

Michael Algorithm

Michael is calculated over something called the *padded MSDU*. This padded MSDU is never transmitted. It is used only as input to Michael. The padded MSDU is the real MSDU plus some extra fields that go into the calculation. The reason for adding these fields is that it protects them against modification when the MIC is checked on the other end. These extra, protected fields include the source and destination MAC addresses, some reserved octets, and a priority octet. A stop octet, with the hexadecimal value 0x5A, is added. Finally, there is a pad of between 4 and 7 zero octets so that the total length of the entity is divisible by four octets. Figure 8-4 illustrates this padded MSDU.

Figure 8-4   *Michael Padded MSDU*

Source Address	Destination Address	Reserved	Priority	MSDU	Stop Octet	Padding
6 octets	6 octets	3 octets	1 octet		1 octet	4 to 7 octets
		0x000000	0x00		0x5A	0x00 values

Michael uses a 64-bit key formatted as two 32-bit words, K[0] and K[1]. The padded MSDU and the key words are passed as input to Michael. The output of Michael is two 32-bit words, which make a 64-bit hash. The pseudocode in Example 8-3 describes the Michael algorithm, using the symbols described earlier in Table 8-1.

Example 8-3   *Michael Algorithm*

```
Michael (Key, MSDU)
    Key: array[2] of int32
    MSDU: array [Length] of int32
    Length: integer         # length of the padded MSDU in 32-bit words
    left := Key[0]; right := Key[1]
    for i := 0 to (n-1):
        left := left XOR MSDU[i]
        (left, right) := Block (left, right)
    end for
    return (left, right)
end Michael
```

continues

Example 8-3 *Michael Algorithm (Continued)*

```
Block() is defined as:
Block (left, right)
    left, right: int32
    right := right XOR (left << 17)
    left := (left + right) MOD 2^32
    right := right XOR (XSWAP(left))
    left := (left + right) MOD 2^32
    right := right XOR (left << 3)
    left := (left + right) MOD 2^32
    right := right XOR (left >> 2)
    left := (left + right) MOD 2^32
    return (left, right)
end Block
```

Preventing Replay Attacks

The second TKIP mechanism is the TKIP Sequence Counter (TSC), which is designed to prevent replay attacks. The WEP specification fails to require that implementers use unique IVs, so it is easy for an attacker to replay packets. Furthermore, the reuse of IVs enables an attacker to reuse a keystream after he has cracked it. The lack of replay prevention in WEP is related to the lack of key management in the original specification. Because no key management is specified, a WEP key was designed to be long lived. Therefore, forbidding reuse of an IV would have lead to an eventual exhaustion of available IVs, which is likely why the designers chose not to require it.

TKIP solves these problems with the TSC. The TSC is a 48-bit counter that starts at 0 and increases by 1 for each packet. TSCs must be remembered because they must never repeat for a given key. Each receiver keeps track of the highest value it has received from each MAC address. If it receives a packet that has a TSC value lower than or equal to one it has already received, it assumes it is a rebroadcast and drops it. Thus, packets can only arrive in sequence.

The ICV and MIC also prevent an attacker from changing the TSC and using it to rebroadcast a packet. Because the TSC in the packet is used in the decryption algorithm, it causes the modified packet to decrypt differently. This results in both the ICV and the MIC not matching the packet. Thus, the decapsulation fails, and the packet is dropped. As mentioned already, the ICV is checked first to make it harder for an attacker to intentionally cause MIC failures and a denial of service (DoS).

This mechanism also prevents a similar attack, which the designers recognized. An attacker could attempt a DoS attack, in which he sends or modifies packets so that they have a future value of the TSC. If the receiver were to update his counter to this new value, the sender would have no knowledge of this jump. He would continue to send packets with proper TSC values, which would look like replayed packets. The specification prevents this threat by specifying that the receiver not update his incoming TSC counter until he successfully verifies the MIC for each packet. As mentioned in the preceding paragraph, an attacker will be unable to get either the ICV or the MIC to decrypt correctly, and this attack will fail.

The TSC is broadcast in the clear in a TKIP packet. The six octets of the TSC (referred to as TSC_0 through TSC_5) are split up for broadcast, as you can see in Figure 8-5.

Figure 8-5   *TKIP Packet Format*

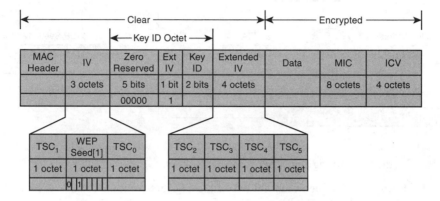

Two octets of the TSC (TSC_0 and TSC_1) are transmitted in octets 3 and 1 of the IV field, which is sent unencrypted. The other four octets are transmitted immediately after the KeyID octet and are also sent unencrypted. This allows the receiver to read the TSC in plaintext and apply it to the decryption algorithm. The TSC is reset to 0 when a new key is negotiated. Therefore, although TSCs are reused, they are never reused with the same key, thus avoiding the reuse problems from which WEP suffers.

Key Mixing Algorithm

The third TKIP algorithm is a key mixing algorithm that is designed to protect the Temporal Encryption Key (TEK). The TEK is a temporary key that can be changed using key management algorithms, as described in the section "Key Management" later in this chapter. It serves as the base key for creating unique per-packet keys. The key mixing algorithm starts with the TEK, which is shared by the sender and the recipient of the message. It combines this TEK with the TSC and the Transmitter Address (TA) to create a unique per-packet, 128-bit WEP seed, which it uses with the WEP algorithm. Because the TSC increases with each packet, the WEP seed changes with each packet. This change includes not only the first 24 bits as in legacy WEP but also the 104-bit WEP key portion. Thus, the attacks that rely on gathering a certain number of packets transmitted with the same WEP key are foiled. In addition, the algorithm specifically avoids certain known-to-be-weak RC4 keys.

The algorithm is depicted in Figure 8-6.

Figure 8-6   *TKIP Key Mixing Algorithm*

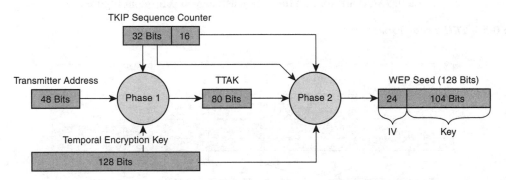

Briefly, the key mixing algorithm works as follows:

- **Phase 1**—The high-order 32 bits of the TSC are combined with the TA and the first 80 bits of the TEK. This phase of the key mixing is an iteration involving inexpensive addition, XOR, and AND operations, plus an S-box lookup reminiscent of the RC4 algorithm. These were chosen for their ease of computation on low-end devices such as APs. Phase 1 produces an 80-bit value called TKIP mixed Transmit Address and Key (TTAK). Note that the only input of this phase that changes between packets is the TSC. Because it uses the high-order bits, it only changes every 64K packets. Phase 1 can thus be run infrequently and use a stored TTAK to speed up processing. The inclusion of the transmitter's MAC address is important to allow a pair of stations to use the same TEK and TSC values and not repeat RC4 keys.

- **Phase 2**—Now the TTAK from phase 1 is combined with the full TEK and the full TSC. This phase again uses inexpensive operations, including addition, XOR, AND, OR, bit-shifting, and an S-box. The output is a 128-bit WEP seed that will be used as the RC4 key in the same manner as traditional WEP. In the phase 2 algorithm, the first 24 bits of the WEP seed are constructed from the TSC in a way that avoids certain classes of weak RC4 keys. The next section describes this construction. In the "TKIP Encapsulation" section later in this chapter, you will see how the per-packet WEP seed is employed in the encryption of the packet.

TKIP Packet Construction

TKIP adds three fields to the standard WEP packet format: the MIC, the Extended IV field, and the Extended IV bit in the KeyID octet.

The six-octet TSC is split into two sections. The least significant two octets, TSC_0 and TSC_1, are placed in the original IV field in positions 3 and 1, respectively. This swapping is done to avoid known weak keys noted in the Fluhrer-Mantin-Shamir paper. Position 2 is filled with a specially crafted octet ([TSC$_1$ | 0x20] & 0x7f) that is also designed to avoid weak key attacks. (These attacks are described in Chapter 6.) The most significant four octets, TSC$_2$ through TSC$_5$, are placed in a new field called the Extended IV field. This field immediately follows the KeyID octet. In the KeyID octet, an additional flag—the Extended IV bit—is set to 1 if the Extended IV field is in use. This indicates to the receiver to extract the six TSC octets from their various locations. Figure 8-5 illustrates the result of this construction. Note that the effect is that the TSC is transmitted in little-endian order, except for octets 0 and 1, which are swapped (as just mentioned). In WEP, the entire IV was in plaintext so that the recipient could read it to know how to decrypt the packet. Similarly, the entire TSC is transmitted in plaintext so that the recipient can use it for decryption.

TKIP Encapsulation

Now that you have seen the format of the TKIP packet, this section describes the process of constructing the packets. TKIP encapsulation is the process of encrypting, fragmenting, calculating integrity checks for, and building the packet. Figure 8-7 illustrates this process.

Figure 8-7   *TKIP Encapsulation*

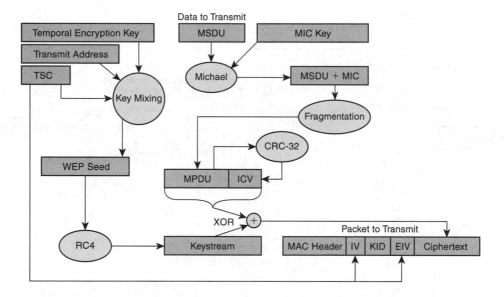

The data to transmit starts as an MSDU. The sender uses the Michael algorithm to calculate the eight-octet MIC over the MSDU and appends it to the MSDU. This process uses the Michael MIC transmit key. If the MSDU plus MIC combination is too large to fit in a single packet, the sender must fragment it. Note that this can split the MIC from the bulk of the MSDU and can even split the MIC across two packets. The result of the fragmentation is one or more MPDUs.

The sender takes each MPDU through the rest of the process. It updates the TSC to get a fresh value and calculates the 128-bit WEP seed using the TKIP key mixing algorithm. In this case, the WEP seed includes the IV, which is calculated (as previously mentioned) from two octets of the TSC. It then performs WEP encryption on the MPDU using the WEP seed. First it calculates a four-octet ICV and appends it to the MPDU. Then it feeds the WEP seed to RC4 and encrypts the MPDU plus ICV to form the ciphertext. Next the sender assembles the packet with the IV, Key ID octet, Extended IV, and ciphertext, as shown in Figure 8-5. The packet is encapsulated in a MAC frame and transmitted.

TKIP Decapsulation

As shown in Figure 8-8, decapsulation is the opposite of encapsulation, with the addition of some integrity checks.

Figure 8-8   *TKIP Decapsulation*

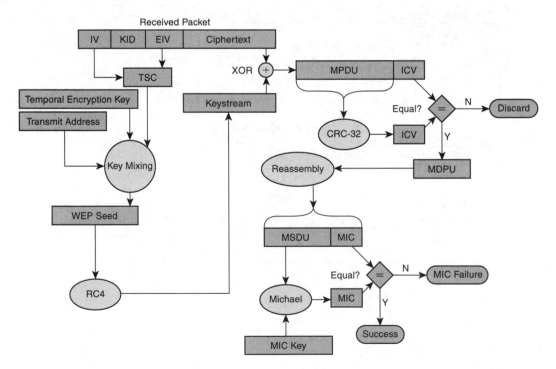

The recipient must recover the plaintext TSC from the IV and Extended IV fields. It verifies that the TSC is greater than the TSC in the previous valid packet it received. It passes the TSC, the transmitter's MAC address, and the TEK through the TKIP key mixing algorithm to compute the same WEP seed that the sender used. The recipient uses this WEP seed as the key to decrypt the packet via RC4. It now has the MPDU plus ICV. The recipient calculates the ICV over the MPDU and verifies that it matches the received ICV. If not, the recipient discards the packet. Next, if more than one MPDU came from a fragmented MSDU, they must be reassembled. At this stage, the recipient can calculate the MIC over the MSDU and compare it to the received MIC. If verification fails, the recipient registers a MIC failure, discards the packet, and takes appropriate countermeasures. If verification succeeds, the recipient has decrypted and verified the integrity of the MSDU and thus has successfully received the data it contains.

CCMP

The other encryption suite protocol introduced in 802.11i is the Counter Mode/CBC-MAC Protocol (CCMP). CCMP is the heart of the Robust Security Network (RSN) portion of 802.11i. It is a stronger set of algorithms than TKIP and also provides confidentiality, integrity, and replay protection. CCMP is based on the Advanced Encryption Standard (AES), which is the current state-of-the-art encryption algorithm. AES is the result of an international competition to produce a strong encryption algorithm. The U.S. government has accepted it as its standard encryption suite. AES has received wide international scrutiny by cryptographic experts and is currently considered to be very secure. It is expressly not patented; therefore, anyone can use it without royalty payments.

Acronym Soup

The name of CCMP comes from acronyms based on other acronyms, including the following:

AES: Advanced Encryption Standard. A standard, strong encryption method.

CTR: Counter mode. Another AES mode, typically used for confidentiality.

CBC-MAC: Cipher Block Chaining Message Authentication Code. This is one of the modes of AES, used for message integrity.

CCM: Short for CTR/CBC-MAC, a mode of AES that combines CTR and CBC-MAC. This mode achieves both confidentiality and integrity.

CCMP: CCM Protocol, or Counter Mode/CBC-MAC Protocol. The security algorithm in 802.11i that uses CCM.

AES has several modes, and CCMP gets its name from their names. CCMP uses the Counter mode for confidentiality and the CBC-MAC mode for integrity. AES also allows for a choice of key and block lengths. CCMP chooses 128 bits for each of these. CCMP chooses an eight-octet MIC and a two-octet length field for use with CCM.

CCMP uses a 48-bit *packet number* (PN), which is similar to the TSC that TKIP uses. The MPDU is similar to the one that TKIP uses. Figure 8-9 illustrates the MPDU format.

Figure 8-9   *CCMP Packet (MPDU) Format*

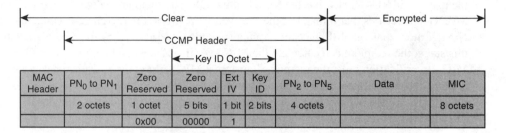

The length of the CCMP header is eight octets, which is four octets longer than the WEP IV/ KeyID header. Like TKIP, it uses a "1" in the Extended IV bit to indicate that there are four extra unencrypted octets in the header. The CCMP header breaks the PN into two parts and puts the two least significant octets at the beginning of the header. It then pads with a reserved octet of zeros. The KeyID octet contains the Extended IV bit and the two KeyID bits. Finally, it follows this with the four most significant octets of the PN. Thus, the PN is transmitted in the clear, in little-endian order, and in two sections. The header is followed by the encrypted section, which contains the data and MIC. The source of these is described in the "CCM Algorithm" section later in this chapter.

CCMP Encapsulation

CCMP encapsulation is the process of encrypting data and wrapping it with appropriate headers for transmission. CCMP encapsulation provides confidentiality, integrity, and replay prevention.

Confidentiality

CCM encryption ensures the confidentiality of data. The block cipher encryption process prevents anyone without the key from reading the message that is in transit. The strength of the AES CTR mode and the protection of the key are the guarantees of this confidentiality.

Integrity

CCM encryption includes the calculation of a Message Integrity Check (MIC) that ensures the integrity of data. This includes protection from replay attacks. CCMP uses a different algorithm than TKIP does: the AES CBC-MAC mode. The MIC is calculated over the data plus some portions of the MAC header, called the *Additional Authentication Data (AAD)*. Although these portions are not encrypted, their inclusion in the integrity check prevents their modification in transit. The AAD includes the entire MAC header except portions that could be changed during retransmission. Thus, it excludes the Duration field and masks to 0 or 1 certain bits of the Frame Control and Sequence Control fields. The protected portions include some Frame Control bits, some Sequence Control bits, QoS control, and the MAC addresses. The AAD contents are illustrated in Figure 8-10.

Figure 8-10   *CCMP Additional Authentication Data Construction*

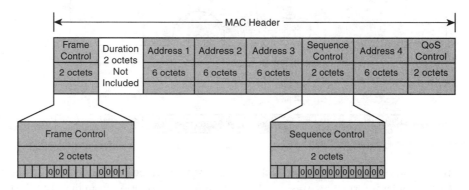

The bits of the Frame Control and Sequence Control fields that are labeled with 0 are the ones zeroed out in the AAD.

Replay Prevention

CCMP employs an incrementing packet counter, called the PN, to prevent packet replay. Along with the destination address (Address 2 from the MAC header) and the Priority field from the MAC header, the PN is part of a nonce. This nonce is included in the CCM encryption algorithm, and it helps ensure that the inputs to CCM are different with every packet. Reuse of a PN with the same Temporal Key would compromise the security of the CCM algorithm.

Encapsulation Process

Figure 8-11 illustrates the CCMP encapsulation process.

Figure 8-11 *CCMP Encapsulation*

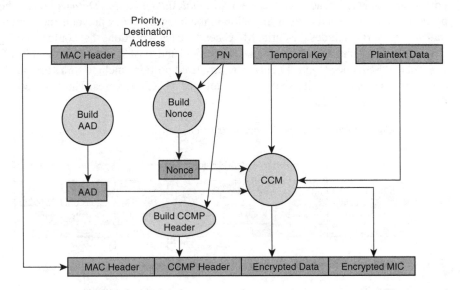

In this figure, you can see how all these processes described previously are put together. The MAC header information is used to build the AAD. Information from the MAC header and the PN are used to build the nonce. The Temporal Key, the MPDU plaintext data payload, the nonce, and the AAD are the inputs to the CCM algorithm. The outputs are the encrypted data and the encrypted MIC. The sender then constructs the CCMP header from the PN and attaches it to the encrypted data plus MIC. The sender appends the MAC to the front of the packet, and it is ready for transmission.

CCMP Decapsulation

CCMP decapsulation is essentially the opposite of encapsulation, as illustrated in Figure 8-12.

The recipient can extract the PN from the CCMP header and the MAC header from the packet. It can verify that the PN has indeed increased and that this is not a replayed packet. It can then calculate the nonce and the AAD. It already has the same Temporal Key that the sender used. From these, it uses the CCM algorithm to decrypt the encrypted data and MIC. It can then recalculate the MIC using the decrypted data and the AAD it has calculated. If they match the MIC from the decryption, the packet and the MAC header have not been modified. It can now be assured that the packet is intact and has arrived securely.

Figure 8-12   *CCMP Decapsulation*

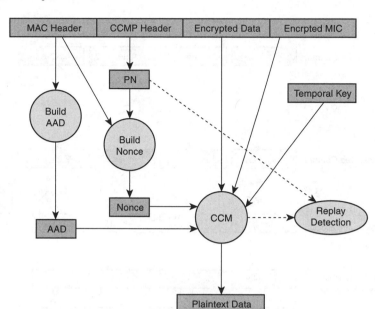

CCM Algorithm

The details of the CCM algorithm are quite complex and are beyond the scope of this book. But it is worth describing the basic concepts to give a feel of the algorithm and how it differs from WEP and TKIP. Chapter 2, "Basic Security Mechanics and Mechanisms," introduced some of the basic concepts of cryptography that are mentioned in this section.

AES is a block cipher, which means it takes a chunk of data and returns a chunk of encrypted data. In CCM, AES takes a 128-bit chunk of data and returns a 128-bit chunk of encrypted data, when provided with a 128-bit key. As previously mentioned, CCM uses two AES modes of operation: Counter mode (CTR) for encryption and Cipher Block Chaining (CBC-MAC) to create the MIC.

CTR is relatively simple. The message is broken into blocks of 128 bits. An arbitrary value, called a *counter,* is encrypted via AES and then XORed with the first block of message to produce the first block of ciphertext. The counter increases by one for each subsequent block of the message, and the encryption is repeated until the whole message is encrypted. The encrypted blocks are concatenated, and you have your ciphertext. This process is illustrated in Figure 8-13.

Figure 8-13   *AES Counter Mode*

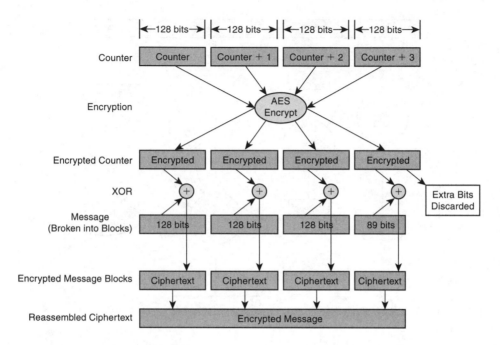

It is important to ensure that identical messages do not look the same when encrypted. If they do, an attacker can gain valuable information if he guesses the nature of the message. CCMP ensures that the counter is different for each packet by using the packet number to start the counter for each packet. Using a different counter each time ensures that the encrypted counter is different each time. This, in turn, ensures that the final ciphertext is different regardless of the contents of the message.

Decryption is the same process. The recipient has to know what the counter value was to start, and both sides use the same algorithm to derive it. The same set of encrypted counters is produced. Because of the properties of XOR, when an encrypted block is XORed with the same encrypted counter a second time, it results in a decrypted message. Thus, both the encryption and decryption processes actually involve using AES to encrypt the counters. This simplifies the implementation and means that the devices only need to implement AES encryption, not AES decryption. This was, in fact, a key motivation of the TGi committee in choosing CTR mode.

Cipher Block Chaining (CBC) is a mode in which each block is encrypted in turn and then fed back into the algorithm. The first block is encrypted first. It is XORed with the second block, and the result is encrypted again. This is XORed with the third block and encrypted again. The process continues until the whole message has been processed. Figure 8-14 illustrates CBC mode.

Figure 8-14 *AES CBC-MAC Mode*

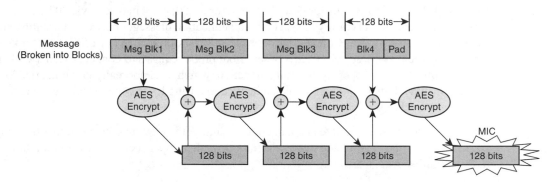

You can see that information is lost in this process. But the goal is not to obtain something reversible, just to obtain something unique and repeatable. This unique result is the MIC, and it can be re-created on the other end by the recipient to verify that the message has not been modified. Again, this process requires only AES encryption, simplifying implementation.

Key Management

One of the big problems in 802.11 is the distribution of keys; it is difficult for an administrator to generate and manage them. If a laptop or card is lost, the security of the site can be compromised. Keys can be compromised during mass distribution, if they are posted on web pages or distributed on CDs or floppy disks. Finally, the security problems make a strong case for developing dynamic keys.

802.11i introduces key management schemes that allow for a separate authentication process to enable the distribution of keys. There are two main phases to this process:

- Master key establishment
- Key exchange

Master key establishment can occur either manually via configuration or dynamically via the 802.1x protocol using EAP. After master keys are established, two parties perform key exchange to generate the transient keys they will use for the session. Although the term "key exchange" is used in the specification and in the literature, in reality this is a negotiation phase in which no actual keys are exchanged.

Master Key Establishment

EAP over LAN (EAPOL) is the preferred method for establishing master keys. 802.1x is a transport protocol used to convey the EAPOL authentication messages between the station and authentication server (AS). (Chapter 7 describes the 802.1x protocol.) For ESSID networks, a station first listens for beacons or actively sends out probe requests to connect to a network. It then authenticates using open system authentication, which does not really do authentication. The station and AP then conduct mutual authentication using EAP, which is where the real authentication takes place.

The station and the AS negotiate and authenticate until both sides are convinced that they are talking to whom they expect and that each side knows the proper secrets. At this point, the AS sends an EAP success message.

The mutual authentication process generates a shared key between the AS and the station. After the key is established, the AS transfers this key to the AP via RADIUS. Thus, this master key is at that point shared between a station and an AP. It is known as the *Pairwise Master Key (PMK)*. Note that the AP is not involved in the key negotiation, except as a conduit for messages. Only at the end, when the PMK is derived, does the AP receive delivery of the PMK from the AS. If a TKIP administrator does not want to use 802.1x, this key can be configured by hand on the client and AP. This is known as a *Preshared Key (PSK)*. For the rest of this discussion, the term "PMK" will include 802.1x PMKs and configured PSKs. How the shared key got to the station and the AP makes no difference from here on. It is important to note that the security of the encryption algorithms depends on the security of the PMKs. If they are predictable or compromised, the rest of the encryption becomes vulnerable.

At this point, key management is ready to begin. First, however, you should understand the different types of keys in 802.11i.

Key Hierarchy

There are two types of keys in 802.11i:

- Pairwise for unicast traffic
- Group for multicast traffic

The main root pairwise key is the PMK, and the main multicast key is the Group Master Key (GMK). The PMK can have a long lifetime and last through multiple associations to an AP. The GMK is a bit more at risk because it is shared among an AP and all its stations. All of the stations know it and might generate many packets with it. Thus, a GMK can be configured to be changed every time a station is disassociated or at a regular interval. On Cisco APs, this time-based reconfiguration is called *broadcast key rotation*. These master keys are used to derive other keys that are described in the next two sections. Table 8-2 summarizes the different types of keys used in 802.11i.

Table 8-2   *Key Types in 802.11i*

Key	Sharing Scheme	Use	Origin
Preshared Key (PSK)	AP and single station	Used in TKIP, WEP, or CCMP.	Configured
Pairwise Master Key (PMK)	AP and single station	Used as long-term stored key to derive other keys.	EAP negotiation
Pairwise Transient Key (PTK)	AP and single station	Used to derive other unicast keys.	Derived from PMK or PSK via 4-way handshake
Group Transient Key (GTK)	AP to single station (ESS networks) OR Single station to multiple stations (IBSS networks)	Used to derive other broadcast/multicast keys. Used in multicast communication.	Derived from PMK or PSK via 4-way handshake; can be renegotiated via group key handshake
Temporal Key (TK)	AP and one or more stations	For TKIP, this is a combination of a Temporal Encryption Key (TEK) and a MIC Key. CCMP has only one key, called the *Temporal Key*.	Derived from PTK
Temporal Encryption Key (TEK)	AP and one or more stations	In TKIP, this is the key used to encrypt packets.	Derived from PTK or GTK
MIC (Michael) Key	AP and one or more stations	In TKIP, this is used to calculate the Michael Message Integrity Check.	Derived from PTK or GTK
EAPOL Key Encryption Key (KEK)	AP and single station	Used in group key handshake to encrypt the new GTK.	Derived from PTK
EAPOL Key Confirmation Key (KCK)	AP and single station	Used in group key handshake to provide integrity for the messages.	Derived from PTK

Pairwise Key Hierarchy

The PMK is the root of all other pairwise keys used in 802.11i. A unique PMK exists between each station and its associated AP. The PMK forms the root of a key hierarchy, as illustrated in Figure 8-15.

Figure 8-15 *802.11i Pairwise Key Hierarchy*

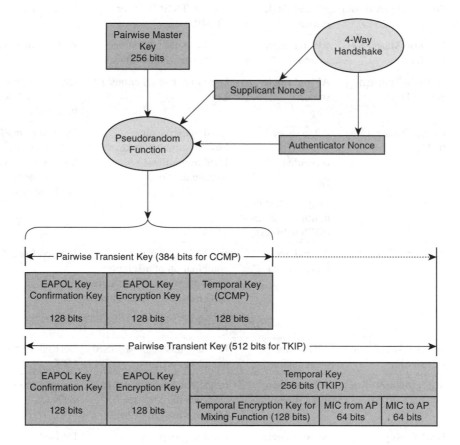

From the PMK, the station and AP derive three keys using a pseudorandom function. The pseudorandom function first generates an intermediate key, the PTK. It takes as input two nonces, or unique numbers, whose origin will be explained later in the section "The 4-Way Handshake." The PTK is then chopped up into three keys: the EAPOL KCK, the EAPOL KEK, and the TK. In TKIP, the TK is 256 bits; in CCMP, it is 128 bits. In the case of TKIP, the 256 bits are further partitioned into the TEK for the mixing function (128 bits), the Michael key for authenticator-to-station traffic (64 bits), and the Michael key for station-to-authenticator traffic

(64 bits). In the case of CCMP, all 128 bits become the CCM key. The pseudorandom function in the pairwise key hierarchy (see Figure 8-15) is the industry-standard SHA-1 cryptographic hash. The Group Key hierarchy can also use SHA-1, but that is not mandated.

Group Key Hierarchy

In a similar fashion, the GMK can be used as the root for the GTK, as illustrated in Figure 8-16.

Figure 8-16   *802.11i Group Key Hierarchy*

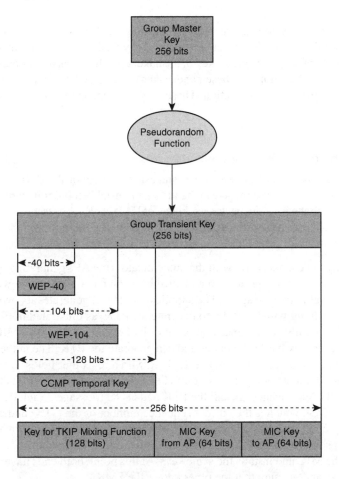

In contrast to the PMK, which is mutually derived, the AP generates the GMK. The AP uses the GMK to generate the GTK, which has a length up to 256 bits and is translated into the various temporal keys used for multicast packets. The GTK can be used with WEP, TKIP, or CCMP. Depending on the encryption protocol used for group communication, its length differs. For

40- or 104-bit WEP, the GTK is used to generate a 40- or 128-bit WEP key. For CCMP, it is used to generate the 128-bit TK. For TKIP, 256 bits are generated and further partitioned, as described earlier for the PTK. If not all the stations support the same encryption protocols, it is possible for a station and AP to support a weaker encryption protocol for group communication than for pairwise communication. For example, in an ESS containing TKIP and CCMP-capable stations, the CCMP-capable stations could use CCMP for communicating with the AP and use TKIP for group communications. TKIP would be the lowest common denominator.

Key Exchange

After master key establishment, both sides share a PMK and are ready to negotiate the transient keys they will use for this particular session. They do this via security handshakes known as the 4-way handshake and the group key handshake. Each has a particular purpose and is performed as necessary. After either of these handshakes occurs, the keys derived are stored and used for pairwise or group communication. These keys are kept as long as they are valid and then destroyed.

The 4-Way Handshake

After a successful EAP authentication and establishment of the PMKs (or if PSKs are being used), a station must use the 4-way handshake to establish the transient keys with the AP. The 4-way handshake is a four-packet exchange of EAPOL-Key messages. It ensures that both sides still share a current PMK to exchange nonces to be used in building the key hierarchy and to exchange the GTK. Figure 8-17 illustrates the 4-way handshake.

The 4-way handshake starts with the authenticator (the AP) generating a nonce value. This nonce serves as replay protection and must be a value not used before with this PMK. It sends this nonce value in Message 1. The supplicant (station) generates its own nonce and uses the two nonces along with the PMK to generate the PTK, as illustrated in Figure 8-15. The supplicant replies with its own nonce and proof of its PMK by including a MIC in Message 2. The authenticator now has both nonces and can generate the PTK. The authenticator verifies the MIC that the client puts in Message 2, along with a few other fields. If the verification is successful, the authenticator generates the GTK if necessary. It sends the GTK in Message 3, which also tells the supplicant to install the PTK and GTK. Message 3 includes the receive sequence counter (RSC), which is the current sequence number of the GTK, and allows the station to detect replayed broadcast messages. The supplicant verifies the MIC in Message 3, installs the keys, and sends Message 4, which is a confirmation. After the reception, the authenticator verifies the MIC and installs the same keys. At this point, both ends have the same pairwise and group keys and are sure that the other knows the PMK.

Figure 8-17   *4-Way Handshake*

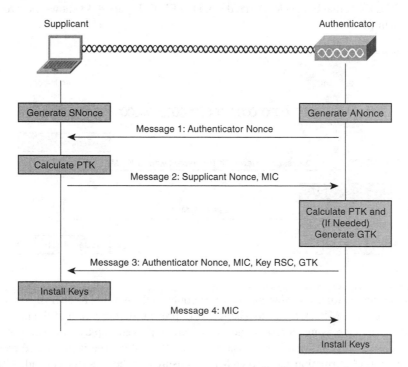

The nonces used in this exchange must be nonrepeating. The easiest way to do this is to have them increase. However, if the nonces are chosen randomly, there is more protection against a precomputed attack against the server or the client. The downside of this approach is having to remember all the previously used nonces to ensure that they are never reused. However, the record of nonces can be cleared when a new PMK is computed.

The Group Key Handshake

In a way similar to the 4-way handshake, the group key handshake facilitates provisioning of a new GTK. The authenticator uses this handshake if only the GTK, but not the PTK, needs changing. The authenticator initiates the group key handshake in the event of a Michael MIC failure in either direction, upon deauthentication or disassociation of a station, or at a specified interval. In addition, a station can request a renegotiation of the GTK, which the authenticator then initiates. The station initiates this request with a special EAPOL-Key packet.

The GTK is only a two-message EAPOL-Key exchange. It uses the EAPOL KEK and the EAPOL KCK that both sides derived from the PMK. Figure 8-18 shows the two-message group key handshake.

Figure 8-18 *Group Key Handshake*

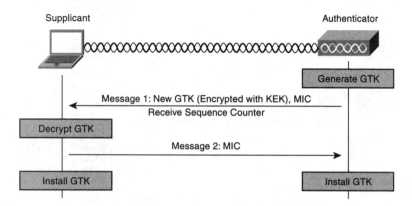

The authenticator sends Message 1, which contains the new GTK, encrypted with the KEK. The message has a MIC, which uses the KCK, to prevent modification of the message in transit. It also has an increasing receive sequence counter to prevent replays. In response, the client sends Message 2 as a confirmation. Message 2 has little in it but the incremented receive sequence counter as confirmation and its own MIC to ensure that the message is valid. After each side has received the other's message, the group keys can be calculated as described in the "Group Key Hierarchy" section.

Security Associations

Security associations are a record of the policy and keys that one or more entities share. In 802.11i, a security association (SA) records the security parameters that a pair or group of stations and APs have negotiated or configured to communicate with each other. These parameters include the cipher suites chosen, MAC addresses of the parties sharing the SA, the keys they have negotiated, SSIDs, and the lifetime of the SA. 802.11i defines several types of security associations, which are illustrated in Figure 8-19.

Figure 8-19 *Security Associations*

PMKSA

The Pairwise Master Key Security Association (PMKSA) is created after a successful 802.1x negotiation as part of EAP, or when a Preshared Key (PSK) is configured. It ties the PMK to a lifetime, the authenticator MAC address, and other authorization information. A PMKSA can be stored for future contact with the same AP. If a station roams to another new AP, it will generate a new PMKSA for it, but when it roams back to the first AP, it can use its original PMKSA.

PTKSA

The Pairwise Transient Key Security Association (PTKSA) is created after the 4-way handshake completes. It is dependent on the PMKSA and is stored for as long as the PMKSA is valid or until the station is deauthenticated. The PTKSA includes the supplicant and authenticator MAC addresses, the pairwise cipher suite selected, and the PTK itself.

GTKSA

The Group Transient Key Security Association (GTKSA) is created during the 4-way handshake or updated during a group key handshake. It stores the GTK, the broadcast/multicast cipher suites, and for which direction the GTK is good. It might also store other authorization or capability parameters such as the SSID. GTKs are unidirectional and are used either for transmitting or receiving. In the case of an AP-based network (ESS), the GTKSA is used between an AP and its associated stations. In the case of an Ad-Hoc mode (IBSS), the GTKSA is used from one station to all other stations.

Security Association Destruction

Transient keys last only as long as a station is associated to an AP. When a station loses association or authentication with an AP, it deletes the transient security associations and all keys associated with them. The PMKSA can persist until it expires.

WPA and Cisco Protocols

802.11i has taken a long time to come to fruition. Although work began in 2001, the standard was only ratified in 2004. Speed is not the primary criterion for standards development, nor should it necessarily be. Standards should be developed under the watchful and considerate eyes of many people, and such consideration takes time. Undue speed can lead to insufficient analysis, which can lead to gaping security holes such as we have seen in WEP. Vendors, however, do view time-to-market as a primary criterion, which has led to some variants of 802.11i.

Cisco Protocols

Cisco was concerned about the lack of solutions for the problems in the WEP protocol. 802.11i was progressing slowly, so Cisco developed its own versions of key mixing and message integrity check algorithms. Cisco Key Integrity Protocol (CKIP) is the Cisco version of the TKIP protocol. It has a key mixing function based on an algorithm presented by Doug Whiting to the 802.11i Task Group. It involves a sequence number to ensure that the actual WEP key changes from packet to packet. Thus, it also thwarts the Fluhrer-Mantin-Shamir attack. Cisco Message Integrity Check serves the same purpose as the 802.11i MIC and is in fact stronger than Michael. It is based on Shai Halevi and Hugo Krawczyk's MMH hashing algorithm. It also prevents replayed packets by using an increasing counter and remembering sequence numbers it has seen. Cisco developed a proprietary rekeying mechanism as part of CKIP. Rather than being derived by both wireless parties, as they are in 802.11i, keys are calculated by the AP and are distributed via EAPOL-Key packets. This makes implementation on the client much easier. These algorithms allowed Cisco to close the WEP holes quickly, but they were not the algorithms eventually selected by the 802.11i Task Group. Thus, Cisco now offers two versions of each of these algorithms: the proprietary Cisco version and the standard 802.11i version. Cisco recommends the 802.11i standard protocols.

WPA

As was mentioned in the introduction to this chapter, WPA is an industry standard, developed from 802.11i drafts by the Wi-Fi Alliance. The alliance adopted as much of the 802.11i version available at the time as it could. It was intended to bring a more immediate standard than the IEEE committee could provide, yet be as forward compatible with 802.11i as possible. The Wi-Fi Alliance did so with the intention of adopting 802.11i when it became finalized. The Wi-Fi Alliance will call the new standard WPA2.

The Wi-Fi Alliance (http://www.wi-fi.org) is an industry association of more than 200 companies, including 802.11 equipment manufacturers, chip foundries, software companies, and many others. Its role is to promote 802.11 gear and to certify interoperability of products. Its members have a strong interest in seeing 802.11 succeed and be as widespread as possible.

Like Cisco, the Wi-Fi Alliance and its other members were concerned about the security problems in 802.11. Security vulnerabilities stood to give the standard a bad name and hurt everyone's sales. This is why the Wi-Fi Alliance developed WPA.

WPA is based on an early draft (version 3.0) of the 802.11i standard, and it primarily implements TKIP, 802.1x authentication, and key management. WPA also includes the requirement to use open key authentication and to obsolete the flawed shared-key authentication. Administrators can use either 802.1x or preshared keys. The PSKs can be configured using either 64 hexadecimal characters or an ASCII pass phrase via a hash algorithm. Like 802.11i, WPA capabilities are advertised in beacons, probe responses, association requests, and reassociation requests.

A network can mix WPA and legacy WEP nodes in what is called *mixed mode*. However, the security of these networks can be compromised using WEP vulnerabilities, and this should be used only temporarily for networks in transition to WPA. WPA is not interoperable with WPA2 because the 802.1x specifications are different.

Security Problems Addressed

Now that you have seen the security mechanisms in 802.11i and WPA, it is fitting to review the vulnerabilities described in Chapter 6 and examine which ones are and are not addressed.

Reconnaissance

802.11i does nothing to address reconnaissance. However, the improvements in encryption, integrity, and authentication significantly strengthen the security of the networks behind them, so they might be less likely to be targeted. Attacks on them will be much less likely to succeed.

DoS Attacks

The disassociation, deauthentication, and transmit-duration attacks are all attacks on the MAC layer. They allow for selective DoS. Unfortunately, 802.11i does nothing to prevent this. These attacks will not be stopped until there is authentication of management and control frames. Hopefully, a future standard will address these. However, it is important to remember that because nothing can be done about radio frequency jamming or interference attacks, there will never be a complete solution to DoS attacks. Wireless networks will always be subject to DoS.

Shared-Key Authentication Attacks

802.11i solves the attacks on the flawed shared-key authentication by obsoleting this authentication method.

MAC Address Spoofing

The standard provides a way to prevent MAC address spoofing by including portions of the MAC address in the MIC calculation. TKIP does this with the padded MSDU that goes into the Michael algorithm. CCMP does this with the additional authentication data included in its MIC calculation. In addition, by providing strong alternative access control methods, it should eliminate the need for authentication based on MAC addresses. MAC address–based authentication was largely a response to not having strong alternatives to keep attackers out.

Message Modification and Replay

The MIC allows a recipient to detect any modification of messages. Because it includes a key that the attacker cannot know, the attacker cannot recalculate it. Also, because it is a hash, the attacker cannot make appropriate modifications to it by flipping bits in the MIC. Thus, the inductive attack is also defeated. Messages cannot be replayed because of the increasing packet counters (TSC in TKIP, PN in CCMP). Finally, the MIC prevents an attacker from changing the packet counter to attempt to rebroadcast a message with a new packet counter.

Dictionary-Based WEP Key Recovery

WEP keys are no longer based on dictionary words, so attackers cannot guess. However, WPA includes a standard for the creation of Preshared Master Keys based on ASCII characters. This opens up the possibility of a dictionary attack. If an attacker can guess the password that was used to generate the PMK, he should be able to successfully communicate with a protected network. If an administrator chooses to use ASCII-based PMKs, he should make sure that the passphrase used is long and includes nonalphanumeric characters. Because it is a one-time configuration and not a user password that will have to be typed more than once, it should be possible to generate it by machine.

WEP Keystream Recovery

802.11i renders WEP keystream recovery useless. CCMP uses a block-based cipher, so there is no keystream to recover. TKIP's key mixing algorithm ensures that each key, and thus each keystream, will be used only once. Although there are still chosen plaintext attacks in which an attacker might be able to recover the keystream, the keystream will not be useful for anything.

Fluhrer-Mantin-Shamir Weak Key Attack

This attack is prevented in the same manner as the preceding attack. The FMS attack relies on receiving a large number of packets encrypted with the same WEP key. CCMP does not use WEP, and TKIP changes the WEP key with each packet. In addition, TKIP specifically places a value in the middle IV octet and swaps the first and third octets of the TSC to prevent known weak RC4 keys. Therefore, even if a future attack based on the weak keys is developed, TKIP should still prevent it.

Rogue APs

802.11i does nothing to prevent rogue APs. Some of the 802.1x EAP methods address this by providing for certificates. By using certificates, the AP is required to prove its identity to the client. If the client is configured correctly, and if the software does not allow the client to circumvent the protections easily, these methods should inhibit rogue APs. There are social engineering attacks in which a rogue AP tries to mimic a real AP to capture traffic or passwords. This is why users for the most part should not be trusted to make decisions about whether an AP is or is not legitimate. It should be left to software safeguards that can verify identity without the user's input.

Security Considerations of EAP

802.11i relies on strong EAP authentication methods to generate the PMKs that serve as the basis for its security. If the underlying keys are compromised, or if the EAP methods used have flaws, the security provided by TKIP and CCMP will also be flawed. 802.11i does not specifically address the security of individual EAP methods.

There is a need for guidelines for EAP methods and the security features they should support. Jesse Walker has written a draft of such a document. Its recommendations include mutual authentication, resistance to dictionary attacks, and the ability to generate keys of at least 128 bits.

Chapter 6 mentions attacks on LEAP and PEAP. 802.11i does not remedy these. Use of strong passwords is the solution for LEAP attacks. Cisco PEAP implementation is not vulnerable to man-in-the-middle (MitM) attacks if used properly with server certificates. PEAP version 2, which is still under development as an Internet Engineering Task Force (IETF) standard, addresses PEAP MitM attacks for all vendors.

Summary

Security problems led to development of the 802.11i standard and a partial implementation of it, known as WPA. 802.11i introduces robust security protocols, including TKIP and CCMP, plus authentication and key management algorithms. TKIP works with existing WEP encryption hardware, whereas CCMP uses the AES algorithm for stronger security. TKIP uses a key mixing algorithm to protect the base Temporal Encryption Key and to help avoid RC4 weaknesses. It uses the Michael algorithm for message integrity but must protect Michael with additional countermeasures. CCMP uses two different modes of AES, one for confidentiality and the other for message integrity.

802.11i includes key management between APs and stations. Master keys are established by one of the EAP authentication methods. The master keys serve as the root of a key hierarchy. Transient keys are negotiated from the master keys using key handshakes. The 4-way handshake is used to prove liveness of the PMK and to establish a fresh PTK. The group key handshake is used to refresh the GTK. 802.11i has taken years to be developed. WPA is a subset of 802.11i that was adopted by the Wi-Fi Alliance to get some of the benefits of 802.11i to market quickly. Cisco also implemented a protocol suite called *CKIP* for the same purpose. 802.11i will supplant CKIP and WPA.

802.11i addresses the known attacks with WEP in addition to some of the other attacks on 802.11 in general. It does not deal with weaknesses in EAP methods such as LEAP and PEAP.

CHAPTER 9

SWAN: End-to-End Security Deployment

Cisco Structured Wireless-Aware Network (SWAN) solution provides integration for Cisco WLAN access points (AP 1200, AP 1100, and AP 350), wireless clients (Cisco, CCX, and non-Cisco/non-CCX clients), CiscoWorks Wireless LAN Solution Engine (WLSE), and Cisco wired switches and routers. This enables scalability, manageability, reliability, and ease of deployment for small, medium, and large enterprise and vertical networks. Furthermore, the SWAN solution enables end-to-end security, end-to-end quality of service (QoS), and Layer 2/Layer 3 mobility. Cisco SWAN solution can scale to manage thousands of APs and thousands of WLAN users across a large network.

This chapter introduces Cisco SWAN architecture. WLAN deployment modes, including standalone AP mode, SWAN nonswitching deployment mode, and SWAN central switching deployment mode, are discussed in detail. SWAN network concepts, along with SWAN network elements, are also discussed. Most of the focus is on enabling end-to-end wireless and wired network security using the SWAN network components. Infrastructure and client 802.1x/EAP (Extensible Authentication Protocol) authentication, radio monitoring functions, Fast Secure Roaming, local 802.1x RADIUS authentication, and security policy monitoring functions are discussed in detail.

Overview of SWAN Security Features

Cisco SWAN solution provides several security features to enable end-to-end security implementation capabilities. These features are as follows:

- Infrastructure and client EAP/802.1x authentication
- Fast Secure Roaming (both Layer 2 and Layer 3) using Cisco Centralized Key Management (CCKM)
- Radio management (RM) functions such as standalone or integrated wireless IDS mode for access points (APs), client-based scanning (Cisco/CCX clients), rogue AP detection and suppression, non-802.11 interference detection, and location management services (including user tracking)
- Local 802.1x RADIUS authentication service
- Security policy monitoring
- Centralized WLAN user data aggregation (via the SWAN central switching mode)

Infrastructure and client EAP/802.1x authentication, Fast Secure Roaming, and radio management functions are bundled as wireless domain services (WDS). Thus, the WDS is used to centralize control functions in a SWAN-enabled wireless and wired network. Using centralization of control functions via WDS, WLAN user mobility is expedited using the Fast Secure Roaming feature, and radio management functions are scaled and easily managed. An AP can function as a WDS server, a WDS client, or both. Alternatively, the WDS services can be run on a Catalyst switch or on a router, in which case the switch or router acts as the WDS server in a SWAN-enabled network. WDS services were introduced in AP IOS release 12.2(11)JA and above.

Infrastructure authentication is used to authenticate WDS client APs to the WDS server. During this process, a shared encryption key is derived via EAP authentication to secure traffic between the WDS client AP and the WDS server. To enable infrastructure authentication, EAP authentication credentials need to be configured on each WDS client AP. Each WDS client AP will authenticate with the RADIUS server through the WDS server to secure the link between itself and the WDS server.

Local 802.1x RADIUS authentication can be enabled on the WDS server or on a WDS client AP at a remote (branch) location to enable fallback RADIUS services. Radio management functions are enabled on the WDS server and WDS client APs, in addition to Cisco and CCX clients, to measure and report radio measurements. It is optional to use Cisco and CCX clients for radio measurements, but it is recommended as a best practice if possible. Using these radio measurements, rogue AP detection/suppression, non-802.11 interference detection, and client tracking features are enabled.

CiscoWorks WLSE provides centralized wireless management functions, including network management, radio management, and security policy monitoring functions, in a SWAN-enabled wireless and wired network. Security policy monitoring can be enabled on the WLSE to monitor for consistent application of security policies across all deployed and managed APs. Alerts are generated for violations such as Service Set Identifiers (SSID), broadcasts, 802.1x EAP settings, and wired equivalent privacy (WEP). Alerts can be delivered by e-mail, syslog, or SNMP trap notifications. Finally, WLSE can be used to monitor for response time (and availability) of RADIUS servers (including Cisco secure access control servers [ACS]). Cisco EAP (LEAP), Protected EAP (PEAP), Flexible Authentication via Secure Tunneling EAP protocol (EAP-FAST), and generic RADIUS authentication types are supported.

SWAN central switching mode enables multiple-layer security defense for WLAN deployment, Layer 3 fast secure roaming, and centralized policy control via the WLAN traffic aggregation switch. SWAN central switching mode is discussed in detail in the next section.

WLAN Deployment Modes and Security Features

Cisco wireless LAN solution can be deployed in different modes to facilitate large, medium, or small branch offices and remote networks. Three basic WLAN deployment modes are available:

- **Standalone AP deployment mode**—In this deployment mode, the AP provides full 802.11 functionality (acting as an 802.11 infrastructure device) along with security, QoS, and Layer 2 mobility.

- **SWAN nonswitching deployment mode**—In this SWAN deployment mode, the AP provides full 802.11 functionality along with QoS functionality. Several security functions, including Layer 2 Fast Secure Roaming, local 802.1x authentication service, and radio management functions, are centralized at the WDS server level.

- **SWAN central switching deployment mode**—In this SWAN deployment mode, the AP provides full 802.11 functionality along with QoS functionality. Both data (802.11 user traffic) and control traffic (Wireless LAN Control Context Protocol [WLCCP] traffic) are aggregated and forwarded through the central switch, such as the Catalyst 6500, equipped with a WLAN services module. The central switch is enabled with a WDS server to provide 802.11 user data aggregation, end-to-end security, Layer 2 fast secure roaming, Layer 3 roaming, WDS scalability, centralized management (including RF management), and QoS functions. The 802.11 user traffic is encapsulated using the generic routing encapsulation (GRE) protocol and is tunneled from the APs to the central switch.

The standalone AP mode is the traditional deployment mode that has been used and will be used in WLAN networks. Hot-spot WLAN networks are likely to use standalone AP deployment mode if the service provider chooses not to deploy the WDS (nonswitching) mode. SWAN nonswitching deployment mode, in which the WDS server typically runs on an AP or a router, can be deployed in small, medium, and branch office networks and in specific hot-spot deployments (for example, in a coffee shop WLAN deployment). Figure 9-1 illustrates the SWAN nonswitching deployment mode in a small, medium, or branch office scenario.

In Figure 9-1, an AP or a router can be used as the WDS server to aggregate all control messages. Fast secure roaming services using the Cisco Centralized Key Management (CCKM) protocol can be deployed for Cisco and CCX clients in this deployment mode. WDS server enables fast secure roaming using the CCKM protocol for EAP/802.1x clients (both Cisco and CCX) associated with Cisco APs. Fast secure roaming services for EAP/802.1x clients are explained in detail later in this chapter. Radio monitoring (RM) services are also enabled using this deployment mode. When RM services are enabled, Cisco APs, Cisco clients, and CCX clients collect RF network information and forward it to the WDS server. Fast secure roaming and RM functions are enabled between the WDS client APs and the WDS server using the WLCCP protocol. Finally, fast secure roaming using CCKM and RM functions is not supported for third-party (that is, non-Cisco and non-CCX) clients.

Figure 9-1   *SWAN Nonswitching Deployment Mode*

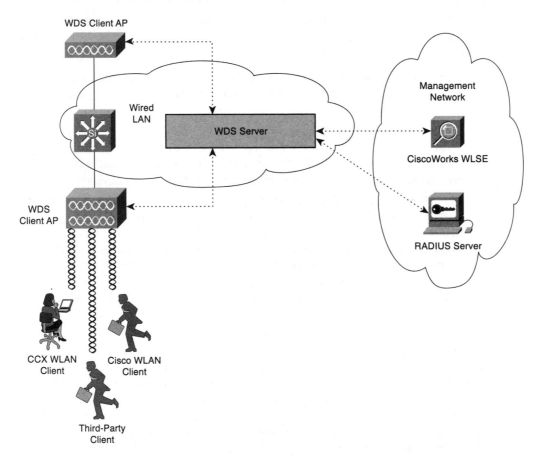

Central switching deployment mode is a newly introduced wired/wireless integration capability on the Cisco Catalyst series switches. Figure 9-2 illustrates a sample deployment topology for the central switching solution. As shown in the figure, the APs can be placed multiple IP hops away from the central switch. GRE tunneling architecture (specifically mGRE tunnel architecture) aggregates the wireless user traffic and transports the user traffic to the central switch. WDS services are enabled on the central switch, where all control traffic is aggregated from the WDS client APs. This single point of ingress provides the capability to apply various security and QoS policies on the central switch. It is recommended that you integrate the central switching mode for WLAN/wired LAN integration at the distribution layer level, but it alternatively can be located in the data center. Finally, note that switching infrastructure between the AP and the central switch is transparent as far as WLAN traffic aggregation and does not need to have WDS services enabled.

Figure 9-2   *SWAN Central Switching Deployment Mode*

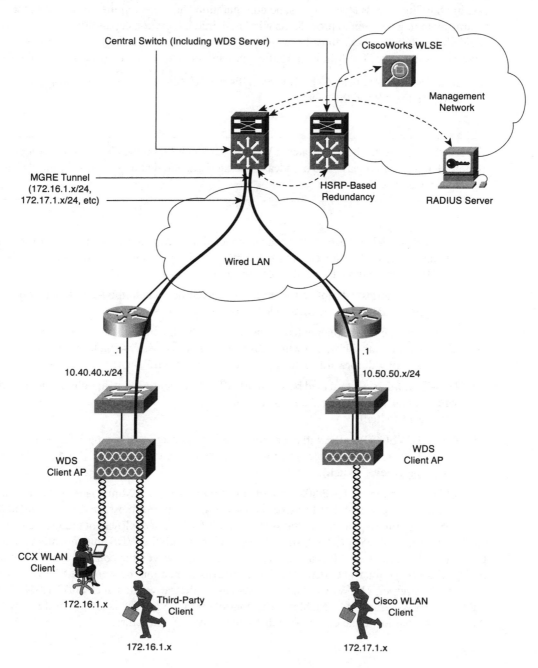

It should be noted that mGRE architecture creates a Layer 3 overlay network on top of the existing building access layer. That is, no configuration change is required to integrate the central switching solution to provide the wireless/wired integration capabilities. However, you could choose to implement an isolated VLAN for wireless users (at each floor level) as a security best practice. The following traffic types are tunneled or natively bridged by the AP:

- IP unicast and multicast WLAN user traffic is GRE tunneled upstream/downstream between the AP and the switch.

NOTE   You are encouraged to check the latest SWAN documentation on the Cisco website for details on how IP unicast, multicast, and broadcast messages are handled in the SWAN central switching deployment mode.

- IP broadcast WLAN user traffic can be tunneled upstream and downstream between the AP and the central switch except for Address Resolution Protocol (ARP) messages. Note that IP broadcast tunneling is disabled by default.
    - ARP queries will not be forwarded to the central switch; the AP will perform proxy ARP using the MAC address of the central switch.
    - Certain client implementations use ARP to check whether a given IP address is in use by other hosts, in which case the ARP messages contain targetIP = srcIP. The AP will forward such ARP requests to the central switch for processing.
- Non-IP traffic is *not* tunneled between the AP and the central switch; rather, non-IP traffic will be locally bridged by the AP via the native infrastructure (for example, the access layer level switch).
- Control (WLCCP) traffic will not be tunneled and is bridged (using the AP's native VLAN if 802.1Q trunking is enabled) by the AP via the native infrastructure (for example, the access layer level switch).

It should be noted that all EAP/802.1x authentication messages, RM messages (such as radio measurements), successful 802.11 associations, and other control messages are forwarded to the WDS server running on the central switch via WLCCP. As a deployment requirement, each AP (referred to as *WDS client AP*) should be configured with the WDS authentication credential. After the WDS client AP is authenticated to the WDS server, the control path is secured (using RC4 encryption and HMAC-MD5 data integrity protection) between the WDS client AP and the WDS server. The WLCCP traffic is sent using the native (management) VLAN of the AP (when VLAN trunking is enabled). The control (WLCCP) traffic is always bridged by the AP and is forwarded to the central switch via the native infrastructure.

Using the central switching integration mode, multiple layers of security can be enforced in which the first layer of security is at the AP level, the second layer of security is at the central switch level, and the third layer of security can be implemented using additional services that are available on the central switch.

Table 9-1 lists the security features that are available in each deployment mode. It should be noted that centralized configuration and software management for APs, bridges, fault monitoring, and trending and reporting functions are grouped as centralized network management.

Table 9-1   *Security Feature Support for WLAN Deployment Modes*

	Standalone AP Mode	SWAN Nonswitching Deployment Mode	SWAN Central Switching Deployment Mode
802.1x/EAP user authentication	Yes	Yes	Yes
WEP, WPA, AES support (data confidentiality)	Yes	Yes	Yes
Multiple VLANs (user groups) support	Yes	Yes	Yes
Layer 2/Layer 3/Layer 4 security filters (AP level)	Yes	Yes	Yes
Admin authentication (TACACS+ or RADIUS)	Yes	Yes	Yes
SSH support on the AP	Yes	Yes	Yes
Local 802.1x RADIUS authentication service	Yes	Yes	Yes
Centralized network management via WLSE	Yes	Yes	Yes
Centralized security policy monitoring via WLSE	Yes	Yes	Yes
Infrastructure authentication	No	Yes	Yes
Layer-2 802.1x fast secure roaming (CCKM)	No	Yes	Yes
Rogue AP detection and suppression via WLSE	No	Yes	Yes
Non-802.11 interference detection	No	Yes	Yes

continues

Table 9-1 *Security Feature Support for WLAN Deployment Modes (Continued)*

	Standalone AP Mode	SWAN Nonswitching Deployment Mode	SWAN Central Switching Deployment Mode
Integrated and standalone (scan-only) wireless IDS modes	No	Yes	Yes
WDS-based user tracking via WLSE	No	Yes	Yes
Layer 3 fast secure roaming and Layer 3 roaming (CCKM-enabled and non-CCKM)	No	No	Yes
Centralized WLAN user data aggregation on the switch (such as single-point of ingress using mGRE tunnels)	No	No	Yes
Centralized security management on the switch (Layer 3/Layer 4 ACLs, rate limiting, and so on)	No	No	Yes

SWAN Infrastructure Authentication

The first phase of deploying a SWAN-enabled WLAN network is to enable infrastructure authentication between WDS client APs and the WDS server. The requirement for infrastructure authentication is to securely authenticate each WDS client AP (as well as each WLSE) to the WDS server and secure the communication between the WDS client APs and the WDS server. This also allows the WDS server to easily identify the authorized APs in a SWAN-enabled network.

Figure 9-3 illustrates the infrastructure authentication message exchange between WDS client APs, the WDS server, and the RADIUS server. The communication link between WLSE and the WDS server is also authenticated and authorized using infrastructure authentication. As shown in Figure 9-3, the WDS client AP(s) and WLSE authenticate via the WDS server to the RADIUS server. This is enabled using EAP authentication between the WDS clients and the WDS server using a user ID and password credentials. It is recommended that you create a unique user ID and password per WDS client AP (and also per WLSE) on the RADIUS server to authenticate with the WDS server. After the WDS client (WDS client AP or the WLSE) is authenticated, a key known as the Context Transfer Key (CTK) is derived simultaneously by the WDS client and the RADIUS server. At the end of successful EAP authentication, the RADIUS server securely communicates the CTK to the WDS server. Using this shared key (CTK) as the master key, encryption keys for WLCCP traffic are derived and periodically refreshed to secure the control traffic between the WDS client and the WDS server.

Figure 9-3 *SWAN Infrastructure Authentication*

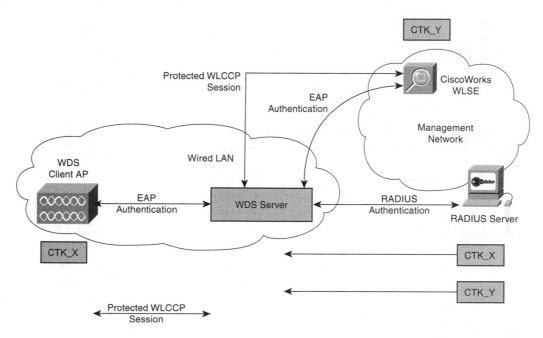

Autodiscovery of authorized APs can be executed on the WLSE using the WDS server, where the WDS server communicates information regarding authorized APs to the WLSE. In this scenario, the Cisco Discovery Protocol (CDP) is not needed, and WLCCP is used to discover and monitor authorized APs throughout the SWAN-enabled WLAN network.

Chapter 12, "WLAN Security Configuration Guidelines and Examples," discusses configuration required on the WDS clients (WDS client APs and the WLSE), the WDS server, and the RADIUS server to enable infrastructure authentication for both SWAN nonswitching deployment mode and the SWAN central switching deployment mode.

Radio Management and Wireless Intrusion Detection

As discussed previously, several RM functions can be enabled using the SWAN deployment modes. A key component of radio measurements is the capability of Cisco APs, in addition to Cisco and CCX (version 2.0 or above), to measure and report measured RF parameters to the WLSE. Using the Cisco SWAN solution, active APs can measure radio parameters while still servicing WLAN clients. Figure 9-4 illustrates radio monitoring using WDS client APs and Cisco CCX clients. As shown in Figure 9-4, collected RM data is sent to the WDS server, which aggregates the RM data and forwards it to the WLSE for analysis.

Figure 9-4 *SWAN Radio Monitoring*

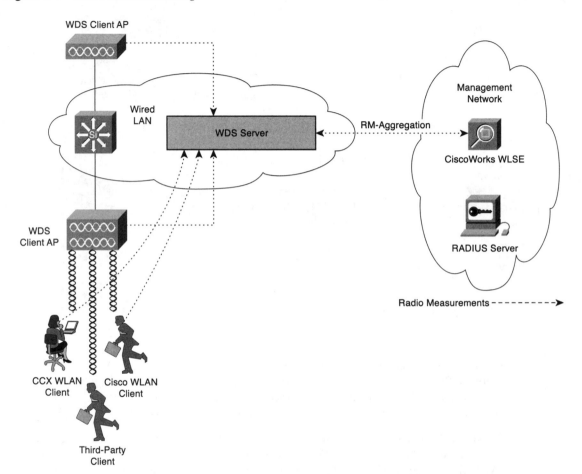

An AP configured on a specific channel can measure 802.11 and non-802.11 activity on that particular channel by gathering beacons, probe responses, the amount of 802.11 activity, and non-802.11 RF energy. When the AP is not transmitting or receiving (such as when it is not servicing an WLAN client), it can jump to an adjacent channel to scan for a short duration of time. The collected RM data is periodically sent to the WDS server. In addition to AP-based scanning, clients (Cisco and CCXv2.0 or above) can be enabled to scan, collect, and report RM data to the WDS server. Using the clients to enable radio monitoring is optional, but it is recommended because it increases the level of accuracy and expands the coverage area of the radio scan. Specifically, the clients can be used to scan areas where there is no AP radio coverage, including fringes of your RF network. The WLAN clients scan and report RM data only when they are associated with the managed (that is, authorized) AP on your network.

To enable WLSE to identify rogue APs, you must discover and identify managed APs and specify their location. You can import a floor plan (GIF/JPEG/BMP format) into the WLSE, and you must identify and place the discovered (that is, managed) APs at appropriate locations on the imported floor plan. After you do this, you can execute the assisted site survey feature to fine-tune the channel and power settings of the access points. The assisted site survey consists of two phases: the AP radio scan and the client walkabout procedure. The WLSE also uses the assisted site survey process to model the RF environment. Chapter 12 discusses the configuration required on the WDS client APs, the WDS server, WLAN clients, and the WLSE to enable radio management features for both SWAN nonswitching deployment mode and the SWAN central switching deployment mode.

After you execute the assisted site survey, it is recommended that you enable radio monitoring on all APs and associated Cisco CCX clients. When the WLSE determines that there are unidentified APs from the collected RM data, it triggers rogue AP alerts. Each rogue AP alert specifies which managed APs are reporting the rogue AP (along with measured signal strength, and so on). Location Manager can be used to triangulate the location of the rogue AP. The WLSE uses the collected RM data, along with the measured signal strength of the rogue AP from the reporting managed APs, to approximate the location of the rogue AP.

Figure 9-5 illustrates two different scenarios of rogue AP detection. In the first scenario, the rogue AP overlaps in RF coverage with the deployed and managed APs; in this case, WDS client AP 1 and 2 detect and report the rogue AP. In the second scenario, a Cisco or CCX client detects and reports the second rogue AP, which is outside the RF coverage area of the managed APs.

After the WLSE detects the rogue AP, the administrator has three choices:

- Use the WLSE to triangulate the location of the rogue AP and physically investigate it. If the rogue AP is within the customer premise and physically located, the administrator can remove it.

- The second option is to trace the rogue AP over the wired network to determine where it is connected (if it connected to the customer's wired network). WLSE uses detected BSSID (that is, MAC address) information of the rogue AP to trace it within the customer's wired network. If the rogue AP is successfully traced, the administrator has the option to shut down the switch port to which the rogue AP is connected.

- The last option is to identify the rogue AP as a "friendly" AP if it is determined to be a valid neighbor's AP. This can be the case in a multitenant environment.

Figure 9-6 illustrates the rogue AP alert that the WLSE generates. The detecting APs and detailed information regarding the rogue AP are displayed.

Figure 9-5 *SWAN Rogue AP Detection*

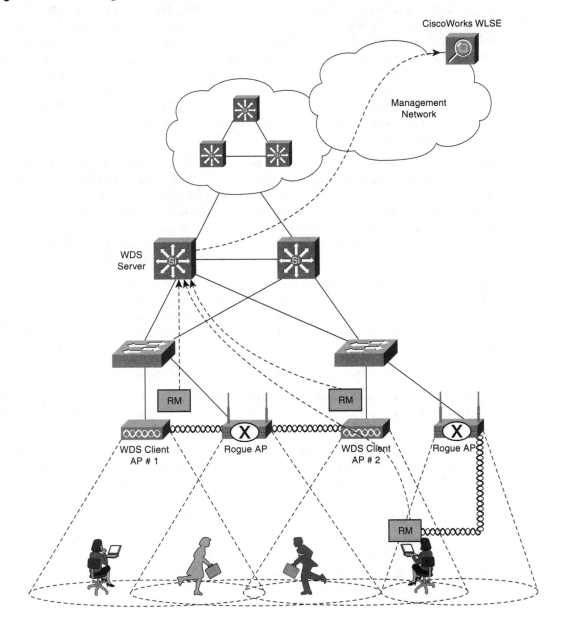

Figure 9-6   *SWAN WLSE Rogue AP Detection Alert*

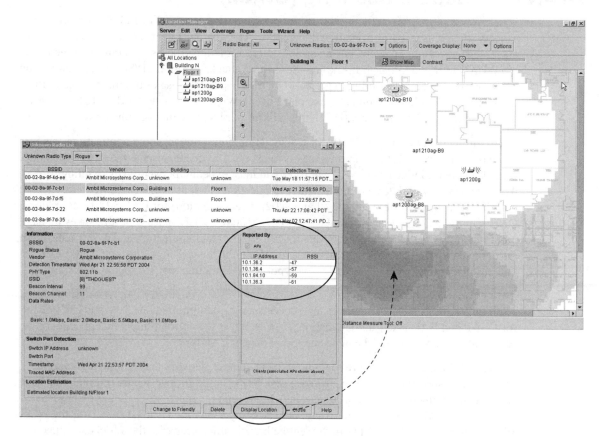

In addition to rogue AP detection and suppression, you can use RM data and user association data to locate users throughout a WLAN network.

Finally, you can use collected RM data to identify non-802.11 RF activity in a WLAN network as well. This is useful for identifying potential denial-of-service (DoS) attacks using RF transmitters (known as RF jamming). The WLSE generates a fault notification when the measured and reported non-802.11 RF activity exceeds a prespecified threshold. In addition to triggering a fault notification, you can configure the WLSE to periodically adjust the channel configuration parameters for the APs based on the collected RM data to avoid non-802.11 RF interference.

SWAN Fast Secure Roaming (CCKM)

When you deploy EAP/802.1x as the security mechanism, you need to address performance aspects when a user roams from an AP to another AP (whether Layer 2 or Layer 3 roam). As discussed in previous chapters, during an 802.11 reassociation process, you must reauthenticate the WLAN user to avoid man-in-the-middle (MitM) attacks. A full EAP/802.1x authentication is likely to increase the roaming delay between the APs. In the case of a remote branch office, if the RADIUS authentication is to take place over a WAN link (such as a RADIUS infrastructure located at the headquarters [HQ]), this will further increase the roaming delay.

The roaming delay during EAP/802.1x reassociation might impact some applications, such as voice over IP (VoIP). If the roaming delay is to exceed 150 ms, the user is likely to notice jitter (that is, decreased voice quality). Therefore, you must expedite between APs roaming for devices enabled with latency/jitter-sensitive applications such as VoIP. The SWAN fast secure roaming feature expedites roaming (that is, 802.11 reassociation) for EAP/802.1x users using Cisco Centralized Key Management (CCKM). Essentially, CCKM is a centralized key management functionality that removes the need for full 802.1x reauthentication and 4-way handshake (as defined by 802.11i/WPA specifications to refresh the unicast keys) during the 802.11 roam process. Refer to Chapter 8, "WLAN Encryption and Data Integrity Protocols," for more discussion on 802.11i and WPA, including unicast key derivation via 4-way handshake.

As of this writing (summer of 2004), fast secure roaming is supported on Cisco and CCX clients for LEAP and EAP-FAST authentication. However, fast secure roaming is independent of the EAP authentication type and can be supported on any EAP type.

Figure 9-7 illustrates fast secure roaming in large campus network and remote branch office scenarios. As shown in the figure, switch-based WDS is used for fast secure roaming in a large campus environment (for scalability reasons). In the remote branch office deployment scenario, you can use an AP or branch office router (and possibly a low-end Catalyst switch) as the WDS. When you use a localized WDS in the remote branch office scenario, the WDS can expedite roaming for CCKM users (for example, LEAP with CCKM and WPA-TKIP enabled VoIP devices) without having to reauthenticate the users to the RADIUS server. As noted previously, this provides a considerable amount of improvement in roaming performance in a remote branch office scenario and accommodates delay/jitter-sensitive applications such as VoIP over WLAN.

During the initial EAP/802.1x authentication process of a WLAN client, credentials are cached on the WDS server. When the client roams, the cached credentials to expedite the roaming process. Thus, SWAN enables infrastructure-based, scalable, and centrally manageable fast secure roaming for EAP/802.1x users. Figure 9-8 illustrates the initial EAP/802.1x authentication process in a SWAN-enabled network for a WLAN client. As shown in the figure, the WLAN client discovers the fast secure roaming–enabled AP during the initial discovery process using WPA Information Element (IE) and associates to the AP (Step 1). During the initial association process, the WLAN client needs to negotiate the ciphers such as Cisco Temporal Key Integrity Protocol (Cisco TKIP, also known as CKIP) or WPA-TKIP (Wi-Fi Protected Access TKIP). This process is similar to initial WPA association.

Figure 9-7   *Fast Secure Roaming Scenarios*

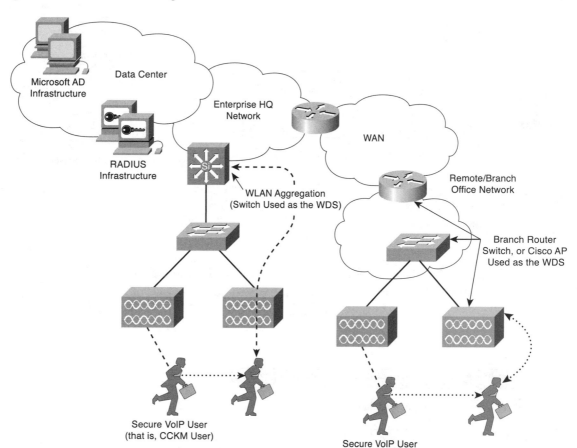

As shown in Figure 9-8, when the initial 802.11 association is successful (Step 2), the WLAN client authenticates with the WDS client AP, which relays the authentication request using the WLCCP protocol to the WDS server (Step 3). The WDS server communicates with the RADIUS server to authenticate the WLAN client. Thus, the WDS client AP does not communicate directly with the RADIUS server. At the end of initial Fast Secure Roaming authentication, both the WLAN client and the RADIUS server derive the Network Session Key (NSK). The RADIUS server securely communicates the derived NSK to the WDS server (Step 4). Subsequently, the WLAN client and the WDS server initiate a 4-way handshake through the WDS client AP where nonces (that is, random numbers) are exchanged to derive the Base Transient Key (BTK) and the Key Refresh Key (KRK), as shown in the figure (Step 5). For more discussion on the 802.11i (and WPA) 4-way handshake and key-derivation process, refer to Chapter 8.

Figure 9-8   *Initial 802.1x CCKM Client Authentication*

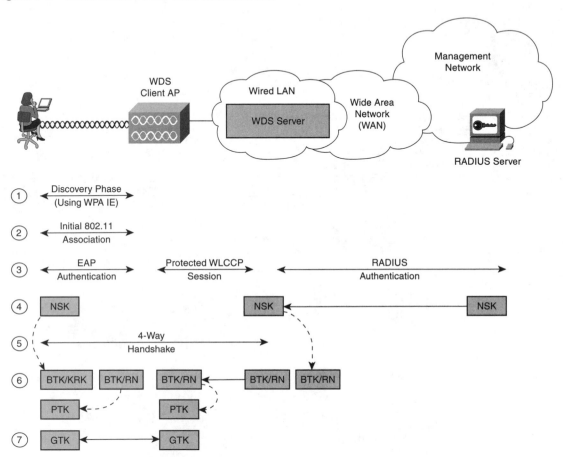

As shown in Figure 9-8, the WDS server securely communicates the BTK and the refresh number (RN) to the WDS client AP (Step 6). In a SWAN-enabled wireless/wired network, the WDS server maintains the keying information (BTK, KRK, and RN) for each CCKM client. The WDS client AP and WLAN client derive the Pairwise Transient Key (PTK) as a function of the BTK. After the PTK is derived, the WDS client AP securely communicates the Group Transient Key (GTK) to the WLAN client (Step 7). See Table 9-2 for a description of keys derived during the Fast Secure Roaming initial authentication process.

Table 9-2   *CCKM Key Hierarchy*

Key	Description
NSK	The NSK is derived at the end of successful EAP authentication by the WLAN client and the RADIUS server.
BTK	The BTK is derived by the WDS server and the WLAN client for the purposes of deriving the actual encryption keys (such as PTK). BTK is a function nonce (that is, random number) exchanged between the WLAN client and the WDS server and NSK.
KRK	The KRK is used during the roaming process to authenticate the WLAN client to the WDS server. KRK is derived as a function of nonces (that is, random numbers) exchanged between the WLAN client and the WDS server and using the NSK.
PTK	The PTK is used to derive the encryption and MIC keys for the user data protection between the WLAN client and the AP. PTK is derived as a function of BTK, refresh number (RN), and BSSID. During the initial authentication, RN is set to 1.
GTK	The AP uses the GTK to transmit broadcast/multicast messages to the WLAN clients. The AP derives and maintains the GTK. GTK is communicated to the WLAN client using a portion of the PTK.

Figure 9-9 shows the reassociation message exchange for a fast secure roaming client. As shown in the figure, the fast secure roaming client sends an 802.11 reassociation message request authenticated using its KRK to the new AP. The new AP (that is, the client WDS AP) relays the reassociation request to the WDS server. The WDS server verifies the reassociation request using the client's KRK. If successful, the WDS server sends the client's BTK and received RN to the new AP. The new AP, in turn, uses the BTK, RN, and its Basic Service Set Identifier (BSSID) to derive the PTK. Finally, the new AP sends its GTK to the WLAN client encrypted using a portion of the PTK. At this point, a full 802.11 reassociation is executed, and the WLAN client can resume its data transfer to the new AP.

As shown in Figure 9-9, the reassociation process is expedited using the WDS server, and a total of three messages are required between the WLAN client and the new AP. Note that in the case of a non-CCKM EAP/802.1x client, a full EAP/802.1x reauthentication is required. In the case of a non-CCKM WPA client, a full EAP/802.1x reauthentication, along with 4-way handshake, is required to reassociate with the new AP. Thus, there is a significant performance improvement in using the SWAN-enabled fast secure roaming implementation for latency-sensitive applications such as VoIP.

Finally, you can deploy fast secure roaming with Cisco TKIP (CKIP) or WPA. When you deploy fast secure roaming with WPA, WPA key management is replaced with fast secure roaming key management (that is, CCKM).

Figure 9-9   *SWAN-Enabled Fast Secure Roaming*

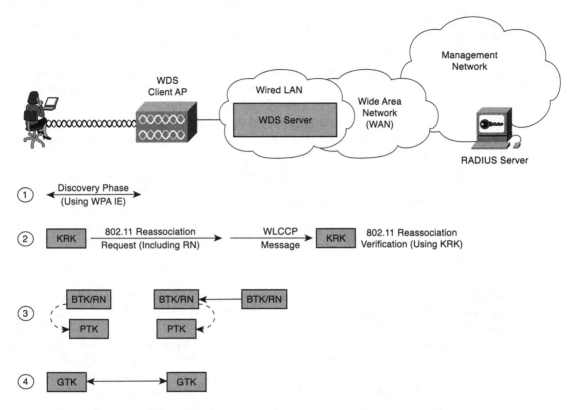

Local 802.1x RADIUS Authentication Service

A primary component of the 802.1x authentication process is the RADIUS server. WLAN users are unable to authenticate and are denied access to the WLAN network if the RADIUS server becomes unavailable. Therefore, it is necessary to provide redundancy for RADIUS services. Depending on the network topology, RADIUS redundancy deployment might differ. In the case of a remote branch office (or a remote store), it is preferred to deploy local redundancy for RADIUS services because the primary RADIUS server is usually located at a central site. Thus, if the primary RADIUS server becomes unreachable (for example, due to WAN link failure), you can use the local fallback RADIUS server. You can use the local 802.1x authentication service available on IOS APs (release 12.2[11]JA and above) or a 2600/3700 series router acting as the WDS server to provide fallback 802.1x RADIUS authentication service for LEAP and EAP-FAST users. You can configure standalone APs or the WDS server running the local 802.1x RADIUS authentication service to periodically monitor the availability of the primary RADIUS server. When the primary RADIUS server becomes available, the WDS server and the standalone APs will revert to using it.

The following is a summary of the local 802.1x RADIUS authentication service capabilities:

- The local 802.1x RADIUS server can reside within an active AP (on a standalone AP, WDS client AP, or an AP acting as the WDS server). Alternatively, the local 802.1x RADIUS server can reside on a branch office router (2600/3700 series).

- The local 802.1x RADIUS server will attach to the standard RADIUS UDP port number (such as UDP port number 1812 for authentication) and listen for RADIUS request packets.

- The local 802.1x RADIUS server handle client authentication and AP infrastructure authentication.

- An operator will manually configure the database of valid users. The database will not be automatically synchronized with the primary RADIUS server. Up to 50 users can be supported on the local 802.1x RADIUS server.

- If a username is removed from the corporate server for security reasons (such as an employee quitting), the operators must remember to remove the name from each of the remote servers.

- Configurable parameters on the local 802.1x RADIUS server are as follows:

  - **NAS settings**—Specifies the IP address and shared secret for an AP

  - **User account configuration**—Username, password (both cleartext and NT-hash formats), and group ID association

  - **Group settings**—IETF attribute 27 (session timeout value), list of allowed SSIDs, client lock-out parameters (number of failed attempts to lock out a client and the lock-out timer before a locked out client is allowed to reauthenticate)

The local RADIUS server is preconfigured on a standalone AP or on the WDS server (if the functionality is available) as the secondary RADIUS server. When the primary RADIUS server becomes unreachable (the default is three consecutive nonresponses from the RADIUS server), the standalone AP or the WDS server falls back to the specified local RADIUS server. Figure 9-10 shows the deployment of a local 802.1x RADIUS authentication service in a remote branch office scenario. When an authenticator (standalone AP or the WDS server) fails to reach the primary RADIUS server after a certain number of tries (the default is three but is configurable), the authenticator falls back to the local RADIUS server (defined as the secondary RADIUS server).

Figure 9-10 *Local 802.1x RADIUS Authentication Service Deployment*

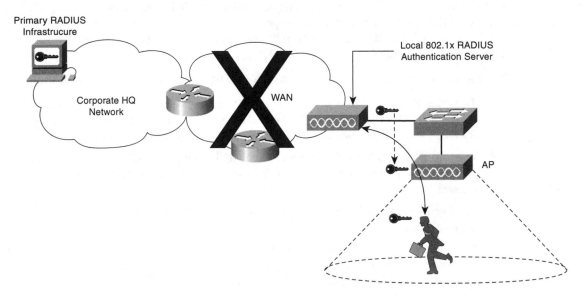

A "dead RADIUS server" timer interval is configurable on each AP to recheck for the availability of the primary RADIUS server(s). At every dead timer interval, the primary servers are re-enabled and tried again on the next authentication. The dead timer setting is a trade-off between timing out on the unreachable servers too often and not seeing the WAN link and servers come up as soon as possible. Thus, it is recommended that you configure an appropriate value for the dead timer depending on the deployment scenario. When the standalone AP or the WDS server tries the main servers while they are down, the radio client trying to authenticate usually reports an authentication timeout.

Summary

After reading this chapter, you should understand the following key concepts:

- Three WLAN deployment modes are available using Cisco products: standalone AP mode, SWAN nonswitching deployment mode, and SWAN central switching deployment mode. SWAN deployment modes enable services such as fast secure roaming (both Layer 2 and Layer 3) for 802.1x users, radio management functions, security policy monitoring, and overall multilayer security defense implementation.

- Infrastructure authentication is required in a SWAN-enabled network to secure the communication link between each WDS client AP and the WDS server.

- Radio monitoring functions are enabled using integrated or standalone AP-based scanning and optional client scanning using Cisco and CCX clients.

- Key RM security functions to deploy are rogue AP detection and suppression, non-802.11 interference detection (to detect possible RF DoS attacks), and WDS-based client tracking.

- Fast secure roaming is provided to expedite roaming for 802.1x clients. This is critical for latency-sensitive applications such as VoIP when using WPA (or 802.1x with dynamic WEP) as the security mechanism.

- The local RADIUS authentication service is provided for the branch/remote office scenarios when the primary RADIUS server (located at corporate HQ) becomes unavailable (for example, due to WAN link failure). You can deploy the local 802.1x RADIUS service on a standalone AP, WDS client AP, or preferably the WDS server.

CHAPTER 10

Design Guidelines for Secure WLAN

Previous chapters in this book discussed the underlying technologies that are necessary to start designing secure WLANs. New WLAN installations are occurring and existing WLANs are being changed as WLAN access is identified as a technical or business requirement, like mobility, for more users.

Many differing technologies can be brought to bear to design secure WLANs, but it is the network designer's responsibility to select the most appropriate security technology. The selection of appropriate security technology must adhere to the WLAN security policy that a corporation has decided on and must also support the technical and business requirements, such as bedside check-in of patients in an emergency room, that are driving the WLAN deployment. This chapter discusses possible WLAN security designs that are based on answering fundamental questions about the services, devices, and policy that the WLAN must support.

Many network designers must consider how to simultaneously support legacy WLAN technologies and requirements along with the new security technologies that are available for securing WLANs. With this in mind, this chapter discusses basic design guidelines for two environments: new WLAN deployments and WLAN deployments that must integrate legacy devices and infrastructure. The primary emphasis will be on new WLAN deployments, and then you will learn how to integrate legacy WLAN deployments. Finally, the chapter closes with a review of how to utilize new security technologies to secure the WLAN.

WLAN Design Fundamentals

The network designer must consider how the security solution impacts several fundamental areas of a WLAN design. This must be done to guarantee that the WLAN security solution and design supports the intended use of the WLAN. For instance, if the mobility of hand-held devices (phones, bar-code readers, and so on) that utilize a persistent, connection-oriented application is a requirement of the WLAN, the network designer must select the appropriate security technology that supports these factors, mobility, and application persistence. The following sections detail other fundamental areas that the network designer must consider.

WLAN Security Policy

Any evaluation of securing a WLAN should start with a review and analysis of the corporation's existing security policy. The primary function of this review and analysis is to determine if the security policy dictates any technical or nontechnical requirements that the network designer must adhere to in selecting the proper security technologies and design. The network designer can do this by asking questions of the policy and determining how the answers affect his WLAN security design. Here are some questions the designer might ask:

- What is the corporate policy for WLAN and application usage?
- Is there an acceptable-use document to which the network designer must make sure WLAN users adhere?
- If the WLAN user is a guest rather than a corporate employee, is a legal disclaimer necessary before he can use the WLAN?
- Is there a policy stating the type of authentication required for WLAN access?
- Is there a policy stating the type of applications that can be accessed while using the WLAN?
- Is there a policy that classifies a particular group of users who can use the WLAN?

The designer must answer these questions and more before he can select the appropriate technologies and designs that will support the WLAN deployment. In all of the design chapters, it is assumed that there is a security policy that dictates that WLAN usage is approved using appropriate security technologies.

Device Support

The network designer should interview the end user requesting the devices' support to determine what options are available for security in the devices. The network designer needs to ask questions such as the following:

- What types of devices will be supported, and what capabilities do they have to support secure connectivity? Some legacy devices, such as legacy handheld scanners, might not have the software, memory, or processor capability to do a security solution like Wired Equivalent Privacy (WEP), much less 802.11i.
- Does the device's radio support advanced security features such as Layer 2 fast secure roaming?

After the network designer answers these questions, he can start to fill out the solution components of the WLAN security design.

Authentication Support

The network designer must also interview users who request WLAN access and ask questions to determine what authentication types might be available. Questions to ask include the following:

- Will the device or device interface have the capability to support advanced authentication techniques?

- Is there a requirement for device- or user-based authentication?

- Will the users be able or inclined to do interactive authentication? (In some environments, such as factory floors, this is impractical due to the device's interface and user expectations of interaction.)

The decision about what types of authentication are available for the WLAN can determine what security frameworks the network designer can select for the WLAN.

Network Services Placement

The network designer needs to consider where the network services for the WLAN are offered, so he should ask questions such as the following:

- Can you leverage existing network services, such as authentications, Domain Name System (DNS), and Dynamic Host Configuration Protocol (DHCP) services, from the existing wired LAN to service the WLAN?

- Are the DNS/DHCP servers protected from denial-of-service (DoS) or worm threats?

- Where will the Wireless Domain Server (WDS) exist in the network?

The answers to these and other questions will determine whether the network designer needs to provision new services for the WLAN or if he can leverage existing network services.

Mobility

The network designer must determine whether the end users who request the WLAN access require mobility in their WLAN application. Here are some examples of questions the network designer might ask to guide his security solution:

- Do I need to support mobility and allow the end users to roam among access points (APs) whether the APs are located on the same IP subnet (Layer 2 roaming) or on different IP subnets (Layer 3 roaming)?

- How fast must the roaming handoff be to support the application?

Application Support

The network designer must determine whether specific application requirements might assist in determining the security framework for the WLAN. Examples of questions the network designer might ask are as follows:

- Are there specific application requirements that will drive the WLAN design? For instance, is there a need to support voice, multicast traffic, or persistent-connection applications that are sensitive to timeouts when roaming?

- If there are application requirements that involve persistent connectivity, does this connectivity involve Layer 2 or Layer 3 roaming, and if so, does it have guidelines for what is the acceptable delay for the application when roaming?

Management of the APs

Network designers determine how to manage the APs on the WLAN. They can determine this by asking themselves what options are available within the existing network infrastructure. Examples of questions the network designer might ask are as follows:

- How can I securely manage the APs and client devices with in-band or out-of-band solutions?

- Can I use virtual local area networks (VLANs) to segregate the APs' management interface from client traffic?

- Will the current wired network design support the extension of a VLAN to the access layer? Would this have an impact on current spanning tree implementations?

- If the AP management traffic cannot be segregated from client traffic, how can I protect the AP from unauthorized access?

- Can I implement router ACLs (RACLs) or VLAN ACLs (VACLs) on the wired switches to limit the IP addresses that can access the AP?

Radio Coverage Design

Radio coverage design impacts how effectively the network designer can perform rogue AP detection. Also, the network designer needs to ask questions such as the following to determine if the radio network impacts the WLAN application:

- How do I design the radio coverage to support the application and mobility requirements?
- Does the security solution impact my ability to roam securely?

Multigroup Access

Finally, the network designer needs to determine if there will be single group access WLAN or if multiple groups with differing security requirements will access the WLAN. The network designer must know the type of access to potentially design for multiple security frameworks implemented on the WLAN. For instance, if guest access and corporate access are required on the WLAN, the network designer might choose to implement two different security mechanisms to support corporate and guest access.

General Security Recommendations

After answering the preceding fundamental questions, the network designer can move on to build the general security baseline. The following sections discuss general security recommendations for the security baseline. All of the following areas are related, and a requirement in one area drives requirements and network design decisions in other areas. For example, assume that a particular application drives the WLAN deployment and that this application has a low tolerance for packet loss to the application server and requires that the client device not change IP addresses during an application session. The application must also cover a large area, which requires multiple APs for sufficient coverage. This requirement drives the need for fast roaming among APs and can preclude one security solution or another. How the security solutions align with the previous fundamentals will determine how the network designer implements the security mechanisms for the WLAN.

The following sections discuss recommendations for the general security requirements for all WLAN designs.

AP Recommendations

The network designer should consider the following recommendations when securing the APs in the WLAN:

- Use central user authentication and authorization for the administration of the APs. By centralizing these functions, the network designer reduces the overhead to administer user authentication and provides scalability and high availability of authentication and authorization services.

- Use encrypted management protocols whenever possible. For instance, use SSH as a replacement for Telnet to gain command-line access to the AP.

- If encrypted management protocols cannot be utilized, make sure that best practices as defined for other infrastructure security devices are used for unencrypted management protocols. For instance, if SNMPv1 is the only SNMP protocol supported, make sure that the SNMP community strings are randomly generated and changed often or, if possible, restrict unencrypted protocols to read-only solutions. Again, if SNMPv1 is required, allow only read-only access to the AP via SNMPv1 if possible. Also, use access control lists (ACLs) to secure the unencrypted management protocols by limiting the IP addresses that can send packets to the AP. You can find best practices for these unencrypted protocols on the Cisco website.

- Remove all unnecessary services on the AP to limit the avenues of exploitation to the device.

- Limit management connectivity so that only the WLAN management platform can connect to the AP. You can accomplish this in a variety of methods. For instance, if it is feasible in the network architecture, the management interface of the AP can be isolated to a particular VLAN in the network. Then ACLs can be applied to the VLAN interface on the APs' default gateway to limit access to the APs to just the WLAN management server.

WLAN Client Recommendations

The network designer should also make sure that the client has sufficient endpoint security controls because the risk of a mobile device, such as a laptop, being used in an attack or carrying a worm is generally quite high. These controls include the following:

- Disable ad-hoc networking mode on all devices to prevent attackers from exploiting this capability. Operating system policy enforcement and compliance tools on the client device are one way to assist in making sure that an attacker does not enable this mode.

- Implement host security measures such as antivirus program and Cisco Security Agent (host intrusion prevention) to protect the device against worms and viruses that can propagate through a public or private WLAN. Host intrusion-prevention products, such as CSA, include personal firewall functionality that limits the capability of other WLAN clients to connect to the WLAN client that CSA is protecting.

Infrastructure Recommendations

These recommendations refer to Catalyst switch features that are helpful in securing the wired side of the WLAN from common threats. This, in turn, improves the overall security posture of the corporation's network when the WLAN is added. Apply these features on the ports that service the WLAN APs:

- Depending on the capabilities of the Catalyst switch, implement RFC 2827 filtering on the access layer or distribution layer switches to prevent spoofed IP addresses from being used on the WLAN. For instance, the 3750 is an L2/L3 switch that can implement this filtering at Layer 3 with standard router ACLs or at Layer 2 with VLAN ACLs (VACLs).

NOTE   Describing the details of these wired LAN security features is outside the scope of this book. Descriptions and configuration examples of these features can be found in the product documentation section of the Cisco website at www.cisco.com.

- Implement Catalyst Layer 2 security features where applicable. These Layer 2 security features include the following:
  - DHCP snooping to protect against rogue DHCP servers or DHCP starvation attacks
  - Dynamic Address Resolution Protocol (ARP) inspection to protect against ARP poisoning attacks

NOTE   In the following sections, you might notice that there are no mitigation techniques for some of the DoS threats identified in Chapter 6, "Wireless Vulnerabilities". Currently, there are no open and interoperable solutions to these threats. It is an inherent risk of the WLAN that you might be subject to a DoS attack. When using unlicensed frequencies, a certain level of SLA/quality of service (QoS) cannot be guaranteed. However, the inherent risk of the WLAN is offset by the productivity gains that are made possible with the WLAN, so the risk is acceptable.

New WLAN Deployments

WLAN designs are newly installed in a variety of areas within home, enterprise, and service provider networks. Two basic options are available for securing a new WLAN: embedded media solutions, such as WPA, and tunneling overlays, such as IPSec and SSL. The following sections discuss these two security frameworks and how to combine these technologies for a highly secure solution. The sections discuss how the security framework functions and compare how the security framework mitigates the threats identified in Chapter 5, "WLAN Basic Authentication and Privacy Methods." Finally, they discuss the impact that the security framework might have on WLAN design fundamentals.

Embedded Security Solutions

WPA is the most widely available standards-based, embedded media solution for securing WLANs. WPA's security scheme relies on the previously discussed 802.1x/EAP for authentication and TKIP for data confidentiality and integrity. 802.11i also relies on 802.1x/EAP for authentication and AES for data confidentiality and integrity. Other embedded media security solutions exist, such as WEP and the Cisco prestandard confidentiality solution, Cisco Key Integrity Protocol (CKIP). For the rest of this chapter, when the text refers to 802.1x/EAP, it is referring generally to the class of security schemes that leverages 802.1/EAP for its authentication and key management. These security schemes include WPA, 802.11i, and the Cisco LEAP security framework. WEP and its use in securing a WLAN is covered later in this chapter.

Because the network is designed to rely on the security embedded in the media, the WLAN extends the existing wired LAN for access by wireless devices. Figure 10-1 depicts the most basic WLAN design option, in which the network services are leveraged from the existing wired resources.

Figure 10-1   *General Embedded Security Design*

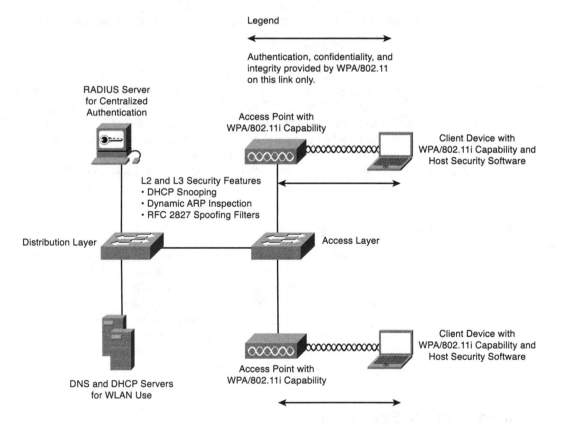

In the figure, the 802.11i or WPA frameworks provide central user authentication and confidentiality. In addition, the figure depicts the possible points of implementation of the host and infrastructure security mechanisms outlined in the "WLAN Design Fundamentals" and "General Security Guidelines" sections earlier in this chapter.

Threat Mitigation

When properly implemented, these security mechanisms allow the network designer to mitigate many of the threats identified in Chapter 6. The following sections list the threats mitigated in this design.

Reconnaissance: Discover Target Network

Although the attacker can still see the SSID of the WLAN through active and passive methods, he cannot discover more than the SSID due to the use of embedded TKIP or AES encryption. It should be noted that the attacker has access to the 802.1x/EAP message exchanges because both protocols are plaintext. There might be portions of information in these exchanges that allow the attacker to gather intelligence about the security scheme of the WLAN and possibly the wired LAN. The network designer must make a decision as to what type of information is available in each EAP authentication type and whether the risk of this information being available is an unacceptable risk for the WLAN.

Network Access: Gain Read Access

Similar to the mitigation of the reconnaissance attack, the embedded encryption algorithms mitigate the attacker's ability to read data from the WLAN (packet sniffers). Additionally, the attacker should not be able to gain read access through a WLAN client because the WLAN should not have ad-hoc mode WLAN enabled and cannot talk to the client directly above the MAC layer. As noted in the preceding section, several EAP authentication types do reveal information about the WLAN. For some EAP authentication types, there might be enough information for an attacker to gain read access to the WLAN. In many instances, applying a best practice for securing the EAP type can mitigate these risks. For instance, when using the LEAP authentication type, the username and password hash are visible to an attacker. This makes the password hash susceptible to an offline dictionary attack. Applying the LEAP best practice of using a strong password policy and periodically changing the LEAP password can mitigate this. If this type of risk is unacceptable, the network designer must again make a decision as to what type of information is acceptable to be viewed within the 802.1x/EAP messages and select the appropriate EAP authentication type to mitigate the risks.

Network Access: Gain Write Access

The centralized authentication of the 802.1x and upper-layer EAP protocols prevent the attacker from being able to gain access to the WLAN, which keeps him from using the WLAN as a source of attack. Additionally, the embedded encryption and integrity mechanisms of the WLAN (TKIP/MIC or AES) prevent the attacker from changing packets in transit or inserting packets into the WLAN.

Design Fundamentals and Embedded Security

In addition to extending the wired LAN services, the network designer must evaluate how the new WLAN addresses the fundamentals of secure WLAN design. The fundamentals discussed in the following sections have notable items with regard to embedded security solutions.

Network Services Placement

In the embedded security design, the proper placement of network services is critical in providing high availability to the WLAN. The primary component to consider in this design is the WDS. The WDS, discussed in Chapter 9, "SWAN: End-to-End Security Deployment," provides local fallback authentication and the security information for Layer 2 fast secure roaming information. As discussed, the WDS can be designated on an AP, switch, or router. Selecting the correct hardware of the WDS depends on the processing resources available on each platform and network topology. For instance, in a large enterprise, a WDS might be located within the switching infrastructure, Catalyst 6500, for scalability considerations. In contrast, in a small, remote office, because the number of APs is probably small, a 2600 might provide an ideal spot for the WDS and could provide fallback authentication if the WLAN to the corporate offices is down.

Mobility

As previously discussed, the Cisco SWAN architecture enables Layer 2 fast secure roaming through the use of the WDS. The general design assumes that the WLAN IP subnet can be contained within a set of distribution switches or that the IP subnet (VLAN) can extend across multiple distribution-layer switches in your network architecture. This is utilized to provide mobility for the design. If either of these conditions is not true, the network designer must use Mobile IP Proxy (MIP) to allow Layer 3 roaming.

Application Support

Because WPA and 802.11i are embedded in the media, they provide support for all Layer 3 protocols, such as IPX and IP. With the capability to support all Layer 3 protocols, the embedded security solutions provide broader application support than most tunneling overlay technologies.

Management of the APs

When utilizing an embedded security framework to secure the WLAN, the APs can be managed through the same IP subnet as the WLAN client traffic or through an isolated management subnet. An isolated management subnet is typically achieved through the use of VLANs on the wired side of the AP; however, in some environments, security policy dictates that this be an entirely separate switching infrastructure for the APs. If a common client and management infrastructure is used to manage the APs, SSH and other encrypted protocols, as previously noted, are useful to secure the management of the APs.

Multigroup Access

Multigroup access can be accomplished by dynamically assigning an authenticated user to a particular VLAN on the switched side of the AP. Hence, a corporate user can be assigned to a VLAN that has unhindered access to the corporate network, whereas a contractor can be assigned to a VLAN that has restricted access to specific hosts on the corporate network.

VPN Overlays

Using VPNs as overlays to the WLAN is the other primary design choice for securing WLANs. When this is the primary design choice, the WLAN is treated as a completely untrusted network and is separated from the corporation's security edge with a VPN gateway device. To gain access to the corporation's resources, the end user must initiate a VPN connection to the VPN device and pass some sort of per-user authentication. Because the WLAN is untrusted, network designers should take the same precautions for WLAN clients as they do for securing remote mobile users who leverage the Internet for corporate access. For example, many corporations require that external users use strong authentication (One Time Passwords or certificates on SmartCards) to gain access to the corporate network. Generally, all VPN overlays adhere to the same corporate policies with regard to the type of password authentication.

In general, all the VPN overlay technologies follow the same base topology for implementation. Figure 10-2 illustrates the topology.

In Figure 10-2, the VPN tunneling framework provides central user authentication and confidentiality. In addition, this figure depicts the host and infrastructure security mechanisms' possible points of implementation from the beginning of the chapter. Also, it is recommended that the WLAN not connect to the Internet natively. If this is done, applications on the WLAN client can connect to Internet services in an insecure manner and allow information to leak to the attacker. For instance, an e-mail program with autoconnect settings turned on might set up a connection to the Internet and provide relevant information to the attacker. For this reason, it is desirable to have some sort of VPN auto-initiation feature with the VPN technology to prevent information from being sent on the WLAN in the clear, before the VPN is established to the VPN gateway. Additionally, it is recommended that network intrusion-detection systems (NIDS) and host intrusion prevention, such as the Cisco Security Agent (CSA), be utilized to protect the servers (DNS, DHCP) that are required to serve the legacy WLAN. The primary purpose of the host security software is to attempt to keep the servers from being exploited and used as stepping stones to gain access to the enterprise network.

Figure 10-2 *General VPN Overlay WLAN Design*

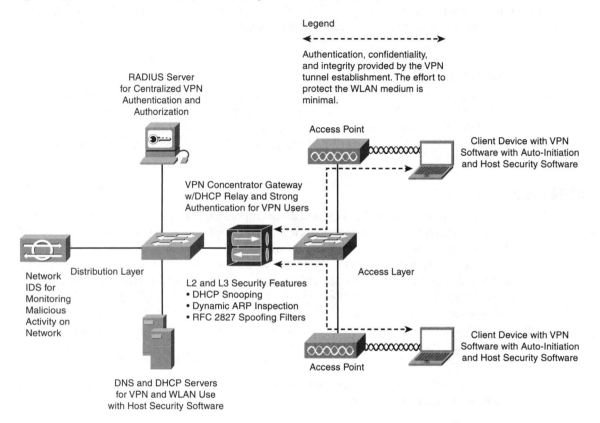

Threat Mitigation

When properly implemented, the security mechanisms in Figure 10-2 allow the network designer to mitigate many of the threats identified in Chapter 6 and described in the following sections.

Reconnaissance: Discover Target Network

Although the attacker can discover the WLAN network topology, he should not be able to determine the network topology behind the VPN gateway device. However, the attacker will have access to any clear-text information that the end host devices transmit before the VPN tunnel is initiated. For instance, many Microsoft Windows operating systems generate broadcasts looking for domain or Active Directory services. Some of this information is available to the attacker. WEP could be employed to make this discovery harder for a low-level attacker, but it is not a valid deterrent for a mid-level or high-level attacker.

Network Access: Gain Read Access

This attack is mitigated by the authentication, encryption, and integrity characteristics of the VPN tunneling technology. However, similar to the reconnaissance threat, the attacker has access to data that is transmitted by the client before the VPN tunnel is established.

Network Access: Gain Write Access

The centralized authentication of the VPN prevents the attacker from being able to gain access to the corporate network. Additionally, the embedded encryption and integrity mechanisms of the VPN will prevent the attacker from changing packets in transit or inserting packets into the communication to the corporate network. This does not prevent the attacker from having write access to the WLAN itself. Therefore, the attacker might be able to launch attacks such as ARP poisoning to attempt man-in-the-middle (MitM) attacks. The VPN protocol should protect against active or passive MitM attacks. There are demonstrated ways to perform MitM attacks against VPN protocols. You should contact your vendor of VPN gateway products to determine the best practices to mitigate a MitM attack.

VPN Overlay Technologies

Three primary types of VPN overlays are implemented to secure WLANs:

- IPSec-based VPNs
- SSL-based VPNs
- SSH-based VPNs

IPSec is the most predominant type of VPN overlay that is used to secure WLANs because it has supported the broadest set of applications. The other two types of VPN overlays, SSL and SSH, are generally more restrictive in their capability to support upper-layer protocols and applications.

IPSec

IPSec VPNs are widely deployed for remote-access VPNs as a replacement for traditional remote-access dial services to secure an organization's traffic across untrusted networks such as broadband mediums like cable and DSL. Because IPSec VPNs are so prevalent in many organizations and many people feel that WLANs are completely untrusted networks, it was a logical extension to use IPSec Remote Access Server (RAS) VPN technology to secure WLANs.

To use IPSec RAS VPNs appropriately for WLANs, the network designer must understand some background on IPSec and its ability to support user authentication and particular applications.

IPSec natively did not have a mechanism for per-user authentication and intended to use widely deployed authentication infrastructures. Originally it was intended that IPSec would leverage a protocol like L2TP to gain user authentication. However, customers and vendors requested that IPSec be extended to support per-user authentication and also the capability to download configuration information such as an embedded tunnel IP address, WINS, and DNS servers for each end user machine. This request led to the development of extensions to the IPSec protocol called *xauth* and *mode config xauth (extended authentication)*, which was created to perform per-user authentication, whereas mode config was created to enable downloading of configuration information (DNS, WINS, and so on) to the RAS VPN client PC if not there. Although these extensions were public drafts, vendors created proprietary implementations of IPSec with these extensions for RAS VPNs.

This resulted in vendor-specific VPN clients not being interoperable among IPSec VPN gateways. However, some implementations of VPN clients are interoperable with multiple vendor IPSec VPN gateways. The most prevalent VPN client that is interoperable with multiple brands of IPSec VPN gateways is the L2TP/IPSec implementation in Microsoft Windows 2000 and XP. On non-PC devices, a prevalent IPSec VPN client that interoperates with many IPSec VPN gateways is called a *movian secure VPN client*.

The network designer needs to be aware of these user authentication, device configuration, and interoperability issues to determine if the end user WLAN devices can support the correct IPSec clients that interoperate with the corporation's RAS VPN solution.

In addition, IPSec is a network-based VPN transport and supports the majority of the upper-layer IP protocol suites natively. It was designed specifically for IP unicast traffic, and the standard makes special mention that it is not intended to support IP multicast traffic. Additional work within the IETF is addressing a standard way to secure multicast traffic. However, there are vendor implementations that can support multicast traffic in an IPSec VPN, most notably the L2TP implementations in which the IP multicast is wrapped in an L2TP IP unicast header and then secured with IPSec. Other implementations use proprietary implementations to support IP multicast. IP multicast support might be an issue because many applications rely on IP multicast to function. Examples include IP video streaming applications like Cisco IP/TV, financial applications, and IP telephony applications like multicast Music-On-Hold in a Cisco Call Manager environment.

There might be other applications that do not interoperate with IPSec, such as applications that embed IP address information as part of their upper-layer protocols. Network designers who already have RAS VPN deployments should be able to identify any applications that might have issues interoperating with IPSec VPNs. If there is not an existing deployment, the network designer needs to test each application that will be used with the IPSec client to validate that it performs properly.

Finally, IPSec gateway devices can typically implement a policy to prevent the client end user from being able to split tunnel. This prevents the IPSec client device from being a stepping stone into the corporate network. This does not prevent a device from being infected while not on the corporate network and subsequently carrying the virus into the network. To mitigate this type of issue, the network designer needs to consider a solution described in the "Admission Control Design" section later in this chapter.

SSL

SSL is predominantly used for securing HTTP-based applications such as web browsing. However, the actual SSL protocol can be used to secure a variety of transport layer protocols. Cisco and other vendors have started to offer the capability to create VPNs utilizing the SSL protocol and specialized SSL gateways that act as gateways to the corporate network. Cisco utilizes the VPN 3000 to offer both IPSec and SSL VPN tunnel termination. The main attraction to SSL-based VPNs is the idea that they enable "clientless" VPNs. This means that the network designer does not have to install or maintain an additional piece of software on the client machine to provide VPN service for WLANs. This is possible because the majority of client device operating systems (OSs) have the SSL protocol implemented in the embedded web browser.

Additionally, because SSL is a transport layer protocol, SSL-based VPNs can support only the protocols that the SSL can encapsulate without additional code on the workstation. To support the capability to tunnel all IP traffic SSL, gateways must download a piece of code to the client (for instance, an ActiveX applet) that puts itself into the IP stack of the client to tunnel all IP packets correctly. This restricts the SSL VPN to certain certified web browsers and operating systems to guarantee interoperability with the applet.

SSH

SSH is a secure alternative to remote terminal programs such as rlogin and Telnet. SSH is actually a suite of protocols that includes scp and sftp. SSH has a port-forwarding feature that makes it capable of acting as a VPN overlay technology. SSH port forwarding allows the client to forward local ports to the computer at the far end of the SSH session. In effect, this allows applications to access enterprise resources that are on the inside of the far-end SSH host for secure access across the WLAN. SSH VPN overlays are similar to SSL VPN overlays for WLAN and provide similar benefits for some situations. For many OSs, SSH is provided by default, thereby allowing SSH to be utilized to protect the WLAN communications. There are two major drawbacks to the use of SSH as a VPN overlay. First, Microsoft operating systems do not provide SSH by default, so a large part of the installation base would have to add SSH as an additional software package. Second, SSH does not support all the IP applications that an enterprise might employ, such as IP multicast. There are ways to configure this to function, but they are typically deployed by advanced users and might not be suitable for general deployment to all WLAN client devices.

Design Fundamentals and VPN Overlays

Keeping the characteristics of the three VPN overlays in mind, it is necessary to review the following fundamentals that have notable items with regard to VPN overlay security solutions. These items might influence the choice of a VPN overlay technology as the proper way to secure a WLAN.

Authentication Support

As has been noted, it is recommended that all VPN users use strong authentication to authenticate the device and users for a VPN overlay. This is recommended because strong authentication—two-factor or certificates—is considered a more secure way of performing user authentication than just a username and static password.

Network Services Placement

For the WLAN client to establish a VPN tunnel, it is recommended that the VPN gateway provide DHCP relay functionality to provide dynamic addressing to the WLAN client. This recommendation allows DHCP to be leveraged on the wired side of the network where centralized management and scalable services are available for DHCP. In some installations, it might be necessary to offer DNS services also for the WLAN client to resolve the domain name of the VPN gateway. Because both DNS and DHCP servers could potentially be reached from outside the VPN gateway, the servers should be protected from attack with the Cisco Security Agent and monitored with network intrusion detection. Also, DNS/DHCP services might be dedicated to WLAN use to reduce the risk that an attack from the WLAN can impact DNS or DHCP services on the wired LAN.

Mobility

VPN overlays require Layer 2 roaming capability to ensure mobility. However, VPN technologies generally do not support Layer 3 roaming and must rely on alternate technologies such as Mobile IP (MIP) to enable this type of mobility. The Layer 3 mobility solution discussed in Chapter 9 and later in this chapter will accommodate Layer 3 mobility for VPN overlays. Also, some current proprietary VPN technologies allow Layer 3 mobility without Mobile IP or other Layer 3 mobility solutions.

Application Support

As noted, there might be challenges with application support when a VPN overlay is utilized to secure a WLAN. A network designer must understand all potential applications that will be utilized on the WLAN and select the appropriate VPN technology to support those applications.

Management of the APs

When you are utilizing a VPN to secure the WLAN, you must manage the APs either through the VPN gateway or through an isolated management subnet. An isolated management subnet is typically achieved through the use of VLANs on the wired side of the AP; however, in some environments, security policy dictates that this be an entirely separate switching infrastructure for the APs. The AP should not accept any connection on the VLAN that corresponds to the VPN subnet because the VPN subnet is considered insecure and no communication should be possible to the AP from this subnet.

Multigroup Access

Multigroup access is accomplished in the VPN gateway by applying different authorizations per group. For instance, a corporate group might be authorized to access all internal networks, whereas a partner group might be restricted to a particular group of hosts or applications on the corporate network.

Combined VPN and Embedded Security Design

In some instances, a network designer might choose to combine the embedded security and VPN overlay security solutions. This combination gives the network designer some additional security benefits compared to either solution by itself. For instance, by making clients authenticate via 802.1x/EAP, the network designer can reduce the risk of someone attacking the network services devices (DHCP and DNS).

When WPA/802.11i and VPNs are the design choice for securing WLANs, the WLAN can be considered an untrusted or a semitrusted network. Therefore, the WLAN is separated from the corporation's security edge with a VPN gateway device. To gain access to the corporation's resources, the client must pass the authentication to the WLAN via 802.1x/EAP. After the client has successfully authenticated and negotiated WLAN encryption keys, the client must initiate a VPN tunnel to the VPN gateway and pass an additional user authentication.

Depending on the authentication methods selected for WPA/802.11 and VPN authentication, the end user *might* need to have an interactive prompt for both authentications. In some instances, dual interaction with the end user might be undesirable to the end user. If this is the case, the network designer might choose to select an authentication technology that can be transparently supplied to both the WPA/802.11i and VPN authentication requests. For instance, a digital certificate for an end user could be leveraged to allow EAP-TLS and an auto-initiated IPSec VPN to authenticate to both security frameworks without user interaction.

In general, the combined security technologies follow the same base topology as the VPN overlay design. Additional security measures to consider in this design are the inclusion of network intrusion detection and host intrusion-prevention software on the hosts that provide network services (DNS, DHCP). The network designer should also leverage any security services that are available in the switching infrastructure, such as dynamic ARP inspection and

DHCP snooping. Figure 10-3 illustrates the topology for the general VPN and embedded security design.

Figure 10-3 *General VPN and Embedded Security Design*

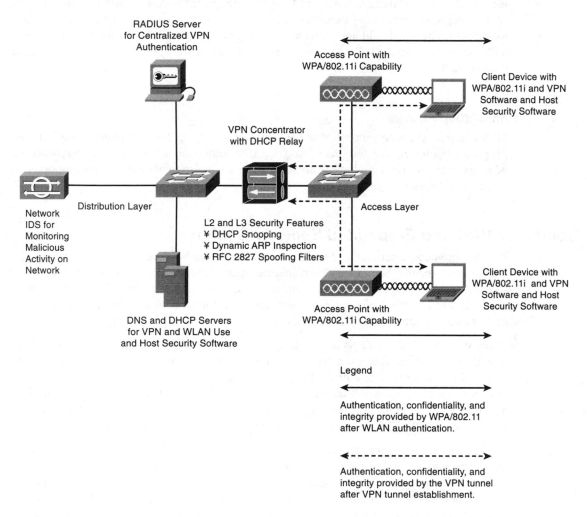

Threat Mitigation

When properly implemented, the security mechanisms in Figure 10-3 allow the network designer to mitigate many of the threats identified in Chapter 5. This section discusses the threats mitigated by this design.

Reconnaissance: Discover Target Network

One of the benefits of combining the embedded security and VPN security frameworks is to defeat an attacker's capability to discover the target WLAN while using a defense-in-depth approach to ensuring the WLAN data's integrity and confidentiality. As discussed in the "Embedded Security Solutions" section of this chapter, there are some potential information leaks with the EAP authentication protocols. In this design, this information leak might be deemed a lesser risk because any information gleaned by the attacker would apply only to authentication to the WLAN and not to the VPN. This is true unless the same user authentication credentials were used to authenticate the user to both the WLAN and the VPN.

Network Access: Gain Read Access

This threat is mitigated by the authentication, encryption, and integrity characteristics of both the embedded security and VPN tunneling technology. It should be noted that if implemented improperly, both the 802.1x/EAP and IPSec authentications can be attacked to gain read access to the WLAN. The threat to the WLAN was discussed in the "Embedded Security Solutions" section of this chapter. However, this design improves on the VPN-only design because the WLAN embedded security does not allow the attacker to have access to data transmitted before the VPN tunnel establishment, except 802.1x/EAP.

Network Access: Gain Write Access

The centralized authentication of the embedded security and VPN security frameworks is the first mitigating factor in gaining write access to a combined security solution. In addition to the authentication, the embedded and VPN security frameworks provide encryption and integrity mechanisms to prevent write access to the WLAN.

Design Fundamentals and the Combined VPN and Embedded Security Design

Keeping the previous characteristics of the VPN overlays and embedded security frameworks in mind, it is necessary to review the following fundamentals that contain notable items with regard to the security solutions.

Authentication Support

In this design scenario, the WLAN might be considered semitrusted because it protects not only the media (embedded security) but also the data via a tunnel. With this in mind, network designers might choose not to require strong authentication for WLAN access. This is entirely a business risk decision for the network designer. Also, as noted previously, the largest issue in this design is how to make the least number of user interactions to authenticate the device to the WLAN and the VPN gateway.

Network Services Placement

Similar to the VPN overlay–only model, it is recommended that the VPN gateway provide DHCP relay functionality to provide dynamic addressing to the WLAN client for the WLAN client to establish a VPN tunnel. In some installations, it might be necessary to offer DNS services for the WLAN client to resolve the domain name of the VPN gateway. Because both DNS and DHCP servers could potentially be reached from outside the VPN gateway, the servers should be protected from attack with the Cisco Security Agent and be monitored by network intrusion detection. As stated previously, dedicating DHCP and DNS servers just for WLAN use is a consideration.

Mobility

VPN overlays require Layer 2 roaming capabilities to ensure mobility. The underlying 802.1x/ EAP must support this Layer 2 mobility. However, VPN technologies generally do not support Layer 3 roaming and must rely on alternate technologies such as Mobile IP to enable this type of mobility. The Layer 3 mobility solution detailed in Chapter 9 and later in this chapter accommodates VPN-overlay Layer 3 mobility. Also, some proprietary VPN technologies allow Layer 3 mobility without Mobile IP or other Layer 3 mobility solutions.

Application Support

As noted, there might be challenges with application support when a VPN overlay is utilized to secure a WLAN. A network designer must understand all potential applications that will be utilized on the WLAN and select the appropriate VPN technology to support those applications.

Management of the APs

When utilizing a combined security solution to secure the WLAN, the APs must be managed either through the VPN gateway or through an isolated management subnet. Because this solution is semitrusted, some network designers might allow the AP to be managed through the VPN gateway rather than through the isolated management subnet.

Multigroup Access

Multigroup access is most easily accomplished in the VPN gateway by applying different authorization per group. For instance, a corporate group might be authorized to access all internal networks, whereas a partner group might be restricted to a particular group of hosts or applications on the corporate network. Although it is possible to accomplish multigroup access in the WLAN via dynamic assignment, this would then require a VPN gateway interface on every VLAN that can handle WLAN traffic. This is not feasible in most network topologies or VPN gateway devices. This makes the VPN gateway the most efficient place to implement authorization because it is the last point of enforcement before accessing the corporate network.

Integration with Existing WLAN Deployments

For many enterprise users, there exists a large amount of legacy WLAN equipment that does not have the capability to utilize one of the previous methods of design to secure WLANs. In this case, the network designer needs to do a detailed threat analysis of the legacy WLAN environment and secure these networks with supplementary technology to the WLAN device, such as firewalls and network intrusion detection.

WPA Upgradeable, WEP Only, and Pre-WEP Devices

The primary legacy technologies to integrate are WPA upgradeable, WEP only, and what is termed "pre-WEP" 802.11 devices. The WEP-only devices are WEP capable, but they do not have the capability to be upgraded to either WPA or 802.11i. As previously noted, WEP can be used as a deterrent against a low class of attacker. However, against a medium and higher grade of attacker, a designer must assume that WEP offers no security whatsoever. Additionally, there are devices that can support WEP with TKIP that will defeat a low- and mid-level attacker, but they do not provide assurance against a patient high-level attacker. Finally, devices exist that do not have the capability to support WEP but do have the capability to interoperate in the 802.11 radios. In this instance, a low-grade attacker can gain access to the WLAN. Network designers must make a business risk decision on what applications are acceptable to run in this environment. The following section attempts to assist the network designer in this decision.

NOTE   In many instances, legacy devices might be based on Frequency Hopping Spread Spectrum (FHSS) WLAN technology operating in the 2.4-GHz range. Sometimes these types of deployments are recommended to customers for apparent security reasons. The capability to obtain these types of radios and put them into a promiscuous mode is harder than with standards-based 802.11 scenarios. However, it is not impossible and should not be relied on for any degree of security. Designers who rely on this fact are relying on "security through obscurity," which is not a recommended practice. The notion of security through obscurity should never be relied on to adequately secure a WLAN. In many instances, these radios do not have an inherent equivalent security scheme comparable to WPA and 802.11i. If an FHSS scheme is selected for RF engineering reasons, it is recommended that the designer investigate using a VPN overlay solution as outlined in the "VPN Overlays" section earlier in this chapter. Alternatively, a designer can look to the vendor to provide a vendor-specific solution.

Integrated Deployments

There are three options for integrating WLANs that have different security schemes. The first option is to dedicate differing WLANs to the differing security domains. For instance, legacy pre-WEP or WEP 802.11b clients would use a dedicated 802.11b WLAN infrastructure, whereas the rest of the corporation would use WPA/802.11i security on a separate 802.11b or

802.11a infrastructure to gain access to the corporation. However, this is not widely done due to the engineering cost in mapping out overlapping WLAN environments with similar 802.11 media, in addition to the high cost of operations for maintaining separate networks.

The second way to integrate legacy clients that support 802.11 WEP is to use WPA's migration mode. WPA migration mode was designed specifically to migrate WEP clients to WPA without having to change the networking infrastructure significantly. However, WPA migration mode still keeps the lowest common denominator as the security measurement for the entire WLAN, namely WEP, so if any WEP is enabled on the WLAN, a mid-level attacker could access the WLAN. For this reason, the Cisco solution for integrating legacy clients is the third option.

The third option utilizes the VLAN capability of the AP to assign clients to the appropriate VLAN, where you can apply the appropriate security technologies for the clients. In this fashion, you can have a VLAN with no WEP and apply additional security checks, such as network IDS and firewalling, to secure the applications on that VLAN. On the same AP, you can have a VLAN that utilizes 802.1x/EAP and TKIP to secure the WLAN. Figure 10-4 depicts the network topology and security mechanisms to accommodate these mixed security schemes.

In Figure 10-4, the devices in the upper-right portion of the drawing represent the newer devices. These newer devices utilize the WPA/802.11 security framework to gain the security benefits outlined in the "Embedded Security Solutions" section earlier in this chapter. The legacy pre-WEP/WEP devices are depicted in the lower-right portion of the figure. The access point utilizes two SSIDs to allow the legacy clients to connect to SSID10, which is mapped to VLAN 10 on the Ethernet side of the AP, and SSID20, which is mapped to VLAN 20 on the Ethernet side of the AP. The trunk from the AP is connected to an Ethernet switch. VLAN 20 is connected directly to the internal network in a manner similar to the embedded security design shown previously in this chapter. VLAN 10 is connected to additional security devices that inspect the traffic for proper behavior and authorization.

Multiple layers of security techniques should be considered for use to secure the pre-WEP/ WEP WLAN and application servers. For instance, multiple layers of filtering are considered in securing the WLAN. This filtering can include any of the following techniques:

- A network designer might want to consider using MAC authentication and MAC filtering with the pre-WEP/WEP devices. Although MAC authentication and filtering can be bypassed with spoofing by an attacker, it still should be considered for the same reasons that WEP should be utilized when there is no other alternative. MAC authentication and filtering mitigate an attack from a low-level attacker. The network designer should note that administering MAC addresses in a large environment might not be worth the effort given the limited benefit. This is a business risk decision that the network designer must make.

Figure 10-4   *Legacy WEP and Pre-WEP Integration*

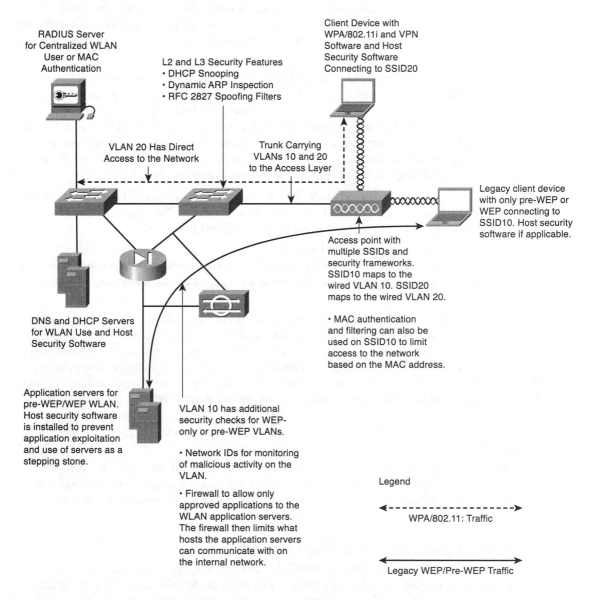

RADIUS Server
for Centralized WLAN
User or MAC
Authentication

L2 and L3 Security Features
• DHCP Snooping
• Dynamic ARP Inspection
• RFC 2827 Spoofing Filters

Client Device with
WPA/802.11i and VPN
Software and Host
Security Software
Connecting to SSID20

VLAN 20 Has Direct
Access to the Network

Trunk Carrying
VLANs 10 and 20
to the Access Layer

Legacy client device
with only pre-WEP or
WEP connecting to
SSID10. Host security
software if applicable.

Access point with
multiple SSIDs and
security frameworks.
SSID10 maps to the
wired VLAN 10. SSID20
maps to the wired VLAN 20.

DNS and DHCP Servers
for WLAN Use and Host
Security Software

• MAC authentication
and filtering can also be
used on SSID10 to limit
access to the network
based on the MAC address.

Application servers for
pre-WEP/WEP WLAN.
Host security software
is installed to prevent
application exploitation
and use of servers as a
stepping stone.

VLAN 10 has additional
security checks for WEP-
only or pre-WEP VLANs.

• Network IDs for monitoring
of malicious activity on the
VLAN.

• Firewall to allow only
approved applications to the
WLAN application servers.
The firewall then limits what
hosts the application servers
can communicate with on
the internal network.

Legend

◄------------------►
WPA/802.11: Traffic

◄------------------►
Legacy WEP/Pre-WEP Traffic

- Security features should be enabled on the network infrastructure to detect and protect against certain types of attack. For instance, dynamic ARP inspection can assist in detecting and preventing ARP attacks against the default gateway of the pre-WEP/WEP WLAN, and DHCP snooping can detect some attacks against the DHCP server that serves the WLAN.

- The firewall is configured to allow the pre-WEP/WEP-only clients to connect to the application servers needed for the WLAN clients to perform their designated functions. In addition, the firewall might perform application layer inspection to allow only proper application commands to pass through the firewall. Also, the firewall as depicted in Figure 10-4 can filter the conversations that the application servers can initiate into the enterprise network, so that if the application server is compromised, there is still another layer of filtering behind it to protect the enterprise network.

- A network intrusion-detection device can inspect all traffic destined to and through the firewall and alert on traffic that matches attack signatures. This alerts the network administrator to potential threats on the pre-WEP/WEP WLAN.

- You can also use Layer 3 and Layer 4 filtering on the access point or the Layer 2 switch to limit what application ports the WLAN can communicate with. The network designer might want to filter these devices if any of the other filtering devices are not available to the WLAN infrastructure.

- It is highly recommended that host intrusion-prevention software, such as the Cisco Security Agent (CSA), be utilized to protect the servers (application, DNS, and DHCP) that are required to serve the legacy WLAN. The primary purpose of the host security software is to attempt to keep the servers from being exploited and used as stepping stones to gain access to the enterprise network. This is the final layer of defense against exploitation that could derive its source from the pre-WEP/WEP WLAN.

Threat Mitigation

When properly implemented, the security mechanisms in Figure 10-4 allow the network designer to mitigate some of the threats identified in Chapter 5 for pre-WEP and WEP-only WLANs. The following sections discuss the threats that must be considered in this design.

Reconnaissance: Discover Target Network

Although the attacker can discover the WLAN network topology, he should be able to determine only a limited subset of the topology behind the firewall device by looking at the characteristics of the traffic for the applications permitted through the firewall. The MAC authentication and filtering will give some protection against this threat for low-level attackers. To further mitigate against an active probing, the network intrusion-detection system should detect some reconnaissance activity and alert the network administrator of this activity. Finally, the attacker will have access to any clear-text information that the end host devices transmit.

With this in mind, it is recommended that the number of applications used on the pre-WEP/ WEP WLAN be kept to a minimum to limit the amount of information that the attacker can glean about the target network.

Network Access: Gain Read Access

This attack is partially mitigated for data on the interior of the firewall by the filtering being done by the firewall. However, on the exterior side of the firewall, the attacker will have the capability to read the WLAN traffic. As previously noted, for this reason, the network administrator must make a business risk decision that the data being transmitted on this WLAN can be read by an attacker with minimal effort.

Network Access: Gain Write Access

This attack is partially mitigated for the data on the interior of the firewall by the filtering done by the infrastructure. As previously noted, depending on the type of filtering being done, there are varying degrees of effectiveness. If the network administrator has chosen to implement MAC-based authentication and filtering for the pre-WEP/WEP WLAN, some level of attackers will be mitigated from gaining write access to the network. In addition, as noted with the application layer inspection provided by the security devices (firewall and network intrusion detection), there is some write protection for the applications that transverse the firewall. However, not all data can be inspected by the firewall, so it is feasible that some application data could be altered outside of the firewall and entered into the application in use on the pre-WEP/ WEP WLAN. Finally, the host security software is intended to mitigate the possibility that the attacker will exploit the write capability to attack the application server and gain access to the host through the application server.

Design Fundamentals

The integration of legacy environments creates some interesting items of note with regard to the design fundamentals for the WLAN. These issues are outlined in the following sections.

WLAN Security Policy

The WLAN security policy is the core component that the network designer uses to determine if he can secure the legacy WLAN sufficiently to allow its deployment alongside other, more advanced WLAN security frameworks.

Device Support, Mobility, and Application Support

Device support is what drives network designers to consider all the alternatives in securing and supporting a legacy WLAN environment. Additionally, it is important to understand that many legacy devices that are pre-WEP or WEP-only cannot support more advanced WLAN features, such as Layer 2 fast secure roaming. The network designer must consider this before adding more application support that requires these new types of features while still trying to maintain the use of the legacy device.

Authentication Support

As discussed, MAC-based authentication is the primary means that is available to determine the identity of a pre-WEP or WEP WLAN device. In addition to the WLAN authentication, the network designer should consider advanced rotating password schemes for the application. Even with a rotating password scheme, an attacker can eventually determine the password for an application. However, in determining the password, the attacker might provide information that a network administrator can use to detect the intrusion attempt. For instance, the network administrator can use failed application authentication attempts to determine that someone is trying to use an old password and alert the person of an attempted intrusion.

Network Services Placement

In the legacy environment, the WLAN clients still might need to access DHCP or DNS resources on the wired enterprise network, so the additional security devices need to either provide these services or allow the WLAN to connect to the services that exist on the wired network. Many firewalls perform DHCP relay or have DHCP server capabilities.

Management of the APs

The AP should not accept any connection on the VLAN that corresponds to the legacy WLAN subnet because the legacy WLAN subnet is considered insecure, and no communication should be possible to the AP from this subnet. The AP should be managed from a dedicated VLAN on the wired side of the network or through the VLAN that corresponds to the WLAN that uses a more advanced security framework.

Radio Coverage Design

In many instances, network designers should limit the transmission power of their radios to make it more difficult for attackers to find their WLANs. An attacker can thwart this mitigation technique by using high-gain antennas. However, it is something to consider because it eliminates a low-level attacker even though it is not a deterrent against a mid-level to high-level attacker.

Multigroup Access

Multigroup access is achieved with the use of multiple SSIDs mapped to wired network VLANs, as previously described in this chapter.

SWAN Central Switch Design Considerations

The SWAN central switch deployment mode, discussed Chapter 9, can have a number of implications on how the network designer layers security in the WLAN deployment. The exact implications depend on which security frameworks (802.1x/EAP or VPN) the network designer has selected for the WLAN deployment.

In embedded security design environments, the central switch deployment primarily affects how you integrate additional security technology, such as firewalls and network intrusion detection, after the end user has accessed the WLAN. Figure 10-5 depicts how multiple WLAN VLANs are tunneled via multipoint Generic Router Encapsulation (mGRE) across access layer or distribution layer Ethernet switches to the 6500 with the Wireless LAN Services Module (WLSM).

Figure 10-5 *Central Switch Design Considerations with Embedded Security*

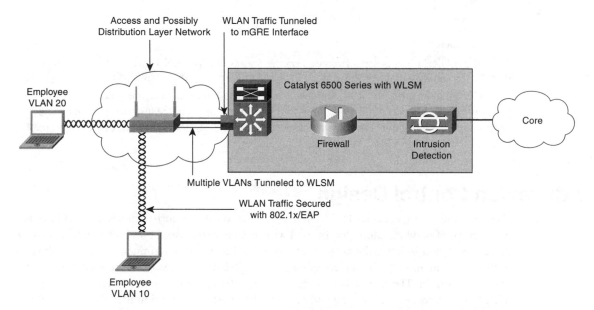

After the mGRE tunnels are terminated on the 6500, the WLAN traffic is routed to the additional network security devices (firewall and network intrusion detection) for inspection. In VPN overlay design environments, the centralized switching mode impacts how and where you position the VPN gateway device and additional security technology. Figure 10-6 depicts how IPSec VPNs from multiple clients on differing WLAN VLANs are tunneled via mGRE across access layer or distribution layer Ethernet switches to the 6500 with the WLSM.

Figure 10-6 *Central Switch Design Considerations with VPN Overlays*

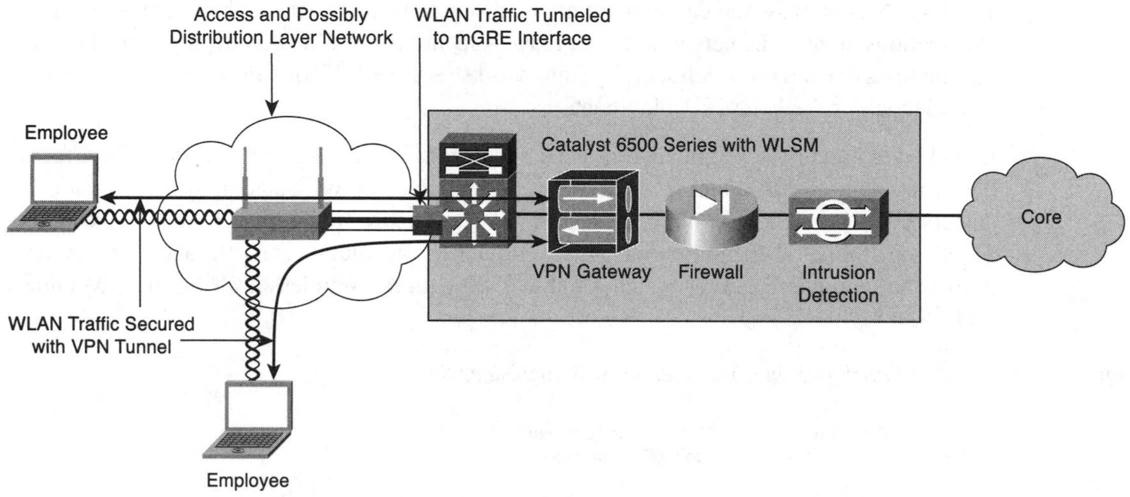

After the mGRE tunnels are terminated on the 65000, the WLAN IPSec VPN traffic is routed to the VPN gateway device that sits between the WLAN and the corporation's core network. Any additional security devices, such as network intrusion detection, are placed after the VPN gateway. There are two main benefits with this design. First, the design offers an easy way to centralize the VPN gateways within a large campus environment. Second, this design enables Layer 3 mobility for VPN users across a large campus.

Admission Control Design

The final topic in this chapter builds on the previous WLAN security frameworks and extends the concept of network admission beyond what has been discussed previously in this book. In this concept, admission to the network at Layer 3 or Layer 2 is determined not only by the user or machine's identity but by the compliance of the WLAN devices to a corporate policy for a variety of criteria. These criteria include antivirus software from vendor XXXX, version YYYY, which must be active and compliant to the latest AV definition files. The intent of this solution is to improve the network's capability to identify, prevent, and adapt to threats. The admission control allows the network designer to make a policy decision on the threat of network clients based on compliance to client security posture.

The solution architecture is designed to allow the access-control decisions to be based on identity information, posture compliance, or both. However, the first phases of the admission-control solution concentrate only on the posture validation. Initial phases of the admission-control solution support Layer 3 access control.

In the context of a WLAN, this access control will initially be determined by a Layer 3 device that sits behind the APs and before the enterprise network. This admission control improves the security posture of the network by being able to validate the security posture of clients that have passed the WLAN authentication but still might be carrying a threat into the enterprise network (such as a worm or a virus). For example, suppose a mobile device has become infected with a virus and deactivates the AV software installed on the mobile device. The corporate policy is that the AV software must be active on the mobile device before access to the network is granted. When the mobile device accesses the WLAN, it is assessed for its compliance to the corporate policy. Because the virus disabled the AV software, the mobile device would fail the policy check and either be denied access to the network or have its access restricted to just accessing remediation services for the virus. Figure 10-7 depicts the network topology for this solution.

Figure 10-7 *Advanced Security Design with Client Policy Compliance*

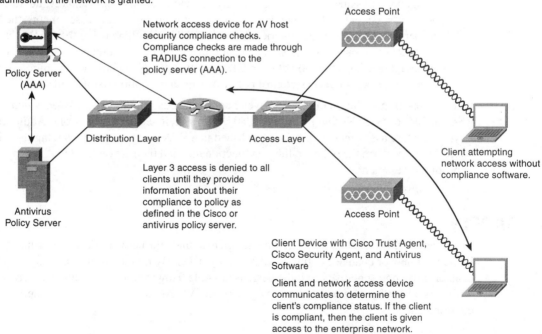

The policy server (AAA) alone can determine compliance of the client by checking a number of criteria. A sample criterion is for AV vendor XXXX, version YYYY to be installed and running before admission to the network is granted.

Policy Server (AAA)

Network access device for AV host security compliance checks. Compliance checks are made through a RADIUS connection to the policy server (AAA).

Access Point

Distribution Layer

Access Layer

Layer 3 access is denied to all clients until they provide information about their compliance to policy as defined in the Cisco or antivirus policy server.

Antivirus Policy Server

Access Point

Client attempting network access without compliance software.

Client Device with Cisco Trust Agent, Cisco Security Agent, and Antivirus Software

Client and network access device communicates to determine the client's compliance status. If the client is compliant, then the client is given access to the enterprise network.

Posture validation can be triggered by any traffic that transverses the gateway. In the Layer 3 mode, posture validation is done by having the Cisco Trust Agent (CTA) be a single point of contact for the host to exchange posture credentials with the network. CTA is intended to aggregate credentials for the client from multiple posture plug-ins and communicating with the network. In Figure 10-7, the network access device (NAD), upon recognition of an incoming client's traffic, issues a challenge for credentials to the client station's CTA via Extensible Authentication Protocol over User Datagram Protocol (EAPoUDP). CTA then gathers its posture credentials and sends them to the NAD. The NAD takes the response from the client and forwards it to the policy server (AAA). The NAD acts as a relay between the client and the policy server. The conversation between the client and the policy server is protected from eavesdropping by tunneling the conversation through Protected Extensible Authentication Protocol (PEAP). The policy server can validate the posture of the client either locally or through an external AV server. When the validation is complete, the NAD enforces the access policy downloaded to it from the policy server. The access policy can be one of the following options:

- Full access
- Restrict access (quarantine)
- Deny access through the NAD
- The restricted access is intended to allow the client to access resources where the client can make changes to its configuration or software installation to become compliant with the posture assessment. At administratively defined intervals, the NAD revalidates the posture assessment of the client. In addition, in between the posture assessments, the NAD also periodically does status queries to determine that the client using the NAD is still the same client that passed the posture validation and that posture credentials have not changed. For clients that do not have CTA installed, the NAD has the capability to query the policy server for access-control policy or a local exception list if available.

Later phases of the solution introduce Layer 2 posture validation via 802.1x/EAP, which makes it applicable for WLANs that utilize WPA/802.11i for their security framework. Additionally, Layer 3 posture assessment can be accomplished in a VPN environment by having the VPN concentrator perform the policy validation functionality and then act on the client's compliance to posture assessment.

Summary

The intent of this chapter was to provide design examples for network designers who want to implement new or change existing WLAN deployments. By no means are the designs in this chapter fully representative of all the designs possible. However, they should give network designers a baseline to work with to design a secure WLAN that is sufficient for their environment.

Operational and Design Considerations for Secure WLANs

This chapter looks at security component best practices for deployment of a secure WLAN. It draws on earlier chapters that describe the Structured Wireless-Aware Network (SWAN) architecture and WLAN design components. This chapter focuses on the following subjects:

- Rogue access point (AP) detection and prevention
- WLAN monitoring and intrusion detection
- WLAN services scaling
- Enterprise guest access

Rogue AP Detection and Prevention

One of the primary concerns that security professionals express with regard to WLANs is rogue APs. Rogue APs can be APs that are connected to the enterprise wired LAN without authorization or APs that are not connected to the wired LAN but that accept associations from clients. Rogue APs can even be APs with a wireless card and a special software package that makes them act as an AP. The rogue APs that are connected to the wired LAN are a security concern because they might not be secured according to a corporation's security policy; this in turn creates a vulnerability in the enterprise network. The rogue APs that are not connected to the wired LAN might accept association requests from clients, which can hamper or deny enterprise clients' access to the corporate WLAN. Also, rogue APs can be classified into two security categories: nonmalicious and malicious.

In the case of nonmalicious APs, the majority of the cases consist of someone installing a rogue AP with the intent being not to bypass the corporation's security policy but to deploy wireless as a convenience or productivity enhancer. The rogue AP installer does not intentionally try to evade detection and uses the default configuration of the AP. The network administrator can often rely on these defaults to identify if there is a conflicting Service Set Identifier (SSID) after the SSIDs are compared to the enterprise WLAN and the Media Access Control (MAC) addresses matching the IEEE OUI for an AP manufacturer.

In the case of malicious APs, the attacker sets up the AP to gain access to the wired network or to disrupt the performance of the WLAN. The attacker can spoof a MAC address to match a legitimate AP, or the attacker can set power, channel, and SSID on the rogue AP to limit its effective coverage area, which in turn minimizes the likelihood of the rogue AP being detected.

Significant technology and manual effort must be expended to mitigate the threat of rogue APs. The primary methods of rogue AP detection are as follows:

- WLAN infrastructure reporting
- Manual rogue AP scanning
- Wired network auditing

This section focuses on these three approaches and covers the pros and cons of each. In most environments, the use of two or all three methods might be appropriate.

SWAN Rogue AP Detection

Chapter 9, "SWAN: End-to-End Security Deployment," discusses SWAN rogue AP detection. However, the network administrator needs to address additional considerations when deploying SWAN rogue AP detection.

The first consideration is covering areas that currently do not have approved WLAN coverage. The network administrator must make a decision about how to best scan these areas for rogue APs. There are two primary options. The first is to do manual rogue AP detection, which is covered in the following section. The second option is based on SWAN and utilizes an AP that is deployed in scan-only mode. In this mode, the AP is not configured to accept WLAN client connections but scans only the frequency channels for AP or client activity. It might transmit beacons, but it will not interfere with the client-to-AP communication. In addition, it will not respond to probes. Finally, scan-only APs are capable of detecting unassociated clients. It is important to detect unassociated clients in areas without authorized WLAN infrastructure because you do not want them to potentially associate to an unauthorized AP. For both options, the network administrator should use a high-gain antenna to maximize the range of the radio for rogue AP detection. For instance, with scan-only APs, you might want to deploy with an omnidirectional, high-gain antenna to get maximum coverage.

NOTE   *Bug lighting* is a term sometimes used to describe attackers' efforts to get unsuspecting clients to associate to a rogue AP. The analogy is that attackers set up a rogue AP and fire up a valid SSID in an attempt to lure unsuspecting clients to their rogue AP, much like a bug light is set up to lure unsuspecting bugs.

The second consideration covers both the 2.4-GHz and 5-GHz frequency ranges when the enterprise has approved only deployments in single frequency ranges. In these deployments, the network administrator must choose a method by which to scan the other frequency range to make sure rogue APs do not utilize that range for unauthorized access. Again, the network administrator needs to choose whether to use manual rogue AP detection or a scan-only AP to provide this coverage. In many cases, network administrators might choose to deploy dual-mode APs with high-gain antennas just to enable the ability to monitor the secondary frequency for rogue APs.

The third consideration is to detect 802.11 ad-hoc mode WLANs occurring within a building. The 802.11 ad-hoc WLANs allow clients to set up a local network in which participants communicate directly with each other. This is known as an *independent basic service set (iBSS) network configuration*. A member of a wired or infrastructure WLAN that participates in an ad-hoc could potentially provide unwilling and unauthorized access to the enterprise network. For this reason, the network administrator might find it necessary to detect these ad-hoc networks. Ad-hoc network detection leverages the SWAN architecture and its radio management (RM) features.

For an ad-hoc network to be created, the participants must issue beacons that synchronize their communication. APs deployed in an infrastructure WLAN can detect these beacons and report them to the Wireless Domain Services (WDS) in their RM messages. The WDS then puts the relevant information into the RM aggregator messages that it sends to the Wireless LAN Solution Engine (WLSE). Figure 11-1 shows this detection and reporting mechanism.

The WLSE then presents several options for displaying the ad-hoc detection information. The WLSE administrator has the option to specify the severity of the ad-hoc detection notification and can choose to determine in what part of the WLAN the ad-hoc network was detected. The WLSE presents the administrator with a list of all the APs that have detected and reported the ad-hoc WLAN and provides the building and floor of the AP, if available.

Manual Rogue AP Detection

The primary technique that has been employed to detect rogue APs has been the manual rogue AP sweep. The network administrator should make manual sweeps for rogue APs because the "supported" infrastructure might not cover the entire geographical area of an enterprise that has network connectivity. For instance, a manufacturing environment typically leverages a wireless environment, but it might not cover the same area as the wired network. For this reason, network administrators are required to use some sort of portable device with a high-gain antenna that actively probes and passively monitors for WLAN activity to detect a rogue AP.

Figure 11-1 *SWAN Ad-Hoc WLAN Detection*

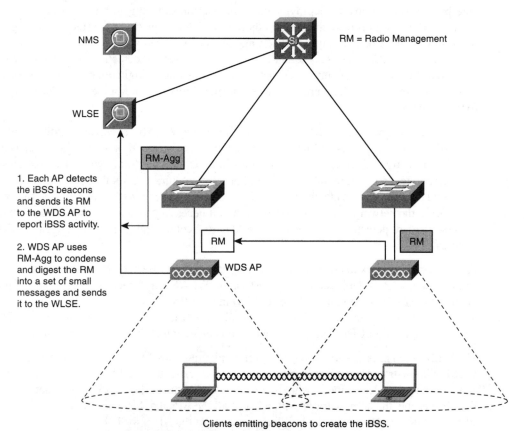

NMS

RM = Radio Management

WLSE

RM-Agg

1. Each AP detects the iBSS beacons and sends its RM to the WDS AP to report iBSS activity.

2. WDS AP uses RM-Agg to condense and digest the RM into a set of small messages and sends it to the WLSE.

RM

RM

WDS AP

Clients emitting beacons to create the iBSS.

If the enterprise has not deployed both 2.4-GHz and 5-GHz WLAN technology (either client APs or scanning-only APs), the network administrator should perform a manual sweep with the alternate 802.11 WLAN technology to detect any rogue APs that might have been put up by offenders using the alternate technology. The network administrator needs to make sure that the tool he uses for manual rogue AP detection also incorporates the use of an active probing component. This is necessary because a rogue AP might turn off its broadcast SSID and "cloak" itself. The network administrator must use an active probing scanner to make the rogue AP respond.

Network-Based Rogue AP Detection

In addition to auditing via the WLAN media network, administrators should investigate ways to integrate several authentication and auditing techniques that leverage the wired LAN to detect or prevent rogue APs.

The first technique is to leverage the existence of 802.1x in all recent model switches and operating systems (OSs). The network administrator must create a policy that states that no client device can connect to the wired network unless it successfully authenticates itself to the network via 802.1x. In this way, the network administrator eliminates a majority of rogue APs because, in many cases of the rogue AP being a nonmalicious installation, the rogue AP is a consumer-brand AP that does not have the ability to act as an 802.1x supplicant.

Note that a determined malicious attacker can circumvent this prevention technique in a variety of ways. For instance, if the attacker has access to a valid set of credentials for 802.1x authentication (such as username and password), he can use an Ethernet hub and a normal client device to authenticate to the infrastructure. After an attacker is authenticated, he can substitute the rogue AP for the "authenticated" client device. Switch security features such as port security, which can limit the number of MAC addresses an Ethernet switch port allows, can make this attack more difficult but not impossible because the attacker can use an advanced client operating system (OS) configuration either to spoof the AP's MAC address or to make an intelligent client device (like a small Linux box) the rogue AP.

The second technique leverages the published IEEE OUI for AP vendors. Several tools, such as APTools (http://winfingerprint.sourceforge.net/aptools.php), allow you to pull the MAC addresses that have been seen on an Ethernet switch and compare them against a list of "approved" AP MAC addresses. If the tool sees a MAC address that is not on the approved list, it prints out the MAC address, which can then be correlated with information from other Cisco network management tools, such as User Resource Tracking, to find the switch name and the switch port to which the AP is attached. Note that this mitigation technique is also vulnerable to an attacker changing the OUI to match a desktop NIC vendor or to spoof the MAC address of an approved AP or desktop.

The final technique involves scanning the network for signatures that identify the rogue AP. The most common scanning techniques include OS fingerprinting and Simple Network Management Protocol (SNMP) scanning. The more prevalent option is the OS fingerprinting technique because it typically is easier to conduct and is more accurate. OS fingerprinting observes characteristics of the individual OS of the AP, such as the way the OS responds to TCP packets with obscure TCP flags and options enabled. OS fingerprinting depends on there being a fingerprint match for the AP point vendor OS. SNMP scanning relies on the rogue AP having SNMP enabled and accessible from the enterprise network. In the case of the malicious rogue AP, this is a highly unlikely scenario. In the nonmalicious rogue AP instance, SNMP scanning is typically effective for detecting rogue AP installations that might be larger than normal and managed by the user or a rogue AP that has SNMP on by default with public and private settings for its read-only and read-write community strings.

WLAN Services Scaling

In the general 802.1x/EAP (Extensible Authentication Protocol) and virtual private network (VPN) designs, large deployments can be taxing on the scalability and availability of network services. Domain Name System (DNS) and Dynamic Host Control Protocol (DHCP) are typically already deployed in a high availability and scalability manner within enterprises due to wired LAN's reliance on these services. The following sections discuss how to address and scale the Remote Authentication Dial-In User Service (RADIUS) and VPN gateway services.

RADIUS Best Practices

RADIUS authentication scalability and high availability is of primary concern to any network designer who must support a WLAN of any size. Several factors impact the scalability and availability of a RADIUS system, including the following:

- Authentication types being used
- RADIUS client configuration for primary and secondary RADIUS servers
- RADIUS logging level
- Type of database used for authentication
- Backup, replication, and synchronization strategy to be employed

Different EAP authentication types put varying amounts of strain on the RADIUS server. For instance, EAP Transport Layer Security (EAP TLS) puts more of a strain on a system than the Lightweight Extensible Authentication Protocol (LEAP) due to the way the EAP types do the mutual authentication. Because of the strain of the EAP authentication types on the server's resources, it might become necessary to load-balance RADIUS requests from APs to multiple RADIUS servers. Figure 11-2 depicts the topology of a group of RADIUS servers being load-balanced for scalability.

Several load balancers (Cisco Content Services Switch, Content Services Module, and so on) support the capability to query the RADIUS server with a fixed username, password, and shared secret to validate that the RADIUS process is still functional. This query is called a "keep alive," and it determines if the RADIUS server should stay in rotation for load balancing. If you are looking to use the RADIUS cluster to collect RADIUS accounting information, remember that you must have a persistent, or "sticky," connection to the same authentication server to make sure that the RADIUS accounting start/stop records from the AP go to the same RADIUS server. This persistence typically is achieved via a source IP persistence configuration. The network administrator must make sure that the load balancer installed in his network can support this persistence with RADIUS accounting.

Figure 11-2 *RADIUS Servers Load-Balanced*

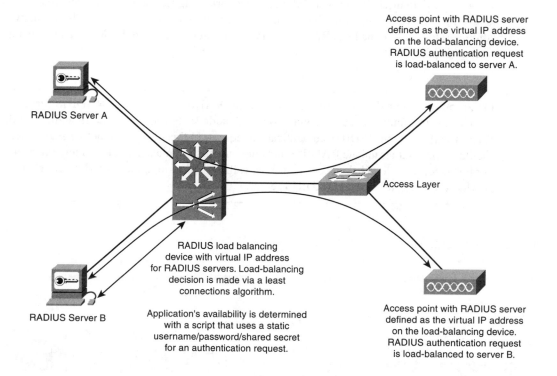

NOTE   *Sticky* or *stickiness* is a term used in server load balancing to denote when a client must remain attached to a real server because there is some sort of state information on the real server with regard to the client. An example is the e-commerce "shopping cart" with which most web purchasers are familiar. The application logic of a shopping cart can sometimes rely on the client always communicating with a particular web server to keep the shopping cart status accurately. SSL-based VPN gateways require that a user be connected to the same SSL VPN gateway until he logs out of the VPN session to provide up-to-date authentication, authorization, and connectivity information.

In addition to having scalability and high availability in the data center, the AP has the capability to designate multiple RADIUS servers in its configuration for local high availability and simple RADIUS scalability. These RADIUS servers are listed in order of preference; the AP tries the first server on the list and proceeds to the second server if the first is unresponsive and times out. A timeout is triggered by the AP settings that include the number of retransmission attempts (three, by default) and a transmission delay between authentication attempts (five seconds, by default). With this capability, the network designer can perform static load-balancing and availability through the static configuration. Figure 11-3 depicts how a network administrator can use the local RADIUS server definition to achieve this load balancing and high availability.

NOTE   In the central switch design, the WLSM acts as the RADIUS client to the RADIUS servers. In this case, you cannot load balance via a source IP address, because only the IP address of the WLSM will be in the RADIUS authentication request. In this design, the network designer should select another unique RADIUS attribute on which to make a load-balancing decision. For instance, some load balancers can use the calling-station-id in the RADIUS request to provide stickiness to a proper RADIUS server.

Figure 11-3   *AP Configuration for Load Balancing and Failover*

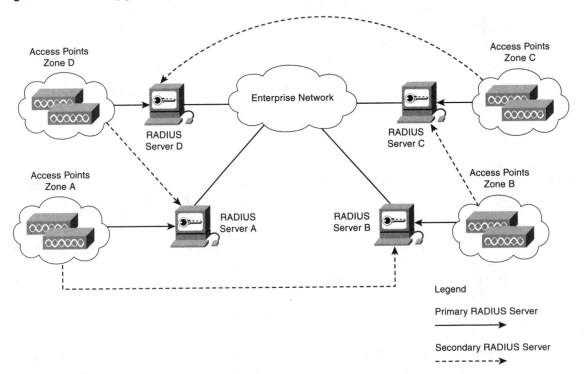

The network designer can achieve simple load balancing by designating that different zones within the enterprise should use different primary RADIUS servers. Zone A uses the IP address of server A as its primary and server B as its secondary. APs in Zone B have server B as their primary server and server A as their secondary server. The IP addresses for the servers that the network designer designates in the AP configuration can be the virtual IP address of a RADIUS load-balancing device in a data center, which can handle dynamic load balancing within the data center.

Another factor in server scalability is the RADIUS logging level. The RADIUS logging level is a value that determines how much information the RADIUS server writes to its log for every RADIUS transaction or server event. The higher the logging level, the more data that is written to the RADIUS log. A high logging level can significantly increase the processing load on the server, which in turn can cause a significant degradation in the servers' authentication performance.

In many instances, the RADIUS server is merely a consolidation and pass-through device for WLAN authentication. With this in mind, network designers must understand that the type and location of the database storing WLAN user authentication credentials impacts both the scalability and high availability of RADIUS from the WLAN client perspective. In most instances, the backend server and underlying database have appropriate scaling and availability built into them because they are also leveraged for other network services like network operating systems or LDAP. However, in some instances, WLAN authentication and RADIUS have seemed to perform poorly because the introduction of the WLAN has overburdened the backend database or because the backend database is not located properly in the network to give timely responses to the RADIUS infrastructure.

Finally, if the user database is stored locally to the RADIUS server, network designers must understand how database replication affects the performance and availability of the RADIUS deployments. The most important thing to note when utilizing a replication strategy is that some RADIUS servers suspend the authentication service during portions of the database replication from a master to a secondary server. In the Cisco Secure Access Control Server (ACS) for Windows database, replication is a top-down design with a cascading method of replication being implemented; this minimizes the time that the authentication server is suspended. Additionally, the network designer might choose not to allow the master server from serving authentication requests directly from clients. This reduces the impact of the authentication service being suspended on the master and allows the master to replicate directly to all of its secondary servers. Finally, if the master and secondary servers reside in differing time zones, the network designer should consider using cascading servers within a time zone. The master server can replicate to a primary server within a time zone during off hours. The primary server within the time zone can then cascade the replication within the time zone. This reduces the impact of the database replication.

VPN Best Practices

If VPN overlays have been selected as either the primary or secondary means of securing a WLAN, a network designer must deal with several issues with regard to large WLAN deployments.

The first issue is scalability of the VPN gateway service. Early VPN gateway devices limited the amount of encryption throughput (10s of Mbps to 100 Mbps) and the number of simultaneous sessions (several hundreds) that they could perform. This limitation led to the development and deployment of several load-balancing technologies. Later releases of VPN gateway products dramatically increased the encryption throughput (multiple Gbps) and simultaneous sessions (several thousand). However, these products still command a price premium and are sometimes not feasible for use as VPN gateway devices to secure a WLAN; therefore, VPN load balancing is still actively deployed for scalability purposes and high availability.

The network administrator's second issue is high availability. Because a VPN is selected to secure the WLAN, it must be available to WLAN users at all times. With this in mind, there are two methods for providing high availability: local high availability and site high availability. Local high availability refers to a way to provide VPN service to a local environment. This environment can be within a data center or even within a large campus. Typically, local high availability is delivered with some sort of local load-balancing device or some extensions to the VPN protocol. Site high availability refers to providing a VPN service for a general VPN service name. So, if a WLAN user is traveling between locations, the network designer wants to provide a similar method of offering VPN service regardless of the location from which the user might be connecting to a WLAN. Because most VPN gateways use a DNS name to establish connectivity, DNS availability becomes a concern for providing site availability. In addition, DNS can be utilized to deliver site-based load balancing for VPN services. In a large WLAN environment, the DNS-based load balancer can make DNS resolution decisions based on the source IP address of the DNS server. For instance, a DNS-based load balancer might resolve a DNS request to VPN cluster A if the request comes from DNS server 1, while resolving a DNS request to a VPN cluster if the request comes from DNS server 2. Figure 11-4 depicts this DNS-based site load balancing.

The following discussions deal with the idea of local high availability. Because the primary VPN deployments are IPSec and SSL-based VPN, these are the only VPN technologies discussed in this section.

IPSec VPN Clustering

You can also use IPSec load balancing built into the IPSec solution. Cisco offers IPSec client load balancing in its VPN 3000. Figure 11-5 depicts the topology of a VPN cluster using the Cisco IPSec clustering and load-balancing technology in the preceding platforms.

Figure 11-4   *Site-Based VPN Load Balancing*

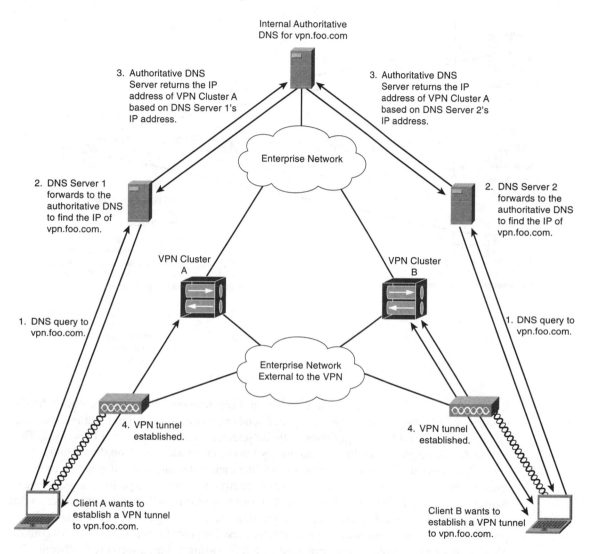

A VPN cluster includes two or more IPSec gateways. A Cisco VPN cluster has one master and multiple secondary devices. The master is designated via an election process among the clustering devices. IPSec clients connect to a cluster virtual IP address. The virtual IP address is an address that is shared among the cluster. The master in the cluster handles any initial IPSec client request. Upon receiving a client request to establish an IPSec tunnel, the master looks at the latest load and availability information that it receives from each secondary device in its keepalive message exchange and its own load-balancing information. Based on the information

Figure 11-5 *IPSec VPN Cluster*

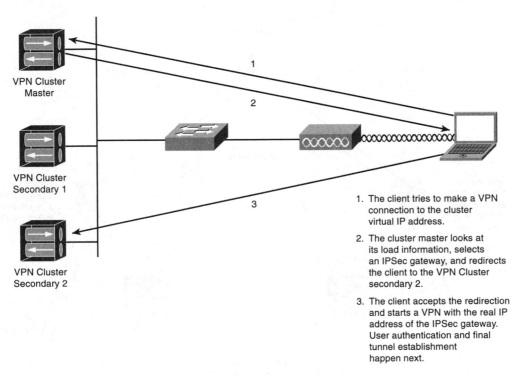

1. The client tries to make a VPN
   connection to the cluster
   virtual IP address.

2. The cluster master looks at
   its load information, selects
   an IPSec gateway, and redirects
   the client to the VPN Cluster
   secondary 2.

3. The client accepts the redirection
   and starts a VPN with the real IP
   address of the IPSec gateway.
   User authentication and final
   tunnel establishment
   happen next.

it finds, the master uses an algorithm to select an IPsec gateway with which the client should continue its IKE negotiation. The master then sends a response to the client that redirects the client to continue its IPSec negotiation with the selected VPN gateway's real IP address. The cluster handles high availability by continually having the master check on the secondaries' status. The secondaries are responsible for sending their status and load information to the master. The slaves, in turn, expect to hear from the master device on a periodic basis. If the master device should fail, the secondary with the highest priority will be the new master so that subsequent IPSec client requests can be serviced. If the secondary devices have identical priority settings, the device with the lowest IP address becomes the master device. All communication among the cluster can be protected with IPSec using a shared secret for authentication.

TIP   The virtual IP address of a VPN 3000 cluster does not respond to a ping echo-request. This can lead to lots of frustration and confusion during troubleshooting if this is not known.

The load is calculated as a percentage of current active sessions divided by the configured maximum-allowed connections.

IPSec External Load Balancer

IPSec can be load-balanced in two ways: An external load-balancing device or a load-balancing algorithm can be built into the IPSec device itself. The former typically is more useful with a mix of IPSec clients because the latter solution requires proprietary extensions to the IPSec protocol. The latter is more cost effective because you are not required to purchase or manage extra devices. In either instance, it is assumed that all the VPN gateways are configured identically to authenticate and authorize all remote clients that might be directed to connect to the VPN gateway.

When using an external load-balancing device, the primary benefit is interoperability (as previously noted) and high availability. Figure 11-6 depicts the basic topology of a load-balancing device balancing connections to a group of IPSec gateways.

When an IPSec peer needs to establish a VPN tunnel through an IPSec load-balancing device, an Encapulating Security Payload (ESP) flow must "follow" its corresponding Internet Key Exchange (IKE) flow; otherwise, the IPSec tunnel will not work. Because of this requirement, the IPSec load-balancing device must match ESP flows to IKE flows. This means that if an IKE flow from client A goes to IPSec gateway B, the corresponding ESP packets from client A must go to IPsec gateway B. ESP flows can alternatively be encapsulated over UDP to transverse Network Address Translation (NAT) and Port Address Translation (PAT) devices. The IPSec load balancer must support this User Datagram Protocol (UDP) wrapping because this NAT transparency feature is default in many IPSec client configurations. In regards to scalability, since IPSec is a stateless protocol, the load-balancing device has no idea how to determine load on the VPN gateway device. The load-balancing device cannot look at the content of the IPSec session and derive load information from the content stream. So, the load balancing device can only use the least-connections algorithm to determine which VPN gateway is least loaded. With regard to high availability, most load balancers do not have the capability to conduct a full IPSec negotiation to determine whether the network behind the VPN gateway is available; therefore, most load-balancing devices determine the availability of the individual VPN gateways via a basic health check, such as with a ping to the device or an initial IKE connection to UDP port 500.

SSL External Load Balancing

SSL VPNs have scaling and high availability challenges that are similar to those of IPSec VPNs. Because SSL VPNs emphasize the idea of a "clientless" VPN, the client does not contain intelligent code to handle load-balancing items such as the IPSec redirection of the VPN 3000. For this reason, most SSL VPN load balancing is done with the use of external load-balancing devices. Load-balancing devices have been used in heavy SSL environments such as

Figure 11-6   *External IPSec Load Balancer*

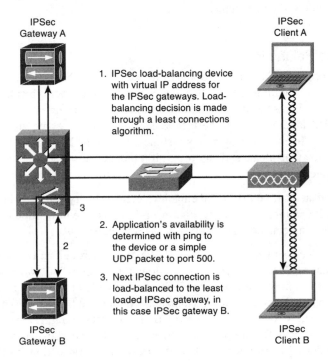

1. IPSec load-balancing device with virtual IP address for the IPSec gateways. Load-balancing decision is made through a least connections algorithm.

2. Application's availability is determined with ping to the device or a simple UDP packet to port 500.

3. Next IPSec connection is load-balanced to the least loaded IPSec gateway, in this case IPSec gateway B.

e-commerce for many years, so there is a well-developed solution set around providing scalable and available SSL solutions. Figure 11-7 depicts the basic topology of a load-balancing device balancing connections to a group of SSL gateways.

SSL typically is load balanced with a least-connections load-balancing algorithm with a stickiness based on source IP address. High availability depends on the SSL health checks that are available on the load-balancing device. These health checks can vary from a simple health check like a ping to a more advanced health check like opening a connection to the SSL VPN device on the SSL VPN port (typically 443), starting the SSL handshake, and then disconnecting.

Enterprise Guest Access

Enterprises generally have guests with high needs to remain productive and in touch, and they have the benefit of an existing network infrastructure that can be leveraged to support their guests. With the growing number of built-in radios in laptops, guests are requesting this type of guest access to utilitize WLANs while working remotely with their company.

Figure 11-7   *External SSL Load Balancer*

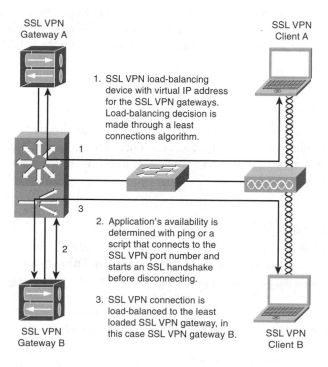

SSL VPN
Gateway A

SSL VPN
Client A

1. SSL VPN load-balancing
   device with virtual IP address
   for the SSL VPN gateways.
   Load-balancing decision is
   made through a least
   connections algorithm.

2. Application's availability is
   determined with ping or a
   script that connects to the
   SSL VPN port number and
   starts an SSL handshake
   before disconnecting.

3. SSL VPN connection is
   load-balanced to the least
   loaded SSL VPN gateway, in
   this case SSL VPN gateway B.

SSL VPN
Gateway B

SSL VPN
Client B

Enterprise Guest Access Requirements

Providing access to enterprise guests poses several unique network requirements. Unlike
traditional enterprise network users, the IT/networking staff does not control the end-to-end
user connection. Instead, enterprise guest networks must support many users with an unknown
variety of devices, configuration, and security. To enable diverse users to easily get connected
without IT support, the guest access network must have a full range of public-access features
that are described in the following sections.

Open Authentication Guest VLAN

For guests to become connected, there must be a way to authenticate with "open authentication." Using their security scheme of choice, network designers can utilize full security for all
their internal users and applications while maintaining a single VLAN with open authentication. This VLAN becomes the guest network.

Traffic Separation of the Guest VLAN to the Edge of the Enterprise

Enterprises require that the guest WLAN traffic not interact with the normal enterprise traffic for security and business-continuity reasons. With this in mind, the network designer must select the proper technology to provide traffic separation for the WLAN as it crosses his enterprise.

Plug-and-Play Connectivity

The network designer must provide a simple connectivity process in which guests can self-activate access. As many as 15 percent of end-user devices are configured with static proxies or DNS configurations. These users must be able to get connected without having to reconfigure their laptops or PDAs.

Cost-Effective and Secure Access Codes

To limit access on the guest network, a network designer might choose to implement an access gateway that can challenge users for valid credentials. The network designer can choose to do this for a variety of reasons, but in many cases the network designer might be required to provide access codes to track and audit who used the guest access for liability reasons. These credentials must be easy to administer and distribute because there is a large volume of guests, many of whom will only need access for a day or even a few hours.

Enterprise Guest Access Design

To provide a technical solution to the preceding requirements, the network designer must utilize several technologies simultaneously. The open authentication for the guest WLAN is easily accommodated using the open authentication in the 802.11 specifications. To provide traffic separation, network designers must combine several technologies to logically separate the guest WLAN from the enterprise network.

One method is to utilize the WLAN VLAN with open authentication to a wired VLAN. In small to medium-size enterprises, the wired guest VLAN can connect directly to the enterprise edge, where a gateway is installed to deal with the last two requirements. However, in large enterprises, it might be impossible to connect the guest VLAN to the enterprise edge if the enterprise does not utilize a Layer 2 core because Layer 2 cores are not as prevalent as Layer 3 cores in many large enterprises. If there is not a Layer 2 core, the network designer must utilize some tunneling protocol either to extend the VLAN across the Layer 3 core or to create an IP-addressable tunnel to encapsulate the guest VLAN traffic and transmit it across the enterprise Layer 3 core. Many technologies exist to perform this function, the most notable being MPLS for extending the guest and GRE for creating an IP-addressable tunnel across the Layer 3 core. Either type of solution should, if possible, leverage a Layer 3 platform that utilizes Virtual Routing Forwardings (VRFs) such as the Supervisor720 for the Catalyst 6500 platform. The use of VRFs creates an independent routing domain for the guest VLAN. This isolation minimizes the risk that a network connectivity issue on the guest VLAN will affect the rest of the enterprise network.

NOTE   The concept of using VRFs and tunneling traffic across the core of a large network is a complex issue. Because this is a WLAN book, it will not delve into this subject in depth. It is suggested that you continue reading up on this subject by visiting the Cisco website and reviewing documentation and design guides relating to this subject.

Another method is to leverage the Wireless LAN Services Module (WLSM) and the central switching design to tunnel the guest traffic to the edge of the corporate network.

Finally, the network designer must address the last two requirements of the guest access: cost effectiveness and secure access codes. These requirements are addressed via the use of a gateway device such as the Cisco Building Broadband Building Manager (BBSM) or the Service Selection Gateway in IOS. It should be noted that gateway devices can be bottlenecks to network throughput, so the network designer must be careful that the guest WLAN traffic doesn't overwelm the gateway device. Figure 11-8 depicts a design that accommodates the requirements for enterprise guest access and that utilizes the technology as previously described.

Figure 11-9 depicts guest access that leverages the WLSM and the central switch design. The inherent tunneling in the solution allows the network administrator to deliver the guest WLAN traffic directly to the corporate edge, where a gateway device can provide the authentication for the guests.

Using the designs in Figures 11-8 and 11-9 as templates, the network designer should be able to refine the design for his environment to provide secure guest WLAN access.

Figure 11-8 *Enterprise Guest Access Design*

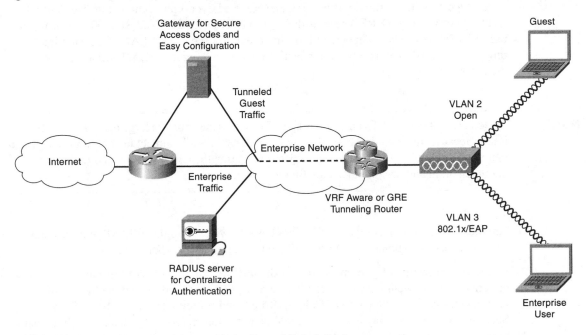

Figure 11-9 *Enterprise Guest Access with the Central Switch Design*

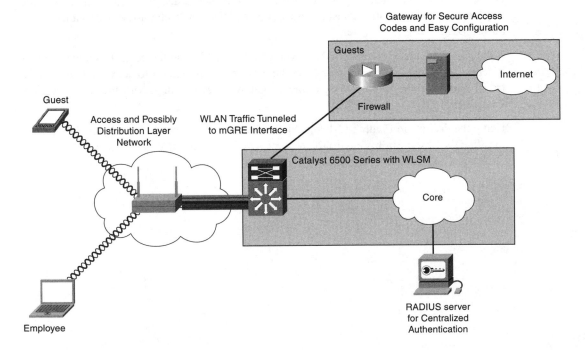

Summary

The intent of this chapter was to provide some best-practice examples of how to deal with some of the operational and design challenges of deploying secure WLANs. The chapter provided guidance on how to handle rogue AP detection and how to scale RADIUS and VPN services and gave the reader options for handling guest access. As always, the best practices that the network designer decides to implement depend upon his particular environment.

WLAN Security Configuration Guidelines and Examples

This chapter provides detailed configuration examples and guidelines for various security implementations such as guest access (open/no Wired Equivalent Privacy [WEP]), static WEP, MAC-address authentication, 802.1x authentication protocol with dynamic WEP, 802.1x authentication protocol with Wi-Fi Protected Access (WPA), WPA Preshared Key (WPA-PSK), multiple Service Set Identifiers (SSIDs) along with wired VLANs, and IP security–based virtual private network (IPSec VPN). It provides secure management configuration examples to secure management traffic to the WLAN infrastructure devices and discusses secure wired policies (for example, Layer 3/Layer 4 ACLs) to match wireless policies.

This chapter covers various WLAN products that are available for deployment from Cisco. It also discusses capabilities of currently available products; however, you are encouraged to consult the Cisco Systems website (http://www.cisco.com) for up-to-date information on products and capabilities.

Cisco WLAN products can be deployed in three modes as discussed in Chapter 9, "SWAN: End-to-End Security Deployment." The possible deployment modes include the following:

- Standalone AP deployment mode
- SWAN nonswitching deployment mode
- SWAN central switching deployment mode

Note that the radio interface configuration for security policies and quality-of-service (QoS) policies is the same across all three deployment modes. Furthermore, the AP locally supports the 802.11/WPA functions across the three modes. However, RADIUS server authentication configuration, RF management, configuration/software management, Layer 3 roaming, and data aggregation are different across the three deployment modes.

Cisco Enterprise Class Wireless LAN Products

Cisco Systems provides multiple WLAN products, including access points (APs), bridges, workgroup bridges, client adapters, network management appliances, and wired/WLAN integration components. For example, various APs are available from Cisco, such as AP1200, AP1100, and so on, for deployment using various 802.11 technologies. Cisco

WLAN products, such as APs and bridges, use Cisco IOS as the operating system. Also, multiple WLAN components and features are available on Cisco Catalyst switching platforms and the router platforms for wireless and wired integration (as part of the Structured Wireless-Aware Network [SWAN] implementation). This section details Cisco products that are currently available for WLAN deployment in enterprise, vertical (retail, health care, education, manufacturing, and so on), and small-to-medium business (SMB) markets. The list of products described in the following sections is not exhaustive; rather, it is a sample of key WLAN products available for deployment.

Cisco Aironet AP1200 Access Point

The Cisco Aironet AP1200 AP is a dual-mode (two-radio) platform. It supports 802.11b, 802.11a, and 802.11g technologies simultaneously with the use of two radios (2.4-GHz and 5-GHz radios). It also supports a pair of antennas per radio. Customers have several antenna choices for 2.4-GHz radio (802.11b and 802.11g), whereas a built-in flexible antenna (omnidirectional and patch) is provided per FCC regulations for the 5-GHz radio (802.11a). The AP1200 supports all EAP authentication protocols (Cisco LEAP, Extensible Authentication Protocol Transport Layer Security [EAP TLS], Protected EAP [PEAP], and so on), RADIUS-based authentication, authorization and accounting, Cisco Temporal Key Integrity Protocol (TKIP), WPA TKIP, Advanced Encryption Standard (AES) for stronger encryption and data integrity, and 802.1Q-based VLANs for user or device differentiation. Furthermore, the AP1200 provides 802.11e-based QoS mechanisms and Layer 3 roaming capabilities (as part of SWAN central switching deployment mode). AP1200 provides built-in network management tools such as HTTP and command-line interface (CLI) management interfaces, Simple Network Management Protocol (SNMP), Telnet, Secure Shell Protocol (SSH), and Trivial File Transfer Protocol (TFTP).

Cisco Aironet AP1100 Access Point

The Cisco Aironet AP1100 is a single-radio platform that supports 802.11b or 802.11g radio (2.4 GHz) and comes integrated with an antenna. The AP1100 supports all EAP authentication protocols (LEAP, EAP-TLS, PEAP, and so on), RADIUS-based authentication, authorization and accounting, Cisco TKIP, WPA TKIP, AES for stronger encryption and data integrity, and 802.1Q-based VLANs for user or device differentiation. Furthermore, the AP1100 provides 802.11e-based QoS mechanisms and Layer 3 roaming capabilities (as part of SWAN central switching deployment mode). AP1100 provides built-in network management tools such as HTTP and CLI management interfaces, SNMP, SSH, Telnet, and TFTP.

Cisco Aironet AP350 Access Point

The Cisco Aironet AP350 is a single-radio platform that supports only 802.11b technology. The AP350 supports all EAP authentication protocols (LEAP, EAP-TLS, PEAP, and so on),

RADIUS-based authentication, authorization and accounting, Cisco TKIP and WPA TKIP for stronger encryption and data integrity, and 802.1Q-based VLANs for user or device differentiation. Furthermore, the AP350 provides 802.11e-based QoS mechanisms and Layer 3 roaming capabilities (Proxy Mobile IP). AP350 provides built-in network management tools such as HTTP and CLI management interfaces, SNMP, SSH, Telnet, and TFTP.

Cisco Aironet BR350 Bridge

The Cisco Aironet BR350 is an 802.11b-based bridge for outdoor deployments. The BR350 enables speeds up to 11 Mbps for long-range, outdoor links deployment of up to 25 miles between buildings. BR350 supports both point-to-point and point-to-multipoint configurations and a broad range of antennas for the outdoor deployments. Cisco LEAP authentication can be used with CKIP to secure the bridged link between the nonroot and root bridges. Furthermore, BR350 supports all EAP authentication protocols and CKIP for WLAN client authentication and data encryption. BR350 supports 802.1Q-based VLAN trunking between root and nonroot bridges, along with VLANs for user or device differentiation. Furthermore, the BR350 provides 802.11e-based QoS mechanisms for traffic prioritization. BR350 provides built-in network management tools such as HTTP and CLI management interfaces, SNMP, SSH, Telnet, and TFTP.

Cisco Aironet BR1410 Bridge

The Cisco Aironet BR1410 is an 802.11a-based bridge that uses the 5.7-GHz unlicensed spectrum for outdoor deployments. The BR1410 enables speeds up to 54 Mbps for long-range, outdoor links deployment between buildings. BR1410 supports both point-to-point and point-to-multipoint configurations and a broad range of antennas for the outdoor deployments. Cisco LEAP authentication can be used with CKIP to secure the bridged link between the nonroot and root bridges. BR1400 supports 802.1Q-based VLAN trunking between root and nonroot bridges. Furthermore, the BR1410 provides 802.11e-based QoS mechanisms for traffic prioritization. BR1410 provides built-in network management tools such as HTTP and CLI management interfaces, SNMP, SSH, Telnet, and TFTP.

Cisco Aironet 802.11b/a/g and Cisco Client Extensions–Enabled Devices

Cisco Aironet 802.11 client adapters and Cisco Client Extensions (CCX)-compliant 802.11 adapters or devices are used to provide wireless network connectivity to a variety of computers, including laptops, PDAs, and workstations. Client adapters using various 802.11 technologies (802.11a/b/g) are available from Cisco. CCX qualified devices (such as laptops) and CCX-qualified 802.11 adapters are non-Cisco client hardware that support various Cisco client functionalities. A list of CCX-qualified client hardware is available at http://www.cisco.com/en/US/partners/pr46/pr147/partners_pgm_concept_home.html.

Worth noting is that major 802.11 chipset manufacturers (including Intel, Aethors, and Broadcom) and laptop manufactures (IBM, Dell, HP, and Toshiba) are included as part of the CCX program.

Cisco Secure Access Server

Cisco Secure ACS provides authentication, authorization, and accounting services to network devices, such as a network access server, PIX Firewall, router, or access point, that function as AAA clients. In a wireless LAN network, the ACS server plays an important role of authenticating WLAN users using EAP authentication protocols (LEAP, EAP-TLS, and PEAP) and creating dynamic session keys for user data encryption between the client and the AP. Along with EAP authentication, Cisco Secure ACS can be used for administrator authentication and authorization. With Cisco Secure ACS, network administrators can quickly administer accounts and globally change levels of service offerings for entire groups of users. Although use of an external user database is optional, support for many popular user repository implementations enables companies to put to use the working knowledge gained from and the investment already made in building their corporate user repositories. Cisco Secure ACS uses the TACACS+ and RADIUS protocols to provide AAA services that ensure a secure environment.

Cisco Wireless LAN Solution Engine

Cisco Wireless LAN Solution Engine (WLSE) is a turnkey network management solution for managing Cisco Aironet wireless LAN infrastructure. It provides centralized, template-based configuration with hierarchical, customer-defined grouping to efficiently manage large numbers of APs and bridges. If desired, plug-and-play configuration allows newly deployed APs and bridges to be automatically configured using the WLSE. The WLSE monitors RADIUS server(s) for LEAP, PEAP, and generic RADIUS authentication service availability. The WLSE further enhances security management by detecting misconfigurations on APs and bridges. The functionality within CiscoWorks WLSE includes proactive monitoring, troubleshooting, notification of performance degradation, and reports for improving capacity planning. The WLSE can also be used for RF management such as the Cisco assisted Site Survey and rogue AP detection capabilities. Refer to Chapter 9 for more details on RF management functions provided by the WLSE.

Catalyst 6500 Wireless LAN Services Module

This services module on the Catalyst 6500 product platform integrated with the Supervisor 720 module supports wireless domain services (WDS) features along with central switching mode to provide end-to-end security, mobility, and manageability for wireless LAN deployments in large and medium-size enterprises and vertical markets. This also allows for wired and wireless integration in a campus environment. This deployment model supports key features such as WDS scalability, Layer 2/Layer 3 fast secure roaming, 802.11 user data aggregation, RF management services, and end-to-end security for wireless and wired LAN integration.

WLAN Security Methods: Configuration Guidelines and Examples

This section provides configuration guidelines and examples for various security policies discussed in the previous chapters. Configuration capabilities are discussed for the IOS-enabled AP and bridging platforms, but the same features can be enabled using WLSE or the centralized WLAN services command-line interface (CLI) available on Catalyst switching platforms.

At the time of this writing, configuration samples are taken from the 12.2(15)JA IOS release. Most of the configuration samples are provided using IOS CLI commands, but the following section briefly discusses configuration via HTML GUI on the access points/bridges. Note that HTML GUI screen changes are made for each IOS release. Refer to WLAN product documentation on the Cisco website for the latest configuration guidelines.

The configuration examples discussed in this section are relevant for an AP in standalone deployment mode; however, radio interface parameters (such as SSID, VLAN assignment, and encryption parameters) are the same across all three deployment modes. Changes specific to SWAN nonswitching deployment mode are discussed in the section "SWAN Nonswitching Deployment: Configuration Guidelines and Examples" later in this chapter, and SWAN central switching deployment mode is discussed in the section "SWAN Central Switching Deployment: Configuration Guidelines and Examples," also later in this chapter.

Navigating the HTML GUI Configuration Pages

Configuration changes can be made on WLAN AP and bridging platforms using a standard web browser. When the web browser is directed to the IOS-enabled access point/bridge (such as http://10.10.10.21), the user is prompted to log in. Factory defaults for user login are "Cisco" for both user ID and password. You should change this, as discussed in the best practices for secure management section. Figure 12-1 is an HTML GUI configuration screen capture for 12.2(13)JA1 IOS release on access point platforms.

Figure 12-1 *HTML GUI Configuration on IOS-Enabled AP*

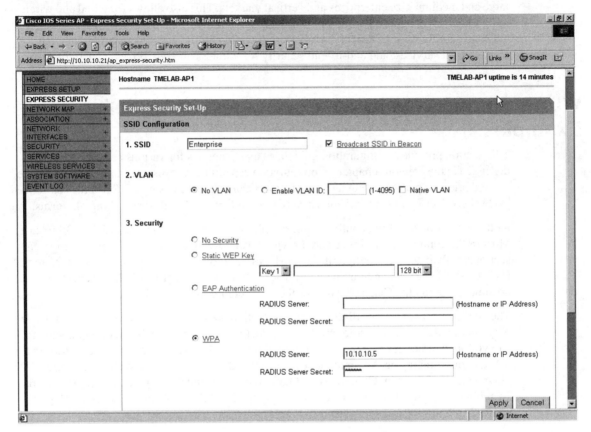

As shown in Figure 12-1, the AP/bridge GUI configuration screen provides express setup page(s) and detailed setup pages for interfaces (both radio and Ethernet), security, and multiple services, including WDS configuration and software management. Navigating the GUI becomes relatively easy when you understand the configuration order for any feature. For example, to configure multiple VLANs for an AP, follow this procedure using the HTML GUI configuration pages:

1 On the Services VLAN page, enable 802.1Q trunking on the AP/bridge by creating the native/management VLAN.

2 On the Services VLAN page, create user VLANs.

3 On the Security SSID page, create SSIDs and map them to VLANs. Specify authentication and key management parameters for each SSID.

4   On the Security Encryption Manager page, specify encryption settings for each VLAN.

5   On the Security Server Manager page, specify RADIUS server parameters.

6   On the Wireless Services page, specify the WDS configuration details (if applicable).

The HTML GUI pages provide status and troubleshooting information (errors, logs, and so on) in addition to configuration options. It is recommended that you navigate the HTML GUI screens on the latest IOS release so that you understand the configuration options available on the AP/bridge.

IOS CLI Configuration Examples and Guidelines

This section details IOS CLI configuration for various WLAN security methods discussed in this book. The intention is to increase your knowledge of how various security methods can be enabled for WLAN deployment. Client and RADIUS server configuration details, along with the AP/bridge IOS CLI configuration, are discussed for various security methods. Along with configuration details, troubleshooting tips are provided (where applicable).

Open/No WEP Configuration

The open/no WEP configuration, shown in Example 12-1, is typically used for guest or hotspot services where Layer 2 authentication and data confidentiality are disabled. Guest mode is typically enabled on the SSID to allow the AP to broadcast the guest/hotspot service SSID.

Example 12-1   *Open/No WEP Configuration on an IOS-Enabled AP/Bridge*

```
TMELAB-AP1#conf t
Enter configuration commands, one per line. End with CNTL/Z.
TMELAB-AP1(config)#int dot11Radio 0
TMELAB-AP1(config-if)#ssid coffee
TMELAB-AP1(config-if-ssid)#authentication open
! Guest mode enables the AP/Bridge to broadcast SSID information
TMELAB-AP1(config-if-ssid)#guest-mode
TMELAB-AP1(config-if-ssid)#end
```

Open/with WEP and WPA-PSK Configurations

The open/with WEP (also known as static WEP) configuration, shown in Example 12-2, typically is used on legacy devices that do not support WPA or 802.11i capabilities. These devices are typically found in vertical markets such as retail and manufacturing. One example would be legacy bar-code scanners used in the retail environment for inventory tracking. Typically, guest mode is enabled on the SSID to allow the legacy 802.11 client devices to discover the WLAN network.

Example 12-2 *Open/with Static-WEP Configuration on an IOS-Enabled AP/Bridge*

```
TMELAB-AP1(config)#int dot11Radio 0
TMELAB-AP1(config-if)#ssid legacy
TMELAB-AP1(config-if-ssid)#authentication open
TMELAB-AP1(config-if-ssid)#guest-mode
TMELAB-AP1(config-if-ssid)#exit
TMELAB-AP1(config-if)#encryption mode wep mandatory
TMELAB-AP1(config-if)#encryption key 1 size 128bit 0 0987654321098765432109876⁵
transmit-key
TMELAB-AP1(config-if)#end
```

As discussed in Chapter 6, "Wireless Vulnerabilities," static WEP has several vulnerabilities. Therefore, it is not recommended for deployment in an enterprise, SMB, or vertical environment.

Figure 12-2 illustrates the static WEP configuration required for a Cisco 350 client NIC adapter. It depicts the Cisco Aironet GUI configuration screen shot.

Figure 12-2 *Static WEP Configuration on a WLAN Client*

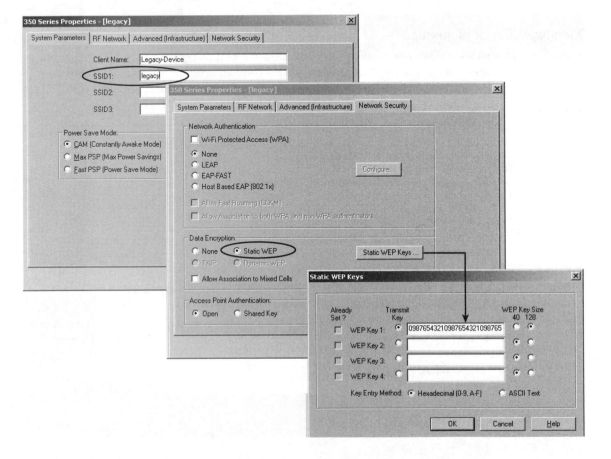

The WPA-PSK (Pre-Shared Key) configuration, shown in Example 12-3, is primarily used for residential deployment but might be of some use in vertical environments in which WPA-DOT1x mode cannot be deployed. WPA-PSK deployment requires a static passphrase to be programmed on the AP and on the WLAN clients. Guest-mode configuration is not required on the SSID but might be desired for applications such as Windows XP native WLAN supplicant to autodiscover the WLAN network.

Example 12-3 *WPA-PSK Configuration on an IOS-Enabled AP/Bridge*

```
TMELAB-AP1(config)#int dot11Radio 0
TMELAB-AP1(config-if)#encryption mode ciphers tkip
TMELAB-AP1(config-if)#ssid msTest2
TMELAB-AP1(config-if-ssid)#authentication open
TMELAB-AP1(config-if-ssid)#authentication key-management wpa
! Specify the pass-phrase for WPA-PSK deployment
TMELAB-AP1(config-if-ssid)#wpa-psk ascii Us3aStrongpAssPhras3
TMELAB-AP1(config-if-ssid)#guest-mode
TMELAB-AP1(config-if-ssid)#end
```

The WPA-PSK passphrase is susceptible to offline dictionary attack; it is recommended that you use a multiple-word passphrase. Figure 12-3 shows the screen capture for a sample WPA-PSK configuration on a Windows XP client.

Figure 12-3 *Sample WPA-PSK Client Configuration*

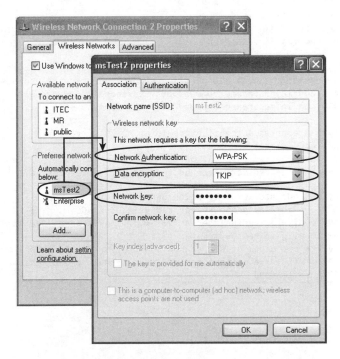

WPA-PSK mode is not recommended for deployment in enterprise or vertical environments due to client management issues and its susceptibility to offline dictionary attack. The IT administrator is required to change the WPA-PSK passphrase due to loss or theft of client devices. Thus, client management issues are primarily related to configuring and continuously updating the WLAN clients with the static passphrase required for WPA-PSK deployment.

MAC Address Authentication Configuration

MAC address authentication can be enabled along with open authentication for any security configuration. A sample configuration sequence to enable MAC address authentication is shown in Example 12-4. As shown in the example, a specific user account for MAC address authentication is added on the AP, and the AP is configured to relay the MAC address authentication request to a RADIUS server. The user account shall be created with the MAC address of the WLAN client adapter as the username and the MAC address of the WLAN client as the password to enable MAC address authentication. Typically, MAC address authentication is enabled for legacy 802.11 devices (which do not support 802.11i/WPA) along with the static WEP configuration. If MAC address authentication is enabled, the AP first checks its local database; if the user account is not found, an authentication request can be relayed to a RADIUS server.

Example 12-4 *Enabling MAC Address Authentication on an IOS-Enabled AP/Bridge*

```
TMELAB-AP1(config)#int dot11Radio 0
TMELAB-AP1(config-if)#ssid legacy
TMELAB-AP1(config-if-ssid)#authentication open mac-address MacAuth
TMELAB-AP1(config-if-ssid)#end
!
! Adding MAC addresses locally on the WLAN AP/Bridge ---
! Mac address of the WLAN NIC card is used as the username and password
TMELAB-AP1(config)#username 00028a4d80cf password 0 00028a4d80cf
TMELAB-AP1(config)#username 00028a4d80cf autocommand exit
!
! Specify MAC address authentication to a RADIUS server:
TMELAB-AP1(config)#aaa new-model
!Specify Radius Server information
TMELAB-AP1(config)#radius-server host 10.10.10.5 auth-port 1812 acct-port 1813 key
tmelab
! Specify MAC address authentication Servers
TMELAB-AP1(config)#aaa group server radius RadiusMAC
TMELAB-AP1(config-sg-radius)#server 10.10.10.5 auth-port 1812 acct-port 1813
TMELAB-AP1(config-sg-radius)#exit
! Specify rad_mac group of servers to be used for MAC address authentication
TMELAB-AP1(config)#aaa authentication login MacAuth group RadiusMAC
TMELAB-AP1(config)#end
```

EAP with Dynamic WEP Configuration

EAP with dynamic WEP configuration has been widely implemented as a result of WEP vulnerability (as discussed in Chapter 6). In this deployment, an encryption key per user is dynamically generated and can be periodically rotated. Multiple EAP protocols (as discussed in Chapter 7, "EAP Authentication Protocols for WLANs") can be used, including Cisco LEAP, EAP-TLS, PEAP, and EAP-FAST. Note that both LEAP and EAP Flexible Authentication via Secure Tunneling (EAP-FAST) should be supported using the "network EAP" type on Cisco client adapters. The network EAP type is a Cisco proprietary authentication type (instead of 802.11 open authentication type) used between the WLAN client and the AP. CCX clients are likely to support LEAP or EAP-FAST using the 802.11 open type plus require EAP configuration. Thus, you should enable network EAP and "open+require EAP" on the APs to ensure that all adapters and EAP types are supported.

The configuration required for EAP/802.1x deployment with dynamic WEP is shown in Example 12-5. As shown in the example, both network EAP and open+require EAP are configured for EAP authentication. Also, broadcast key rotation is enabled for the EAP users. In addition to authentication and encryption parameters configuration, RADIUS server configuration is required to relay the authentication request to a specific RADIUS server.

Example 12-5 *EAP with Dynamic WEP Configuration on an IOS-Enabled AP*

```
TMELAB-AP1(config)#int dot11Radio 0
TMELAB-AP1(config-if)#ssid Enterprise
! Enable LEAP authentication and specify the LEAP list name "LEAP-AUTH"
TMELAB-AP1(config-if-ssid)#authentication network-eap EAP-AUTH
! Enable EAP authentication methods using "Open+Require EAP"
TMELAB-AP1(config-if-ssid)#authentication open eap EAP-AUTH
! Enable broadcast SSID
TMELAB-AP1(config-if-ssid)#guest-mode
TMELAB-AP1(config-if-ssid)#exit
! There are multiple WEP encryption modes available on Cisco APs. Note that WEP-
optional is Cisco proprietary whereas WEP-Mandatory is Standards based.
TMELAB-AP1(config-if)#encryption mode wep mandatory
! Enable Broadcast Key rotation for every 900 seconds (15 minutes)
TMELAB-AP1(config-if)#broadcast-key change 900
TMELAB-AP1(config-if)#exit
! Configure RADIUS server parameters for EAP authentication
TMELAB-AP1(config)#aaa new-model
! Specify Radius Server information
TMELAB-AP1(config)#radius-server host 10.10.10.5 auth-port 1812 acct-port 1813 key
tmelab
! Specify EAP authentication servers
TMELAB-AP1(config)#aaa group server radius RadiusEAP
! Specify 10.10.10.5 server as an EAP authentication server
TMELAB-AP1(config-sg-radius)#server 10.10.10.5 auth-port 1812 acct-port 1813
TMELAB-AP1(config-sg-radius)#exit
```

continues

Example 12-5 *EAP with Dynamic WEP Configuration on an IOS-Enabled AP (Continued)*

```
! Specify rad_eap group of servers to be used for EAP authentication
TMELAB-AP1(config)#aaa authentication login EAP-AUTH group RadiusEAP
! Configure miscellaneous RADIUS server parameters
TMELAB-AP1(config)#radius-server attribute 32 include-in-access-req format %h
TMELAB-AP1(config)#radius-server authorization permit missing Service-Type
TMELAB-AP1(config)#radius-server vsa send accounting
TMELAB-AP1(config)#end
```

Example 12-6 *Debug Help*

```
TMELAB-AP1#debug dot11 aaa authenticator process
TMELAB-AP1#debug dot11 aaa authenticator state-machine
!
! An example EAP authentication sequence
TMELAB-AP1#
*Mar  1 00:16:07.447: dot11_auth_dot1x_start: in the dot11_auth_dot1x_start
*Mar  1 00:16:07.447: dot11_auth_dot1x_send_id_req_to_client: sending identity request
for 0007.8592.0c8a
*Mar  1 00:16:07.448: dot11_auth_dot1x_send_id_req_to_client: Started timer
client_timeout 30 seconds
*Mar  1 00:16:07.450: dot11_auth_parse_client_pak: Received EAPOL packet from
0007.8592.0c8a
*Mar  1 00:16:07.450: dot11_auth_dot1x_run_rfsm: Executing
Action(CLIENT_WAIT,EAP_START) for 0007.8592.0c8a
*Mar  1 00:16:07.450: dot11_auth_dot1x_send_id_req_to_client: sending identity request
for 0007.8592.0c8a
*Mar  1 00:16:07.450: dot11_auth_dot1x_send_id_req_to_client: Started timer
client_timeout 30 seconds
*Mar  1 00:16:07.451: dot11_auth_parse_client_pak: Received EAPOL packet from
0007.8592.0c8a
*Mar  1 00:16:07.451: dot11_auth_parse_client_pak: id is not matching req-id:1resp-
id:2, waiting for response
*Mar  1 00:16:07.456: dot11_auth_parse_client_pak: Received EAPOL packet from
0007.8592.0c8a
*Mar  1 00:16:07.456: dot11_auth_dot1x_run_rfsm: Executing
Action(CLIENT_WAIT,CLIENT_REPLY) for 0007.8592.0c8a
*Mar  1 00:16:07.456: dot11_auth_dot1x_send_response_to_server: Sending client
0007.8592.0c8a data to server
*Mar  1 00:16:07.457: dot11_auth_dot1x_send_response_to_server: Started timer
server_timeout 60 seconds
*Mar  1 00:16:07.468: dot11_auth_dot1x_parse_aaa_resp: Received server response:
GET_CHALLENGE_RESPONSE
*Mar  1 00:16:07.468: dot11_auth_dot1x_parse_aaa_resp: found eap pak in server response
*Mar  1 00:16:07.468: dot11_auth_dot1x_run_rfsm: Executing
Action(SERVER_WAIT,SERVER_REPLY) for 0007.8592.0c8a
*Mar  1 00:16:07.468: dot11_auth_dot1x_send_response_to_client: Forwarding server
message to client 0007.8592.0c8a
```

Example 12-6 *Debug Help (Continued)*

```
*Mar  1 00:16:07.469: dot11_auth_dot1x_send_response_to_client: Started timer
client_timeout 30 seconds
*Mar  1 00:16:07.476: dot11_auth_parse_client_pak: Received EAPOL packet from
0007.8592.0c8a
*Mar  1 00:16:07.476: dot11_auth_dot1x_run_rfsm: Executing
Action(CLIENT_WAIT,CLIENT_REPLY) for 0007.8592.0c8a
*Mar  1 00:16:07.476: dot11_auth_dot1x_send_response_to_server: Sending client
0007.8592.0c8a data to server
*Mar  1 00:16:07.476: dot11_auth_dot1x_send_response_to_server: Started timer
server_timeout 60 seconds
*Mar  1 00:16:07.481: dot11_auth_dot1x_parse_aaa_resp: Received server response:
GET_CHALLENGE_RESPONSE
*Mar 1 00:16:07.481: dot11_auth_dot1x_parse_aaa_resp: found eap pak in server response
*Mar  1 00:16:07.481: dot11_auth_dot1x_run_rfsm: Executing
Action(SERVER_WAIT,SERVER_REPLY) for 0007.8592.0c8a
*Mar  1 00:16:07.482: dot11_auth_dot1x_send_response_to_client: Forwarding server
message to client 0007.8592.0c8a
*Mar  1 00:16:07.482: dot11_auth_dot1x_send_response_to_client: Started timer
client_timeout 30 seconds
*Mar  1 00:16:07.484: dot11_auth_parse_client_pak: Received EAPOL packet from
0007.8592.0c8a
*Mar  1 00:16:07.484: dot11_auth_dot1x_run_rfsm: Executing
Action(CLIENT_WAIT,CLIENT_REPLY) for 0007.8592.0c8a
*Mar  1 00:16:07.485: dot11_auth_dot1x_send_response_to_server: Sending client
0007.8592.0c8a data to server
*Mar  1 00:16:07.485: dot11_auth_dot1x_send_response_to_server: Started timer
server_timeout 60 seconds
*Mar  1 00:16:07.490: dot11_auth_dot1x_parse_aaa_resp: Received server response: PASS
*Mar  1 00:16:07.490: dot11_auth_dot1x_parse_aaa_resp: found session timeout 600 sec
*Mar 1 00:16:07.490: dot11_auth_dot1x_parse_aaa_resp: found eap pak in server response
*Mar 1 00:16:07.491: dot11_auth_dot1x_parse_aaa_resp: found leap session key in server
response
*Mar  1 00:16:07.491: dot11_auth_dot1x_parse_aaa_resp: leap session key length 16
*Mar  1 00:16:07.491: dot11_auth_dot1x_run_rfsm: Executing
Action(SERVER_WAIT,SERVER_PASS) for 0007.8592.0c8a
*Mar  1 00:16:07.491: dot11_auth_dot1x_send_response_to_client: Forwarding server
message to client 0007.8592.0c8a
*Mar  1 00:16:07.492: dot11_auth_dot1x_send_response_to_client: Started timer
client_timeout 30 seconds
*Mar  1 00:16:07.492: %DOT11-6-ASSOC: Interface Dot11Radio0, Station SRISUNDA-W2K
0007.8592.0c8a Associated KEY_MGMT[NONE]
```

Using the configuration guidance provided in Example 12-5, the EAP with dynamic WEP
configuration on the AP/bridge supports LEAP, PEAP, EAP-FAST, EAP-TLS, or any other
EAP authentication method. Figure 12-4 shows the LEAP client configuration required on the
Cisco Aironet Client Utility (ACU) supplicant using a Cisco 350 PCMCIA client adapter.

Figure 12-4 *Sample LEAP Client Configuration*

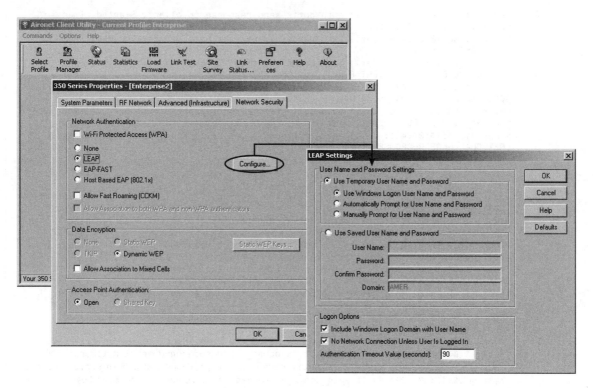

Figure 12-5 shows the PEAP client configuration required on a Windows XP client operating system using the Windows native EAP supplicant.

Figure 12-6 shows the EAP-FAST client configuration required on the Cisco ACU using the Cisco 350 PCMCIA client adapter.

Figure 12-7 shows the EAP-TLS client configuration required on a Windows XP client operating system using the Windows native EAP supplicant.

Figure 12-5   *Sample PEAP Client Configuration*

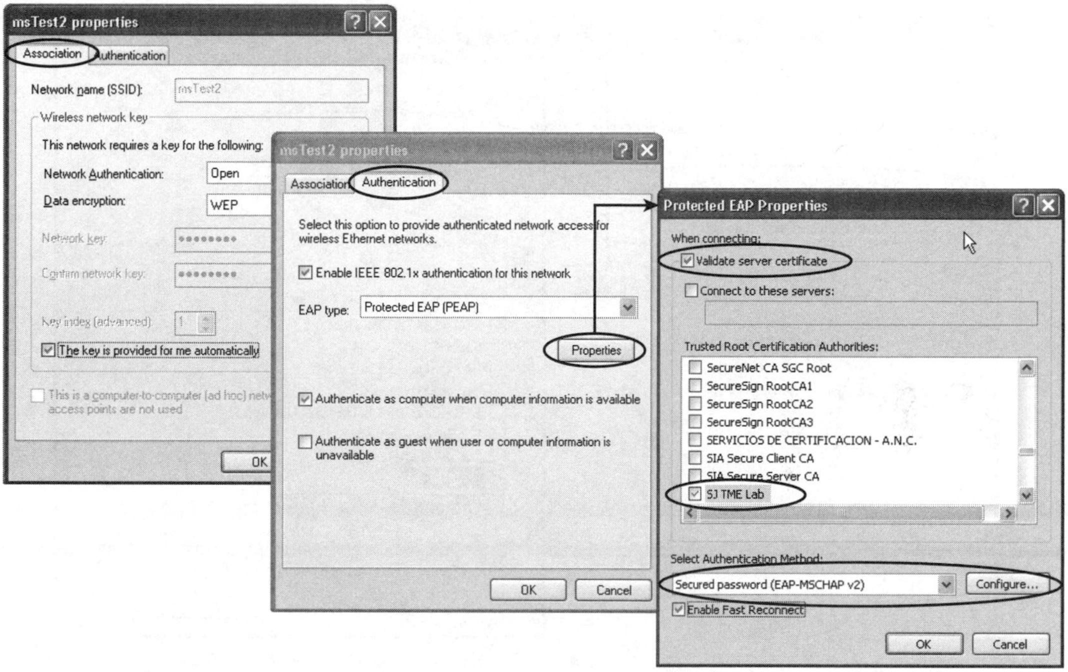

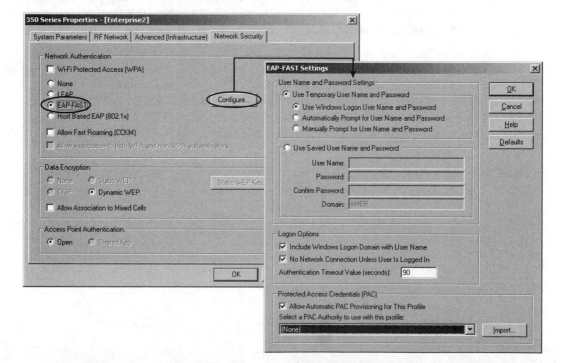

Figure 12-6   *Sample EAP-FAST Client Configuration*

Figure 12-7   *Sample EAP-TLS Client Configuration*

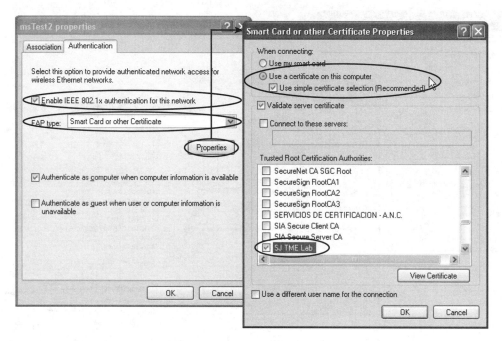

Figure 12-8 shows the PEAP client configuration required on a third-party EAP supplicant and available from Meetinghouse Data Communication (MDC). Note that third-party supplicants such as the MDC EAP supplicant are embedded and provided with CCX clients.

Along with client and AP configuration, RADIUS server configuration is required to enable EAP authentication. Specifically, you must add each AP (in standalone mode, also known as non-SWAN mode) as a AAA client on the RADIUS server database, and you must configure appropriate EAP protocol parameters. Alternatively, you can use wildcard addressing (for example, 10.10.10.*) while specifying the AAA client on the RADIUS server to support multiple standalone APs with a single AAA client entry. Figure 12-9 shows how you can add the AP as a AAA client on the Cisco Secure ACS RADIUS server.

Figure 12-8   *PEAP Configuration on a Third-Party EAP Supplicant*

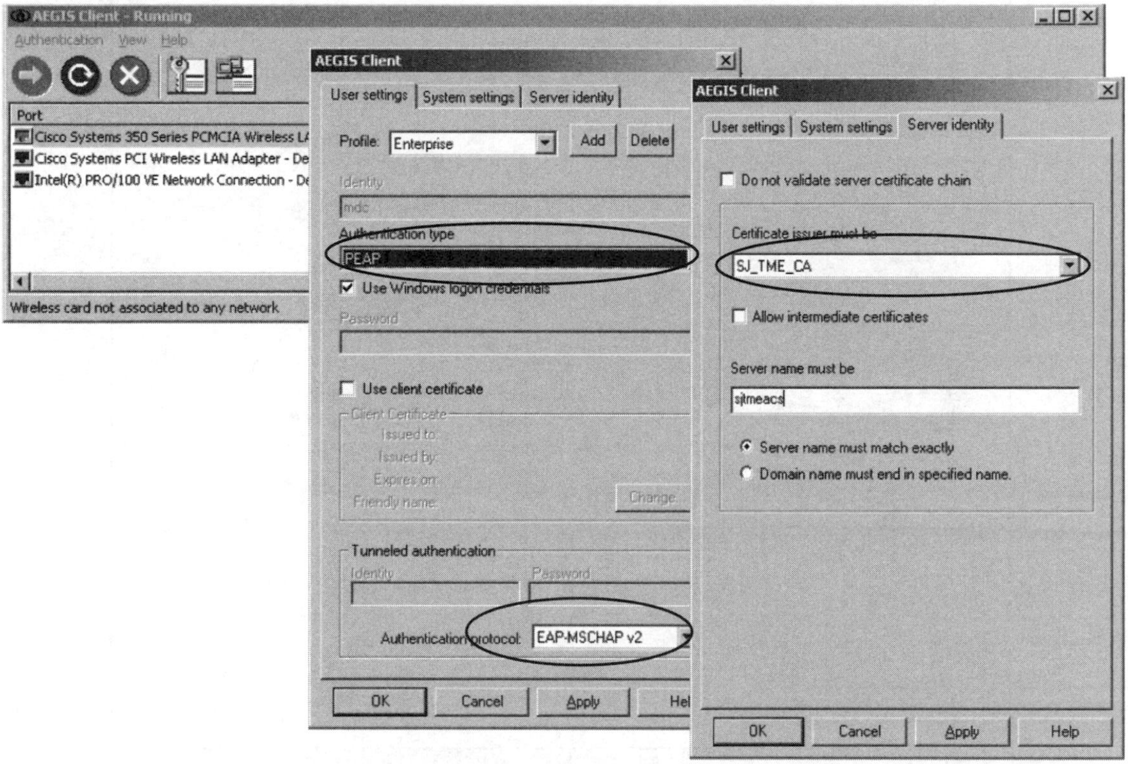

In addition to the AAA client settings, you must specify EAP protocols (LEAP, PEAP, EAP-FAST, or EAP-TLS) on the RADIUS server. Figure 12-10 shows the required EAP parameter configuration on the Cisco Secure ACS server. You should enable and configure on the RADIUS server only the EAP protocols that are deployed in your network.

Figure 12-9 *Basic RADIUS Server Configuration*

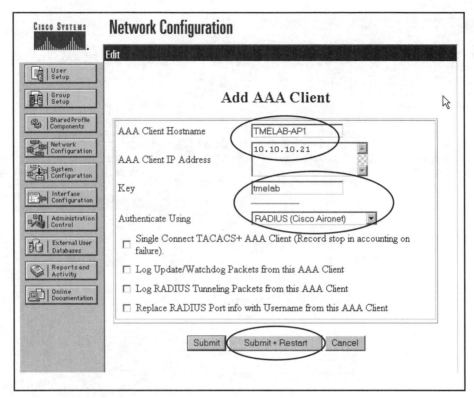

Along with the AAA client and EAP protocol settings, you can alter user-group (or user) settings to periodically reauthenticate the user to the WLAN network. You can configure Internet Engineering Task Force (IETF) parameter 27 at the user or user-group level to periodically reauthenticate WLAN users.

WPA-DOT1x Configuration

As discussed in Chapter 8, "WLAN Encryption and Data Integrity Protocols," several improvements were made in the 802.11i specification to increase the cryptographic strength of RC4 implementation in 802.11 products. This resulted in a data confidentiality and integrity protocol known as TKIP (refer to Chapter 8 for more details). WPA-DOT1x configuration mode enables the network administrator to implement EAP authentication, with WPA-TKIP used for data confidentiality and data integrity. Typically, an enterprise WLAN rollout would use WPA-DOT1x security configuration to provide Layer 2–based user authentication and data confidentiality. Note that you can deploy any EAP protocol (such as LEAP, PEAP, EAP-TLS, or EAP-FAST) along with WPA.

Figure 12-10 *EAP Parameter Configuration on a RADIUS Server*

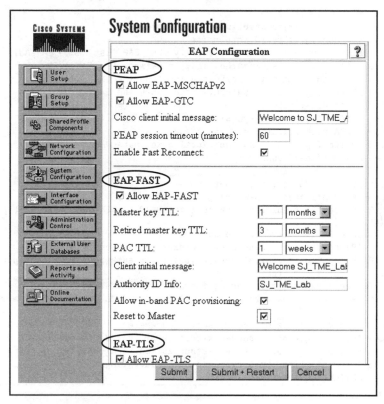

Example 12-7 provides the configuration sequence required to enable WPA on Cisco APs/ bridges. As shown in the example, TKIP needs to be configured as the cipher for WPA mandatory deployment mode. Along with the authentication and cipher settings, you must specifiy RADIUS configuration to enable the AP (standalone mode) to relay EAP authentication requests to the RADIUS server.

Example 12-7 *WPA-DOT1x Configuration on an IOS-Enabled AP*

```
TMELAB-AP1(config)#int dot11Radio 0
! Enable cipher negotiation and specific data confidentiality protocols that can be
negotiated.
! Note that TKIP, WEP128, and WEP40 are standards based. CKIP, CKIP-CMIC, and CMIC
modes are Cisco proprietary and are known as Cisco TKIP modes.
TMELAB-AP1(config-if)#encryption mode ciphers ?
  ckip       Cisco Per packet key hashing
  ckip-cmic  Cisco Per packet key hashing and MIC (MMH)
  cmic       Cisco MIC (MMH)
  tkip       WPA Temporal Key encryption
  wep128     128 bit key
```

continues

Example 12-7 *WPA-DOT1x Configuration on an IOS-Enabled AP (Continued)*

```
  wep40      40 bit key
TMELAB-AP1(config-if)#encryption mode ciphers tkip
TMELAB-AP1(config-if)#ssid Enterprise
! Enable LEAP authentication and specify the LEAP list name "EAP-AUTH"
TMELAB-AP1(config-if-ssid)#authentication network-eap EAP-AUTH
! Enable EAP authentication methods using "Open+Require EAP"
TMELAB-AP1(config-if-ssid)#authentication open eap EAP-AUTH
! Enable broadcast SSID
TMELAB-AP1(config-if-ssid)#guest-mode
! Enable WPA authenticated key management
TMELAB-AP1(config-if-ssid)#authentication key-management wpa
TMELAB-AP1(config-if-ssid)#end
!
! Configure RADIUS Server parameters
TMELAB-AP1(config)#aaa new-model
TMELAB-AP1(config)#radius-server host 10.10.10.5 auth-port 1812 acct-port 1813 key 0
tmelab
! Configure RADIUS server group settings
TMELAB-AP1(config)#aaa group server radius EAP-Servers
TMELAB-AP1(config-sg-radius)#server 10.10.10.5 auth-port 1812 acct-port 1813
TMELAB-AP1(config-sg-radius)#exit
! Configure a radius server group for EAP authentication
TMELAB-AP1(config)#aaa authentication login EAP-AUTH group EAP-Servers

! Configure miscellaneous RADIUS server parameters
TMELAB-AP1(config)#radius-server attribute 32 include-in-access-req format %h
TMELAB-AP1(config)#radius-server authorization permit missing Service-Type
TMELAB-AP1(config)#radius-server vsa send accounting
TMELAB-AP1(config)#end
```

On the WLAN client, you need to configure WPA and a specific EAP protocol to enable the WPA-DOT1x mode. Typically, WPA configuration is independent of the EAP protocol configuration. Thus, follow the recommendations in the previous section as far as configuring LEAP, EAP-TLS, PEAP, or EAP-FAST. Figure 12-11 illustrates WPA configuration for a Cisco EAP-FAST client.

Figure 12-12 illustrates the WPA configuration on a Windows XP client.

Figure 12-11 *Sample EAP-FAST with WPA Client Configuration*

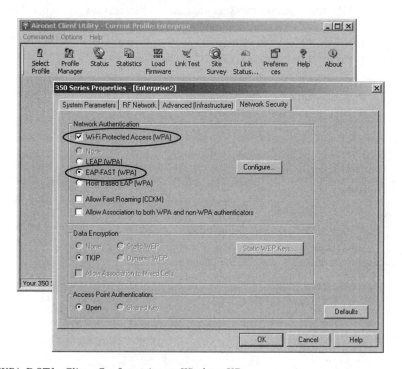

Figure 12-12 *WPA-DOT1x Client Configuration on Windows XP*

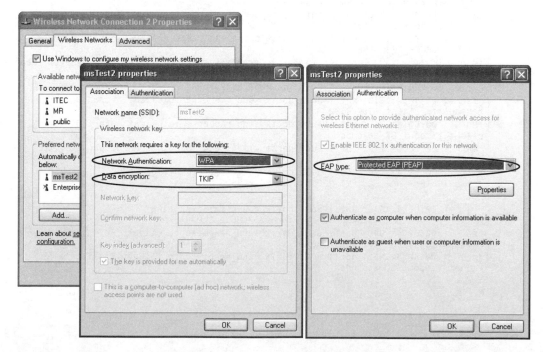

Finally, the RADIUS server configuration is the same as described in the previous section for enabling EAP authentication and specific EAP authentication protocols. Thus, note that no additional configuration is required on the RADIUS server for WPA-DOT1x deployment as compared to EAP/802.1x with dynamic WEP deployment. Example 12-8 illustrates the debug commands for troubleshooting WPA-DOT1x deployment.

Example 12-8 *Debug Information (WPA-DOT1x)*

```
TMELAB-AP1#debug dot11 aaa authenticator process
TMELAB-AP1#debug dot11 aaa authenticator state-machine
!
! An example WPA-DOT1x authentication sequence (PEAP/with WPA client authentication)
TMELAB-AP1#
*Mar  1 00:50:41.175: dot11_auth_dot1x_start: in the dot11_auth_dot1x_start
*Mar 1 00:50:41.175: dot11_auth_dot1x_send_id_req_to_client: sending identity request
for 0007.8592.3b99
*Mar  1 00:50:41.176: dot11_auth_dot1x_send_id_req_to_client: Started timer
client_timeout 30 seconds
*Mar  1 00:50:41.696: dot11_auth_parse_client_pak: Received EAPOL packet from
0007.8592.3b99
*Mar  1 00:50:41.696: dot11_auth_dot1x_run_rfsm: Executing
Action(CLIENT_WAIT,EAP_START) for 0007.8592.3b99
*Mar  1 00:50:41.696: dot11_auth_dot1x_send_id_req_to_client: sending identity request
for 0007.8592.3b99
*Mar  1 00:50:41.696: dot11_auth_dot1x_send_id_req_to_client: Started timer
client_timeout 30 seconds
*Mar  1 00:50:41.706: dot11_auth_parse_client_pak: Received EAPOL packet from
0007.8592.3b99
*Mar  1 00:50:41.706: dot11_auth_dot1x_run_rfsm: Executing
Action(CLIENT_WAIT,CLIENT_REPLY) for 0007.8592.3b99
*Mar  1 00:50:41.706: dot11_auth_dot1x_send_response_to_server: Sending client
0007.8592.3b99 data to server
*Mar  1 00:50:41.706: dot11_auth_dot1x_send_response_to_server: Started timer
server_timeout 60 seconds
*Mar  1 00:50:41.716: dot11_auth_dot1x_parse_aaa_resp: Received server response:
GET_CHALLENGE_RESPONSE
*Mar 1 00:50:41.716: dot11_auth_dot1x_parse_aaa_resp: found eap pak in server response
*Mar  1 00:50:41.716: dot11_auth_dot1x_run_rfsm: Executing
Action(SERVER_WAIT,SERVER_REPLY) for 0007.8592.3b99
*Mar  1 00:50:41.716: dot11_auth_dot1x_send_response_to_client: Forwarding server
message to client 0007.8592.3b99
*Mar  1 00:50:41.716: dot11_auth_dot1x_send_response_to_client: Started timer
client_timeout 30 seconds
*Mar  1 00:50:41.719: dot11_auth_parse_client_pak: Received EAPOL packet from
0007.8592.3b99
*Mar  1 00:50:41.720: dot11_auth_dot1x_run_rfsm: Executing
Action(CLIENT_WAIT,CLIENT_REPLY) for 0007.8592.3b99
…..
*Mar  1 00:50:41.915: dot11_auth_dot1x_run_rfsm: Executing
Action(SERVER_WAIT,SERVER_REPLY) for 0007.8592.3b99
*Mar  1 00:50:41.915: dot11_auth_dot1x_send_response_to_client: Forwarding server
message to client 0007.8592.3b99
*Mar  1 00:50:41.915: dot11_auth_dot1x_send_response_to_client: Started timer
client_timeout 30 seconds
```

Example 12-8 *Debug Information (WPA-DOT1x) (Continued)*

```
*Mar  1 00:50:41.923: dot11_auth_parse_client_pak: Received EAPOL packet from
0007.8592.3b99
*Mar  1 00:50:41.923: dot11_auth_dot1x_run_rfsm: Executing
Action(CLIENT_WAIT,CLIENT_REPLY) for 0007.8592.3b99
*Mar  1 00:50:41.923: dot11_auth_dot1x_send_response_to_server: Sending client
0007.8592.3b99 data to server
*Mar  1 00:50:41.923: dot11_auth_dot1x_send_response_to_server: Started timer
server_timeout 60 seconds
*Mar  1 00:50:41.931: dot11_auth_dot1x_parse_aaa_resp: Received server response: PASS
*Mar  1 00:50:41.931: dot11_auth_dot1x_parse_aaa_resp: found session timeout 600 sec
*Mar  1 00:50:41.931: dot11_auth_dot1x_parse_aaa_resp: found eap pak in server response
*Mar  1 00:50:41.931: dot11_auth_dot1x_parse_aaa_resp: Found AAA_AT_MS_MPPE_SEND_KEY
in server response
*Mar  1 00:50:41.931: dot11_auth_dot1x_parse_aaa_resp: AAA_AT_MS_MPPE_SEND_KEY session
key length 32
*Mar  1 00:50:41.931: dot11_auth_dot1x_parse_aaa_resp: Found AAA_AT_MS_MPPE_RECV_KEY
in server response
*Mar  1 00:50:41.931: dot11_auth_dot1x_parse_aaa_resp: AAA_AT_MS_MPPE_RECV_KEY session
key length 32
*Mar  1 00:50:41.931: dot11_auth_dot1x_run_rfsm: Executing
Action(SERVER_WAIT,SERVER_PASS) for 0007.8592.3b99
*Mar  1 00:50:41.932: dot11_auth_dot1x_send_response_to_client: Forwarding server
message to client 0007.8592.3b99
*Mar  1 00:50:41.932: dot11_auth_dot1x_send_response_to_client: Started timer
client_timeout 30 seconds
*Mar  1 00:50:41.993: %DOT11-6-ASSOC: Interface Dot11Radio0, Station dynamic-
xp0007.8592.3b99 Associated KEY_MGMT[WPA]
TMELAB-AP1#show dot11 associations
802.11 Client Stations on Dot11Radio0:
SSID [Enterprise] :
MAC Address    IP address      Device       Name          Parent        State
0007.8592.3b99 10.10.10.20     350-client   dynamic-xp    self          EAP-Assoc
Others:   (not related to any ssid)
```

IPSec VPN over WLAN Configuration

As discussed in Chapter 10, "Design Guidelines for Secure WLANs," IPSec VPN deployment over WLAN provides Layer 3–based user authentication and data confidentiality. IPSec VPN over WLAN deployment is an alternative to 802.11i deployment, or you can deploy it in combination with 802.11i to provide both Layer 2– and Layer 3–based user authentication and data confidentiality. Typically, either 802.11i or IPSec VPN over WLAN is deployed in an enterprise or vertical environment. Example 12-9 provides a configuration example for IPSec VPN over WLAN deployment in which policies (filters) are put in place to limit traffic through the access points. 802.11i features are disabled in the configuration example provided; however, if IPSec VPN is implemented with 802.11i, these filters are not necessary but could be implemented optionally by the network administrator.

Example 12-9 *AP IOS CLI Configuration for IPSec VPN Inbound and Outbound Filters*

```
interface Dot11Radio0
 no ip address
 ! Apply filters to both in-bound and out-bound traffic on the radio interface
 ip access-group IPSecVPN_InBound in
 ip access-group IPSecVPN_OutBound out
 no ip route-cache
 !
 ssid Enterprise
  authentication open
  guest-mode
 !
 speed basic-1.0 basic-2.0 basic-5.5 basic-11.0
 rts threshold 2312
 station-role root
 ! Enable Layer 2 filters at the host level on the AP
 ! Bridge group ACLs are used since radio and Ethernet interfaces are bridged together
 ! Thus, ACLs would be applied on the BVI interface(s)
 l2-filter bridge-group-acl
 bridge-group 1
 bridge-group 1 subscriber-loop-control
 bridge-group 1 input-type-list 200
 bridge-group 1 output-type-list 200
 bridge-group 1 block-unknown-source
 no bridge-group 1 source-learning
 no bridge-group 1 unicast-flooding
 bridge-group 1 spanning-disabled
 !
interface FastEthernet0
 no ip address
 no ip route-cache
 duplex auto
 speed auto
 bridge-group 1
 no bridge-group 1 source-learning
 bridge-group 1 spanning-disabled
 !
 ! Define ACL for inbound IPSec VPN traffic to the AP
ip access-list extended IPSecVPN_InBound
 permit esp any any
 permit icmp any any
 permit udp any any eq domain
 permit udp any any eq bootpc
 permit udp any any eq isakmp
 deny   ip any any
 !
 ! Define ACL for outbound VPN traffic to the WLAN clients
ip access-list extended IPSecVPN_OutBound
 permit icmp any any
 permit esp any any
 permit udp any any eq bootps
 permit udp any any eq domain
```

Example 12-9 *AP IOS CLI Configuration for IPSec VPN Inbound and Outbound Filters (Continued)*

```
 permit udp any any eq isakmp
 deny   ip any any
!
! Ethertype filters are used to allow IP (0x0800) and ARP (0x0806) traffic only
access-list 200 permit 0x0806 0x0000
access-list 200 permit 0x0800 0x0000
access-list 200 deny   0x0000 0xFFFF
```

If 802.11i is disabled for the IPSec VPN over WLAN deployment, the WLAN client should be configured for open/with no WEP.

Along with filters on the APs, IPSec VPN over WLAN policies should be reinforced at the Layer 3 termination point of the IPSec VPN user VLAN (most likely at the distribution layer level), as shown in Example 12-10.

Example 12-10 *Recommended ACLs for the VPN User VLAN on the Layer 3 Termination Switch*

```
! This configuration was captured from the Cisco SAFE WLAN implementation lab
! The following are ACLs for the IPSec VLAN 83 mapping to subnet 10.1.83.0/24
! VPN termination gateway is located in the 10.1.50.0/24 subnet
!
! ACL 182 is defined to permit IPSec traffic to the VPN gateway subnet
! ACL 182 is applied to in-bound traffic on the switch port
! That is, ACL is applied to traffic from the AP to the VPN termination gateway
access-list 182 permit esp 10.1.83.0 0.0.0.255 10.1.50.0 0.0.0.255
access-list 182 permit udp 10.1.83.0 0.0.0.255 eq isakmp 10.1.50.0 0.0.0.255 eq isakmp
! Permit full ICMP for troubleshooting
access-list 182 permit icmp 10.1.83.0 0.0.0.255 10.1.50.0 0.0.0.255! Permit DHCP
requests for initial IP assignment for wireless client
access-list 182 permit udp host 0.0.0.0 eq bootpc host 255.255.255.255 eq bootps
access-list 182 permit udp 10.1.83.0 0.0.0.255 eq bootpc host 255.255.255.255 eq bootps
access-list 182 permit udp 10.1.83.0 0.0.0.255 eq bootpc host 10.1.11.50 eq bootps
! Deny all other traffic, don't log Windows file share broadcasts
access-list 182 deny udp 10.1.83.0 0.0.0.255 any eq netbios-ns
access-list 182 deny udp 10.1.83.0 0.0.0.255 any eq netbios-dgm
access-list 182 deny ip any any log
!
!
! ACL 183 is applied to out-bound traffic on the switch port
! ACL 183 allows traffic from the VPN gateway subnet to IPSec VPN user VLAN
access-list 183 permit esp 10.1.50.0 0.0.0.255 10.1.83.0 0.0.0.255
access-list 183 permit udp 10.1.50.0 0.0.0.255 eq isakmp 10.1.83.0 0.0.0.255 eq isakmp
! Permit Full ICMP for troubleshooting
access-list 183 permit icmp 10.1.50.0 0.0.0.255 10.1.83.0 0.0.0.255
! Permit DHCP responses for the initial IP assignment for the wireless client
access-list 183 permit udp host 10.1.11.50 eq bootps host 255.255.255.255 eq bootpc
access-list 183 permit udp host 10.1.11.50 eq bootps 10.1.83.0 0.0.0.255 eq bootpc
! Deny all other traffic
access-list 183 deny ip any any log
```

Multiple Security Profiles (SSIDs/VLANs) Configuration

Cisco WLAN products support multiple SSIDs (also known as wireless VLANs) and wired VLANs. It is recommended that you deploy multiple VLANs to support multiple security policies on the same WLAN infrastructure. Typically, an SSID is mapped to a wired VLAN and defines a unique security policy. Chapter 13, "WLAN Deployment Examples," provides examples of how multiple SSIDs and VLANs can be used in enterprise and vertical environments. The configuration discussed in this section applies to all three WLAN deployment modes discussed in Chapter 9. However, in SWAN central switching deployment mode, most of the user traffic is not sent over the defined wired VLAN on the AP; rather, it is forwarded via the defined Layer 3 GRE tunnel on the AP.

The native VLAN of the trunk between the AP/bridge and the access (that is, closet) switch serves as the management VLAN for the AP/bridge. It is not allowed to configure management VLAN to be anything other than the native VLAN (mapped to BVI1 interface) of the AP/bridge. IP address identity should be configured on the BVI1 interface to allow management traffic to terminate on the AP/bridge. Note that IP address identity configuration is allowed only for the BVI1 interface on the AP/bridge. Typically, WLAN user traffic is not allowed on the native/ management VLAN. (That is, native VLAN is not mapped to an SSID.) Three VLANs are created in Example 12-11. VLAN 10 is defined as the native/management VLAN for the AP, whereas VLANs 11 and 12 are defined as user VLANs. The Example 12-11 configuration sequence applies for standalone AP and SWAN nonswitching deployment modes.

Example 12-11 *Multiple SSID and VLAN Configuration on an IOS-Enabled AP*

```
! Create Management/native VLAN on the radio interface
TMELAB-AP1(config)#int dot11Radio 0.10
TMELAB-AP1(config-subif)#encapsulation dot1Q 10 native
! Map the management VLAN to bridge group 1 (BVI1)
TMELAB-AP1(config-subif)#bridge-group 1
TMELAB-AP1(config-subif)#exit
! Create Management/native VLAN on the Ethernet interface
TMELAB-AP1(config)#int fastEthernet 0.10
TMELAB-AP1(config-subif)#encapsulation dot1Q 10 native
! Map the management VLAN to bridge group 1 (BVI1)
TMELAB-AP1(config-subif)#bridge-group 1
TMELAB-AP1(config-subif)#exit
! Create User VLAN-id 11
TMELAB-AP1(config)#int dot11Radio 0.11
TMELAB-AP1(config-subif)#encapsulation dot1Q 11
TMELAB-AP1(config-subif)#bridge-group 11
TMELAB-AP1(config-subif)#exit
TMELAB-AP1(config)#int fastEthernet 0.11
TMELAB-AP1(config-subif)#encapsulation dot1Q 11
TMELAB-AP1(config-subif)#bridge-group 11
TMELAB-AP1(config-subif)#exit
! Create User VLAN-id 12
TMELAB-AP1(config)#int dot11Radio 0.12
```

Example 12-11   *Multiple SSID and VLAN Configuration on an IOS-Enabled AP (Continued)*

```
TMELAB-AP1(config-subif)#encapsulation dot1Q 12
TMELAB-AP1(config-subif)#bridge-group 12
TMELAB-AP1(config-subif)#exit
TMELAB-AP1(config)#int fastEthernet 0.12
TMELAB-AP1(config-subif)#encapsulation dot1Q 12
TMELAB-AP1(config-subif)#bridge-group 12
TMELAB-AP1(config-subif)#exit
TMELAB-AP1(config)#
! Enable WPA for user VLAN-id 11
TMELAB-AP1(config)#int dot11Radio 0
TMELAB-AP1(config-if)#encryption vlan 11 mode ciphers tkip
TMELAB-AP1(config-if)#broadcast-key vlan 11 change 3600
! Enable static WEP for user VLAN-id 12
TMELAB-AP1(config-if)#encryption vlan 12 mode wep mandatory
TMELAB-AP1(config-if)#encryption vlan 12 key 1 size 128bit 09876543210987654321098765
! Map SSID "Enterprise" to user VLAN-id 11
TMELAB-AP1(config-if)#ssid Enterprise
TMELAB-AP1(config-if-ssid)#vlan 11
! Enable WPA-DOT1x on SSID "Enterprise"
TMELAB-AP1(config-if-ssid)#authentication open eap EAP-AUTH
TMELAB-AP1(config-if-ssid)#authentication key-management wpa
TMELAB-AP1(config-if-ssid)# exit
! Map SSID "Legacy" to user VLAN-id 12
TMELAB-AP1(config-if)#ssid Legacy
TMELAB-AP1(config-if-ssid)#vlan 12
TMELAB-AP1(config-if-ssid)#authentication open
TMELAB-AP1(config-if-ssid)#guest-mode
TMELAB-AP1(config-if-ssid)#exit
!
! Note: Specify RADIUS server parameters as discussed in previous examples
```

By default, you map each SSID statically to a VLAN, as shown in Example 12-11. However, you can overwrite this SSID-to-VLAN ID mapping and dynamically reassign the user to a different wired VLAN (also known as a dynamic VLAN assignment). Dynamic VLAN assignment is enabled using the 802.1x authentication; the RADIUS server's returned VLAN ID overrides the default VLAN mapping on the AP. Furthermore, dynamic VLAN assignment segments users into user groups and enforces a unique security policy per user group (that is, per wired VLAN). Typically, one SSID is deployed along with multiple wired VLANs per AP to enforce user-group policies across an enterprise network. You can achieve dynamic VLAN assignment on the Cisco WLAN products using the user or user-group IETF tunnel parameters 64 (tunnel type: set to "VLAN"), 65 (tunnel medium type: set to "802"), and 81 (tunnel private group ID: set to VLAN-ID). Figure 12-13 illustrates RADIUS server screen captures for dynamic VLAN assignment configuration using the user or user-group IETF tunnel parameter settings.

Figure 12-13 *Dynamic User VLAN Assignment RADIUS Server Configuration*

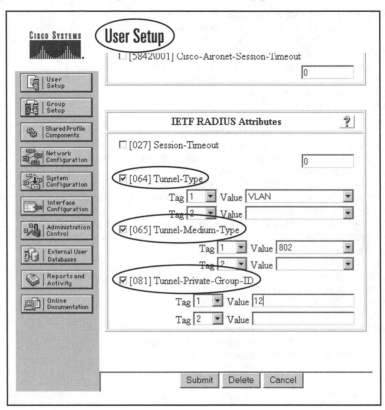

Note that in SWAN central switching deployment mode, you must reassign the WLAN client to a different mGRE tunnel. (Reassigning the client to a different wired VLAN does not have an effect on the user traffic flow.)

You can use the show command shown in Example 12-12 on the AP to verify a client's VLAN assignment.

Example 12-12 *AP IOS "show" Command to Verify Client's VLAN/SSID Assignment*

```
TMELAB-AP1#sh dot11 associations all-client
Address          : 0007.8592.3b99         Name: dynamic-xp
IP Address       : 10.12.12.23            Interface        : Dot11Radio 0
Device           : 350-client                      Software Version: 5.30
State            : EAP-Assoc              Parent          : self
SSID             : Enterprise             VLAN            : 12
Hops to Infra    : 1                      Association Id   : 41
Clients Associated: 0                     Repeaters associated: 0
Key Mgmt type    : NONE                   Encryption       : WEP
Current Rate     : 11.0                   Capability       : ShortHdr
Supported Rates  : 1.0 2.0 5.5 11.0
```

Example 12-12 *AP IOS "show" Command to Verify Client's VLAN/SSID Assignment (Continued)*

```
Signal Strength    : -39  dBm      Connected for    : 175 seconds
Signal Quality     : 78 %           Activity Timeout : 18 seconds
Power-save         : Off             Last Activity   : 8 seconds ago
Packets Input      : 45             Packets Output   : 1
Bytes Input        : 8878           Bytes Output     : 82
Duplicates Rcvd    : 0             Data Retries      : 0
Decrypt Failed     : 0             RTS Retries       : 0
MIC Failed         : 0
MIC Missing        : 0
```

You can map multiple SSIDs to the default VLAN when 802.1Q trunking is disabled on the AP. This is less secure than using multiple VLANs with SSIDs, but it might be useful in a scenario in which 802.1Q VLAN trunking is not supported by the wired infrastructure. Example 12-13 shows the configuration required to enable two SSIDs (one configured for WPA-DOT1x mode and the other configured for WPA-PSK mode) where both SSIDs are mapped to the default VLAN (that is, 802.1Q trunking is disabled). Alternatively, in a retail deployment environment, you could have two SSIDs in which one is configured for EAP/802.1x with dynamic WEP and the other is configured for static WEP mapping to the default VLAN. This would be useful when both EAP/802.1x and legacy clients have to be supported on the same wired VLAN (perhaps due to an ongoing migration from legacy to EAP/802.1x clients). Finally, note that this deployment option limits the capability to enforce unique security policies on the wired network side for specific user groups (or device groups).

Example 12-13 *Multiple SSID to Default VLAN Mapping on an IOS-Enabled AP*

```
!
TMELAB-AP1(config)#int dot11Radio 0
! Enable WPA TKIP Cipher
TMELAB-AP1(config-if)#encryption mode ciphers tkip
!
! Enable SSID "Enterprise" and configure WPA-DOT1x mode
TMELAB-AP1(config-if)#ssid Enterprise
TMELAB-AP1(config-if-ssid)#authentication open eap EAP-AUTH
TMELAB-AP1(config-if-ssid)#authentication key-management wpa
!
! Enable SSID "WPA-PSK" and configure WPA-PSK mode
TMELAB-AP1(config-if)#ssid Legacy
TMELAB-AP1(config-if-ssid)#authentication open
TMELAB-AP1(config-if-ssid)#authentication key-management wpa
TMELAB-AP1(config-if-ssid)#wpa-psk ascii AReY0UableT0F0llowAl0ng?PleaseD0s0
TMELAB-AP1(config-if-ssid)#guest-mode
TMELAB-AP1(config-if-ssid)#end
!
! Note: Specify RADIUS server parameters for EAP authentication (as discussed in the
WPA-DOT1x configuration example)
```

SWAN Nonswitching Deployment: Configuration Guidelines and Examples

This section addresses configuration guidelines for SWAN nonswitching deployment mode. This deployment mode is discussed in detail in Chapter 9. Security, Layer 2 fast secure roaming, local authentication, and management functions are centralized at the wireless domain services (WDS) server level. You can deploy an AP, Catalyst switch, or branch-office router (Cisco 2600 or 3700 series) as the WDS server. In this deployment mode, the control traffic (known as WLCCP traffic) flows through the WDS server, whereas the data traffic (actual 802.11 user traffic) is forwarded via the normal route. Note that this is different from the central switching model, in which both control and user data is forwarded through the central switch.

The WLAN security methods discussed in the section "WLAN Security Methods: Configuration Guidelines and Examples" also apply to SWAN nonswitching deployment mode. One of the major changes made in the SWAN nonswitching deployment mode is that 802.1x/EAP authentication messages are relayed through the WDS server. In this scenario, the WDS client AP still controls user access into the network; however, the WDS server becomes the authenticator. In EAP/802.1x authentication, these changes are used to expedite Layer 2 fast secure roaming for 802.1x/EAP clients. Along with fast secure roaming, the RF data aggregation function and the local authentication service can be enabled on the WDS server. Note that the local authentication service is independent of the WDS functions; however, it is recommended that you enable it on the WDS server because all EAP/802.1x authentication messages are relayed through the WDS server.

Basic WDS Configuration

Basic WDS configuration involves enabling WDS server service on the selected WDS server(s), enabling WDS client service on the appropriate APs, and enabling infrastructure authentication between the WDS server and the WDS client APs. Note that the WDS client APs use WLCCP (UDP, Port # 2887) to communicate with the WDS server. Example 12-14 illustrates the configuration sequence required to enable a WDS server for the SWAN nonswitching deployment mode. As discussed in Chapter 9, WDS client APs reside in the same subnet as the WDS server and autodetect the WDS server. Note that you can refer to the WDS server in this deployment mode as the Layer 2 WDS server. As shown in Example 12-14, you must configure a specific priority for the Layer 2 WDS server; the WDS server with the highest configured priority within a subnet is selected as the active WDS server.

Example 12-14 *WDS Server Configuration (SWAN Nonswitching Deployment Mode)*

```
!
! Enable WDS server mode and specify priority for the WDS server
WDS-SERVER(config)#wlccp wds priority 99 interface bVI 1
! Enable infrastructure and client authentication types
WDS-SERVER(config)#wlccp authentication-server infrastructure WLCCP-AUTH
WDS-SERVER(config)#wlccp authentication-server client leap LEAP-AUTH
WDS-SERVER(config-wlccp-auth)#exit
WDS-SERVER(config)#wlccp authentication-server client eap EAP-AUTH
WDS-SERVER(config-wlccp-auth)#exit
! Configure WDS server to communicate with the RADIUS server
WDS-SERVER(config)#aaa new-model
WDS-SERVER(config)#radius-server host 10.10.10.5 auth-port 1812 acct-port 1813 key
tmelab
! Specify RADIUS server group for client EAP authentication
WDS-SERVER(config)#aaa group server radius rad-eap
WDS-SERVER(config-sg-radius)#server 10.10.10.5 auth-port 1812 acct-port 1813
WDS-SERVER(config-sg-radius)#exit
! Specify RADIUS server group for infrastructure authentication
WDS-SERVER(config)#aaa group server radius rad-wlccp
WDS-SERVER(config-sg-radius)#server 10.10.10.5 auth-port 1812 acct-port 1813
WDS-SERVER(config-sg-radius)#exit
WDS-SERVER(config)#aaa authentication login LEAP-AUTH group rad-eap
WDS-SERVER(config)#aaa authentication login EAP-AUTH group rad-eap
WDS-SERVER(config)#aaa authentication login WLCCP-AUTH group rad-wlccp
```

Along with configuring the WDS server, you must configure WDS client service on each AP, as shown in Example 12-15.

Example 12-15 *Configuring WDS Client Mode on an Access Point (SWAN Nonswitching Deployment Mode)*

```
! Specify infrastructure authentication credentials for the WDS client AP
TMELAB-AP1(config)#wlccp ap username ap1 password tmelab
TMELAB-AP1(config)#end
```

You can use debug commands shown in Example 12-16 to troubleshoot infrastructure and client authentication problems.

Example 12-16 *Debug Information on the WDS Server (SWAN Nonswitching Deployment Mode)*

```
! View WDS server status and number of registered APs and WLAN clients
WDS-SERVER#show wlccp wds
      MAC: 000c.30e9.0711, IP-ADDR: 10.10.10.22    , Priority: 5
      Interface BVI1, State: Administratively StandAlone - ACTIVE
      AP Count: 1    , MN Count: 0
! View registered WDS client AP information
WDS-SERVER#show wlccp wds ap
    MAC-ADDR       IP-ADDR         STATE          LIFETIME
000c.8500.0156   10.10.10.21     REGISTERED      553
WDS-SERVER#
! Other useful commands on the WDS Server ---
WDS-SERVER#debug wlccp wds
```

continues

Example 12-16 *Debug Information on the WDS Server (SWAN Nonswitching Deployment Mode) (Continued)*

```
!
!
Debug information on the WDS client AP:
! View registration status and view authenticated WDS server info
TMELAB-AP1#show wlccp ap
 WDS = 000c.30e9.0711, 10.10.10.22
 state = wlccp_ap_st_registered
 IN Authenticator = 10.10.10.22
 MN Authenticator = 10.10.10.22
TMELAB-AP1#
```

Fast Secure Roaming (CCKM) Configuration

As discussed in Chapter 9, fast secure roaming functionality (CCKM protocol) expedites Layer 2 roaming for EAP/802.1x clients. In addition to the basic WDS configuration sequence provided in Examples 12-14 and 12-15, further configuration is required, as shown in Example 12-17, on a WDS client AP to enable fast secure roaming. Note that, as shown in Example 12-17, WPA-TKIP or Cisco TKIP (CKIP) is used as the cipher, whereas CCKM is used as the key management protocol.

Example 12-17 *Configuring Fast Secure Roaming on a WDS Client AP*

```
!
! Enable CCKM roaming for LEAP or EAP-FAST with WPA-TKIP clients
TMELAB-AP1(config)#int dot11Radio 0
! Enable WPA-TKIP cipher for the WLAN clients
TMELAB-AP1(config-if)#encryption mode ciphers tkip
TMELAB-AP1(config-if)#ssid Enterprise
TMELAB-AP1(config-if-ssid)#authentication network-eap LEAP-AUTH
! Enable CCKM key management for fast secure roaming clients
TMELAB-AP1(config-if-ssid)#authentication key-management wpa cckm
TMELAB-AP1(config-if-ssid)#end
!
          OR
!
! Enable CCKM for LEAP or EAP-FAST with Cisco TKIP clients
TMELAB-AP1(config)#int dot11Radio 0
! Enable CKIP cipher for fast secure roaming clients
TMELAB-AP3(config-if)#encryption mode ciphers ckip-cmic
TMELAB-AP1(config-if)#ssid Enterprise
TMELAB-AP1(config-if-ssid)#authentication network-eap LEAP-AUTH
! Enable CCKM key management for fast secure roaming clients
TMELAB-AP3(config-if-ssid)#authentication key-management cckm
TMELAB-AP1(config-if-ssid)#end
```

There is no need to configure RADIUS server information on the WDS client AP because all authentication messages are relayed through the WDS server. After you enable WDS mode, it is important to enable all authentication types (LEAP, EAP, MAC address, and infrastructure) on the WDS server. This is required whether or not fast secure roaming is implemented for any EAP type. (All EAP authentication messages are relayed through the WDS server.)

Figure 12-14 illustrates the fast secure roaming configuration required for an EAP-FAST client. As shown, you can enable the WPA-TKIP cipher along with fast secure roaming (CCKM). The EAP-FAST implementation on Cisco clients requires you to configure the network EAP authentication type on the WDS client APs and on the WDS server.

Figure 12-14 *Fast Secure Roaming Configuration for EAP-FAST Client*

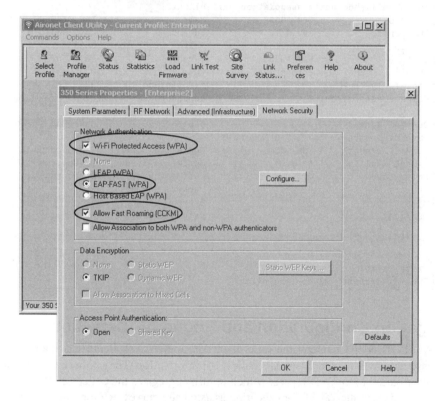

In the event of client authentication failures, you can use debug commands, as shown in Example 12-18, on the WDS client AP and on the WDS server to debug the authentication problems.

Example 12-18 *Debug Information on the WDS Client AP*

```
TMELAB-AP1#debug wlccp ap mn
*Mar  1 03:06:12.247: wlccp_ap_mn: Pre Reg Req: Association for 0007.8592.3b5a
*Mar  1 03:06:12.247: wlccp_ap_mn: Pre Reg Req: sent ksc 1 *
*Mar  1 03:06:12.247: wlccp_ap_mn: Pre Reg Req: bssid 0007.85b3.581e key type 2
*Mar  1 03:06:12.247: wlccp_ap_mn: Pre Reg Req: ssid Enterprise
*Mar  1 03:06:12.247: wlccp_ap_mn: Pre Reg Req: sent msc 14 *
*Mar  1 03:06:12.251: wlccp_ap_mn: PreReg Reply: eap_server_type 17
*Mar 1 03:06:12.251: wlccp_ap_mn: ap_proc_prereg_reply assoc for 0007.8592.3b5a
*Mar  1 03:06:12.252: wlccp_ap_mn: PreReg Reply: got MSC 15 *
*Mar  1 03:06:12.273: wlccp_ap_mn: MN Reg Req: ssid Enterprise,
 bssid 0007.85b3.581e, auth 8, ip 0.0.0.0 flag 1
*Mar  1 03:06:12.276: wlccp_ap_mn: MN registration reply status SUCCESS, NO ERROR
TMELAB-AP1#show dot11 associations all-client
Address           : 0007.8592.3b5a      Name              : TME_LAB2_PC1
IP Address        : 10.10.10.47         Interface         : Dot11Radio 0
Device            : 350-client          Software Version  : 5.30
State             : EAP-Assoc           Parent            : self
SSID              : Enterprise          VLAN              : 0
Hops to Infra     : 1                   Association Id    : 2
Clients Associated: 0                   Repeaters associated: 0
Key Mgmt type     : CCKM                Encryption        : TKIP
Current Rate      : 11.0                Capability        : ShortHdr
Supported Rates   : 1.0 2.0 5.5 11.0
Signal Strength   : -36  dBm            Connected for     : 118 seconds
Signal Quality    : 83 %                Activity Timeout  : 23 seconds
Power-save        : Off                 Last Activity     : 3 seconds ago
Packets Input     : 42                  Packets Output    : 15
Bytes Input       : 5388                Bytes Output      : 1511
Duplicates Rcvd   : 0                   Data Retries      : 5
Decrypt Failed    : 0                   RTS Retries       : 0
MIC Failed        : 0
MIC Missing       : 0
Other Useful commands ---
TMELAB-AP1#debug wlccp leap-client
```

RF Aggregation Configuration and Rogue AP Detection

As discussed in Chapter 9, the WDS client APs and WLAN clients (Cisco and CCXv2 or above) associated with WDS client APs collect RF information. They collect and forward the RF information to the WDS server, which in turn aggregates the collected RF information and forwards it to the WLSE for executing assisted site-survey, RF topology mapping, location management, and rogue AP detection services.

The WDS server must be configured to communicate with the WLSE using the WLCCP protocol. This requires the WLSE to authenticate with the WDS server and secure the WLCCP link between itself and the WDS server. SNMP community parameters must also be configured on all WDS client APs and on the WDS server. (See Example 12-19.) This enables the WLSE to manage the WDS servers and the WDS client APs.

Example 12-19 *WDS Server and WDS Client AP Configuration for Enabling RF Management*

```
!
! Configure the WDS server to communicate with the WLSE
WDS-SERVER(config)#wlccp wnm ip address 10.10.10.9
!
! SNMP community string configuration required on both WDS server and the WDS client APs
WDS-SERVER(config)#snmp-server view iso iso included
WDS-SERVER(config)#snmp-server community tmelab-ro view iso RO
WDS-SERVER(config)#snmp-server view iso iso included
WDS-SERVER(config)#snmp-server community tmelab-rw view iso RW
```

The WLSE functions as the Wireless Network Manager (WNM) component of SWAN. Follow this procedure for setting up WLSE 2.5 or above for RF management services:

1 Configure SNMP read and read-write communities to use with the WDS server and the WDS client APs.

   On the WLSE web-based GUI, navigate to Devices > Discover > Device Credentials > SNMP Communities.

2 Configure Telnet/SSH credentials to use to log in to the WDS server and WDS client APs.

   Enter the Telnet/SSH credentials on the WLSE GUI interface found at Devices > Discover > Device Credentials > Telnet/SSH user password.

3 Configure WLCCP credentials to authenticate the WLSE to each WDS server.

   Using the WLSE GUI, navigate to Devices > Discover > Device Credentials > WLCCP Credentials. Enter the WLCCP username and password.

4 Click on Save to save the configured WLSE parameters.

5 Ensure that the WLSE has discovered the WDS server and moved it to the "managed" state. You can execute this by using the WLSE GUI via Devices > Discovery > Managed/Unmanaged options.

6 Use the Radio Manager Assisted Site-Survey wizard to carry out the initial deployment of managed APs.

Consult the WLSE documentation posted on the Cisco website for the proper syntax for entering the previous credentials and also for carrying RF management services.

Along with configuring the WDS server, WDS client APs, and WLSE, the WLAN clients must
be configured to enable radio management. The client scanning feature is not mandatory but
can be enabled on Cisco and CCXv2 clients to increase the accuracy of RF management/
security features such as rogue AP detection. Figure 12-15 shows enabling the radio management feature on a Cisco 350 client adapter. (The feature is enabled by default.)

Figure 12-15   *Enabling Radio Management on a Cisco Client*

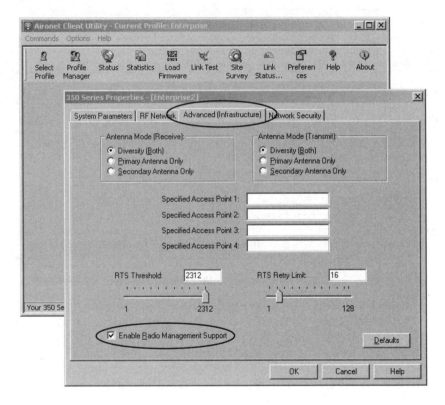

Figure 12-16 shows a rogue AP alert generated by the WLSE. As shown in Figure 12-15, you
can use Location Manager in WLSE version 2.5 or higher to narrow the location of the detected
rogue AP. Furthermore, the WLSE 2.7 release and above provides rogue AP suppression via
switch port tracing and allowing the administrator to shut down the switch port to which the
rogue AP is attached. Note that this (rogue AP suppression via switch port shutdown) requires
CDP to be enabled on your wired network.

Figure 12-16   *Rogue AP Alert on WLSE*

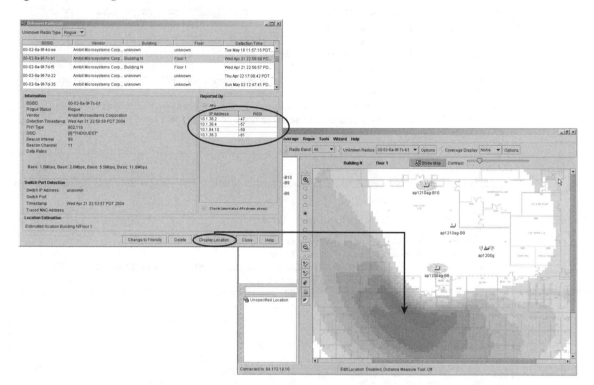

Local Authentication Configuration (RADIUS Fall-Back Service)

You can enable local authentication service on the WDS server in a branch office scenario to provide fall-back RADIUS service during WAN link failure conditions. You can also use it as the primary RADIUS server in a small office scenario; however, note that accounting/auditing services are not available on the local authentication server. Furthermore, local authentication service is only supported for LEAP and EAP-FAST authentication types. Example 12-20 provides the configuration sequence required to enable local authentication service for LEAP users. Note that local authentication service is independent of WDS functions, but it is recommended that you enable it on the WDS server because all EAP/802.1x authentication messages (CCKM and non-CCKM) are relayed through the WDS server.

Example 12-20 *Local LEAP Authentication Service Configuration on the WDS Server*

```
! Enable local authentication service on the WDS server for LEAP clients
WDS-SERVER(config)#aaa new-model
WDS-SERVER(config)#aaa authorization exec default local
WDS-SERVER(config)#aaa authentication login default local
WDS-SERVER(config)#radius-server local
! Add AP(s) as AAA client(s) along with shared secret for RADIUS authentication
WDS-SERVER(config-radsrv)#nas 10.10.10.21 key 0 tmelab
! Add user account information under the local radius service for specific users
WDS-SERVER(config-radsrv)#user tmeuser101 password 0 tmelab
WDS-SERVER(config-radsrv)#end
WDS-SERVER#
```

You can use debug commands to verify local authentication service (on the local authentication server), as shown in Example 12-21.

Example 12-21 *Debug Commands for Local Authentication Service*

```
WDS-SERVER#debug radius local-server error
WDS-SERVER#debug radius local-server client
! Use the following show command to look at local authentication statistics
WDS-SERVER#show radius local-server statistics
Successes            : 2        Unknown usernames     : 0
Client blocks        : 0        Invalid passwords     : 0
Unknown NAS          : 0        Invalid packet from NAS: 0
NAS : 10.10.10.21
Successes            : 2        Unknown usernames     : 0
Client blocks        : 0        Invalid passwords     : 0
Corrupted packet     : 0        Unknown RADIUS message : 0
No username attribute : 0       Missing auth attribute : 0
Shared key mismatch  : 0        Invalid state attribute: 0
Unknown EAP message  : 0        Unknown EAP auth type  : 0
Username                 Successes  Failures  Blocks
tmeuser101                   2         0         0
```

Securing Bridge-to-Bridge Links

Root bridge to nonroot bridge communications can be secured with LEAP authentication and Cisco TKIP. It is strongly recommended that you use this or IPSec VPN over bridged links to secure the data traffic.

Examples 12-22 and 12-23 provide a deployment example for securing the root to nonroot bridged link using LEAP/with Cisco TKIP configuration. Example 12-22 shows a root bridge configuration in which LEAP authentication is enabled to authenticate the nonroot bridges. As shown in the example, Cisco TKIP is enabled to provide data confidentiality and to protect data integrity between the root and nonroot bridges.

Example 12-22 *Security Configuration Required on the IOS-Enabled Root Bridge*

```
ROOT-BRIDGE(config)#int dot11Radio 0
ROOT-BRIDGE(config-if)#ssid bridgedLink
! Enable LEAP authentication and specify the LEAP list name "LEAP-AUTH"
ROOT-BRIDGE(config-if-ssid)#authentication network-eap LEAP-AUTH
! Enable infrastructure mode association with the non-root bridges
ROOT-BRIDGE(config-if-ssid)#infrastructure-ssid
ROOT-BRIDGE(config-if-ssid)#exit
! Enable encryption parameters
ROOT-BRIDGE(config-if)#encryption mode wep mandatory mic key-hash
! Enable broadcast key rotation for every 900 seconds (15 minutes)
ROOT-BRIDGE(config-if)#broadcast-key change 900
ROOT-BRIDGE(config-if)#exit
! Configure radius server parameters for EAP authentication
ROOT-BRIDGE(config)#aaa new-model
! Specify Radius server information
ROOT-BRIDGE(config)#radius-server host 10.10.10.5 auth-port 1812 acct-port 1813 key
tmelab
! Specify EAP authentication servers
ROOT-BRIDGE(config)#aaa group server radius rad-eap
! Specify 10.10.10.5 server as an EAP authentication server
ROOT-BRIDGE(config-sg-radius)#server 10.10.10.5 auth-port 1812 acct-port 1813
ROOT-BRIDGE(config-sg-radius)#exit
! Specify rad-eap group of servers to be used for LEAP authentication
ROOT-BRIDGE(config)#aaa authentication login LEAP-AUTH group rad-eap
! Configure miscellaneous radius server parameters
ROOT-BRIDGE(config)#radius-server attribute 32 include-in-access-req format %h
ROOT-BRIDGE(config)#radius-server vsa send accounting
ROOT-BRIDGE(config)#end
```

Example 12-23 shows the nonroot configuration in which LEAP authentication is enabled to protect the bridged link to the root bridge. Note that you must specify LEAP authentication credentials (username and password) on the nonroot bridge. Even though it is not explicitly configured in Example 12-23, Cisco TKIP is negotiated as the cipher when the bridged link is initially "brought up" between the root and nonroot bridges. (This is because the root bridge is configured with Cisco TKIP.)

Example 12-23 *Configuration on the IOS-Enabled Nonroot Bridge*

```
NR-BRIDGE1(config)#int dot11Radio 0
NR-BRIDGE1(config-if)#ssid bridgedLink
! Enable LEAP authentication and specify the LEAP list name "LEAP-AUTH"
NR-BRIDGE1(config-if-ssid)#authentication network-eap LEAP-AUTH
! Enable infrastructure mode association with the root bridge
NR-BRIDGE1(config-if-ssid)#infrastructure-ssid
! Specify username and password for LEAP authentication
NR-BRIDGE1(config-if-ssid)#authentication client username nonRoot1 password 0 tmelab
NR-BRIDGE1(config-if-ssid)#end
```

The same debug commands for the EAP/802.1x authentication on the AP can be used on the root bridge to debug the nonroot bridge authentication problems.

Secure WLAN Management Configuration Guidelines

This section discusses the configuration commands for secure management best practices, as outlined in Chapter 10.

By default, Telnet access is enabled on the APs. It is recommended that you disable Telnet access and enable SSH access to the APs. Example 12-24 illustrates the configuration required to disable Telnet access on the AP.

Example 12-24 *Commands to Disable Telnet Access to the AP*

```
access-list 111 permit tcp any any neq telnet
line vty 0 4
 access-class 111 in
line vty 5 15
 access-class 111 in
!
```

Example 12-25 shows commands required to enable SSH access and disable HTTP access on the IOS-enabled APs or the bridges. By default, HTTP access is enabled on the APs for management. It is recommended that you disable HTTP access or restrict HTTP access to the AP (management traffic only).

Example 12-25 *Commands to Enable SSH Access on the AP/Bridge*

```
! Commands to enable SSH version 1.5 on the APs/Bridges
! Domain-name is simply used as a seed to generate the RSA keys for the SSH sessions
TMELAB-AP1(config)#ip domain-name tmelab.cisco.com
TMELAB-AP1(config)#crypto key generate rsa general-keys modulus 1024
! Command to disable HTTP access to the AP
TMELAB-AP1(config)#no ip http server
```

Administrator authentication is locally enabled on the APs. If desired, RADIUS or TACACS+ can be used for administrator authentication. You can use the commands shown in Example 12-26 on a standalone AP or on the WDS client AP to enable TACACS authentication.

Example 12-26 *TACACS Configuration Required for Administrator Authentication*

```
!
TMELAB-AP1(config)#aaa new-model
! Specify TACACS+ server information
TMELAB-AP1(config)#tacacs-server host 10.10.10.5 key tmelab1
TMELAB-AP1(config)#aaa group server tacacs+ tac-admin
TMELAB-AP1(config-sg-tacacs+)#server 10.10.10.5
TMELAB-AP1(config-sg-tacacs+)#exit
! Remove default user account
TMELAB-AP1(config)#no Username Cisco
! Configure to check the local user database first and then the TACACS server for user
authentication and authorization
TMELAB-AP1(config)#aaa authentication login default local group tac-admin
```

Example 12-26   *TACACS Configuration Required for Administrator Authentication (Continued)*

```
TMELAB-AP1(config)#aaa authorization exec default local group tac-admin
! If desired, enable http authentication/authorization via TACACS
TMELAB-AP1(config)#ip http authentication aaa
```

Along with the preceding configuration on the AP/bridge, you must add the AP/bridge as "TACACS+(IOS)" AAA client on the AAA server. Also, make sure to create the appropriate user accounts on the AAA server and to provide the appropriate level of access for each user. For example, when using Cisco Secure ACS server, user or user-group settings for the "TACACS(IOS)" privilege level parameter can be specified from level 1 to 15 for the administrative user (1 = read only, whereas 15 = read and write permissions).

A hacker can potentially spoof the default gateway MAC address for a guest VLAN or in a hotspot scenario to carry out man-in-the-middle (MitM) attacks. It is recommended that you lock down the default gateway MAC address to prevent these attacks in a hotspot or guest VLAN deployment scenario. Example 12-27 prevents the hacker from using the default gateway (10.10.10.1) MAC address to carry out MitM attacks. As shown in Example 12-27, the MAC address of the default gateway (DG) is added to the association access list. This prevents anyone from using the DG MAC address and associating to the AP. (That is, it prevents DG MAC address spoofing.)

Example 12-27   *Black Listing the Default Gateway MAC Address on the AP*

```
! Black listing the default gateway mac-address to prevent MitM attacks in a hot-spot/
guest access scenario
TMELAB-AP1#sh arp
Protocol  Address          Age (min)  Hardware Addr   Type   Interface
Internet  10.10.10.1             0   0004.dd82.29c0  ARPA   BVI1
Internet  10.10.10.27            0   0009.6b50.bd45  ARPA   BVI1
Internet  10.10.10.24           33   000c.850f.256a  ARPA   BVI1
Internet  10.10.10.22           34   000c.30e9.0711  ARPA   BVI1
Internet  10.10.10.21            -   000c.8500.0156  ARPA   BVI1
! Create an association access list to deny client(s) from using the DG mac-address
dot11 association mac-list 700
access-list 700 deny   0004.dd82.29c0   0000.0000.0000
access-list 700 permit 0000.0000.0000   ffff.ffff.ffff
```

Public Secure Packet Forwarding (PSPF) prevents a client that is associated to an AP from communicating with other clients on the same WLAN cell. This feature should be enabled on guest VLANs and on hotspot deployments to prevent hacker attempts to compromise WLAN user devices. As shown in Example 12-28, PSPF can be enabled on the radio interface and on the radio subinterface(s).

Example 12-28 *Port Security (PSPF) Configuration Commands*

```
! Enabling PSPF (port security) on the Radio interface
TMELAB-AP1#conf t
TMELAB-AP1(config)#int dot11Radio 0
TMELAB-AP1(config-if)#bridge-group 1 port-protected
```

It is a recommended practice to restrict management traffic to the AP/bridge. If VLANs are enabled on the AP/bridge, management traffic can be separated from the user traffic, and ACLs can be applied on the management VLAN. You can implement the following best practices to secure management traffic between the AP/bridge and the management servers (WLSE, AAA, and so on):

- Restrict network management and radio management traffic between APs and the WLSE:
  - Allow SNMP traffic between the APs and the WLSE.
  - Allow WLCCP traffic (UDP, 2887) between the APs and the WDS.
  - Allow WLCCP traffic (UDP, 2887) between the WDS and the WLSE.
  - Allow SSH (TCP, port 22) and HTTP traffic between management servers and the APs.
  - Allow TFTP traffic between the APs and the WLSE.
- Restrict RADIUS traffic between APs and the RADIUS server:
  - Allow authentication traffic: UDP, port 1812 or 1645.
  - Allow accounting traffic: UDP, port 1813 or 1646.
- Restrict other traffic types:
  - Allow DHCP traffic between APs and the DHCP server.
- Deny all other traffic to the APs.

SWAN Central Switching Deployment: Configuration Guidelines and Examples

This section addresses configuration guidelines for SWAN central switching deployment mode. This deployment mode is discussed in detail in Chapter 9. Using the central switching deployment mode, both control and user traffic is aggregated by the central switch that is equipped with a WLAN services module. Thus, this deployment mode enables a single point of ingress for both WLAN user and control traffic into the wired network.

The WLAN security methods discussed in the section "WLAN Security Methods: Configuration Guidelines and Examples" also apply to the central switching deployment mode. One of the major changes made in the SWAN central switching deployment mode is that SSID/VLAN is mapped to an mGRE tunnel terminating on the central switch. WDS services such as fast secure roaming, discussed in the section "SWAN Nonswitching Deployment: Configuration Guidelines and Examples," also apply to central switching deployment mode.

Refer to Figure 9-2 for a sample SWAN central switching deployment. Example 12-29 illustrates the configuration required for an AP integrated as part of the central switching deployment mode (using Catalyst 6500 equipped with the wireless LAN services module as the central switch). Note that three VLANs are configured: two VLANs (VLAN 2 and VLAN 3) for user VLANs and the third as the native/management VLAN (VLAN 10). Note that RADIUS server information is not specified because all authentication messages are relayed to the RADIUS infrastructure via the WDS server.

Example 12-29   *AP Configuration: Central Switching Deployment Mode*

```
!
interface Dot11Radio0
! Configure encryption parameters for user VLANs 2 and 3
 encryption vlan 2 mode ciphers tkip
 encryption vlan 3 mode wep mandatory mic key-hash
 !
 ! Map SSID "Enterprise22" to network-id 22 (locally mapped to VLAN 2)
 ssid Enterprise22
    vlan 2
    authentication open eap eap-methods
    mobility network-id 22
 ! Map SSID "Enterprise33" to network-id 33 (locally mapped to VLAN 3)
 ssid Enterprise33
    vlan 3
    authentication open eap eap-methods
    authentication network-eap eap-methods
    authentication key-management cckm
    mobility network-id 33
 !
interface Dot11Radio0.2
 encapsulation dot1Q 2
 no ip route-cache
 bridge-group 2
 bridge-group 2 subscriber-loop-control
 bridge-group 2 block-unknown-source
 no bridge-group 2 source-learning
 no bridge-group 2 unicast-flooding
 bridge-group 2 spanning-disabled
!
interface Dot11Radio0.3
 encapsulation dot1Q 3
 no ip route-cache
 bridge-group 3
 bridge-group 3 subscriber-loop-control
 bridge-group 3 block-unknown-source
 no bridge-group 3 source-learning
 no bridge-group 3 unicast-flooding
 bridge-group 3 spanning-disabled
```

continues

Example 12-29 *AP Configuration: Central Switching Deployment Mode (Continued)*

```
!
interface Dot11Radio0.10
 encapsulation dot1Q 10
 no ip route-cache
 bridge-group 1
 bridge-group 1 subscriber-loop-control
 bridge-group 1 block-unknown-source
 no bridge-group 1 source-learning
 no bridge-group 1 unicast-flooding
 bridge-group 1 spanning-disabled
!
!
interface FastEthernet0
 no ip address
 . . .
!
interface FastEthernet0.2
 encapsulation dot1Q 2
 no ip route-cache
 bridge-group 2
 no bridge-group 2 source-learning
 bridge-group 2 spanning-disabled
!
interface FastEthernet0.3
 encapsulation dot1Q 3
 no ip route-cache
 bridge-group 3
 no bridge-group 3 source-learning
 bridge-group 3 spanning-disabled
!
interface FastEthernet0.10
 encapsulation dot1Q 10
 no ip route-cache
 bridge-group 1
 no bridge-group 1 source-learning
 bridge-group 1 spanning-disabled

!
interface BVI1
 ip address 10.10.10.15 255.255.255.0
 no ip route-cache
!
ip default-gateway 10.10.10.1
….
! Configure SNMP parameters to enable management by WLSE
snmp-server community snmpro RO
snmp-server community snmprw RW
snmp-server enable traps tty
bridge 1 route ip
!
! Specify WLCCP infrastructure authentication credentials
```

Example 12-29 *AP Configuration: Central Switching Deployment Mode (Continued)*

```
wlccp ap username cisco1 password 7 13061E010803
! Specify central switch WDS IP address
wlccp ap wds ip address 10.99.99.10
! Enable mGRE tunneling to the central switch
wlccp ap mobility
!
```

Supervisor configuration to enable central switching deployment mode on the Catalyst 6500 switch is provided in Example 12-30. As shown in the example, each mGRE tunnel interface is mapped to a network ID on the supervisor. Also, a loopback interface is defined as the source for each mGRE interface. Loopback interfaces and mGRE interfaces must be reachable to the APs (that is, must be routable). The loopback interface address is used as the destination IP address for an mGRE tunnel by the AP, whereas the mGRE tunnel interface address is the default gateway for the WLAN clients. Note that tunnel is in "untrusted" mode by default. If the tunnel is untrusted, DHCP snooping must be enabled within the tunnel, as shown in the example. Note that along with trusted/untrusted and DHCP snooping features, several existing security features of the Catalyst 6500 platform equipped with Supervisor 720 module are applicable to the mGRE interface(s) defined on the supervisor. These include L2-L4 access control lists (ACLs), router ACLs (RACLs), VLAN ACLs (VACLs), TCP Intercept (a feature used to prevent TCP SYN flooding attacks), and Route Processor (RP) rate-limiters (a feature used to prevent denial-of-service [DoS] attacks such as ICMP ping flooding). Finally, you must define VLAN to communicate with the WLAN service module on the supervisor.

Example 12-30 *Catalyst 6500 Supervisor Configuration: Central Switching Deployment Mode*

```
!
hostname sup720
!
. . .
! Define the VLAN on which WLAN communication to the supervisor is enabled
wlan module 3 allowed-vlan 99
! Enable ip dhcp snooping globally on the switch
! Note that dhcp snooping is required for the "untrusted" tunnels
ip dhcp snooping
mls ip multicast flow-stat-timer 9
no mls flow ip
no mls flow ipv6
...
!
vlan 99
 name to-WLSM
!
. . .
! Define Loopback interface22 as the source for Tunnel22
interface Loopback22
 description tunnel_source for network-ID_22
 ip address 10.10.100.22 255.255.255.0
! Define Loopback interface33 as the source for Tunnel33
```

continues

Example 12-30 *Catalyst 6500 Supervisor Configuration: Central Switching Deployment Mode (Continued)*

```
interface Loopback33
 description tunnel source for network-ID 33
 ip address 10.10.101.33 255.255.255.0
!
! Define mGRE Tunnel22 mapping to network-ID 22
interface Tunnel22
 description to Enterprise22 SSID
 ip address 10.22.22.1 255.255.255.0
 ip helper-address 10.20.20.4
 no ip redirects
 ip dhcp snooping packets
 tunnel source Loopback22
 tunnel mode gre multipoint
 mobility network-id 22
!
! Define mGRE Tunnel33 mapping to network-ID 33
interface Tunnel33
 description to_Enterprise33 SSID
 ip address 10.33.33.1 255.255.255.0
 ip helper-address 10.20.20.4
 no ip redirects
 ip dhcp snooping packets
 tunnel source Loopback33
 tunnel mode gre multipoint
 mobility network-id 33
!
. . .
! Define interface for VLAN 99 on the Supervisor
interface Vlan99
 description to_WLSM
 ip address 10.99.99.1 255.255.255.0
. . .
! Configure routing to advertise 10.x.x.0 subnets
router eigrp 100
  network 10.0.0.0
  no auto-summary
!
```

Example 12-31 illustrates the configuration required on the wireless LAN service module of the Catalyst 6500 switch. As illustrated in the example, a VLAN for communication with the supervisor must be defined (and match what is defined on the supervisor). Along with this, you must specify WLCCP infrastructure and EAP/802.1x, client authentication configuration for RADIUS servers. Finally, you must specify SNMP community strings to communicate with the WLSE.

Example 12-31 *Catalyst 6500 WLSM Configuration: Central Switching Deployment Mode*

```
aaa new-model
!
aaa authentication login wlccp-infra group radius
aaa session-id common
. . .
!
wlan vlan 99
 ipaddr 10.99.99.10 255.255.255.0
 gateway 10.99.99.1
 admin
!
!
ip classless
ip route 0.0.0.0 0.0.0.0 10.99.99.1
. . .
! Configure SNMP parameters to be managed by WLSE
snmp-server community snmprw RW
snmp-server community snmpro RO
snmp-server enable traps tty
! Define radius server parameters
radius-server host 10.1.1.11 auth-port 1812 acct-port 1813
radius-server key cisco123cisco
radius-server authorization permit missing Service-Type
!
! Enable infrastructure and client EAP/802.1x authentication
wlccp authentication-server infrastructure wlccp-infra
Wlccp authentication-server client any wlccp-infra
! Define WLSE information
wlccp wnm ip address 10.1.1.100
```

Summary

This chapter provided configuration examples for the best practices and design examples discussed throughout this book. IT also discussed configuration examples for the standalone AP and SWAN deployment modes. Security methods discussed, such as guest access, EAP/802.1x deployment with dynamic WEP, and EAP/802.1x with WPA, apply across all deployment modes. Always check the Cisco website (http://www.cisco.com) for the latest product configuration documentation.

CHAPTER 13

WLAN Deployment Examples

This chapter discusses several WLAN deployment examples across large, medium, and small enterprise networks and across vertical markets such as retail, education, healthcare, and manufacturing. Whereas Chapter 10, "Design Guidelines for Secure WLANs," discussed deployment guidelines and best practices for securing WLANs, this chapter applies the aforementioned deployment guidelines and best practices uniquely for each customer scenario to give you snapshots of different WLAN security deployments, each with unique deployment criteria. Deployment challenges and issues are also discussed with each example. If applicable, a deployment/topology diagram is given for a deployment example.

Large Enterprise Deployment Examples

This section details typical large-enterprise WLAN deployments. WLAN deployment in large enterprise networks can be considered to have three phases. The first phase is usually a pilot deployment with limited coverage (typically for executive users who require mobility throughout one or multiple floors). The security design and implementation issues are resolved in the initial phase. In the second phase of deployment, meeting rooms throughout multiple buildings typically are covered to provide WLAN connectivity. Management issues are resolved as the deployment starts to grow in terms of the number of WLAN infrastructure elements and WLAN users. The third and last phase of deployment is to expand coverage throughout the enterprise. In the last phase, scalability issues have to be addressed and any infrastructure/client-management issues revisited. The security deployment model determined in the first phase holds unless the customer runs into major management and scalability issues. In the main campus environment, WLAN connectivity is likely to be secondary connectivity (with wired connectivity being primary), whereas in a branch office environment, WLAN connectivity is likely to be considered the primary network connectivity mechanism.

Large Enterprise WLAN Deployment Example I

The first example is taken from a large enterprise WLAN deployment in a high-tech company. This customer deployment covers all main areas of multiple campuses across the globe (in multiple cities) and several branch offices. The majority of the user community tends to be technology savvy and good at adopting new technologies. In this deployment, wired connectivity is considered the primary network connectivity, and wireless is provided as the secondary network connectivity throughout the campuses. In some remote offices, WLAN connectivity is considered the primary network connectivity.

The customer deployment criteria are as follows:

- Mutual authentication and strong encryption for WLAN users.
- Single sign-on required; desire to tie the Windows login to WLAN user authentication.
- Authenticate WLAN users to Microsoft back-end Active Directory (AD) infrastructure.
- No public-key infrastructure (PKI) (digital certificate) requirement for user authentication.
- Desire to deploy WLAN ubiquitously across the globe.
- Plan to deploy wireless voice over IP (VoIP).
- Provide guest access service across main campus buildings.

The customer deployment environment includes the following:

- WLAN users standardized on Windows 2000 and XP; however, a small subset of the users has Linux, Mac OS X laptops and Windows CE personal digital assistants (PDAs).
- WLAN users standardized on Cisco Aironet adapters or embedded CCX laptops.
- Microsoft AD infrastructure is deployed globally.
- Central (corporate and regional headquarters [HQ]) to remote sites have redundant WAN links. Redundant WAN links can be relied on to provide reliable RADIUS service to authenticate remote WLAN users.
- A subset of the user community (sales representatives and support personal) is mobile within a country and at times across the globe.
- Guest users can bring in laptops with any OS and any WLAN vendor network interface card (NIC) adapter.

WLAN Security Deployment Details

Given the preceding deployment criteria and deployment environment, EAP/802.1x with Temporal Key Integrity Protocol (TKIP) (WPA [Wi-Fi Protected Access] model) was selected as the deployment model to provide Layer 2–based user authentication and data confidentiality for employees. In this specific scenario, the customer selected Cisco LEAP for mutual authentication and dynamic Wired Equivalent Privacy (WEP) for strong encryption in the initial phase of the deployment. LEAP was selected due to the customer's desire for noncertificate-based user authentication (that is, non-PKI). Furthermore, LEAP deployment was facilitated with the use of Cisco Aironet client adapters and the CCX laptops where LEAP support is natively provided. Initially, WLAN connectivity was enabled only for Windows 2000 and XP users. In the second phase of deployment, WLAN access was expanded to Mac OS, Linux, and Windows CE (PDA) users.

For users with Cisco Aironet client adapters, single sign-on was facilitated using the Aironet Client Utility (ACU) configured to obtain LEAP authentication credentials via Windows user login. For users with CCX laptops, single sign-on was facilitated using securely stored user authentication credentials on the user's laptop. The deployment was expanded to allow wireless access for 25,000 employees worldwide.

In the initial phase, dynamic WEP was deployed to facilitate a quick deployment. Because of known WEP weaknesses (as discussed in Chapter 6, "Wireless Vulnerabilities"), the encryption key was rotated every 15 minutes using IETF parameter 27 (also known as *session-timeout*, which is a per-user or user-group IETF parameter) on the RADIUS server. To provide strong data confidentiality, users were slowly migrated to WPA. Along with migration to WPA, strong password policy was instituted for WLAN users to enable LEAP authentication. The IT administrator instituted a minimum of 10 characters with at least two nonalphanumeric characters in a user's password as the strong password policy. A long-term migration to EAP-FAST is planned for the Cisco Aironet client adapter and CCX users to minimize risk due to offline dictionary attacks.

Wired/Wireless LAN Integration and WLAN Infrastructure and User Management Details

In deploying WLAN throughout the campus environment, a single VLAN per building was deployed to accommodate WLAN devices and WLAN users. This provided the IT administrator with the flexibility to enforce specific wired security policies for the WLAN devices and users. This also enabled seamless Layer 2 mobility within a building. However, this meant spanning a single VLAN at the building distribution layer level and was against the overall wired deployment policy, which mandated limiting the size of wired VLANs. Limiting the size of wired VLANs usually means enforcing Layer 3 routed links between distribution and access layer level switches. In the initial deployment phase, the compromise was made for security purposes (isolating WLAN devices/users per building) and for enabling seamless Layer 2 roaming, however.

As the deployment grew to a large size (500+ access points and 10,000 WLAN users), the IT department had to automate WLAN infrastructure management and user management. The IT department has a "home-grown" network management system to facilitate infrastructure management. Wireless LAN Solution Engine (WLSE) was incorporated as part of this to enable automated software and firmware management for APs along with configuration management. WLSE version 2.5 (or above) and AP IOS release 12.2(13)JA (or above) are incorporated (as part of the SWAN architecture) to automate RF site survey (using the assisted site-survey feature). Furthermore, WLSE along with SWAN network elements (switches/routers, APs, and clients) were configured to scan and detect rogue APs. Specifically, distribution layer switches (Catalyst 6500 switches with Supervisor 720 module and the Wireless LAN Service Module [WLSM]) were configured to enable Wireless Domain Services (WDS) to facilitate SWAN-related features, such as RF monitoring, rogue AP detection, and fast secure roaming for VoIP devices.

To facilitate large-scale WLAN user deployment, automated IT tools (such as Altiris client management solution) were used to push out the Aironet Installation Wizard and Aironet Client Utility (ACU) configuration (generated using the Aironet Configuration Administration Tool [ACAT]) to all users with Aironet client adapters and CCX-certified laptops.

Figure 13-1 provides the overall deployment architecture and topology of this customer's network. As seen in the figure, WLAN was deployed for multiple buildings in a large campus environment. Standard campus design practices were implemented for the wired deployment in access, building distribution, core, data center, and Internet access modules.

Note that integration of WLSM into Catalyst 6500 switches at the distribution layer level (as shown in Figure 13-1) removes the need to span user VLANs across the distribution switch. Each wired VLAN per floor can be GRE tunneled into the supervisor using the Catalyst 6500 WLSM integration model. Preferably, WLSM integration can be performed starting in the first phase of deployment to minimize changes to the existing wired network when integrating wireless into a large campus-wired network.

AAA and External User Database Infrastructure Implementation Details

In addition to management issues, AAA infrastructure scalability and availability issues had to be resolved. To facilitate large-scale EAP/802.1x authentication, AAA (RADIUS server) infrastructure had to be scaled for large campuses, and redundancy had to be provided for large campus and remote office deployment scenarios. Central network operation centers (NOCs) were used for large campuses (using the DATA center as the NOC), and RADIUS servers were deployed in regional NOCs to address remote office deployments.

Four Cisco Secure ACS RADIUS servers were deployed in the central NOC for the main campus HQ where 10,000+ WLAN users are facilitated. A minimum of two Cisco Secure ACS RADIUS servers were deployed per regional NOC. A load balancer (such as Cisco Catalyst 6500 server content switching module or the 6500 Supervisor IOS load balancing feature) was used to load balance among multiple RADIUS servers. In the remote office deployment, the APs were configured to use the regional RADIUS infrastructure as the primary RADIUS server, and the central NOC (that is, corporate NOC) was configured as the secondary RADIUS infrastructure (to be used under regional NOC failure conditions only).

NOTE	RADIUS server scaling for EAP authentication is based on many factors. The number of WLAN users, the number of APs, authentication timeout, and the EAP protocol used are some of the factors that you should consider. For more details, visit the Cisco website and explore deployment guidelines for this. Specifically, refer to http://www.cisco.com/en/US/products/sw/secursw/ps2086/products_white_paper09186a00801495a1.shtml.

Figure 13-1   *Large Enterprise WLAN Deployment I Example*

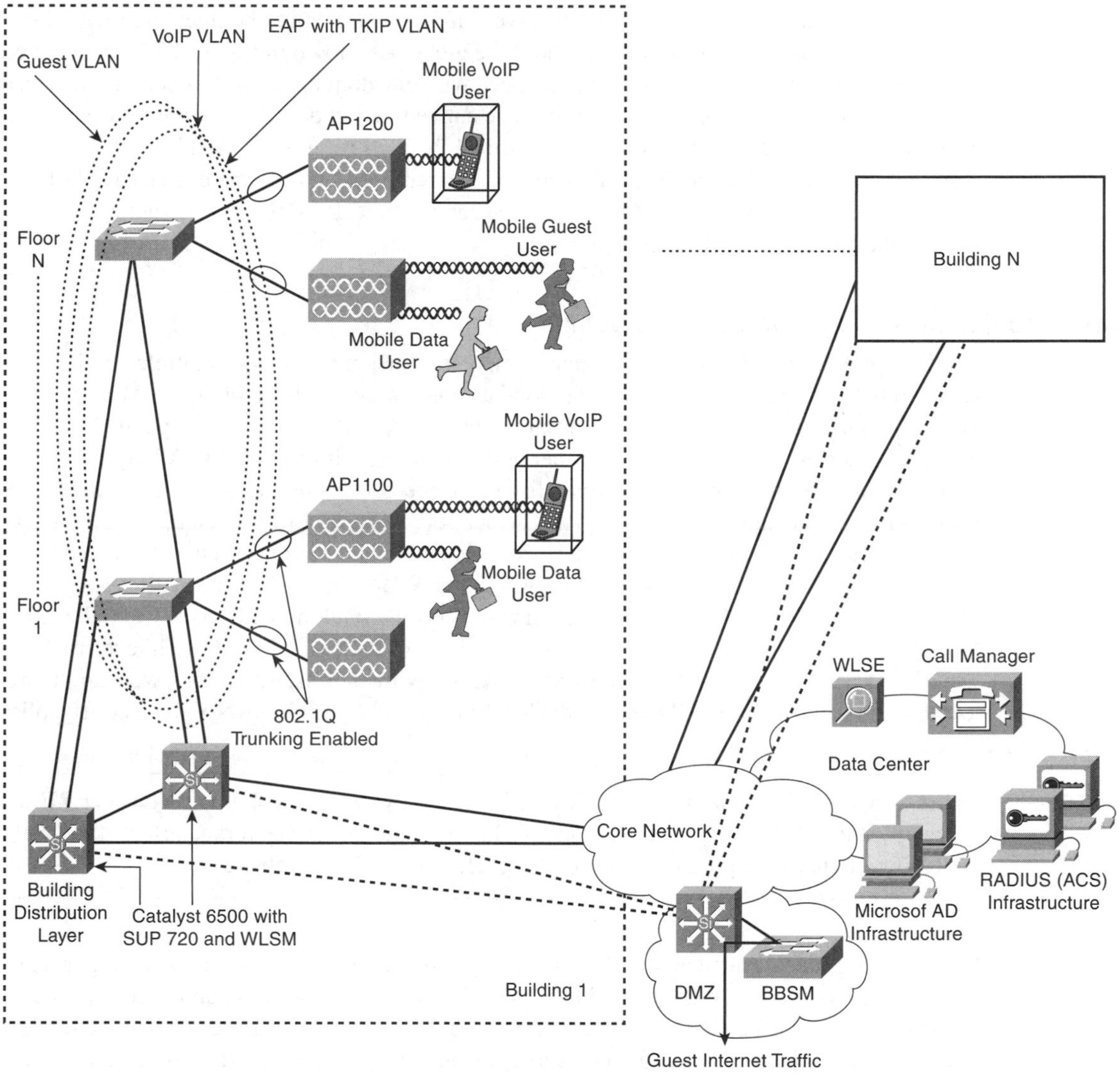

In the initial deployment, one key issue for RADIUS server infrastructure scalability was session rekey timing. Initially, every user was configured for reauthentication every 15 minutes (while WEP was deployed for encryption); as a result, RADIUS server infrastructure was impacted (due to an increased number of user authentication requests per minute). However, in the long run, migration to WPA eliminated the rekey (that is, reauthentication) timing requirement, which significantly improved the RADIUS server's scalability and performance.

Along with RADIUS server scalability issues, Microsoft AD scalability and availability had to be increased for WLAN user authentication. To facilitate users who roamed from site to site (which was possible globally), RADIUS server infrastructure had to be integrated with the Microsoft AD domains deployed throughout the globe. As shown in Figure 13-2, data centers (both central and regional NOCs) were equipped with one domain controller per AD domain to facilitate users who roam globally (to minimize authentication delay) and to provide sufficient availability and scalability. As shown in Figure 13-2, WDS running in each branch office is configured to use the RADIUS infrastructure in the regional NOC as the primary RADIUS server. In the event of regional NOC failure, the central NOC RADIUS infrastructure would be used as the backup RADIUS server.

VoIP and Guest Services Deployment Details

In a large enterprise WLAN network deployment, expansion to include multiple applications needs to be addressed. One of the initial nondata applications to be deployed is VoIP over WLAN. To facilitate unique security requirements for VoIP deployment, a separate WLAN/wired VLAN was deployed per floor or per building (along with the existing VLAN[s] for data users). Using the multiple VLANs capability in Aironet APs, four VLANs were created. The initial VLAN was maintained for the data users, a second VLAN was created for VoIP WLAN users, a third VLAN was created for guest access (discussed later in this chapter), and a fourth VLAN was created as the management VLAN for the WLAN infrastructure. VoIP VLAN/SSID was configured to allow EAP authentication with WPA-TKIP along with Cisco Centralized Key Management (CCKM) for fast secure roaming (as part of the Cisco SWAN architecture). Cisco 7920 WLAN VoIP devices were deployed for WLAN VoIP access, where they were configured to use LEAP and WPA-TKIP along with CCKM to comply with WLAN VoIP security policy.

NOTE	Apart from considering security policies for VoIP deployment, you should reconsider RF site-survey for the WLAN network. Specifically, the robustness of RF coverage affects the VoIP over WLAN quality. For more details on this, refer to the Cisco website.

Guest services deployment across the main campus building was facilitated by configuring the guest VLAN as open/no WEP and using a Layer 3-based service access control device (such as BBSM) to authenticate guest users via secure HTTP. Typically, guest user authentication is implemented to prevent unauthorized users from accessing an enterprise's guest network and using the network connectivity for malicious activities. As shown in Figure 13-1, guest traffic from each access switch was groomed at the building distribution layer switch, and a generic routing encapsulation (GRE) tunnel was used to transport the guest traffic to the Internet access module (typically, this would be the demilitarized zone [DMZ]) within the main campus network. A BBSM-like device was used at the Internet access module to authenticate guest users and allow Internet access. BBSM was configured to use HTTP redirect to authenticate guest users to the RADIUS infrastructure. Using a web-based online Intranet signup page, guest users were provisioned with temporary accounts on the RADIUS infrastructure.

Figure 13-2   *Large Enterprise Branch Office WLAN Deployment Example*

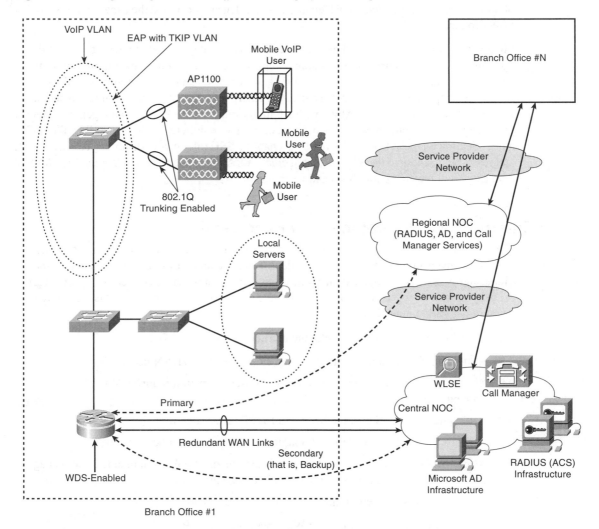

Summary of Large Enterprise WLAN Deployment Example I

The main challenges in this deployment were ongoing client management, RF management, rogue AP detection, and security. The requirement to continuously upgrade software/firmware is a significant challenge for the IT department, and efforts were undertaken to automate this process using readily available client management tools and home-grown applications. RF management and rogue AP detection required significant manpower during initial deployment.

However, the deployment of SWAN architecture (WLSE 2.5 or above along with 12.2[13] JA or above on APs) minimized the RF deployment burden and provided the capability to scan and detect rogue APs.

Finally, security is an ongoing challenge; the IT department must keep up with the latest developments in WLAN security and maintain an up-to-date security implementation to minimize risks due to commonly known WLAN vulnerabilities. The IT department uses the SWAN RF monitoring capability to continuously scan the enterprise WLAN deployment and detect any unauthorized WLAN activity. Along with RF monitoring, secure WLAN management policies were deployed to secure the WLAN infrastructure. These policies include enabling TACACS authentication on the WLAN infrastructure, enabling SSH (along with disabling Telnet access), and restricting access to the WLAN management VLAN (as discussed in Chapter 12, "WLAN Security Configuration Guidelines and Examples").

Large Enterprise WLAN Deployment Example II

This deployment example is also taken from a large enterprise WLAN deployment in a high-tech company. Similar to Example I, this deployment covers multiple campuses across the globe, and WLAN is deployed as an overlay network. (That is, wired connectivity is considered primary and wireless secondary.) In some remote offices, WLAN connectivity is considered the primary network connectivity.

The following are the customer deployment criteria:

- Mutual authentication and strong encryption exists for WLAN users.
- Single sign-on is required; you do not want user intervention during WLAN authentication.
- Authenticate WLAN users to back-end LDAP infrastructure.
- A desire exists to deploy WLAN ubiquitously across the globe.
- Minimize client management. Minimize the number of SW components to be managed on the WLAN client for user authentication and encryption.

The customer deployment environment includes the following:

- WLAN users are standardized on Windows 2000 and XP.
- The LDAP infrastructure is deployed globally.
- The majority of the NIC cards are Cisco PCMCIA cards (80 percent of the users); however, the rest of the WLAN clients are non-Cisco and are from a mixed vendor base.
    - Non-Cisco clients are supported on the Windows XP OS platform only.

- Central (corporate and regional HQ) to remote sites have redundant WAN links.
  - Redundant WAN links can be relied on to provide reliable RADIUS service to authenticate remote WLAN users.
- A subset of the user community (sales representatives and support personal) is mobile within a country and at times across the globe.

WLAN Security Deployment Details

Given the preceding deployment criteria and deployment environment, along with the customer's desire to implement IEEE 802.11i security recommendations, EAP/802.1x with TKIP (WPA model) was selected as the deployment model to provide Layer 2-based user authentication and data confidentiality. In this specific scenario, the customer selected EAP-FAST (EAP- Flexible Authentication via Secure Tunneling) and PEAP/MS-CHAPv2 (protected EAP with MS-CHAPv2) for mutual authentication along with WPA for strong encryption in the initial phase of the deployment. EAP-FAST was selected as the mutual authentication solution for Cisco Aironet clients, whereas PEAP/MS-CHAPv2 was selected as the authentication solution for non-Cisco/non-CCX clients.

EAP-FAST implementation on Cisco clients provides strong mutual authentication using user ID/password as the user authentication credential, along with the use of Protected Access Credential (PAC) as discussed in Chapter 7, "EAP Authentication Protocols for WLANs." In addition, both EAP-FAST and WPA are supported on Cisco clients for Windows 2000 and XP operating systems. Similar to EAP-FAST, PEAP/MS-CHAPv2 provides strong mutual authentication using user ID/password as the user authentication credential. PEAP/MS-CHAPv2 was selected for non-Cisco clients because EAP-FAST is not supported on them. However, non-Cisco clients standardized on Windows XP can take advantage of native OS support of PEAP/MS-CHAPv2 and WPA security features.

EAP-FAST deployment on Cisco Aironet clients was facilitated with the use of ACU, which was configured to locally store the user authentication credential (username/password). PEAP/MS-CHAPv2 deployment on non-Cisco/non-CCX clients was facilitated using Windows native EAP supplicant, which was configured to allow PEAP/MS-CHAPv2 authentication. Cisco Secure ACS (Release 3.2.3 and above) was deployed to authenticate both EAP-FAST and PEAP/MS-CHAPv2 users. RADIUS server certificates were bought from a public PKI entity (for example, VeriSign) and installed on the RADIUS servers to enable PEAP authentication. Note that the choices here are either to use an enterprise (private) PKI entity to issue RADIUS server certificates or to use a public PKI entity to issue RADIUS server certificates to enable PEAP authentication. If you are using a private PKI entity, the trusted root CA certificate (and possibly sub-CA certificates) needs to be distributed to the WLAN clients configured to execute PEAP authentication. It is a deployment requirement to configure the trusted root CA (and any sub-CAs) on a PEAP-enabled WLAN client.

Wired/Wireless LAN Integration

To minimize changes on the existing wired infrastructure to integrate WLAN, a pair of Catalyst 6500 switches at the data center level was integrated with the Wireless LAN Service Module (WLSM) (and Supervisor 720) to enable centralized WLAN traffic aggregation. As discussed in Chapter 9, "SWAN: End-to-End Security Deployment," this deployment model provides a single point of ingress for all WLAN user traffic and control traffic. WLSM provides a scalable WDS for radio management and fast secure roaming services. Furthermore, the 6500 WLSM integration model removes the need to span user VLANs across the distribution switch to enable seamless roaming across the enterprise network. Each wired VLAN per floor can be GRE-tunneled into the supervisor using this deployment model.

Deployment Challenges

One of the major challenges in the initial deployment was that the EAP-FAST automatic provisioning for LDAP back-end user DB was not supported. Automatic provisioning enables the per-user PAC to be dynamically provisioned on the user's device. Manual PAC provisioning could be used for LDAP back-end user databases (supported in ACS 3.2.3 release and above) but was rejected due to ease of deployment concerns. Another challenge was that PEAP/MS-CHAPv2 authentication is not supported with the LDAP back-end database. To address these major deployment challenges, the customer was able to create an automated "out-of-band" (using wired connectivity) mechanism for enabling wireless users. A user who desired wireless access was directed to an internal company website and was required to authenticate to the back-end LDAP DB and specify a separate username/password for wireless access. After the user was provisioned on the RADIUS infrastructure (using an automated script), he was notified via e-mail. The user was instructed (via the confirmation e-mail) to configure his or her laptop with the username/password for WLAN authentication.

Lastly, users were provisioned on the root RADIUS server, and configuration of the root RADIUS server was distributed to the nonroot RADIUS servers worldwide (using the Cisco Secure ACS features). This facilitates users who roam between several regions to use the same authentication credential to gain network access.

AAA Infrastructure Implementation Details

As previously discussed in Example I, AAA infrastructure scalability and availability issues had to be resolved. To facilitate large-scale EAP/802.1x authentication, the AAA (RADIUS server) infrastructure had to be scaled for large campuses and redundancy had to be provided for large campus and remote office deployment scenarios. Central NOCs were used for large campuses (using the data center as the NOC), and RADIUS servers were deployed in regional NOCs to address remote office deployments. For more information, refer to the "AAA and External User Database Infrastructure Implementation Details" section earlier in this chapter.

Summary of Large Enterprise WLAN Deployment Example II

Major deployment challenges in this example were related to chosen EAP protocols and back-end user DB compatibility. However, the customer was able to overcome these challenges using out-of-band (over the wired network) provisioning of user authentication accounts on the RADIUS infrastructure.

Finally, in addition to authentication and data confidentiality needs, the customer deployed the Cisco SWAN solution to enable RF management (including rogue AP detection) and to enable a central point of ingress for all WLAN traffic into the wired LAN network. WLSE, IOS-enabled Cisco Aironet APs, Catalyst 6500 switches equipped with the WLSM, and Cisco/non-Cisco clients were integrated to enable the SWAN solution.

Vertical Deployment Examples

This section covers WLAN deployment examples in key vertical markets, including retail, education, healthcare, manufacturing, and finance. Wireless access is used as the primary network access method in certain verticals such as retail and healthcare. An example (or two) for each vertical market is provided in this section, detailing WLAN applications, overall deployment criteria, and WLAN security implementation specifics to accommodate each unique environment.

In a retail deployment, multiple APs typically are deployed across a store. (The number of required APs depends on the store's size.) The WLAN APs and infrastructure are connected to a store's wired infrastructure, which in turn is connected to the central HQ via a WAN link. The WLAN link BW typically is limited between the central HQ and the store, and the backup connectivity mechanism is dialup ISDN, where usage is limited to critical applications such as credit card transaction processing. One of the major challenges in WLAN deployment for a retail environment is legacy handhelds. Legacy handhelds deployed to work with 900-MHz and frequency hopping (FH) wireless technologies are prevalent in the retail environment. These handhelds use DOS or a vendor-proprietary operating system and have limited processor capability. Typically, these handhelds are deployed in hundreds per store and take a long time to be replaced with newer Windows CE–based devices. Migrating the legacy handhelds to be 802.11b compliant and providing sufficient security are the major design and implementation challenges.

WLAN deployment in healthcare also brings specific challenges. Healthcare professionals tend to be highly mobile, and proper RF, mobility, and security design play a key role in ensuring continuous and secure connectivity throughout a health institution. Deployment criteria such as Layer 3 roaming and session persistence must be considered in conjunction with a security deployment in a healthcare environment. Session persistence is required because users could temporarily roam out of a WLAN coverage area, during which time the user application sessions must be sustained (that is, the WLAN infrastructure should not disconnect the user). Additionally, the Health Insurance Portability and Accountability Act (HIPPA) in the United

States or equivalent laws around the world must be complied with for a healthcare WLAN deployment.

A WLAN deployment in an education environment such as a university campus also has unique requirements. For example, the IT department might standardize on WLAN infrastructure; however, students are allowed to bring any laptop with their choice of OS and WLAN NIC adapter. This creates challenges with standardizing on a specific WLAN security mechanism for the user community, including the students and faculty/staff. Typically, WLAN connectivity is considered the primary connectivity mechanism for students to access learning materials. User authentication is considered a must to only allow access to valid users; however, data confidentiality is not considered a must because nonconfidential learning material is typically shared over the WLAN medium. However, both user authentication and data confidentiality are usually required for faculty and teaching staff to secure their communication over the WLAN.

Mobility is a key requirement in a manufacturing environment in which mobile workers (such as forklift drivers within a warehouse) use several applications, including inventory management. Similar to the healthcare environment, fast Layer 2/Layer 3 roaming and session persistence become critical in a manufacturing environment to facilitate the mobile workers. Also, similar to the retail environment, legacy devices along with new Windows CE devices (multivendor clients) must be facilitated.

Finally, a security deployment criterion to provide strong mutual user authentication along with data confidentiality are musts in financial environments. Due to strong regulatory requirements to protect individual financial data, strict security deployment criteria are used to ensure identity verification and end-to-end data protection. Typically, multiple layers of security (such as Layer 2 and Layer 3 user-based authentication and data confidentiality) are deployed in a financial WLAN deployment scenario.

Retail WLAN Deployment Example I

This deployment example is taken from a retail WLAN deployment. WLAN has been extensively deployed and used in retail store applications for the past two decades, including in inventory tracking (bar-code scanning), wireless-enabled cashier machines, wireless-enabled scales, printers, and so on. This deployment example is taken from a large-scale WLAN rollout for thousands of retail stores across the United States to provide primary network connectivity at each store. In this deployment scenario, one of the major deployment challenges was to enable user authentication and data confidentiality for legacy handhelds.

The customer deployment criteria include the following:

- Legacy DOS-based handheld scanners (for example, Symbol PDT 6800 series scanners at http://www.symbol.com/) are supported.

- Wireless printers and wireless VoIP devices are supported.

- Mutual authentication and strong encryption (minimum dynamic WEP) are preferred.
- No PKI (digital certificate) requirement exists for user authentication.

The customer deployment environment includes the following:

- A reliable 64-Kbps Frame Relay link exists between a store and the corporate or regional HQ. A redundant WAN link is provided via dialup ISDN and limited for critical services (such as banking transactions).
- Multiple devices types, including legacy DOS-based handheld scanners used for inventory tracking, new handheld PDAs (based on Palm OS) used for inventory tracking, VoIP handsets, wireless-enabled scales, printers, and cash registers, are deployed across each store.
- A combination of Cisco Aironet 350 PCMCIA and non-Cisco (or non-CCX) adapters are deployed in different handhelds.
- Microsoft AD infrastructure is deployed at the central HQ only.
- A Cisco 2600 series router is used per store along with multiple Catalyst 3500 series switches.

WLAN Security Deployment Details

In this deployment scenario, a single "wireless cell" cannot be used to accommodate unique security requirements per device type. This is primarily due to the customer requirement to support legacy DOS-based handheld devices (static WEP capable only) and newer PDA devices (EAP/802.1x capable) along with VoIP devices. Therefore, multiple "virtual" wireless cells were deployed in which each virtual WLAN cell had a unique security implementation to suit a specific device type. Multiple virtual cells were enabled with the use of multiple wireless VLANs (SSIDs) in each store. Each SSID was mapped to a unique, wired VLAN where Layer 3/Layer 4–based policies were implemented on the store router. This enabled the administrator to enforce a specific security policy per wireless/wired VLAN. Figure 13-3 illustrates the overall deployment topology for this customer scenario. As shown in the figure, multiple SSIDs and VLANs are deployed to accommodate multiple security profiles (as desired for various devices) using a single WLAN infrastructure.

Static WEP was enabled on the legacy wireless VLAN as the security mechanism for legacy DOS-based handheld scanners and wireless-enabled scales due to limited capabilities on these devices. In addition to static WEP, MAC address authentication was enabled to authenticate the legacy devices and the wireless-enabled scales. MAC addresses of these devices were centrally stored on the RADIUS infrastructure at the HQ site. However, these MAC addresses were locally stored on the WDS to MAC-address authenticate legacy devices during WAN link outage. Network access to these devices was limited to specific inventory servers using Layer 3 (IP address–based) ACLs on the store router.

Figure 13-3 *Retail WLAN Deployment Example I*

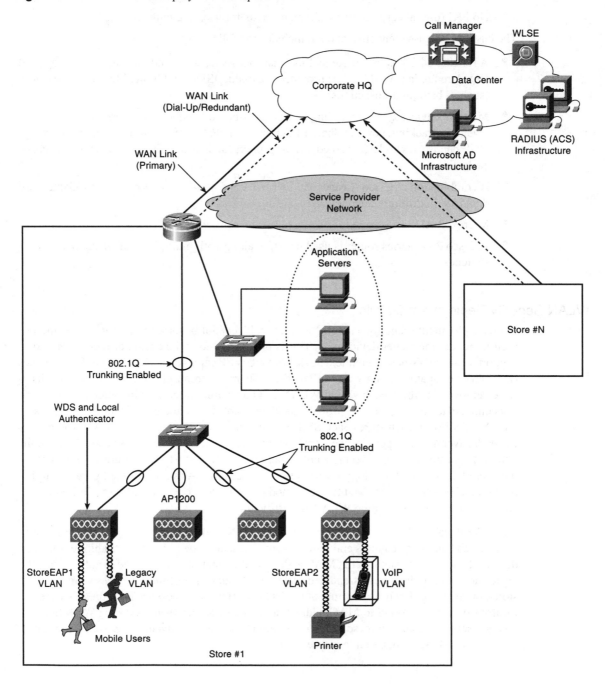

New Palm OS handheld devices were integrated with Cisco Aironet PCMCIA adapters, and LEAP was enabled for mutual authentication with dynamic WEP for data confidentiality. The LEAP authentication credential was securely stored on the Palm OS device. Palm OS devices were deployed on wireless VLAN "storeEAP1" (configured to enable LEAP authentication with dynamic WEP) and were given appropriate network access rights using Layer 3/Layer 4 ACLs on the store router.

Wireless VoIP devices were deployed on a third SSID/VLAN (VoIP VLAN) and were given voice QoS along with access to Call Manager and VoIP voice gateway at each store. Cisco 7920 VoIP handsets were deployed with LEAP authentication, CCKM, and WPA-TKIP on the VoIP VLAN. CCKM enable fast secure roaming (as part of the Cisco SWAN solution) by expediting 802.1x roaming between APs for VoIP users. Without fast secure roaming implementation for VoIP users, 802.1x reauthentication would have been executed over the WAN link in this deployment scenario, which can result in variable (and possibly lengthy) delays during roaming between APs. Thus, the fast secure roaming feature significantly improved roaming performance to minimize delay and jitter for VoIP users in this deployment scenario.

On wireless VLAN "storeEAP2," LEAP was enabled with dynamic WEP for wireless-enabled printers (such as HP Jet direct 680n with 802.11b internal wireless print server). Employees used printing services across the store for various purposes. As with other devices, access to the wireless-enabled printers was limited using Layer 3 and Layer 4 ACLs on the store router.

A strong password policy was implemented for all LEAP-enabled devices (Cisco 7920 hand-sets and wireless-enabled printers) to mitigate risks due to the offline (passive) dictionary attack scenario. The IT department required a 16-character password with four nonalphanumeric char-acters to generate passwords for LEAP authentication. A user ID/password combination was securely stored on each device for LEAP authentication.

Finally, a fifth VLAN was created as the management VLAN for the APs. The management VLAN was not mapped to the radio interface, and access was restricted via AP's Ethernet interface with the use of Layer 3 and Layer 4 ACLs on the store router. ACLs on the store router were used to limit access to AP's management VLAN to allow only RADIUS and management traffic between the AP and the management (RADIUS server and WLSE) devices.

WDS and AAA Infrastructure Implementation Details

WDS was enabled on an AP1200 per store to enable fast secure roaming for VoIP devices and local authentication service for all LEAP devices. Alternatively, WDS services can be enabled on the store router if a Cisco 26xx or Cisco 36xx/37xx router is used as the store router.

In addition to using WDS to facilitate fast secure roaming via CCKM, RF management was enabled via WDS to facilitate RF monitoring at the store level, including functionality such as rogue AP detection. WLSE version 2.5 (and above) and AP IOS release 12.2(13) JA (and above) are required to enable RF monitoring functionality.

Each LEAP-enabled device at the store level was configured with a unique user account at the HQ RADIUS user database. LEAP user accounts for each store are grouped and maintained at the HQ RADIUS user database. In addition to this, user accounts for a specific store are distributed via WLSE template–based configuration to populate WDS at each store with appropriate user accounts. When devices are added and removed from each store, the HQ RADIUS database and the appropriate store local database (on the local store WDS) are updated.

When the primary WAN link is available, an initial LEAP authentication request is sent to the primary RADIUS infrastructure via the WAN link. However, when the WAN link fails, a local authentication service on the WDS AP authenticates the LEAP users during the initial client association and during 802.1x reauthentication (if required).

Deployment Challenges

One of the biggest challenges in this retail deployment was client management with regard to managing client firmware, drivers, and configuration. The Wavelink Avalanche solution was used to manage WLAN firmware, drivers, and configuration on clients from multivendors. Configuration management on the clients included static WEP-key management and LEAP authentication profile management. Another challenge was to configure a local WDS per store with the LEAP authentication credential for LEAP-enabled devices. As discussed previously, each LEAP-enabled device was configured with a unique authentication credential (username and password). WLSE was used to automate WDS configuration per store. A generic template was created using WLSE for WDS configuration across stores and a separate WDS template per store with unique configuration information such as relevant LEAP authentication credentials for LEAP-enabled devices used at each store.

Summary of Retail WLAN Deployment Example I

As discussed in this example, it is important to a provide a wired/wireless LAN infrastructure to accommodate multiple device types, each with its unique security requirement at the store level. In addition, the deployment model should provide capabilities to migrate from legacy retail deployment to a new deployment supporting 802.11i-capable devices.

Local WDS is required at each store level to facilitate fast secure roaming and RF management. Additionally, local authentication service is enabled on the WDS AP to facilitate fallback radius authentication service during the primary WAN link outage. However, the fallback (local) authentication service implementation does mandate that ongoing maintenance of the local user database is synchronized with the central HQ user database.

Retail WLAN Deployment Example II

This example is also taken from a retail WLAN deployment. WLAN connectivity was implemented as the primary network connectivity for several in-store applications, including inventory management. This example has deployment characteristics that are similar to Retail

Example I. The overall architecture is such that legacy and new devices must be facilitated over a WLAN network, store-to-HQ WAN connectivity is nonredundant, and multivendor clients are deployed for various in-store applications.

The customer deployment criteria are as follows:

- Support legacy DOS-based handheld scanners (such as Symbol PDT 6800 series scanners).

- Enable a long-term transition to 802.11i standards–based security implementation.

  — Migrate legacy devices to new handheld PDAs (based on Windows CE).

- Support wireless-enabled web tablets (HTML, web browser–enabled WLAN devices mounted on shopping carts) provided by retailer to shoppers.

  — Wireless-enabled web tablets are used to advertise special offers to shoppers.

- Mutual authentication and strong encryption are preferred.

- Possibly provide public hotspot service to customers at the deli section in the future.

The customer deployment environment is as follows:

- Reliable 64-Kbps Frame Relay link between a store and the corporate or regional HQ. Redundant WAN link is provided via dialup 28.8 Public Switched Telephone Network (PSTN) link and is limited for critical services (such as banking transactions).

- Multiple device types, including legacy DOS-based handheld scanners used for inventory tracking, new handheld PDAs (based on Windows CE) used for inventory tracking, and wireless-enabled tablets, are deployed at each store.

- Multivendor WLAN NIC adapters (including Cisco NIC adapters) and embedded clients are deployed to facilitate in-store retail applications.

- A Cisco 3700 series router is used per store along with 2900 series Catalyst switches.

Like Retail Example I, Cisco WLAN infrastructure (in this case, AP1100s) was used to enable multiple SSIDs and VLANs within the store. A dedicated wired switch (Cisco Catalyst 2900) was deployed per store to accommodate WLAN devices and users. Along with an additional wired switch, a Cisco 3700 router with firewall services was used to provide isolation between wired and wireless networks.

As shown in Figure 13-4, one wireless VLAN (SSID mapped to wired VLAN) was created to facilitate legacy DOS-based handheld devices. This VLAN, called *legacy*, was configured with static WEP. Legacy devices were only allowed to communicate with the inventory servers on the wired segment. Access privileges were limited to legacy VLAN using stateful firewall features on the in-store router (Cisco 3700). A second VLAN named legacy was created to allow only devices configured with EAP authentication and WPA. PEAP/MS-CHAPv2 was selected as the EAP protocol to facilitate the multivendor NICs used on PDAs (Windows-CE 4.2 or above) and web tablets (Windows XP based). However, the local RADIUS server was deployed due to lack of local authentication support for PEAP. A user authentication credential (user ID/password) was securely stored on each PEAP-capable device. Broader access

Figure 13-4 *Retail WLAN Deployment Example II*

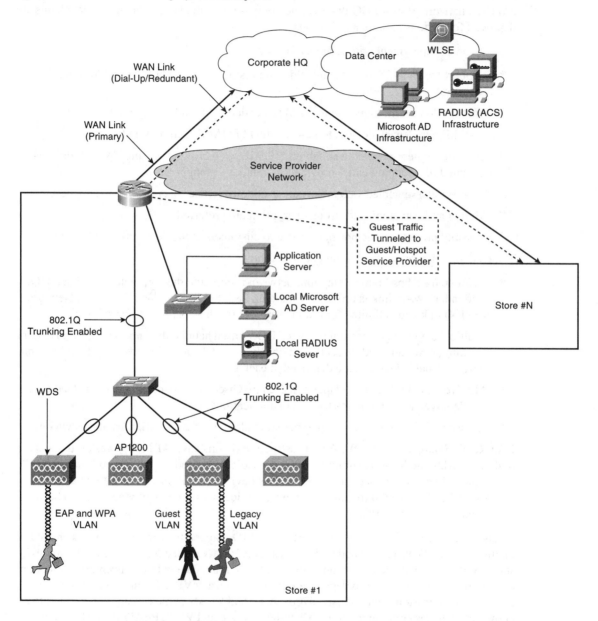

privileges were allowed for legacy VLAN (as compared to legacy VLAN) using Cisco 3700 stateful firewall capabilities. A third VLAN could be implemented in the future to facilitate hotspot services for deli customers. Guest traffic could be groomed at the store router and tunneled to the hotspot service provider network. Stateful firewall services on the 3700 series routers could be used to enforce appropriate security policy on the hotspot VLAN.

Cisco SWAN solution was implemented using WLSE 2.5 (and above) and a minimum of 12.2(13)JA IOS release on the APs. This enabled RF monitoring at the store level, including rogue AP detection and unauthorized activity detection on the hotspot VLAN.

As with Retail Example I, client management was one of the biggest challenges as far as managing multivendor client firmware, drivers, and configuration. The Wavelink Avalanche solution was used to manage WLAN firmware, drivers, and configuration on clients from multivendors. Configuration management on the clients included static WEP-key management and periodic static-WEP key rotation.

University WLAN Deployment Example

This WLAN deployment example is taken from a university environment. WLAN coverage is provided across the university to give students and staff access to the university network as well as Internet access. Typically, university deployments tend to be open architecture that is oriented to accommodate different types of devices, operating systems, and WLAN NIC adapters.

The customer deployment criteria include the following:

- Authenticate students to back-end LDAP DB using HTTP redirect (application layer level authentication).
- Provide mutual authentication and strong data confidentiality for staff.
- Detect unauthorized WLAN activity across the campus network.
- Support VoIP over WLAN deployment for staff and maintenance personnel.

The customer deployment environment is as follows:

- Students can bring any WLAN-enabled laptop for network access.
    - The administrator does not and cannot standardize client OS or client NIC adapter.
    - Students are given a university account.
- Staff members are standardized on Windows 2000 and Windows XP operating systems, along with Cisco Aironet 802.11a/b/g client NIC adapters.
- Staff and student authentication credentials are kept in an LDAP database.
- Cisco Secure ACS is standardized for the RADIUS infrastructure.
- Cisco 7920 VoIP handsets are deployed across the campus.

Based on the previous deployment criteria and the deployment environment, multiple SSIDs/ VLANs were enabled on the Aironet APs and wired infrastructure to accommodate students and staff. Figure 13-5 shows the use of multiple VLANs/SSIDs in a university WLAN deployment scenario. As shown in the figure, 802.1Q trunking was enabled to the APs to facilitate mapping of SSIDs to wired VLANs.

Figure 13-5 *University WLAN Deployment Example*

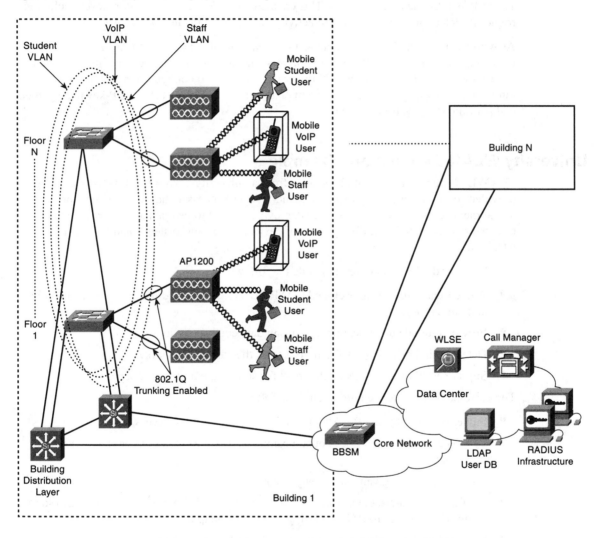

The wireless Student VLAN was provisioned with open/no WEP (that is, open access) across the campus as a result of the inability to standardize on any security model due to the nonstandardized client environment. All traffic from Student VLAN was routed to the core network, where Cisco Building Broadband Service Manager (BBSM) control led user access into the campus network. BBSM blocked all access at the Layer 3 level for unauthenticated users. Further, using the HTTP redirect functionality available on BBSM, unauthenticated students were redirected to the login web page. Using secure HTTP, students are requested to provide an authentication credential to BBSM, which in turn authenticates the student to the back-end LDAP DB. Note that secure HTTP is required to secure student authentication credentials from eavesdroppers. After successful authentication, student traffic is allowed into the campus network to access learning materials or the Internet. Note that data confidentiality is not provided here due to the nonstandardized client environment.

A second VLAN named "Staff" was provisioned across the campus to enable WLAN access with EAP/802.1x with the TKIP model. PEAP/GTC with WPA was implemented to provide mutual authentication and strong data confidentiality for staff users across the campus. The PEAP/GTC supplicant on the Cisco Aironet 802.11a/b/g client adapter was configured to obtain the LDAP DB authentication credential from the user and authenticate the user to the RADIUS infrastructure via back-end LDAP DB.

A third VLAN was created for VoIP deployment (named "VoIP"). LEAP with WPA was implemented for the VoIP VLAN to facilitate mutual authentication and strong data confidentiality. The IT administrator used a strong password policy of 14 characters with a combination of alphanumeric and nonalphanumeric characters to create the LEAP authentication credential for Cisco 7920 devices. VoIP authentication credentials were locally stored on the Cisco Secure ACS infrastructure. Also, the Cisco 7920 devices were configured to securely store the LEAP authentication credential. Fast secure roaming using the CCKM protocol was enabled on the VoIP VLAN.

Finally, a fourth VLAN was created as the management VLAN for the APs. The management VLAN was not mapped to the radio interface, and access was restricted via AP's Ethernet interface with the use of Layer 3 and Layer 4 ACLs at the distribution layer level (the Layer 3 termination point for the management VLAN). Layer 3 (IP address–based) and Layer 4 (for example, protocol-based) ACLs were used to limit access to AP's management VLAN to allow only RADIUS and management traffic between the AP and the management (RADIUS server and WLSE) devices.

WDS functionality was initially enabled on an active AP1200 (the AP services 802.11 clients and functioning as the WDS) or standalone AP1200 (the AP functions as the WDS and does not service 802.11 clients) located at each building to enable the SWAN solution and to facilitate fast secure roaming and RF management. RF management (also referred to as radio management) services include rogue AP detection and suppression, client anomaly detection, non-802.11 interference detection, and so on. WLSE version 2.5 and above and AP IOS release 12.2(13)JA and above are required to enable fast secure roaming and RF management services. As the network grows from a medium to large size (more than 200 APs), WDS functionality will be migrated to Catalyst 6500 switches equipped with WLSM to be deployed either at the building aggregation layer level or possibly at the data center level.

Wired deployment policies are not discussed in detail in this example, but the IT administrator implemented access controls for student, staff, and VoIP VLANs at the building distribution layer level (the Layer 3 termination point for these VLANs). Layer 3 and higher ACLs, in addition to policy-based routing (PBR) or the VPN virtual routing and forwarding (VRF) feature, can be used at the distribution layer level switch. For the student traffic aggregation, GRE tunnels can aggregate the student traffic from each building to a central aggregation point in the core network to be authenticated via the BBSM (or a BBSM-like device). Catalyst 6500 WLSM integration provides a much easier way to aggregate student, staff, and VoIP traffic to a central point in the wired network and apply appropriate security policies and an appropriate level of network access for each group of users.

One of the challenges in this deployment is the inability to provide data confidentiality to students due to the nonstandardized client environment. The long-term goal is to deploy WPA for students using Windows 2000 and XP platforms. However, if the student uses a non-Microsoft OS that does not support WPA, a third-party supplicant can be purchased with a per-supplicant license fee.

Financial WLAN Deployment Example I

This deployment example is taken from a financial WLAN deployment. In this scenario, WLAN deployment is considered an overlay network deployment and is used for non-mission-critical financial applications. Initially, WLAN is deployed within restricted areas with the intention of expanding coverage globally across all locations.

The customer deployment criteria are as follows:

- WLAN users have mutual authentication and strong encryption.

    — Hardware token–based One Time Password (OTP) authentication is the preferred user authentication method.

- Minimize client management. Minimize the number of SW components to be managed on the WLAN client for user authentication and encryption.

- Monitor WLAN deployment to detect unauthorized activity.

The customer deployment environment is as follows:

- Wireless LAN users are standardized on Windows 2000 and XP.

- WLAN users are standardized on Cisco Aironet client NICs and embedded CCX laptop clients.

- RSA secure ID infrastructure is deployed for OTP authentication.

- Central (corporate and regional HQ) to remote sites have redundant WAN links.

    — Redundant WAN links can be relied on to provide reliable RADIUS service to authenticate remote WLAN users.

- A subset of the user community (sales representatives and support personal) is mobile within a country and at times across the globe.

- The long-term plan is to migrate to 802.11i-compliant AES implementation on WLAN clients and WLAN infrastructure.

Based on the preceding deployment criteria and deployment environment, EAP/802.1x with WPA was chosen as the security model. The initial deployment covered about 1000 users at multiple locations (primarily executive staff). PEAP/GTC was implemented to facilitate OTP user authentication. Cisco Aironet client NIC adapters and CCXv2 laptops were chosen to support both PEAP/GTC and WPA. Selected clients were upgradeable to 802.11i-compliant AES implementation via firmware and software upgrade. User laptops were configured for PEAP/GTC authentication with WPA. The user was required to enter an OTP authentication credential using his or her hardware-based token. ACS infrastructure was configured to relay PEAP/GTC user authentication to the RSA secure ID server. A public PKI entity (such as VeriSign) was used to issue RADIUS server certificates for the ACS infrastructure for PEAP authentication. PEAP/GTC clients were configured to trust the certificate from this public PKI entity and belonging to the "FinancialCompany.com" domain. Note that most operating systems (including Windows) are usually populated with trusted PKI entity certificates.

The Cisco AP1200 platform was deployed to facilitate dual-band (802.11a/b/g) deployment and to provide 802.11i-compliant security features (including AES). Deployment topology similar to that described in "Large Enterprise Example I" was used to facilitate future expansion and to support multiple types of applications. Initially, this meant deploying a single VLAN per building to accommodate the WLAN data users and, as the WLAN user population grew, possibly segmenting the users into multiple VLANs per building. Using isolated VLANs for WLAN deployment allowed the IT administrator to implement specific security policies per WLAN VLAN.

Finally, the SWAN solution was implemented to enable RF monitoring and rogue AP detection capabilities. This required WLSE 2.5 or above and AP IOS release 12.2(13)JA or above. This allowed the IT administrator to monitor for any unauthorized WLAN activity. As the network grows from medium to large, Catalyst 6500 equipped with WLSM can be considered to scale WDS services and to centrally aggregate both WLAN user and control traffic. Alternatively, the Catalyst 6500 WLSM deployment model (also known as the SWAN central switching deployment mode, discussed in Chapter 9) can be used from the beginning as the WLAN network grows from small (fewer than 50 APs) to large (more than 200 APs) across a large campus network. Secure management policy was implemented; Telnet was disabled and SSH was enabled. HTTP, SNMP, RADIUS, Wireless LAN Control and Context Protocol (WLCCP), and SSH traffic to the APs were restricted to allow access only from management servers (such as WLSE, Cisco Secure ACS, and so on).

One of the major challenges in this deployment was client management due to a continuous need to upgrade client firmware, drivers, and software to provide the latest security capabilities. IT tools such as the Altiris client management solution can automate client firmware, drivers, software, and configuration. Cisco ACAT tool can create an enterprise client configuration for Cisco Aironet adapters. Also, Cisco Installation Wizard packages drivers, firmware, and software together to enable automated upgrades.

Financial WLAN Deployment Example II

This example is also taken from a large financial WLAN deployment. In this scenario, WLAN deployment is the primary network used for mission-critical financial applications. Typical applications used over WLAN in this implementation were electronic trading applications, e-mail access, and intranet/Internet web browsing.

The customer deployment criteria are as follows:

- Mutual authentication and strong encryption exists for WLAN users.
- Provide user authentication and data confidentiality at both Layer 2 and Layer 3 levels.
- Minimize manual user logon intervention to one time at the most and implement two-factor user authentication.
- Minimize client management. Minimize the number of SW components to be managed on the WLAN client for user authentication and encryption.
- Monitor WLAN deployment to detect unauthorized activity.

The customer deployment environment is as follows:

- WLAN users are standardized on Windows 2000 and XP.
- WLAN users are standardized on Cisco Aironet client NIC adapters and embedded CCX laptops.
- The WLAN network is deployed at multiple locations across the globe.
- RSA secure ID infrastructure is deployed to facilitate OTP user authentication.

Based on the preceding customer deployment criteria, EAP/802.1x with WPA and IPSec VPN over WLAN models were implemented to provide user authentication and data confidentiality at both Layer 2 and Layer 3 levels. OTP user authentication was implemented with IPSec VPN to facilitate two-factor authentication as required by the company security policy. EAP-FAST authentication with WPA was implemented as the Layer 2 security model. The user authentication credential was securely stored on the laptop to minimize user intervention during the Layer 2 authentication and authorization phase. Overall, the user is only required to provide the authentication credential once during the initial logon.

The typical IPSec VPN over WLAN deployment model leaves the WLAN network (Layer 2 network) unprotected (that is, EAP/802.1x with WPA is not implemented) possible DHCP starvation attacks and DNS targeted attacks are possible. These attacks are possible because IPSec VPN users require DHCP services and possibly DNS services before successfully authenticating with the network. However, the combined Layer 2 and Layer 3 security model prevents these attacks albeit with increased deployment complexity. In this deployment scenario, successful Layer 2 authentication enables the user to obtain a DHCP IP address and enables DNS services. However, all other traffic is blocked until successful Layer 3 IPSec VPN authentication and authorization. Layer 3 and Layer 4–based ACLs are used at the distribution layer level to allow only DHCP, DNS, RADIUS, and IPSec traffic into the network. The IPSec VPN session is also terminated at the distribution layer level (such as the VPNSM module on the Catalyst 6500 switch).

As shown in Figure 13-6, a single, isolated VLAN per building was created for WLAN users. If necessary, WLAN was segmented to one VLAN per X number of floors based on the number of users (to scale for broadcast traffic). Additionally, isolated VLANs were added in the long run for different applications such as VoIP and guest access. RADIUS and OTP authentication infrastructures were centralized at the corporate HQ for main campus deployment and the branch offices.

Cisco SWAN solution was implemented to enable RF monitoring and rogue AP detection capabilities. In this implementation, WDS was enabled on the Catalyst 6500 switch equipped with WLSM at the distribution switch level (as shown in Figure 13-6) to enable RM data aggregation and forwarding to WLSE. This allowed the IT administrator to monitor for any unauthorized WLAN activity across the main campus deployments and at remote sites. As discussed in Chapter 9, all WLAN user traffic and control traffic is aggregated using the SWAN central switching deployment mode (such as using the Catalyst 6500 WLSM integration model). In addition to WLSM, the VPN Service Module (VPNSM) was integrated at the distribution switch level to terminate IPSec VPN users and allow access into the campus network.

Secure management policy was implemented; Telnet was disabled and SSH was enabled. HTTP, SNMP, RADIUS, WLCCP, TFTP, and SSH traffic to the APs was restricted to allow access only from management servers (such as WLSE, Cisco Secure ACS, and so on).

The major challenge in this deployment was to maintain client configuration and software components to facilitate both Layer 2 and Layer 3 security model implementations. Specifically, WPA/EAP supplicant and the VPN supplicant had to be maintained in the long term. Client-automated maintenance tools were created to facilitate this process.

Finally, note that if the WAN links between remote sites and the corporate HQ fail, WLAN users at remote sites cannot gain WLAN network access. This was deemed appropriate because most of the applications required servers located at the corporate HQ.

Healthcare WLAN Deployment Example I

This example is taken from a healthcare deployment. WLAN penetration has increased in hospital and patient clinic environments. WLAN deployment facilitates seamless roaming for medical staff members who use 802.11-enabled laptop and PDA-based devices to access patient care information.

Figure 13-6 *Financial WLAN Deployment Example II*

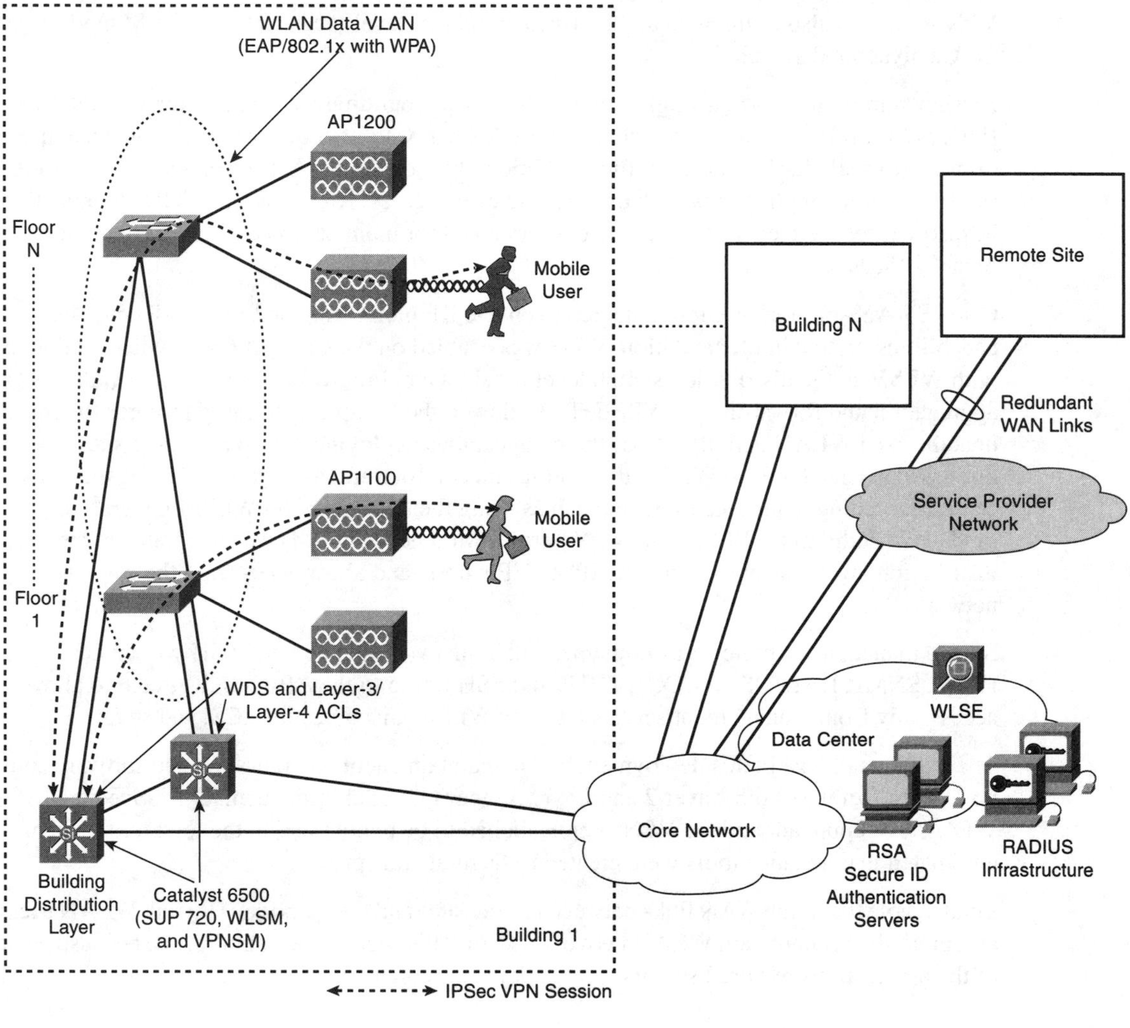

The healthcare mobile applications include the following:

- **Mobile carts**—These are mobile patient-care workstations that provide "point of care" services. Typically, mobile carts are used to access patient care information and are integrated with various healthcare applications. A mobile cart is assembled with various types of computer hardware, including a flat-screen LCD panel, CPU, hard disk, wireless network adapter, and external battery. Mobile carts are available from vendors such as Stinger Industries, Elliott DATA systems, and Tremont Medical.

- **e-dictation**—This application is typically run on wireless-enabled iPAQ-based PDAs to automate radiology reporting and so on. Healthcare professionals use voice-recognition software along with predefined templates to record and transmit patient-care information over WLAN.

- **Patient monitoring**—Real-tme patient monitoring applications are typically enabled over WLAN.

The customer deployment criteria are as follows:

- A desire exists to deploy WLAN ubiquitously across all clinics and hospitals.

- A scalable WLAN infrastructure can support 100,000+ users in 300+ locations.

- Mutual authentication and strong encryption exist for WLAN users.

- Single sign-on integrates WLAN authentication with Windows login.

- Authenticate WLAN users to back-end AD infrastructure.

- Applications include mobile carts and patient monitoring.

- A desire exists to deploy wireless VoIP applications (on-call paging and so on).

- Minimize client management. Minimize the number of SW components to be managed on the WLAN client for user authentication and encryption.

- Detect unauthorized WLAN activity across clinics and hospitals.

- A long-term strategy exists to migrate to PDAs and tablets.

- A requirement exists to meet HIPPA compliance for securing patient information.

The customer deployment environment is as follows:

- Wireless LAN users are standardized on the Windows 2000 platform (with long-term migration planned for Windows XP).

- Microsoft AD infrastructure is deployed for user authentication.

- Client adapters are standardized on embedded clients (CCXv2-compliant laptops).

- Central and regional HQs (corporate NOC and regional NOCs) to remote sites have redundant WAN links.

  — Redundant WAN links can be relied on to provide reliable RADIUS service to authenticate remote WLAN users.

  — Each remote NOC and the central NOC have multiple RADIUS servers.

- The user community (doctors and nurses) is mobile across clinics and hospitals.

Figure 13-7 describes the deployment topology for this implementation example. EAP/802.1x with TKIP was selected as the deployment model based on the preceding deployment criteria and deployment environment. PEAP/MS-CHAPv2 with WPA was deployed for mobile carts (with CCXv2-compliant PCs running Windows XP and Windows 2000 operating systems). LEAP, WPA TKIP, and CCKM were selected as the solution to enable fast secure roaming for

VoIP devices (such as Cisco 802.11-enabled 7920 VoIP devices). To accommodate multiple security solutions, multiple VLANs/SSIDs were enabled on the Cisco WLAN infrastructure.

Figure 13-7 *Healthcare WLAN Deployment Example I*

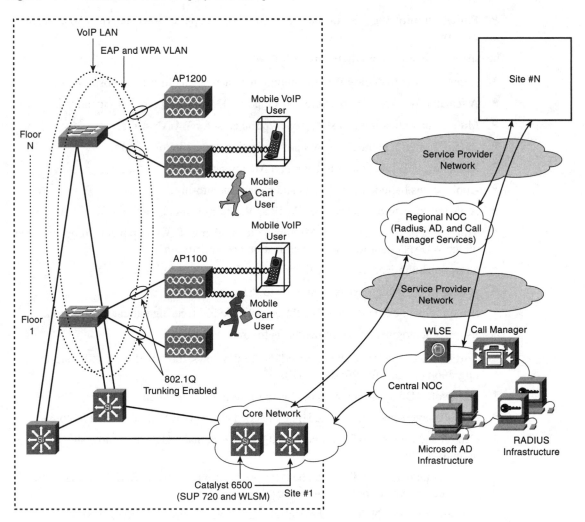

Wireless VLAN "EAPandWPA" was provisioned for mobile cart devices that were configured with PEAP and WPA. A second wireless VLAN "VoIP" was provisioned for 802.11-enabled VoIP devices configured with LEAP, WPA-TKIP, CCKM, and voice QoS. The IT administrator used strong password policy to create 15-character passwords with multiple nonalphanumeric characters to be used for LEAP authentication on VoIP devices. A unique user ID/password was securely stored on each LEAP-enabled VoIP device. Additionally, wired Layer 3 ACLs were applied to the "VoIP" VLAN to limit access to the CallManager and the VoIP gateway.

Both PEAP and LEAP authentication credentials were stored in the distributed AD infrastructure to authenticate mobile health professionals between different clinics and hospitals. RADIUS and AD infrastructure were deployed at each regional NOC and the central NOC. RADIUS server certificates for PEAP authentication were obtained from a public PKI entity (such as VeriSign), and PEAP clients were configured to trust only certificates from VeriSign and those belonging to HealthcareCompany.com, where the company's domain information is incorporated within the RADIUS server certificate. This eliminated the requirement to distribute the trusted root CA entity certificate. (Microsoft and most operating systems by default contain trusted public PKI entity certificates.)

One of the major deployment issues addressed was RADIUS server scalability. To scale to support multiple thousands of users per region, multiple RADIUS servers were deployed at each regional NOC and at the central NOC. (Multiple ACS servers were deployed at the central NOC, and a minimum of two ACS servers were deployed per regional NOC.) A load balancer product (such as Cisco Catalyst 6500 server content switching module) was used to load balance between multiple RADIUS servers. WLAN infrastructure at each clinic was configured to communicate with a regional or central NOC RADIUS infrastructure as the primary server and a different NOC as the secondary NOC. This provided redundancy for RADIUS servers during primary NOC failure.

Cisco SWAN solution was deployed to enable WDS, which facilitated fast secure roaming (requires AP IOS release 12.2[11]JA and above). In addition to fast secure roaming, RF monitoring was implemented to enable the wireless IDS capability including rogue AP detection (requires WLSE 2.5 and above and AP IOS release 12.2[13]JA and above). Initially, WDS was deployed on a single-radio AP1200 at each clinic and hospital (one per subnet). As the WLAN deployment grew, WDS functionality was migrated to the Cisco switching infrastructure (the Catalyst 6500 switch equipped with Supervisor 720 module and the WLSM).

Long-term migration is planned to enable 802.11i-standardized AES implementation for the mobile carts. This requires a driver, firmware, and supplicant update on the CCX-compliant WLAN NIC adapter (used on the mobile carts). Thus, the need to upgrade the CCX clients to add new security and management features is an ongoing operational challenge. Client management applications such as Altiris automated this process.

Healthcare WLAN Deployment Example II

This example is taken from a distributed healthcare deployment. WLAN deployment facilitates seamless roaming for medical staff members who use WLAN and laptop-based devices to access patient care information. In this example, the WLAN deployment covers approximately 600+ clinics throughout a country.

The customer deployment criteria include the following:

- A desire exists to deploy WLAN ubiquitously across all 600+ clinics.
- Mutual authentication and strong encryption exists for WLAN users.
- Provide local fall-back EAP authentication service to users on the local clinic AP.
- 802.11-enabled laptops (for physicians and nurses) can facilitate instantaneous access to patient-care information and so on.
- Minimize client management. Minimize the number of SW components to be managed on the WLAN client for user authentication and encryption.
- Remotely monitor RF activity across all clinics, including rogue AP detection.
- HIPPA compliance is required (user-based authentication and strong data encryption).

The customer deployment environment is as follows:

- Distributed WLAN infrastructure supports 3000 users in 600+ locations (on average 5 users per location).
- Each clinic has one AP1200 deployed (maximum two APs deployed at some clinics).
- Most of the staff is restricted to one location with the exception of specialists, who roam among multiple locations.
- Wireless LAN users are standardized on the Windows XP platform.
- Client adapters are standardized on embedded clients (CCXv2-compliant laptops).
- Microsoft AD infrastructure is deployed for user authentication.
- Each clinic has one WAN link for connectivity to the central NOC.
  - Under WAN link failure conditions, the dialup ISDN link provides connectivity for mission-critical services (credit card transactions and so on).

Figure 13-8 illustrates the deployment topology for this example. As shown in the figure, sites 1 to N (N represents the clinic number) have the WLAN network deployed in a distributed fashion. Based on the preceding customer deployment criteria and deployment environment, EAP/802.1x with WPA was selected as the security model. Specifically, Cisco LEAP was selected due to the local authentication feature requirement under WAN link failure conditions. LEAP accounts were created for physicians and nurses on the RADIUS infrastructure. The IT administrator used a strong password policy of a 14-character password with at least four nonalphanumeric characters to create a strong LEAP authentication credential to minimize risks due to offline dictionary attacks. The LEAP authentication credential was securely stored using the WLAN supplicant on each CCX-compliant laptop.

Figure 13-8 *Healthcare WLAN Deployment Example II*

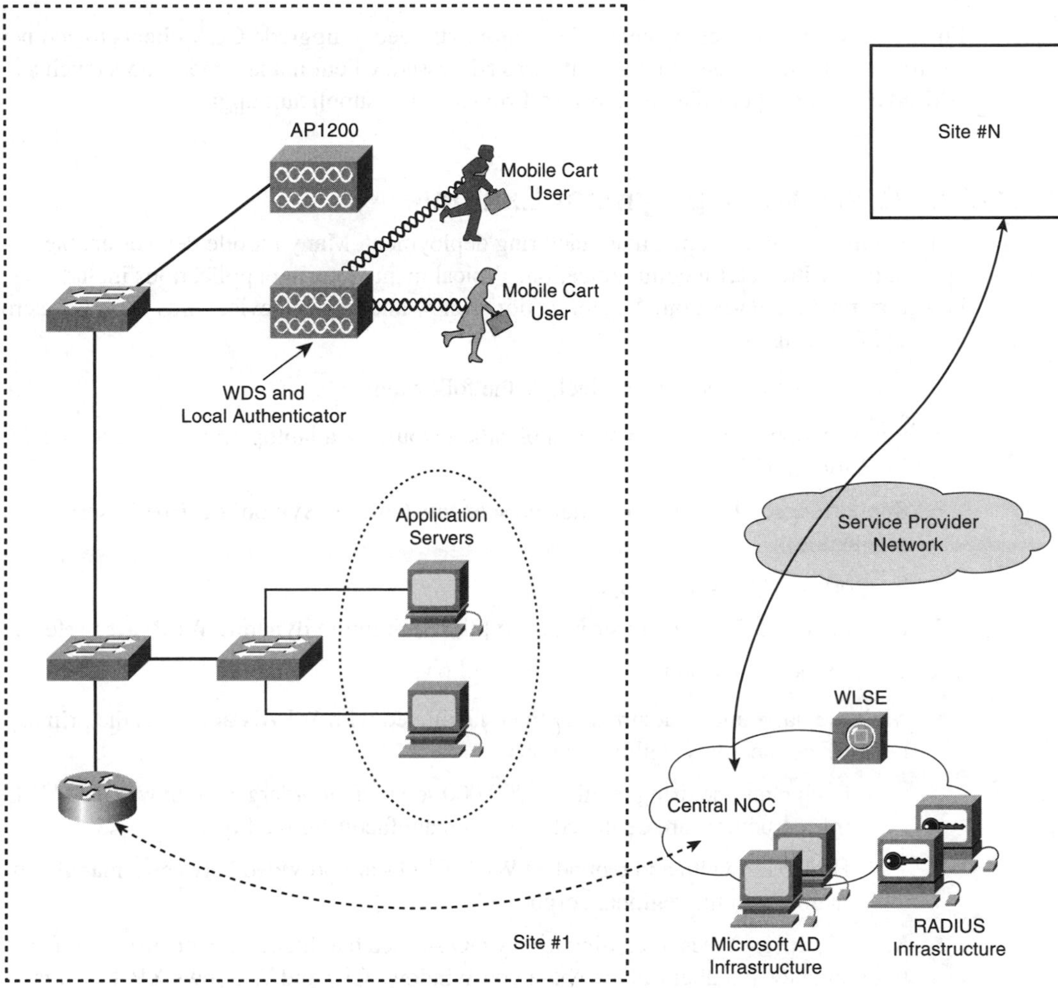

An AP1200 per location (most of the locations contained only one AP) was configured as the local authenticator. The LEAP authentication credential for all users per local location was securely stored on the AP. One of the challenges in this deployment was to populate LEAP authentication user accounts per location and continuously synchronize the local database with the central RADIUS database. Along with the local authentication service, WDS was deployed to enable radio management services, including rogue AP detection. AP IOS release 12.2(13) JA or above and WLSE 2.5 or above are required to enable radio management services, including rogue AP detection, rogue AP suppression, and RF monitoring. In this deployment,

WLSE was centrally positioned at the HQ, where RF management data was collected over the WAN link via WDS at each clinic.

Finally, as with other deployments, the continuous need to upgrade CCX clients to add new security and management functionality was addressed. Client management tools (such as Altiris) automated periodic client driver, firmware, and supplicant upgrades.

Manufacturing WLAN Deployment Example

This example is taken from a manufacturing deployment. Many mobile devices enable applications with stateful communication. Typical manufacturing applications include inventory tracking and so on. A combination of new and legacy devices was deployed across the manufacturing floor.

The customer deployment criteria include the following:

- Support mobile users. A typical application would be a laptop on a forklift to enable inventory tracking.

- Support legacy DOS-based handheld scanners (such as Symbol PDT 6800 series scanners).

- Support wireless VoIP devices.

- Mutual authentication and strong encryption (minimum dynamic WEP) are preferred.

The customer deployment environment is as follows:

- Multiple, large manufacturers are to be facilitated with WLAN access as the primary network connectivity within a country.

   — Each manufacturing facility is 200,000 square feet or larger. Both wired and WLAN infrastructures are deployed across a manufacturing facility.

   — High bandwidth and redundant WLAN links are provided between a manufacturing facility and the regional/corporate NOCs.

- Multiple device types, including legacy DOS-based handheld scanners used for inventory tracking, new handheld PDAs (based on Windows CE) and Windows XP–based laptops used for inventory tracking, and WLAN-enabled VoIP handsets, are deployed across the manufacturing floor.

- A combination of Cisco Aironet client adapters and non-Cisco/non-CCX adapters is deployed in different devices along with CCXv2 certified laptops.

- Microsoft AD infrastructure and Cisco Secure ACS infrastructure are deployed at each manufacturing location and at the central HQ.

- Cisco Catalyst 3500 series switches are deployed at the building access layer level, and Catalyst 6500 switches are deployed at the building distribution layer level.

As shown in Figure 13-9, multiple SSIDs and VLANs were enabled on Cisco APs to facilitate multiple levels of security. Each SSID was mapped to a unique wired VLAN where Layer 3 and

Layer 4–based policies were implemented on the building distribution Layer 3 switch. This enabled the administrator to enforce the specific security policy per wireless/wired VLAN.

Figure 13-9   *Manufacturing WLAN Deployment Example*

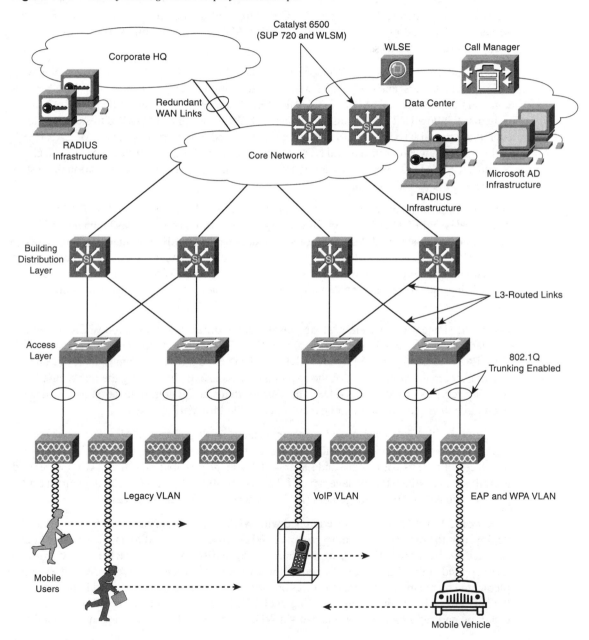

On wireless VLAN, the "Legacy" static WEP was enabled as the security mechanism for legacy DOS-based handheld scanners due to limited capabilities on these devices. In addition to static WEP, MAC address authentication was enabled to authenticate the legacy devices. MAC addresses of these devices were stored on the regional RADIUS infrastructure and on the HQ RADIUS infrastructure. The regional NOC RADIUS infrastructure was used as the primary server for MAC address authentication, and HQ RADIUS infrastructure was used as the secondary (or fall-back) server.

New PDA devices based on the Windows CE OS and Windows XP laptops were integrated with CCX client adapters, and EAP-FAST was enabled for mutual authentication with WPA for data confidentiality. A second SSID/VLAN called "EAPandWPA" was enabled on the WLAN infrastructure to allow EAP-FAST authentication with WPA. Similar to MAC address authentication, the regional NOC RADIUS infrastructure was used as the primary server for EAP-FAST authentication, whereas the central NOC was used as the redundant fall-back server. The Cisco Secure ACS RADIUS server was configured to relay the EAP-FAST authentication request to the Microsoft AD infrastructure.

A third VLAN/SSID called "VoIP" was created to facilitate Cisco 7920 wireless VoIP handsets. This wireless/wired VLAN was given voice QoS along with access to CallManager and VoIP voice gateway. Cisco 7920 VoIP handsets were deployed with LEAP authentication, CCKM, and WPA-TKIP to enable fast secure roaming on the VoIP VLAN. A separate VoIP account was provisioned per user on the Microsoft AD infrastructure, along with strong password policy with a minimum 10-character password using a combination of alphanumeric and nonalphanumeric characters.

On the "EAPandWPA" wireless VLAN, fast secure roaming was configured (CCKM was enabled) for PDAs (Windows CE–based) and Windows XP–based mobile laptop devices using EAP-FAST authentication with WPA-TKIP for data confidentiality. When EAP-FAST and LEAP users roam from AP to AP, the roaming process is expedited using the fast secure roaming services available via WDS. This ensures that stateful communication is maintained for mobile devices and jitter and latency are controlled for VoIP devices.

Finally, a fourth VLAN was created as the management VLAN for the APs. The management VLAN was not mapped to the radio interface, and access was restricted via the AP's Ethernet interface with the use of Layer 3 and Layer 4 ACLs on the distribution switch. ACLs were used to limit access to the AP's management VLAN to only allow RADIUS and management traffic between the AP and the management (RADIUS server and WLSE) devices.

A pair of Catalyst 6500 switches equipped with WLSMs and supervisor 720 modules was deployed at the data center level to groom all WLAN user traffic and to enable scalable WDS services for the entire WLAN network. Appropriate security policies for each user/device group were applied at the WLAN traffic aggregation switch level. (Layer 3/Layer 4 ACLs were implemented on the mGRE tunnel interfaces on the Catalyst 6500 supervisor.) In addition to using the WDS to facilitate fast secure roaming via CCKM, RF management (including rogue AP detection and suppression) was enabled via WDS to facilitate RF monitoring at each facility.

One of the biggest challenges in this manufacturing deployment was client management with regard to managing client firmware, drivers, and configuration. The Wavelink Avalanche solution was used to manage WLAN firmware, drivers, and configuration on clients from multivendors. Configuration management on the clients included static WEP-key management, LEAP authentication profile, and EAP-FAST authentication profile management. Overall, this deployment provides capabilities to facilitate legacy and new handheld devices, typical manufacturing applications, and VoIP over WLAN.

Small and Medium Businesses and SOHO WLAN Deployments

This section covers examples from small, medium, and SOHO (small office, home office) deployments. In small office and SOHO scenarios, WLAN is considered the primary network connectivity and is preferred to wired Ethernet connectivity. This is primarily due to the desire to minimize overall network deployment costs (that is, eliminate wiring costs). In the medium office scenario, WLAN could be deployed either for primary network connectivity or as an overlay deployment (mainly providing coverage for meeting rooms).

Medium Enterprise WLAN Deployment Scenario Example

In this example, WLAN was deployed as the primary network connectivity for an office of approximately 1000 employees. All users were at a single physical location.

The customer deployment criteria and deployment environment are as follows:

- Strong user authentication and strong encryption exist.
- Support single sign-on integrates WLAN authentication with Windows logon.
- Users are standardized on Windows XP platform and CCX-enabled laptops.
- Cisco Secure ACS and Microsoft AD infrastructure are deployed.

Given the preceding deployment requirements and deployment environment, the customer implemented PEAP/MS-CHAPv2 with WPA as the WLAN security policy. Windows XP supplicant was configured to enable PEAP/MS-CHAPv2 authentication using the user's Windows logon credentials to facilitate single sign-on. An X.509v3 compliant server certificate was self-issued using Cisco Secure ACS 3.3 and above. The self-issued server certificate was used for PEAP authentication. The ACS server was configured to authenticate PEAP users via Microsoft AD server.

RF monitoring functionality, including rogue AP detection, was enabled using Cisco SWAN solution. This required WLSE 2.5 or above, AP IOS release 12.2(13)JA or above, and CCXv2 or above for WLAN clients.

Small Office WLAN Deployment Example

In this example, WLAN connectivity was enabled as the primary network connectivity for approximately 100 users at a single location. The customer did not have the IT budget to deploy RADIUS infrastructure for WLAN user authentication. Also, the customer had not deployed Microsoft AD infrastructure. However, the customer did standardize on the Cisco WLAN infrastructure and clients for WLAN deployment. Figure 13-10 illustrates this deployment topology.

Figure 13-10 *Small Office WLAN Deployment Example*

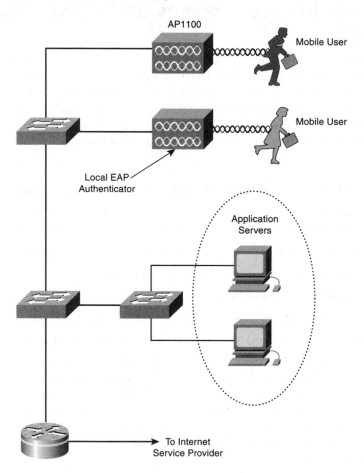

LEAP with WPA was selected as the security model, where the local RADIUS server on the IOS-enabled APs (12.2[11] JA1 release or above) facilitated LEAP authentication. The IT administrator used a strong password policy to generate 15-character passwords with a combination of alphanumeric and nonalphanumeric characters. The LEAP authentication credential was securely stored on each laptop.

SOHO WLAN Deployment Scenario Example

This example provided a secure WLAN deployment at home to enable remote connectivity for a full-time telecommuter. In this example, WPA-PSK mode was used between the WLAN client and the AP to secure the link layer. However, the client was required to launch and terminate the IPSec VPN tunnel with corporate HQ to enable access to corporate applications. A long passphrase (greater than 20 characters) created using a combination of alphanumeric and non-alphanumeric was used as the WPA-PSK passphrase (to minimize risk due to offline dictionary attacks). Figure 13-11 illustrates this deployment topology.

Figure 13-11   *SOHO WLAN Deployment Example*

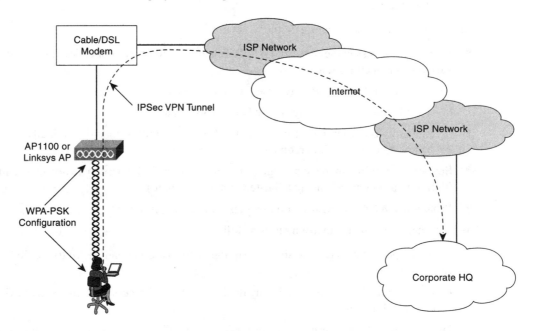

Hotspot (Public WLAN) Deployment Examples

This section covers hotspot WLAN deployment examples. Today, hotspot WLAN deployments (also known as public WLAN access) are prevalent across coffee shops, airports, and hotels. At some locations, hotspot service is provided for free, whereas in other locations, a service fee (a flat fee or usage-based fee) is charged. The deployment scenarios covered in this section include large-scale WLAN deployment in coffee shops by a single service provider and WLAN deployments in airports.

Coffee Shop WLAN Hotspot Deployment Example

This example discusses a single service provider's deployment of hotspot service across hundreds of coffee shops. Internet access is provided as the primary service, and users are charged for the service. The service provider uses two different models to charge the users. The first model is a prepaid service in which the user is charged on a per-minute basis for Internet access. The second model is a flat service for an unlimited number of minutes for a fixed monthly fee.

When users initially try to access the Internet, they are authenticated using a web browser that is redirected to a web server. Users provide authentication credentials to the service provider using a secure HTTP browser. After the user is successfully authenticated, he is given full access to the Internet.

The customer deployment criteria do the following:

- Block user access to the network (HTTP, Telnet, and all other applications) until after successful authentication.
    - Use HTTP redirect to force users to authenticate via regional NOC.
    - Authenticate users using secure HTTP (SSL-enabled).
- Dynamically provision new users. A new subscriber is provisioned dynamically via central NOC using a valid credit card.
- Support two billing models: a usage-per-minute model (using a prepaid account) and an unlimited usage model (using a flat-fee monthly account).
- Protect the WLAN infrastructure in an open access environment.

The customer deployment environment is as follows:

- Each hotspot location (coffee shop) is equipped with a router and an AP to facilitate Internet access.
- Customers are allowed to bring in any device for WLAN access (as long as the device supports an Internet browser).
- Users are billed per hour or can be provisioned an unlimited access account (based on a monthly fee).
- A reliable WAN link exists between a coffee shop and the regional NOC. Internet traffic from authenticated users (valid users) is directed to the Internet gateway via the regional NOC.
- Regional NOCs are connected to the central NOC via a service provider network using high-bandwidth WAN links. User authentication traffic is directed to the central NOC where the AAA server, customer DB, and billing server are located.

The WLAN infrastructure was configured with open/no WEP access at each coffee shop to allow users to associate to the network at the Layer 2 level. However, Cisco SSG function was used at the Layer 3 level on the regional NOC router to control user access. Specifically, HTTP redirect was used to authenticate users via the central NOC using secure HTTP protocol. A user must possess a prepaid account or a monthly fee account to authenticate successfully. Also, a user was allowed to provision a new account using HTTP direct via the central NOC. In this scenario, the user provides credit card information via secure HTTP to the service provider and dynamically provisions an account. After the user is successfully authenticated, the SSG gateway at the regional NOC allows the user traffic to be routed to the regional ISP gateway. Figure 13-12 illustrates the customer deployment.

Figure 13-12   *Coffee Shop Hotspot Deployment Example*

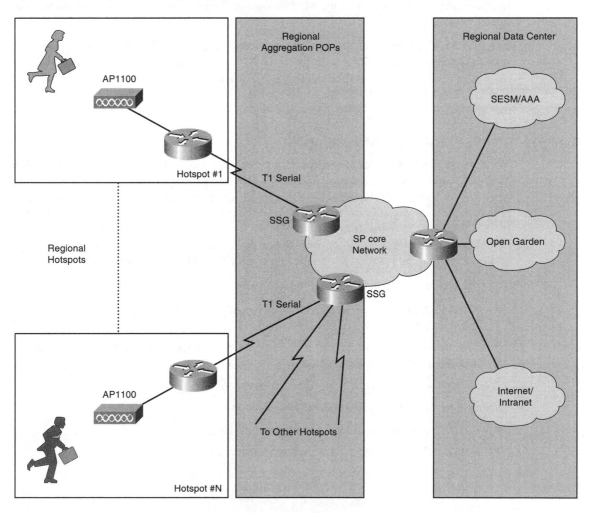

It is critical to protect the WLAN infrastructure in a hotspot deployment. In this deployment, secure management practice was implemented for the APs. This meant disabling Telnet access and enabling SSH access to the APs. SSH, SNMP, HTTP, and RADIUS traffic to the APs was restricted only to servers residing in regional and central NOCs. (WLAN users were disallowed access to the AP.) WLSE was deployed at the central NOC to manage configuration and firmware on the APs. Additionally, RF monitoring was enabled to detect unauthorized activity at hotspot locations. WLSE 2.5 and above, along with 12.2(13)JA AP IOS release or above, is required to enable RF monitoring. To facilitate RF monitoring, the WDS service was enabled on an AP per hotspot location.

In addition to enabling the previous features to secure the WLAN infrastructure, Public Secure Packet Forwarding (PSPF) was implemented to provide some level of security for WLAN hotspot users. PSPF function on the AP disallows communication between users who are associated to the same AP.

Finally, a MAC-address filter was created with a default gateway (DG) MAC address to disallow association of any WLAN user using the DG MAC address. This prevents denial-of-service (DoS) and man-in-the-middle (MitM) attacks using the DG MAC address. This function is available on 12.2(13)JA AP IOS release and above.

Airport WLAN Deployment Example

WLAN is typically deployed at an airport for private and public use. Private use of a WLAN by airlines for operational functions such as baggage handling and passenger check-in is common across many airports. Public use such as hotspot deployment to facilitate Internet access is also common across many airports. It has become common practice to leverage a single WLAN infrastructure for both private and public WAN deployment examples, hotspot WLAN deployment examples, coffee shop WLAN hotspot deployment examples, and public usage at an airport. This example captures details of a typical WLAN deployment at an airport.

The customer deployment criteria are the following:

- A single WLAN infrastructure is used to provide services to multiple parties: both "private" and public WLAN access.

- Typical private use: An airline employee uses WLAN access to execute customer check-in and baggage-handling functions.

- Allow a service provider to provide hotspot service.

The customer deployment environment is as follows:

- WLAN coverage is provided throughout the airport.

- Both wireless and wired infrastructure is owned by the airport authority.

- Airlines own their back-end infrastructure for private applications (such as customer check-in and baggage handling).
- A hotspot (public Internet access) service provider router is located on the airport premises.

Multiple SSID and VLAN functionalities on the Cisco AP platforms were used to provide both public and private access using a single WLAN infrastructure. A private SSID/VLAN was created according to specifications by an airline for its private usage. For example, an airline company might choose to implement IPSec over WLAN as the security model to secure its private data over the shared WLAN infrastructure. In this scenario, each end client must be equipped with a VPN client, and the IPSec session would terminate on the VPN concentrator located at the airline's back-end infrastructure (the airline's private wired LAN). However, one of the challenges with IPSec over WLAN is end-device support. For example, the VPN client might not be available for WLAN-enabled handheld devices used by airline employees for baggage tracking and handling activities.

Alternatively, the airline could choose to implement EAP/802.1x with WPA over the WLAN security model for these handheld devices (if possible) and then securely tunnel the traffic to the airline's private LAN. If not EAP/802.1x with WPA over the WLAN security model, another security mechanism to consider would be SSL-enabled VPN. In this scenario, each handheld device would use an SSL-enabled application to secure transactions with an SSL-enabled VPN concentrator located at the airline's private VLAN.

Figure 13-13 illustrates the overall topology for an airport wireless LAN and wired LAN deployment. As shown in the figure, multiple SSIDs and wired VLANs facilitate both private and public applications over the same WLAN infrastructure. Up to 16 SSIDs and VLANs (including management VLAN for the APs) can be enabled on the Cisco wireless LAN infrastructure.

To facilitate hotspot service, an open/no WEP SSID/VLAN was provisioned across the airport on all APs. Traffic from the hotspot VLAN was GRE-tunneled to the service provider's router (SSG-enabled) located on the airport premises. The service provider used the same model described in the coffee shop example to dynamically provision users, authenticate users, and allow Internet access for valid users. Refer to the coffee shop example for additional information on providing hotspot Internet access services.

Summary

As discussed throughout this chapter, the customer's deployment criteria determined the deployment model used in each deployment example. The customer adjusted the selected deployment model to suit his deployment environment. However, each scenario presented unique deployment challenges based on the selected deployment model. The customer usually made a trade-off between desired security strength and ease of deployment.

Figure 13-13 *Airport WLAN Deployment Example*

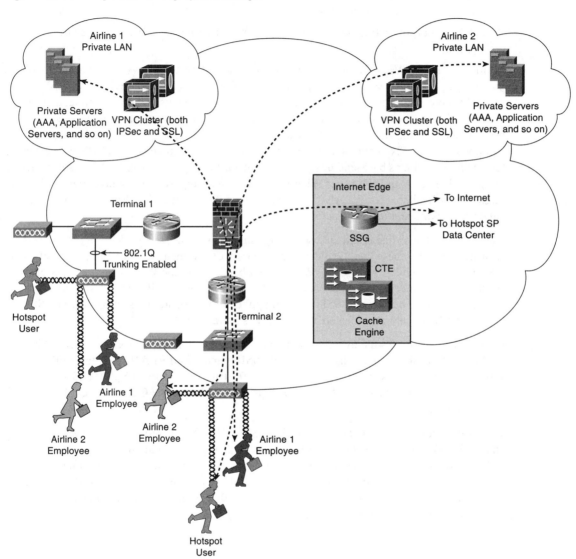

Resources and References

This appendix lists web-based resources for many of the book resources. Because web references have a tendency to change, this is included to help you search in case the link has changed.

General Tools

802.11-Security.com — http://802.11-security.com

Air-Jack (wlan_jack, essid-jack) — http://802.11ninja.net

AiroPeek — http://www.wildpackets.com

Airsnarf — http://airsnarf.shmoo.com

Airsnort — http://airsnort.shmoo.com

APTools — http://winfingerprint.sourceforge.net/aptools.php

Bernard Aboba's "Unofficial 802.11 Security Web Page" — http://www.drizzle.com/~aboba/IEEE

bsd-airtools (dstumbler, dwepcrack, dwepcrack, prism2dump) — http://www.dachb0den.com/projects/bsd-airtools.html

Cantenna — http://www.cantenna.com

Ethereal — http://ethereal.com

Goonda.com — http://www.goonda.org/wireless

KisMAC — http://www.binaervarianz.de/projekte/programmieren/kismac

Kismet — http://www.kismetwireless.net

Libradiate — http://www.packetfactory.net/Projects/libradiate

MacStumbler — http://www.macstumbler.com

monkey_jack — http://rdi.st/blackhat/baird_lynn/airjack-v0.5.1-alpha/tools/monkey_jack.c)

Network Stumbler—http://www.netstumbler.com

Omerta—http://www.ecediinc.com/la/libnet@securityfocus.com/0353.html

Prismdump—http://developer.axis.com/download/tools

Security Wizards Wireless Resources—http://www.secwiz.com/Default.aspx?tabid=24

Sniffer Wireless—http://www.networkassociates.com

Tcpdump—http://tcpdump.org

void11—http://www.wlsec.net/void11

WarBSD—http://www.warbsd.com

WarLinux—http://sourceforge.net/projects/warlinux

Wellenreiter—http://www.wellenreiter.net

wep_crack and wep_decrypt—http://www.goonda.org/wireless/prism2

WEPCrack—http://wepcrack.sourceforge.net

Defensive Tools

AirMagnet—http://www.airmagnet.com. This multifaceted commercial tool does attack detection and network troubleshooting.

fakeap—http://www.blackalchemy.to/Projects/fakeap/fake-ap.html. Luckily, some tool writers work on the side of the network administrators creating thousands of random beacons to confuse wardrivers and wardrivers but would not work against a targeted attack to be used to distinguish the fake from the real APs.

Cryptography and Cryptanalysis

Arbaugh, William A. "An Inductive Chosen Plaintext Attack Against WEP/WEP2." Submission to IEEE-802.11, doc# IEEE 802.11-01/230. http://www.cs.umd.edu/~waa/attack/v3dcmnt.htm. May 2001.

Bellardo, J. and S. Savage. "802.11 Denial-of-Service Attacks: Real Vulnerabilities and Practical Solutions." Proceedings of the USENIX Security Symposium. Washington, D.C. August 2003. http://www.cs.ucsd.edu/users/savage/papers/UsenixSec03.pdf.

Borisov, Nikita, Ian Goldberg, and David Wagner. "Intercepting Mobile Communications: The Insecurity of 802.11." 7th Annual Conference on Mobile Computing and Networking. July 2001.

Fluhrer, S., I. Mantin, and A. Shamir. "Weaknesses in the Key Scheduling Algorithm of RC4." In Proc. 8th Workshop on Selected Areas in Cryptography, LNCS 2259. Springer-Verlag, 2001. http://www.drizzle.com/~aboba/IEEE/rc4_ksaproc.pdf.

Schneier, B. "Attack Trees." *Dr. Dobb's Journal*. December 1999. http://www.schneier.com/paper-attacktrees-ddj-ft.html.

Walker, Jesse. *Unsafe at Any Key Size: An Analysis of the WEP Encapsulation*. IEEE doc #802.11-00/362, October 2000.

Cryptography and Cryptanalysis Websites

http://wombat.doc.ic.ac.uk/foldoc/foldoc.cgi?RC4

http://www.cisco.com/warp/public/cc/pd/witc/ao350ap/prodlit/1515_pp.h

http://www.cypherspace.org/adam/rsa/rc4.html

http://www.ncat.edu/~grogans/main.htm

http://www.ssh.fi/support/cryptography/algorithms/symmetric.html

http://www.wow-com.com/industry/tech/

Wireless Standards and Associations

There are several standards bodies and industry associations. The Wi-Fi Alliance is a trade industry association that made its mission to promote the use of wireless networks. The IEEE and the IETF are independent standards for wireless networking and many other technologies.

Wi-Fi Alliance

Wi-Fi Alliance—http://www.wifialliance.com

Wi-Fi Protected Access (WPA)—http://www.wifialliance.com/OpenSection/protected_access.asp

IEEE

802.11 document site—http://www.802wirelessworld.com/index.jsp

802.1x mailer—http://www.ieee802.org/1/private/email/

Current status of 802.11i—http://grouper.ieee.org/groups/802/11/Reports/tgi_update.htm

IEEE 802.1 maintenance page for latest drafts—http://www.ieee802.org/1/pages/802.1aa.html

IEEE LAN/MAN standards—http://standards.ieee.org/reading/ieee/std/lanman/

Linksec mailer—http://www.ieee802.org/linksec/email/mail1.html

Official 802.11i website—http://grouper.ieee.org/groups/802/11/

The Unofficial 802.11 Security Web Page—http://www.drizzle.com/~aboba/IEEE/ (good site for IEEE WLAN information)

IETF

EAP archives—http://mail.frascone.com/pipermail/eap/

IETF EAP site—http://www.ietf.org/html.charters/eap-charter.html

IETF EAP WG—http://www.drizzle.com/~aboba/EAP/eapissues.html

IETF EAP WG charter—http://www.ietf.org/html.charters/eap-charter.html

Jesse Walker's IETF Internet draft (February 2004)—http://www.ietf.org/internet-drafts/draft-walker-ieee802-req-04.txt

RFC search—http://www.rfc-editor.org/rfcsearch.html

Working drafts of IETF EAP—http://ietf.levkowetz.com/drafts/eap/rfc2284bis/

Other Sites

ArcFour algorithm—http://www.mozilla.org/projects/security/pki/nss/draft-kaukonen-cipher-arcfour-03.txt

C implementations of 802.11i algorithms—http://www.deadhat.com/wlancrypto/

Cisco Aironet Security—http://www.cisco.com/go/aironet/security

Configuring load-balancing on VPN 3000 concentrators—http://www.cisco.com/en/US/partner/products/hw/vpndevc/ps2284/products_tech_note09186a0080094b4a

Deploying Cisco Secure ACS for Windows in a Cisco Aironet environment—http://www.cisco.com/en/US/products/sw/secursw/ps2086/products_white_paper09186a00801495a1.shtml

Latest PPP assignments—http://www.iana.org/assignments/ppp-numbers

LEAP article in *Packet* magazine (for manager types)—http://www.cisco.com/warp/public/784/packet/exclusive/apr02.html

INDEX

Numerics

3 DES (triple Data Encryption Standard), 18
4-way handshake, 222
802 RM, 61
802.11-Security.com, 399

A

AAA
    MAC-based authentication, 116
    servers, 6
    shared-key authentication, 118
access
    attack objectives, 128
    enterprise guest, 300–303
    multigroup, 259
access control, 157
    EAP-FAST, 187
        frame format, 189
        functional entities, 188
        message exchange, 191
    EAP protocols
        EAP-MD5, 170
        EAP-OTP, 171
        EAP-TLS, 171, 174
        EAP-TTLS, 176
        frames, 163–168
        layered framework, 159–162
        three-party model, 158
    LEAP, 185
    PEAP, 176
        frame format, 177–179
        message exchange, 180–182
access points. *See* APs
accounting, 114
    RADIUS protocol, 47
    TACACS+ protocol, 44
Ack (acknowledge), 36
addresses (IPv6), 53
ad-hoc mode security, 155
administrator authentication, 346
admission control, 282–283
adoption (IPv6), 54

AES CBC-MAC mode, 217
AES counter mode, 216
AH (Authentication Header), 55
AirJack, 139, 399
AirMagnet, 400
airport WLAN hotspot deployment example,
    394–395
Airsnarf, 399
AirSnort, 149, 399
algorithms
    Diffie-Hellman, 19, 30–31
    encryption strengths/weaknesses, 23
    MIC, 196
    Michael algorithm, 204–205
antennae, 6
applications
    MAC-based authentication, 116
    open authentication, 114
    shared-key authentication, 118
    WLAN design considerations, 258
APs (access points), 6–7, 14, 81
    configuration for load balancing and
        failover, 294
    rogue, 154
        detecting, 287–291
        SWAN, 243
    WLAN design considerations, 258
ArcFour algorithm, 402
asymmetric encryption, 19–20
attack trees, 126–127
    access, 128
    DoS, 128
attacks, 288
    asymmetric encryption, 22
    authentication, 140
    brute-force attacks, 23
    DoS, 128, 138
        disassociation and deauthentication, 139
        transmit duration, 140
    inductive attacks, 144
    key recovery attacks, 146
        dictionary-based, 146
        EAP protocols, 150–153
        Fluhrer-Mantin-Shamir attack,
            147–149
    keystream recovery, 142

attacks (*continued*)
  man-in-the-middle, 26
  objectives, 126
    access, 128
    attack trees, 126–128
  reaction attacks, 143–144
  reconnaissance, 127, 130
    sniffing, 130–132
    SSIDs, 130
    wardriving, 133–136
  reply attacks, preventing, 206
  rogue APs, 287
auditing, 114
authenticated data exchange, 22
authentication, 13, 34, 96–97
  administrator, 346
  attacks, 40
  CAs (certificate authorities), 32
  digital certificates, 31
  EAP protocols, 157
    EAP-MD5, 170
    EAP-OTP, 171
    EAP-TLS, 171, 174
    EAP-TTLS, 176
    frames, 163–168
    layered framework, 159–162
    three-party model, 158
  EAP-FAST, 187
    frame format, 189
    functional entities, 188
    message exchange, 191
  Kerberos, 48–49
  LEAP, 185
  MAC-based, 115–116
  mechanics, 111
  open, 113–114
  PEAP
    frame format, 177–179
    message exchange, 180–182
    PEAP, 176
  PPP, 34–35
    CHAP, 38
    EAP, 40–42
    link layer, 35
    negotiations, 35
  private key algorithms, 21
  RA, 45

  RADIUS protocol, 46
  shared-key, 116–118
  SWAN infrastructure authentication, 240
  TACACS+ protocol, 42–43
  WLAN design fundamentals, 257
Authentication Header (AH), 55
authentication servers, 48
authenticators, 40, 159
authorization, 13
  RADIUS, 46
  TACACS+ protocol, 43
availability, 13

B

BBSM (Building Broadband Service Manager), 374
beacon frames, 94
Bernard Aboba's "Unofficial 802.11 Security Web Page," 399
birthday paradox, 143
bridges, 6
brute-force attacks, 23
BSD UNIX, reconnaissance attacks, 137
bsd-airtools, 136, 399
BSS (Basic Service Set), 81
bug lightning, 288
Building Broadband Service Manager (BBSM), 374

C

Catalyst 6500 Wireless LAN Services Module, 310
CCK (Complementary Code Keying), 70
CCKM (Cisco Centralized Key Management), 246, 249
CCM algorithm, 215
CCMP, 196
  CCM algorithm, 215
  decapsulation, 214
  encapsulation, 212–213
  overview, 211
CCX (Cisco Client Extensions), 5, 309
central switching deployment mode (SWAN), 348–352
certificate authorities, 31
certificates, 31–32

CHAP (Challenge-Handshake Authentication
  Protocol), 37
    compatibility, 40
    EAP-MD5, 170
    vulnerabilities, 40
choreography. *See* exchanges
Cisco Aironet 802.11b/a/g, 309
Cisco Aironet AP350 AP, 308
Cisco Aironet AP1100 AP, 308
Cisco Aironet AP1200 AP, 308
Cisco Aironet BR350 AP, 309
Cisco Aironet BR1410 AP, 309
Cisco Client Extensions (CCX), 309
Cisco Compatible Extensions (CCX), 5
Cisco protocols, 226
Cisco Secure ACS, 310
Cisco Trust Agent (CTA), 283
Cisco Centralized Key Management (CCKM), 246,
  249
Cisco Structured Wireless Aware Network.
  See SWAN
Cisco Wireless LAN Solution Engine (WLSE), 310
CKIP (Cisco Key Integrity Protocol), 195, 246
client adapters, 6–7
clients, WLAN design recommendations, 260
coffee shop WLAN hotspot deployment example,
  391–394
collisions, 143
communication, 48
compatibility (CHAP), 40
Complementary Code Keying (CCK), 70
Compound Session Key (CSK), 182
confidential messages, 24
confidentiality, 13–15
    CCMP, 212–213
    digital signatures, 29
    public key algorithms, 19–22
    symmetric key encryption, 16–17
configuring
    MAC address authentication, 316
    WLAN security
        bridge-to-bridge links, 344–345
        HTML GUI configuration pages, 311–312
        IOS CLI configuration, 313–320, 324,
          329–335
        management configuration, 346–347
coverage areas, 81

creating digital signatures, 26
cryptography, 31
    asymmetric encryption, 19–20
    digital signatures, 26, 29
        creating, 27
        verifying, 28
    hash functions, 24–26
    keys
        CAs (certificate authorities), 32
        public, 31
    resources, 400
    symmetric encryption, 18–19
CSK (Compound Session Key), 182
CTA (Cisco Trust Agent), 283
cypher text, 22

D

data, 19
    frames, 104
    integrity, 20–22
    WEP, 121
Data Encryption Standard (DES), 19, 48
deauthentication, 99
deauthentication attacks, 139
decapsulation
    CCMP, 214
    TKIP, 211
    WEP, 202
decrypting
    cypher text, 22
    Kerberos, 51
    recovered keystreams, 146
    WEP, 123
demilitarized zones (DMZs), 114
deploying
    IPSec VPN over WLAN, 331
    SWAN central switching deployment mode, 281,
      348–352
    SWAN nonswitching deployment mode, 336
        fast secure roaming (CCKM) configuration,
          337–339
        local authentication configuration (RADIUS
          fall-back service), 343
        RF aggregation configuration, 340–342
        WDS configuration, 337–343

deploying (*continued*)
 WLANs, 235
  embedded security solutions, 261–264
  financial WLAN examples, 376–379
  healthcare WLAN examples, 379–384
  integration with existing systems, 275–280
  large enterprise examples, 355–356, 358–364
  manufacturing WLAN examples, 386–388
  medium enterprise WLAN deployment example, 389
  security features, 239
  small office WLAN deployment example, 390
  SOHO WLAN deployment example, 391
  SWAN central switching deployment mode, 238
  SWAN nonswitching deployment mode, 235
  university example, 373–375
  vertical market examples, 365–371
  VPN overlays, 265–270
DES (Data Encryption Standard), 19, 48
designing
 SWAN central switch design considerations, 281
 WLANs
  admission control, 282–283
  AP management, 258
  AP recommendations, 259–260
  application support, 258
  authentication support, 257
  client recommendations, 260
  combined VPN/embedded security design, 271–274
  device support, 256
  embedded security solutions, 262–264
  fundamentals, 255
  infrastructure recommendations, 260
  integration with existing systems, 275–280
  mobility, 257
  multigroup access, 259
  network services placement, 257
  new deployments, 261
  radio coverage, 258
  security policies, 256
  VPN overlays, 265–270
DFS (Dynamic Frequency Selection), 62, 76

dictionary-based attacks, 146
 LEAP, 151
Diffie-Hellman algorithm, 19, 30–31
digital certificates, 31–32
Digital Signature Standard (DSS), 29
digital signatures, 13, 26–29
 confidentiality, 29
 verifying, 28
disassociation attacks, 139
disassociations frames, 102
distributing public keys, 31
distribution service (DS), 82
DMZs (demilitarized zones), 114
DoS (denial-of-service) attacks, 128, 138
 disassociation and authentication, 139
 IEEE 802.11i, 227
 transmit duration, 140
DS (distribution service), 82
DSS (Digital Signature Standard), 29
Dynamic Frequency Selection (DFS), 62, 76

E

EAP (Extensible Authentication Protocol), 40, 163
 802.1x, 150
 attacks, 150
  dictionary attacks, 151
  PEAP man-in-the-middle attacks, 153
 authentication mechanisms
  EAP-MD5, 170
  EAP-OTP, 171
  EAP-TLS, 171, 174
  EAP-TTLS, 176
 flexibility, 42
 frames, 163
  request/response, 165
  success/failure, 167–168
 LEAP. *See* LEAP
 packet types assigned by IANA, 166–167
 security, 229
 Tunneled EAP (TEAP), 187
 vulnerabilities, 176
 with dynamic WEP configuration, 317–319
EAP over LAN protocol. *See* EAPOL

EAP-FAST, 187
  client configuration, 320
  frame format, 189
  functional entities, 188
  message exchange, 191
  with WPA client configuration, 326
EAP-GTC, 171
EAPOL (EAP over LAN protocol), 183–185
  master key establishment, 218
EAPOL Key Confirmation Key (KCK), 220
EAPOL Key Encryption Key (KEK), 220
EAP-OTP, 171
EAP-TLS, 171, 174
  client configuration, 322
EAP-TTLS, 176
ECP chaining mechanism, 17
e-dictation, 381
embedded security
  central switch design, 281
  combined with VPN overlay security solutions,
    271–274
  design fundamentals, 264
  threat mitigation, 262
EMSK (Extended Master Session Key), 182
Encapsulating Security Payload (ESP), 55
encapsulation
  CCMP, 212–213
  TKIP, 210
  WEP, 200–201
encryption, 14, 52
  algorithms, 23
  asymmetric encryption, 19–20
  digital signatures, 26–29
  hash functions, 24–26
  private key, 20
  symmetric encryption, 18–19
  symmetric key encryption, 15
encryption protocols
  CCMP, 211
    CCM algorithm, 215
    decapsulation, 214
    encapsulation, 212–213
  TKIP
    decapsulation, 211
    encapsulation, 210
    key mixing algorithm, 207
    Michael MIC, 204–205

  overview, 203
  packet construction, 209
  preventing reply attacks, 206
WEP, 197–198
  decapsulation, 202
  encapsulation, 200–201
  RC4, 198–199
enterprise guest access, 300–303
ERO (European Radiocommunications Office), 76
ESP (Encapsulating Security Payload), 55
Ethereal, 132, 399
ETSI (European Standard Organizations and
  Regulations), 77
European Radiocommunications Office (ERO), 76
exchanges
  association frames, 100–102
  authentication, 96–97
  data frames, 104
  deauthentication, 99
  disassociation frames, 102
  reassociation frames, 102
exclusive OR (XOR), 202
Extended Master Session Key (EMSK), 182
Extensible Authentication Protocol. *See* EAP

F

failover (AP configuration), 294
fakeap, 400
fast secure roaming (CCKM), 338–339
FCC regulations, 67
FCS (frame check sequence), 198
financial WLAN deployment examples, 376–379
Fluhrer-Mantin-Shamir attack, 147
FMS (Fluhrer-Mantin-Shamir) attack, 147, 228
frame check sequence (FCS), 198
frame types
  CHAP (Challenge-Handshake Authentication
    Protocol), 38
  PAP (Password Authentication Protocol), 35
frames, 89
  association frames, 100–102
  beacon frames, 94
  data frames, 104
  deauthentication frames, 99
  disassociation frames, 102

frames (*continued*)
>EAP, 163
>>request/response, 165
>>success/failure frames, 167–168
>EAP-FAST, 189
>FCS, 198
>MAC frame, 90
>management, 90
>PEAP, 177–179
>probe request frames, 95
>probe response frames, 95
>reassociation frames, 102
functions (hash functions), 24–26

G

GMK (Group Master Key), 218
Goonda.com, 399
group key handshake, 223
group key hierarchy, 221
Group Master Key (GMK), 218
GTKSA (Group Transient Key Security Association), 225
guest services (large enterprise WLAN deployment), 360

H

handshakes (CHAP), 37
hash functions, 24–26
headers
>AH (Authentication Header), 55
>ESP (Encapsulating Security Payload), 55
healthcare WLAN deployment examples, 379–384
hotspot WLAN deployment examples, 391–395
HTML GUI configuration pages, 312

I–J

IANA (Internet Assigned Numbers Authority), 166–167
IAPP (Inter-Access Point Protocol), 73

iBSS (independent basic service set)
>mode, 83
>network configuration, 289
ICV (Integrity Check Vector), 143, 198
IDEA (International Data Encryption Algorithm), 19
identity protocols, 34
IEEE (Institute of Electrical and Electronic Engineers), 60
>802 standard, 60–63
>online resources, 401
IEEE 802.11, 69, 84
>authentication, 111
>compared to WPA, 66
>services, 88
IEEE 802.11a, 70–71
IEEE 802.11b, 70
IEEE 802.11e, 73–75
IEEE 802.11f, 73
IEEE 802.11h, 76–78
IEEE 802.11i, 195–196
>CCMP, 211
>>CCM algorithm, 215
>>decapsulation, 214
>>encapsulation, 212–213
>development, 225
>dictionary-based WEP key recovery, 228
>key management, 217
>>key exchange, 222–223
>>key hierarchy, 218–221
>>master key establishment, 218
>>security associations (SAs), 224–225
>message modification and replay, 228
>rogue APs, 229
>security problems addressed, 227
>TKIP, 203
>>decapsulation, 211
>>encapsulation, 210
>>key mixing algorithm, 207
>>Michael MIC, 204–205
>>packet construction, 209
>>preventing reply attacks, 206
>WEP, 197–198
>>decapsulation, 202
>>encapsulation, 200–201
>>RC4, 198–199
>WEP keystream recovery, 228
IEEE 802.11k, 75

IEEE 802.1x
  EAPOL, 184–185
  overview, 183
IETF, 402
IKE (Internet Key Exchange), 56
IKMP (Internet Key Management Protocol), 56
independent basic service set (iBSS)
  mode, 83
  network configuration, 289
indexes (SPI), 55
inductive attacks, 144
initialization vectors. *See* IVs
Institute of Electrical and Electronic Engineers.
  See IEEE
integrating WLAN deployments, 275–280, 357
integrity, 13, 24–26
  CCMP, 212–213
  ICV, 143, 198
  public key algorithms, 19–22
  WEP, 121
Inter-Access Point Protocol (IAPP), 73
International Data Encryption Algorithm (IDEA),
  19
Internet Assigned Numbers Authority (IANA),
  166–167
Internet Key Exchange (IKE), 56
Internet Key Management Protocol (IKMP), 56
intrusion detection (SWAN), 243
IOS CLI configuration, 313–320
  IPSec VPN over WLAN configuration, 329–331
  multiple security profiles configuration, 332–335
  WPA-DOT1x configuration, 324
IP, 55
IPng (IP: The Next Generation), 52
IPSec, 54
  authentication header (AH), 55
  external load balancers, 299
  key management, 56
IPSec VPN clustering, 296–297
IPSec VPN over WLAN configuration, 329–331
IPSec VPNs, 267
IPv6, 52
  address structure and representation, 53
  headers, 53
  scalability, 54

ISPs, 47
IV (initialization vectors), 17, 143, 197
  generating (WEP), 122
  inductive attacks, 144
  traffic injection, 145

K

KCK (EAPOL Key Confirmation Key), 220
KDC (key distribution center), 48–50
KEK (EAPOL Key Encryption Key), 220
Kerberos
  authentication, 48–49
  replies, 51
  requests, 51
key exchange, 222
  4-way handshake, 222
  group key handshake, 223
key management, 15, 29, 217
  IPSec, 56
  key exchange, 222–223
  key hierarchy, 218
    CCKM, 249
    group key hierarchy, 221
    Pairwise key hierarchy, 220
  master key establishment (EAPOL), 218
  PEAP, 182
key mixing algorithm (TKIP), 207
key pairs, 23
key recovery attacks, 146
  dictionary-based, 146
  EAP protocols, 150–153
  Fluhrer-Mantin-Shamir attack, 147–149
Key Scheduling Algorithm (KSA), 147, 199
keylength (WEP), 121
keys
  CAs (certificate authorities), 32
  cryptography, 31
  digital certificates, 31
  hierarchy, 218–220, 249
  key management. *See* key management
  secret keys, 30
  WEP, 197
keyspace, 23

keystream recovery
keystream dictionaries, 141
RC4, 142
reaction attacks, 143
uses for recovered keystreams, 145
KisMAC, 399
Kismet, 135, 399
KSA (Key Scheduling Algorithm), 147, 199

L

LAN/MAN RM (Reference Model), 60
LAN/MAN standards, 60
large enterprise WLAN deployment, 355–356
AAA and external user database infrastructure
implementation, 358–359
deployment challenges, 364
security deployment, 363
security details, 356
VoIP and guest services, 360
wired/wireless LAN integration, 357
layered framework for authentication, 159–162
LEAP, 185
client configuration, 319
dictionary-based attacks, 151
EAP-FAST. *See* EAP-FAST
legacy devices/systems, 276
Libradiate, 399
Light Weight Access Point Protocol (LWAPP), 79
link layer (PPP), 35
Linux reconnaissance attacks, 137
LLC (Logical Link Control), 61
load balancing
AP configuration, 294
IPSec external load balancers, 299
IPSec VPN clustering, 297
RADIUS, 292
site-based VPN, 296
SSL external load balancers, 299
local authentication configuration (RADIUS fall-back
service), 343
Logical Link Control (LLC), 61
LOGIN port (TACACS protocol), 42
LWAPP (Light Weight Access Point Protocol), 79

M

MAC address authentication, configuring, 316
MAC address spoofing, 141, 227
MAC frame, 90
MAC Protocol Data Unit (MPDU) 184, 203
MAC Service Data Unit (MSDU), 203
MAC-based authentication, 115–116
MacStumbler, 135, 399
management frames, 90
man-in-the-middle attacks, 26, 153
manual rogue AP detection, 289
manufacturing WLAN deployment examples, 386–
388
master keys, 218
Master Session Key (MSK), 182
medium enterprise WLAN deployment example, 389
message digest, 24
messages
authentication, 113
exchanges, 93
EAP-FAST, 188, 191
LEAP, 185
PEAP, 180–182
TLS, 172
MIC (Message Integrity Check) algorithm, 196
Michael algorithm, 204–205
Michael MIC, 204–205
Mini Stumbler, 134
mobility, WLAN design considerations, 257
monkey_jack, 139, 399
MPDU (MAC Protocol Data Unit), 184, 203
MSDU (MAC Service Data Unit), 203
MSK (Master Session Key), 182
multiple security profiles (SSIDs/VLANs), 332–335

N

NAD (network access device), 283
Nak (negative acknowledge), 36
negotiations (PPP), 35
Network Stumbler, 134, 400
network-based rogue AP detection, 291
networks
Robust Security Network, 196
wireless. *See* wireless networks
NICs, 6

NMS (network management servers), 6
nonswitching deployment mode (SWAN), 336
    fast secure roaming (CCKM) configuration, 337–339
    local authentication configuration, 343
    RF aggregation configuration, 340–342
    WDS configuration, 337–343

O

Omerta, 139, 400
open authentication, 113–114
open authentication guest VLAN, 301
open/no WEP configuration, 313
open/with WEP (static WEP) configuration, 313

P–Q

PAC TLV frame format (EAP-FAST), 189
packets
    EAP packet types assigned by IANA, 166–167
    PAP, 36
    TKIP, 209
Pairwise key hierarchy, 220
Pairwise Master Key (PMK), 218
Pairwise Master Key Security Association (PMKSA), 225
Pairwise Transient Key (PTK), 220
Pairwise Transient Key Security Association (PTKSA), 225
PAP (Password Authentication Protocol), 35–37
passwords, 34–35
PEAP (Protected EAP), 64
    arbitrary parameter exchange, 178
    client configuration, 320
    configuration on a third-party EAP supplicant, 322
    frames, 177–179
    key management, 182
    man-in-the-middle attacks, 153
    message exchange, 180, 182
plaintext attacks, 142
PLCP (Physical Layer Convergence Protocol), 70
PMK (Pairwise Master Key), 218

PMKSA (Pairwise Master Key Security Association), 225
PPDU (PLCP Protocol Data Unit), 70
PPP (Point-to-Point Protocol), 34
    link layer, 35
    negotiations, 35
    online resources, 402
Preshared Key (PSK), 218
pre-WeP devices, 275
PRGA (Pseudorandom Generation Algorithm), 199
Prismdump, 132, 400
privacy, 119–122
private key encryption, 20
probe request frames, 95
probe response frames, 95
processing WEP, 120–122
Protected EAP (PEAP), 64
protocols
    CHAP, compatibility, 40
    Cisco, 226
    IKE (Internet Key Exchange), 56
    IPSec, 54–55
    IPv6, 52
        address structure and representation, 53
        headers, 53
        scalability, 54
    Kerberos
        authentication, 48–49
        replies, 51
        requests, 51
    PPP, 34
        CHAP, 38
        EAP, 40–42
        link layer, 35
        negotiations, 35
        PAP, 35–36
    RADIUS (Remote Address Dial-In User Service), 45
        accounting, 47
        authentication, 46
        authorization, 46
        transactions, 47
    shared-key authentication, 117
    TACACS+, 42
        accounting, 44
        authentication, 43
        authorization, 43

transactions, 44
Pseudorandom Generation Algorithm (PRGA), 199
PSK (Preshared Key), 218
PSPF (Public Secure Packet Forwarding), 347
PTK (Pairwise Transient Key), 220
PTKSA (Pairwise Transient Key Security
  Association), 225
public keys
  creating, 31
  distributing, 31
  encryption, 22
Public Secure Packet Forwarding (PSPF), 347
public WAN deployment examples, 391–395
public WLAN (PWLAN), 85

R

radio coverage design, 258
radio management
  enabling on a Cisco client, 342
  SWAN, 242–243
Radio Manager Assisted Site-Survey wizard, 341
radio technologies in, 802.11, 68
RADIUS (Remote Address Dial-In User Service)
  protocol, 45–46
  accounting, 47
  authentication, 46
  authorization, 46
  best practices, 292–293
  EAP parameter configuration on RADIUS server,
    323
  Local authentication configuration (RADIUS fall-
    back service), 343
  server load balancing, 292
  SWAN, 250
  transactions, 47
RC4 (Rivest Cipher 4), 19, 198
  history of, 121
  keystream dictionaries, 141
  keystream recovery, 142
  KSA, 147
  two phases, 121
reaction attacks, 143
reason codes, 104–105

reconnaissance, 127

reconnaissance attacks, 130
  sniffing, 130–132
  SSIDs, 130
  wardriving, 133–136
refresh number (RN), 248
Remote Address Dial-In User Service. *See* RADIUS
removing certificates, 32
replies (Kerberos protocol), 51
reply attacks, preventing, 206
REPLY message, 43
reply packets (PAP), 36
request packets (PAP), 36
request/response frames (EAP), 165
requests (Kerberos protocol), 51
resolves, 21
response, 40
retail WLAN deployment
  example 1, 366
    challenges, 370
    security, 367
    WDS and AAA infrastructure, 369
  example 2, 371
revoking certificates, 32
RF aggregation configuration, 340–342
Rivest Cipher 4 (RC4), 19
RN (refresh number), 248
Robust Security Network, 196
rogue APs, 154
  detecting, 287
    manually, 289
    network-based, 291
    SWAN, 288–289
  IEEE 802.11i, 229
  SWAN, 243
routers, wireless aware, 6

S

SAs (security associations), 55, 224–225
scalability
  IPv6, 54
  RADIUS best practices, 292–293

VPN best practices, 296–299

security, 8, 13
    access control, 157
        EAP frames, 163–168
        EAP-FAST, 187–191
        EAP-MD5, 170
        EAP-OTP, 171
        EAP-TLS, 171, 174
        EAP-TTLS, 176
        layered framework, 159–162
        LEAP, 185
        PEAP, 176–180, 182
        three-party model, 158
    accounting, 44
    ad-hoc mode, 155
    attacks
        access, 128
        authentication, 140
        DoS, 128, 138–140
        key recovery attacks, 146–153
        objectives, 126–128
        reaction attacks, 143
        reconnaissance, 127, 130–136
    authentication
        Kerberos, 48–49
        MAC-based, 115–116
        mechanics, 111
        open, 113–114
        PAP, 35–36
        PPP, 35
        shared-key, 116–118
        TACACS, 42
        TACACS+ protocol, 42
    authorization, 43
    bridge-to-bridge links, 344–345
    brute-force attacks, 23
    CAs (certificate authorities), 32
    confidentiality, 15–17
    configuring, 307
    cryptography
        asymmetric encryption, 19–20
        digital signatures, 26–29
        hash functions, 24–26
        symmetric encryption, 18–19
    digital certificates, 31

digital signatures, 13
EAP, 229
embedded security solutions
    design fundamentals, 264
    threat mitigation, 262
encryption, 14
HTML GUI configuration pages, 311–312
IOS CLI configuration, 313–320
    IPSec VPN over VLAN configuration, 329–331
    multiple security profiles configuration, 332–335
    WPA-DOT1x configuration, 324
Kerberos protocol, 51
key management, 29, 217
    key exchange, 222–223
    key hierarchy, 218–220
    master key establishment, 218
    SAs, 224–225
protocols, 38
retail WLAN deployment, 367
rogue APs, 154, 287–291
SWAN, 233–234
    802.11x RADIUS authentication service, 250
    fast secure roaming, 246
    infrastructure authentication, 240
    radio management, 242–243
    rogue APs, 243
    WLAN deployment, 239
threat mitigation
    combined VPN/embedded security design, 273
    integration with legacy devices, 278–279
VPN overlays, 265
    design fundamentals, 270
    technologies, 267–269
    threat mitigation, 266
WEP, 123
    key recovery attacks, 146–153
    keystream and plaintext recovery, 141, 143–145
WLAN design concerns
    AP recommendations, 259–260
    client recommendations, 260
    infrastructure recommendations, 260

WLAN management configuration, 346–347
WLANs standards, 65
security associations. *See* SAs
security domain conceptual model, 8
security parameter index (SPI), 55
security policies (WLAN design), 256
Security Wizards, 400
seeds (WEP), 121, 197
sender authentication, 22
Service Set Identifier (SSID), 114
services, 87
    IEEE 802.11, 88
    state transitions, 92
shared-key authentication, 116–118
shared-key authentication attacks, 140, 227
sign, 29
signatures, digital, 26–28
site-based VPN load balancing, 296
small office WLAN deployment example, 390
Sniffer Wireless, 400
sniffing, 130–132
SOA (services-oriented architecture) paradigms, 53
SOHO (small office, home office), 389
SOHO WLAN deployment example, 391
SPI (security parameter index), 55
spoofing
    IEEE 802.11i, 227
    MAC addresses, 141
SSH, 269
SSID (Service Set Identifier), 114, 130, 287
SSL, 269
SSL external load balancing, 299
STA (station), 7, 81
standards
    ERO, 76
    ETSI, 77
    FCC regulations, 67
    IEEE 802, 60
    IEEE 802.11, 69
    IEEE 802.11a, 70–71
    IEEE 802.11b, 70
        channel allocation, 70
    IEEE 802.11e, 73–75
    IEEE 802.11f, 73
    IEEE 802.11h, 76–78
    IEEE 802.11k, 75
    LAN/MAN, 60
    layered framework for authentication, 160–162

WLANs, 7, 59, 62–63
WPA, 65
START message, 43
state diagrams, 91–93
state transitions, 92
static WEP configuration, 313
status codes, 106–107
stickiness, 293
Structured Wireless Aware Network. *See* SWAN
success/failure frames (EAP), 167–168
supplicants, 159
    third-party, 322
SWAN (Cisco Structured Wireless Aware Network),
    4, 233
    802.11x RADIUS authentication service,
        250
    central switching deployment, 281,
        348–352
    fast secure roaming, 246
    infrastructure authentication, 240
    nonswitching deployment, 336–343
    radio management, 242–243
    rogue AP detection, 243, 288–289
    security, 233–234
    WLAN deployment, 235
        central switching deployment mode,
            238
        nonswitching deployment mode, 235
        security features, 239
switches (wireless aware), 6
symmetric encryption, 18–19
symmetric key encryption, 15–17

T

TACACS, administrator authentication, 346
TACACS+ protocol, 42
    accounting, 44
    authentication, 43
    authorization, 43
    transactions, 44
Task Group i (TGi), 195
tcpdump, 132, 400
TEAP (Tunneled EAP), 187
TEK (Temporal Encryption Key), 207
Temporal Encryption Key (TEK), 207
Temporal Key (TK), 220

TGi (Task Group i), 195
third-party supplicants, 322
threat mitigation
    combined VPN/embedded security design,
        273
    integration with legacy devices, 278–279
    VPN overlays, 266
three-party model, 158
three-way handshakes (CHAP), 37
timing, 37
TK (Temporal Key), 220
TKIP
    decapsulation, 211
    encapsulation, 210
    key mixing algorithm, 207
    Michael MIC, 204–205
    overview, 203
    packet construction, 209
    preventing reply attacks, 206
TKIP Sequence Counter (TSC), 206
TLS (Transport Level Security), 64, 172
    EAP-TLS, 174
    EAP-TTLS, 176
TLV frame format (PEAP), 178
TPC (Transmit Power Control), 62, 76
traffic injection, 145
transactions
    RADIUS protocol, 47
    TACACS+ protocol, 44
Transmit Power Control (TPC), 62, 76
trees. *See* attack trees
troubleshooting
    rogue APs, 287
        manually, 289
        network-based, 291
        SWAN, 288–289
    WDS server configuration, 337
trust model (open authentication), 114
TSC (TKIP Sequence Counter), 206
Tunneled EAP (TEAP), 187

U–V

university WLAN deployment example, 373–375

upgrading, integrating design with existing WLAN
    deployments, 275
vertical market WLAN deployment, 365
    financial WLAN deployment examples,
        376–379
    healthcare WLAN deployment examples, 379–
        384
    manufacturing WLAN deployment examples,
        386–388
    retail WLAN example 1, 366
        challenges, 370
        security, 367
        WDS and AAA infrastructure, 369
    retail WLAN example 2, 371
    university WLAN deployment example, 373–375
void11, 139, 400
VoIP (Voice over IP), large enterprise WLAN
    deployment, 360
VPNs (virtual private networks)
    IPSec, 54
    overlays, 265
        best practices, 296–299
        central switch design, 281
        combined with embedded security design,
            271–274
        design fundamentals, 270
        technologies, 267–269
        threat mitigation, 266
vulnerabilities
    EAP, 176
    MAC-based authentication, 116
    open authentication, 114
    shared-key authentication, 118
    WEP, 123
    wireless networks, 125

W

WarBSD, 137, 400
wardriving, 133–136
WarLinux, 137, 400
WDS (Wireless Domain Services), 289
websites
    cryptography and cryptoanalysis, 401

general tools, 399–400

IEEE resources, 401

websites (*continued*)

IETF resources, 402

WiFi Alliance, 226, 401

Wellenreiter, 135, 400

WEP (Wired Equivalent Privacy), 18, 65, 108–109, 197–198

　CCMP, 211

　　CCM algorithm, 215

　　decapsulation, 214

　　encapsulation, 212–213

　decapsulation, 202

　encapsulation, 200–201

　ICV, 143

　IEEE 802.11i, 195–196

　IVs, 24

　keys, 197

　key management, 122

　key recovery attacks, 146

　　dictionary-based, 146

　　EAP protocols, 150–153

　　Fluhrer-Mantin-Shamir attack, 147–149

　keystream and plaintext recovery, 141–143

　　uses for recovered keystreams, 145

　pre-WEP devices, 275

　privacy mechanics, 119

　processing model, 120–122

　RC4, 199

　seed, 197

　TKIP, 203

　　decapsulation, 211

　　encapsulation, 210

　　key mixing algorithm, 207

　　Michael MIC, 204–205

　　packet construction, 209

　　preventing reply attacks, 206

　vulnerabilities, 123

　WEP-only devices, 275

wep_crack and wep_decrypt, 400

WEPCrack, 149, 400

WGBs (workgroup bridges), 6

Wi-Fi Alliance, 65

　websites, 226, 401

Wi-Fi Protected Access. *See* WPA

wireless-aware routers, 6

wireless-aware switches, 6

Wireless Domain Services (WDS), 289

Wireless LAN Association (WLANA), 67

Wireless LAN Services Module (WLSM), 4, 303

Wireless LAN Solution Engine (WLSE), 357

wireless LANs. *See* WLANs

wireless networks

　security

　　ad-hoc mode, 155

　　authentication attacks, 140

　　DoS attacks, 138

　　　disassociation and deauthentication, 139

　　　transmit duration, 140

　　reconnaissance attacks, 130–136

　　rogue APs, 154

　supplicants, 159

　vulnerabilities, 125

wireless service provider (WSP), 82

WLANA (Wireless LAN Association), 67

WLANs (wireless LANs), 3

　authentication, 96–97

　basic topology, 84

　Cisco Enterprise class, 307–308

　　Catalyst 6500 Wireless LAN Services Module, 310

　　Cisco Aironet 802.22b/a/g, 309

　　Cisco Aironet AP350 AP, 308

　　Cisco Aironet AP1100 AP, 308

　　Cisco Aironet AP1200 AP, 308

　　Cisco Aironet BR350 AP, 309

　　Cisco Aironet BR1410 AP, 309

　　Cisco Secure ACS, 310

　　WLSE, 310

　components, 6

　deauthentication, 99

　deploying

　　financial WLAN examples, 376–379

　　healthcare WLAN examples, 379–384

　　large enterprise examples, 355–364

　　manufacturing WLAN examples, 386–388

　　university example, 373–375

　　vertical market examples, 365–371

　deployment modes, 235

　　security features, 239

　　SWAN central switching deployment mode, 238

　　SWAN nonswitching deployment mode, 235

　designing

admission control, 282–283
AP management, 258
AP recommendations, 259–260
application support, 258
authentication support, 257
client recommendations, 260
combined VPN/embedded security design, 271–274
device support, 256
embedded security solutions, 262–264
infrastructure recommendations, 260
mobility, 257
multigroup access, 259
network services placement, 257
new deployments, 261
radio coverage, 258
security policies, 256
VPN overlays, 265–270
elements and characteristics, 81
enterprise guest access, 300–303
frames, 89, 102–104
associations frames, 100–102
beacon frames, 94
MAC frame, 90
management, 90
probe request frames, 95
probe response frames, 95
reassociations frames, 102
integration with existing systems, 275–280
limitations, 4
medium enterprise deployment example, 389
public, 85
reason codes, 104–105
security, 8
bridge-to-bridge links, 344–345

HTML GUI configuration pages, 311–312
IOS CLI configuration, 313–324, 329–335
management configuration, 346–347
standards, 64
security domain conceptual model, 8
services, 87
IEEE 802.11, 88
state transitions, 92
services scaling
RADIUS best practices, 292–293
VPN best practices, 296–299
small office deployment example, 390
SOHO deployment example, 391
standards, 7, 59, 62–63
state diagram, 91–93
status codes, 106–107
SWAN, 4
WEP, 108–109
WLSE (Cisco Wireless LAN Solution Engine), 310, 357
WLSM (Wireless LAN Services Module), 4, 303
WPA (Wi-Fi Protected Access), 65, 226, 261
compared to IEEE 802.11, 66
WPA upgradeable devices, 275
WPA-DOT1x configuration
debug information, 328
WPA-PSK configuration, 315
WSP (wireless service provider), 82

X–Z

XOR (exclusive OR), 202
XTACACS protocol, 42

Cisco Press

Learning is serious business.

Invest wisely.

ciscopress.com

CISCO SYSTEMS

Cisco Press

Your **first-step** to networking starts here

Are you new to the world of networking? Whether you are taking your first networking class or simply need a better understanding of a specific technology to choose your next networking class, Cisco Press First-Step books are right for you.

➤ **No experience required**

➤ **Includes clear and easily understood explanations**

➤ **Makes learning easy**

Check out each of these First-Step books that cover key networking topics

- **Computer Networking First-Step**
  ISBN: 1-58720-101-1

- **LAN Switching First-Step**
  ISBN: 1-58720-100-3

- **Network Security First-Step**
  ISBN: 1-58720-099-6

- **Routing First-Step**
  ISBN: 1-58720-122-4
  September 2004

- **TCP/IP First-Step**
  ISBN: 1-58720-108-9
  October 2004

- **Wireless Networks First-Step**
  ISBN: 1-58720-111-9

Visit **www.ciscopress.com/firststep** to learn more.

What's your next step?

Eager to dig deeper into networking technology? Cisco Press has the books that will help you move to the next level. Learn more at **www.ciscopress.com/series**.

ciscopress.com

Learning begins with a first step.

CISCO SYSTEMS

Cisco Press

NETWORK BUSINESS SERIES

JUSTIFY YOUR NETWORK INVESTMENT

Network Business books deliver:

A clear and approachable writing style—no in-depth technical knowledge required

Technology overviews that promote informed decision making

Implementation scenarios that outline various business models

ROI and TCO metrics that assist with complex technology decisions

Interviews with industry leaders that provide real-world insights on technology decisions

Detailed case studies that showcase relevant technologies

Look for Network Business titles at your favorite bookseller

The Case for Virtual Business Processes
Young / Jude • ISBN: 1-58720-087-2

IP Telephony Unveiled
Brown • ISBN: 1-58720-075-9

Planet Broadband
Yassini • ISBN: 1-58720-090-2

Power Up Your Small-Medium Business
Aber • ISBN: 1-58705-135-4

The Road to IP Telephony
Carhee • ISBN: 1-58720-088-0

Taking Charge of Your VoIP Project
Walker / Hicks • ISBN: 1-58720-092-9

The Business Case for E-Learning
Kelly / Nanjiani • ISBN: 1-58720-086-4 • Coming Soon

Network Business Series.   **Justify Your Network Investment.**

Visit **www.ciscopress.com/series** for details about the Network Business series and a complete list of titles.

CISCO SYSTEMS

Cisco Press

FUNDAMENTALS SERIES
ESSENTIAL EXPLANATIONS AND SOLUTIONS

When you need an authoritative introduction to a key networking topic, **reach for a Cisco Press Fundamentals book**. Learn about network topologies, deployment concepts, protocols, and management techniques and **master essential networking concepts and solutions**.

Look for Fundamentals titles at your favorite bookseller

802.11 Wireless LAN Fundamentals
ISBN: 1-58705-077-3

**Cisco CallManager Fundamentals:
A Cisco AVVID Solution**
ISBN: 1-58705-008-0

Data Center Fundamentals
ISBN: 1-58705-023-4

IP Addressing Fundamentals
ISBN: 1-58705-067-6

IP Routing Fundamentals
ISBN: 1-57870-071-X

Voice over IP Fundamentals
ISBN: 1-57870-168-6

Visit **www.ciscopress.com/series** for details about the Fundamentals series and a complete list of titles.

Learning is serious business.
Invest wisely.

CISCO SYSTEMS

Cisco Press

CISCO CERTIFICATION SELF-STUDY
#1 BEST-SELLING TITLES FROM CCNA® TO CCIE®

Look for Cisco Press Certification Self-Study resources at your favorite bookseller

Learn the test topics with **Self-Study Guides**

Gain hands-on experience with **Practical Studies** books

Prepare for the exam with **Exam Certification Guides**

Practice testing skills and build confidence with **Flash Cards and Exam Practice Packs**

Visit **www.ciscopress.com/series** to learn more about the Certification Self-Study product family and associated series.

Learning is serious business.
Invest wisely.

Cisco Press

Learning is serious business.

Invest wisely.

CISCO SYSTEMS

Cisco Press

CCIE PROFESSIONAL DEVELOPMENT
RESOURCES FROM EXPERTS IN THE FIELD

CCIE Professional Development books are the **ultimate resource for advanced networking professionals**, providing practical insights for effective network design, deployment, and management. **Expert perspectives, in-depth technology discussions, and real-world implementation advice** also make these titles essential for anyone preparing for a CCIE® exam.

CISCO SYSTEMS

CCIE® Professional Development
Routing TCP/IP
Volume I

A detailed examination of interior routing protocols

ciscopress.com

Jeff Doyle, CCIE No. 1919

Look for CCIE Professional Development titles at your favorite bookseller

Cisco BGP-4 Command and Configuration Handbook
ISBN: 1-58705-017-X

Cisco LAN Switching
ISBN: 1-57870-094-9

Cisco OSPF Command and Configuration Handbook
ISBN: 1-58705-071-4

Inside Cisco IOS Software Architecture
ISBN: 1-57870-181-3

Network Security Principles and Practices
ISBN: 1-58705-025-0

Routing TCP/IP, Volume I
ISBN: 1-57870-041-8

Routing TCP/IP, Volume II
ISBN: 1-57870-089-2

Troubleshooting IP Routing Protocols
ISBN: 1-58705-019-6

Troubleshooting Remote Access Networks
ISBN: 1-58705-076-5

Visit **www.ciscopress.com/series** for details about the CCIE Professional Development series and a complete list of titles.

Learning is serious business.
Invest wisely.

CISCO SYSTEMS

Cisco Press

NETWORKING TECHNOLOGY GUIDES
MASTER THE NETWORK

Turn to Networking Technology Guides whenever you need **in-depth knowledge of complex networking technologies**. Written by leading networking authorities, these guides offer theoretical and practical knowledge for **real-world networking applications and solutions**.

Look for Networking Technology Guides at your favorite bookseller

Cisco Access Control Security: AAA Administration Services
ISBN: 1-58705-124-9

Cisco CallManager Best Practices: A Cisco AVVID Solution
ISBN: 1-58705-139-7

Designing Network Security,
Second Edition
ISBN: 1-58705-117-6

Network Security Architectures
ISBN: 1-58705-115-X

Optical Network Design and Implementation
ISBN: 1-58705-105-2

Top-Down Network Design, Second Edition
ISBN: 1-58705-152-4

Troubleshooting Virtual Private Networks
ISBN: 1-58705-104-4

CISCO SYSTEMS

Cisco Access Control Security:
AAA Administration Services

Hands-on techniques for enabling authentication, authorization, and accounting

ciscopress.com   Brandon Carroll

Visit **www.ciscopress.com/series** for details about Networking Technology Guides and a complete list of titles.

Learning is serious business.
Invest wisely.

ciscopress.com

SEARCH THOUSANDS OF BOOKS FROM LEADING PUBLISHERS

Safari® Bookshelf is a searchable electronic reference library for IT professionals that features more than 2,000 titles from technical publishers, including Cisco Press.

With Safari Bookshelf you can

- **Search** the full text of thousands of technical books, including more than 70 Cisco Press titles from authors such as Wendell Odom, Jeff Doyle, Bill Parkhurst, Sam Halabi, and Karl Solie.

- **Read** the books on My Bookshelf from cover to cover, or just flip to the information you need.

- **Browse** books by category to research any technical topic.

- **Download** chapters for printing and viewing offline.

With a customized library, you'll have access to your books when and where you need them—and all you need is a user name and password.

TRY SAFARI BOOKSHELF FREE FOR 14 DAYS!

You can sign up to get a 10-slot Bookshelf free for the first 14 days. Visit **http://safari.ciscopress.com** to register.

Learning is serious business.   **Invest wisely.**

CISCO SYSTEMS

Cisco Press

3 STEPS TO LEARNING

STEP 1

STEP 2

STEP 3

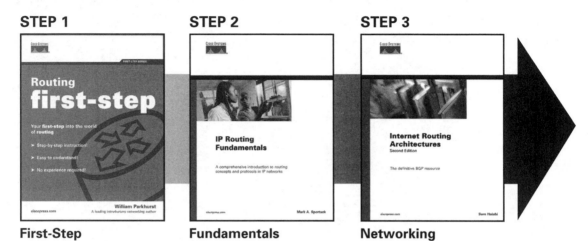

First-Step

Fundamentals

**Networking
Technology Guides**

STEP 1   **First-Step**—Benefit from easy-to-grasp explanations.
No experience required!

STEP 2   **Fundamentals**—Understand the purpose, application,
and management of technology.

STEP 3   **Networking Technology Guides**—Gain the knowledge
to master the challenge of the network.

NETWORK BUSINESS SERIES

The Network Business series helps professionals tackle the
business issues surrounding the network. Whether you are a
seasoned IT professional or a business manager with minimal
technical expertise, this series will help you understand the
business case for technologies.

Justify Your Network Investment.

Look for Cisco Press titles at your favorite bookseller today.

Visit **www.ciscopress.com/series** for details on each of these book series.

Cisco Press

Learning is serious business.

Invest wisely.